Digital Dynamics in Nordic Contemporary Art

Digital Dynamics in Nordic Contemporary Art

Edited by
Tanya Toft Ag

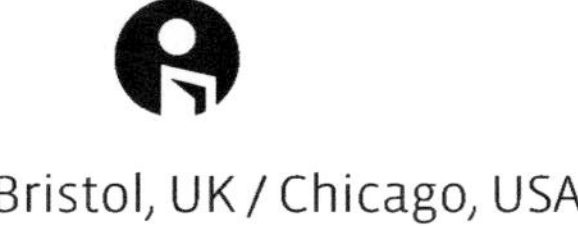

intellect Bristol, UK / Chicago, USA

First published in the UK in 2019 by
Intellect, The Mill, Parnall Road, Fishponds, Bristol, BS16 3JG, UK

First published in the USA in 2019 by
Intellect, The University of Chicago Press, 1427 E. 60th Street,
Chicago, IL 60637, USA

A catalogue record for this book is available from the
British Library.

Copy-editors: MPS and Michael Eckhardt
Cover designer: Aleksandra Szumlas and Kirstine Edith Toft
Cover art: Jana Winderen, *Jana Winderen* (2014), Krísuvik, Iceland.
Index: Max Alvares and Tanya Toft Ag
Photo by Finnbogi Pétursson. Courtesy of the artist
Production managers: Katie Evans and Jelena Stanovnik
Typesetting: Contentra Technologies

Print ISBN: 978-1-78320-948-4
ePDF ISBN: 978-1-78320-950-7
ePUB ISBN: 978-1-78320-949-1

Printed and bound by Hobbs, UK.

Supported by

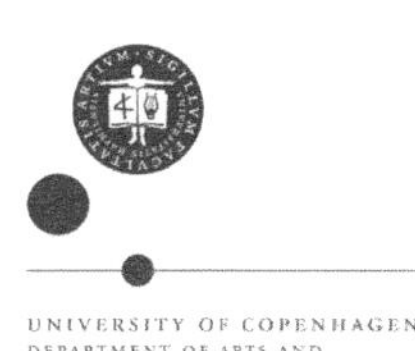

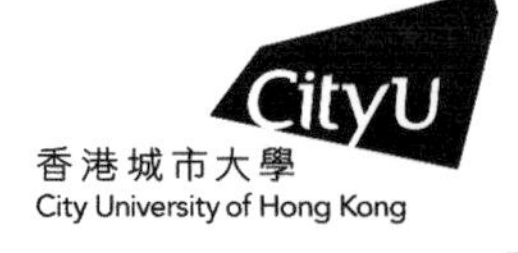

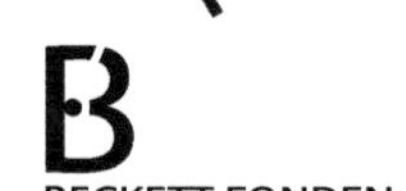

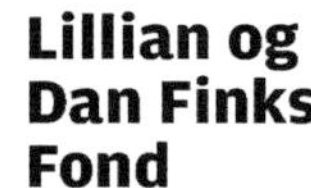

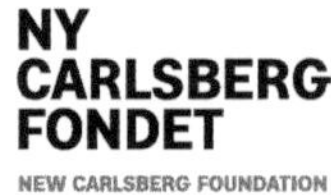

Contents

Foreword

This book is initiated with intentions of contributing insight and reflection on how contemporary art is changing in the era of the digital. It embraces an expanded field of contemporary art, one that evolves not only within the confines of the domain of fine art, but also in synergies with other domains that, with the digital, are brought into closer proximity to art, and which might bring the art into closer encounters with society and its evolution. As we are still in an early phase of cultural and societal change with the digital, we are equally at a very early – though critical – stage of seeking out how the digital announces new roads for art's enquiry and role in society, which is the main objective of the book's investigation. I would like to first of all thank all the close to 100 participants of this book project – artists, curators, authors and assistants – for sharing your thinking and time to make the book happen.

This book did not come about swiftly. It has evolved through a slow but thorough process of ongoing conceptualization, research, writing and feedback. As initiator of the book, my curiosity on what we see happening in art and artistic discourse today, influenced by the digital dynamics that restructure society, has grown from almost a decade's research in this domain. The examination of this condition, particularly in a Nordic contextual perspective, is furthermore a result of curatorial practice and research within and beyond this context, which has allowed for encounters and exchanges with artists, curators, architects, innovation designers, cultural producers and scholars, whose inspiration and ideas have contributed to fine-tuning the book's conception and approach.

During this time, I have been mostly geographically located outside of the Nordic region. Sometimes, you realise how distinct and specific things are when you are distanced from them. While closely collaborating with curator Nina Colosi in the framework of her exhibition initiative Streaming Museum in New York City, I had the opportunity to research art, discourses and trajectories in the domain of digital, video and other media art in the Nordic context especially during our development of the curatorial project titled *Nordic Outbreak*. Unfolding throughout 2013 and 2014, this initiative presented video art by 32 Nordic artists in public spaces across New York City and on tour throughout the Nordic region. I want to thank you deeply, Nina, for developing and carrying out this project with me, which made an essential foundation for the becoming of this book. With *Nordic Outbreak*, a basic premise of the book was established of examining expanded formats, cross-genre and site-contextual significances of contemporary digital art in relation to various urban contexts – and as such, seek to grasp the reality of contemporary art of today as evolving and contingent phenomena.

On tour through the Nordic region, *Nordic Outbreak* visited Helsinki, Copenhagen, Reykjavik, Stavanger, Nuuk and Umeaa, in collaboration with KIASMA Museum for Contemporary Art and Media Facades Festival in Helsinki, Danish Architecture Centre, Screen City Festival in Stavanger, Reykjavik Art Museum, Katuaq the Cultural Centre of Greenland, as well as Umeaa in Sweden on the occasion of the city named European Capital of Culture in 2014. Throughout the *Nordic Outbreak* project, I had the pleasure of collaborating with and learning from Daniela Arriado, Birta Gudjonsdottir, Kati Kivinen, and Jacob Lillemose, who were invited as guest curators. Also, with curators with whom I collaborated in the various Nordic contexts, Signe Cecilie Jochumsen and Dan Lestander, as well as scholars and curators Erkki Huhtamo, Margrét Elísabet Ólafsdóttir, Björn Norberg, Minna Tarkka, and Jonatan Habib Engqvist, all to whom I am deeply thankful for furthering my understanding of art in the expanded digital domain and its specific conditions and artistic implications in the various local Nordic art contexts.

An early conception of the book especially developed on the basis of a symposium held at Scandinavia House in New York City within the framework of the *Nordic Outbreak* programme, which continued in the form of talks and panels on the Nordic tour. On these occasions some of the book's contributors were brought together and shared perspectives and ideas that have since amounted into chapters for the book.

My deep thanks also goes to my former research assistant Laura Goldschmidt at Copenhagen University. Laura and I developed the methodology of interviewing artists in the Nordic art context together, and she has been an invaluable and persistent companion in the process of identifying the artists, inviting for and collecting their testimonials. Her insightful master's thesis examining a 'digital avant-garde' in the Nordic context – also based on some of the artist testimonials in the book – is a noteworthy side outcome of these research efforts (Laura Goldschmidt, 'Digital avant-garde: The mobilization of an acute avant garde through digital art in the Nordic countries', 2016). Later in the process, I gratefully received help with data handling and distribution of the book from the wonderful Chananthorn Vinitwatanakhun (Lilly), and skillful design assistance for the book's cover by Kirstine Edith Toft (my sister).

I would like to thank the artists and curators who have helped me with nuancing my understanding of the Nordic art context, whom I have met during the processes of curating the *Voyage to the Virtual* exhibition at Scandinavia House (2015) – with special thanks to Ariana Tiziani and Kyle Reinhart, some of whom have contributed their artist testimonial to this volume, the *Here All Alone* (2015) in Copenhagen, allowing for inspiring conversations with Swedish artist Anders Weberg, and during my involvement with the Screen City Biennial in Stavanger, Norway (since 2016), which has provided a curatorial and research framework for examining digital dimensions and implications of contemporary art in the urban context of Stavanger. Thank you, Daniela (Arriado), for inviting me in to develop the biennial and discourse around the 'expanded' moving image in this context with you.

I would also like to thank specific curators from the Nordic context who particularly inspired the thinking grounds of the book through in-depth interviews conducted in 2013, and who were important initiators within this realm of contemporary art in the Nordic context: Daniela Arriado – initiator of Screen City Biennial (was Screen City Festival in 2013 and 2015), Magdalena Malm – initiator of Mobile Art Production (2008–12) and Trevor Davies – initiator of the LightSound project (2008–10) and director of Copenhagen International Theatre. I thank you all for sharing your insightful perspectives on discourses and trajectories when operating on uncertain, experimental, interdisciplinary and media-material grounds in the domain of contemporary art – in this particular context.

I hope that this book will prove a helpful resource for researchers, artists, curators and others with an interest in the broad domain of digital art, as reference and perhaps an empirical point of departure for further research. I especially hope that by 'hearing' the artists voices, and voices by authors of diverse perspectives and areas of expertise, the book will stimulate and broaden thinking in the field of contemporary art as this is evolving and changing with digital culture and technologies. In particular, that it will further acknowledgement and support of new ways in which art can participate in forming society and our cultural horizons. It is thus my hope that the book will prompt others to pick up where the chapters and scope of the book end – continue with pursuing and examining in more depth the crucial questions raised in the book concerning the expanded domain, matter and inquiries of contemporary (digital) art.

Most ambitiously, and with particular regards to the Nordic context as the main domain of investigation, I hope the book will inspire the field of art (its gatekeepers, critics, fund distributors and initiators) towards greater open-mindedness when it comes to emerging forms and 'genres' of art, and encourage reformulations of how to assess art's quality – perhaps sometimes found in experimentation rather than reference – and considered value in society. To this extend I am grateful to the Nordic Culture Point, Lilian og Dan Finks Fond (The Royal Danish Academy of Sciences and Letters), Ny Carlsberg Fondet, Beckett-Fonden and Scandinavia House in New York City for supporting the book and its premise of contribution to the contemporary field of art. Also to my publisher Intellect and namely production editors Katie Evans and Jelena Stanovnik, who saw the potential of the book and patiently allowed for it to develop in focus and scope throughout the process. Support in all aspects for this project is important not only in order to maintain art's relevance as the antenna of our species but also to encourage continuous pursuits of new avenues for art and art's significance – in whatever forms, manifestations and inquiries it will explore – as an ethical, conscious and critical participant in (and on the critical verge of) the (digital) shaping of our future societies.

Tanya Toft Ag

Introduction

Tanya Toft Ag

A growing number of artists today evolve their art by means of 'the digital'. This concept evokes a condition in which society and our evolutionary system is intertwined with information technology and our everyday lives are organized by digital culture. Ever since digital electronics became ubiquitous in society, replacing and upgrading mechanical and analogue electronic technology during the last half of the twentieth century, digital culture has profoundly influenced how artists work, the intuitions and imaginations they work from, and their orientations and inquiries.

This book sets out to examine art's changing trajectories, meanings and roles – or 'genres' – in our present condition influenced by the digital. Especially, how the digital affects current artistic thinking as a point of departure for artistic discourse. While digital tools, software and environments increasingly constitute pencil, paint and canvas, the digital's influence on art is no longer a matter of experimentation with technologies in the peripheries of the world of contemporary art. Contemporary art reflects the increasingly digital organization of our life-worlds. It emerges contingently with the ubiquitous and intelligent digital technologies of our contemporaneity that structure our networked society, cultures and social relations.

With very few exceptions, almost all art made today is affected by dynamics of the digital because it is produced within digital culture. This also goes for art that does not employ digital technologies or materiality. This book approaches *digital art* in terms of art that derives from practices in which digital technologies provide an essential dimension to the artwork's conception, production and aesthetic materiality, as well as its exhibition. Rather than seeking to define and categorize new forms of artistic expression with the digital however, the book examines contemporary digital art as in a contingent condition with the dynamics of digital culture.

At the centre of the book's project is thus a concern with how contemporary art is affected by and responding to historically specific dynamics of governing structures, which to a large extent are connected to the dynamics of the digital today. The term *digital dynamic*, as appears in the book's title, announces a certain trajectory conditioned by digital culture that restructures our sociopolitical and cultural life worlds as a process of change over time. A digital dynamic might involve a force, frequency or energy that has come about by digital-technological development, released by the invention of a technology, system, infrastructure or interface that catalyses through our societal system and worldly ecologies. It might manifest in what we could call a trend, a patterned activity, or in schemes of innovation, producing motion and stimulating change. Digital dynamics reflect prominent diachronic forces in digital culture that also effect orientations in contemporary art and arts inquiries. The book's attention to broader societal digital dynamics, which structure the individual chapters, allows for broader perspectives on recent and current emergences in art in relation to society and development in technology. The aim is thus to excavate the deeper socio-cultural levels at which art's conceptual, material and operational inquiries reconfigure in digital culture today; to embrace a contemporary moment in which the digital is reconditioning art's form, presentation, and meaning – as well as its appropriation, manifestation, distribution, application and potential participation in processes of change.

In the late nineteenth century, artists broke with traditions to create art for the modern age, emphasizing innovation and experimentation in forms, materials and techniques in order to create artworks that better reflected modern society. Modern art emerged in technological dynamics of the Industrial Revolutions of the eighteenth and nineteenth centuries during which technology made a foundation for building the modern society by way of optimizing manufacturing and transportation, effecting urbanization with profound social, economic and cultural conditions for life – and for the artist. New technology, such as for example photography, introduced new methods in artistic practice for depicting and interpreting the world with aims of expanding people's worldview and providing access to new ideas. In modern art the technological medium was easily associated with representational form in cinema, photography and, notably, advertising. This book however avoids a point of departure for examining digital art in a model of representational discourse anchored in modernist ideals.

While representational discourse has largely dominated art theory since the beginning of the twentieth century, the digital art of today can however be seen to challenge the structures of representation – such as categories, forms and the fixation of meaning – and to deconstruct the very material of representational images. This book tries to avoid fixed ideas of art's form and categorization by genre, as well as established conceptions of 'legitimate' modes in which art has been considered to be autonomous and critical. It approaches contemporary art – digital art – as a zone of convergence of disciplines, practice methodologies and elements of everyday life with which art is contingent. Rather than seeing 'digital art' as a kind of genre or sub domain of fine art, the book pays attention to how contemporary art resonates with the contemporary society and its sociopolitical reality, as the art inquires into human perceptions, habits and actions. It explores a broader cultural–societal perspective on how art evolves with digital culture and expands into new territories and eventually into new modes of existence for art in society. The book takes this holistic point of departure in order to take into account the complexity in aesthetic modes by which contemporary art engages critically with our contemporaneity today.

Today, digital technologies are simultaneously tools for artistic practice and part of artists' everyday lives. The digital influences not only the tools and materials available for producing art, or the process of conceptualizing, planning and disseminating an artwork. Technological innovations and an increasingly digital, networked organization of contemporary culture contribute to a growing collective thought and awareness. Network culture and easy mobility enables artists to communicate, exchange ideas and collaborate across place. The proliferation of artists' websites, the online documentation of art installations, the digitization of analogue art, digital archives for video and new media art, as well as online video- and file-sharing services, shape an open landscape of increasing accessibility, visibility and interchange of aesthetics. Artists can maintain a more or less real-time overview of the art field, obtain knowledge of art groups or initiatives elsewhere and quickly pick up on tendencies and orientations in the global art world. Moreover, artists can reflect on their practice in relation to everything else produced, presented and documented *while* producing their artwork.

In acknowledgement of this condition, the book departs from the premise that the influence of digital technology on contemporary art begins before the artwork is produced, and even before the conception of an artistic idea. It begins where the artist intuitively finds inspiration, sees or feels an urgent need to respond to the world, and considers her or his capacity to act in the given societal or worldly conditions. Therefore, methodologically, the book examines first of all how the artist is implicated with contemporary realities and visions as a human being living in networked structures and connected to certain modes of discourse, forms of life, conceptions of thought and configurations of the common in our digitally organized reality today. It finds its point of departure in artists' own reflections on how the digital is changing their practices and position of agency today.

In the early stages of the book's development, during autumn 2015 and spring 2016, 78 artists were interviewed who employ concepts, materials and/or tools of digital culture as an integral component in their practices. These artists have generously granted their individual testimonials in response to questions inquiring into how the digital influences their work and working conditions; notably, how they consider the digital to enable, motivate or even evolve their artistic expressions in response to their contemporary societal context.

An extensive sample of these testimonials constitutes the first part of the book. They are organized thematically for the purpose of assisting the reader's navigation, but they are also offered as a resource for others to draw out different thematic lineages or patterns of artistic thinking. The testimonials present a kind of collective intelligentsia, offering an empirical window into how a current 'image of thought' in contemporary art evolves with the digital. They are collected during a time in which many artists (and many interviewed for this book) have practiced both before and during the introduction of digital technologies to mainstream society. Their reflections on how they have adopted digital tools in their practice, adjusted to a changing global and networked field of art, and how their coping with digital culture informs their inquiries, make a rich compound of knowledge that is crucial to archive for current and future understandings and analysis of this pivotal moment in the history of contemporary art – happening globally and in this book examined in a western, Scandinavian context.

The artist testimonials add up to what can be described as a collective 'image of thought' – a concept I borrow from philosopher Gilles Deleuze – as a sense of a common, collective and implicit mode of understanding that comes before actual thinking and which guides the creation of artistic concepts. Deleuze's notion of the term however carries a great deal of concern, as a dogmatic image that leads us to presuppose things, providing common pictures of what it means to live in the present while preventing us from authentic modes of thinking. While I use the term here in a less deterministic manner – and in the belief that artists might be among those of us who are more liberated from presupposed logics and repetitions – artists are nonetheless also cultural participants. The digital is a metapsychological phenomenon that facilitates our current adjustment to the present and the conditions of our communicative existence – for artists, authors and citizens alike.

With these considerations in mind, the book examines the overall questions: how does the digital participate in evolving contemporary art and aesthetics? How can we characterize an 'image of thought' emerging in the context of the digital era as orienting current artistic practices and discourse? And how may this 'image of thought' affect, encourage or enable contemporary modes of political aesthetics and resonance in the art? The book casts these questions from a point of departure in the life world of the artist as the visionary starting point for art's production and evolution.

Some readers might criticize the focus on 'digital' dynamics as announcing a special condition for contemporary art. They could argue that contemporary art is contemporary art, no matter the tools and materialities it is made from, and hence there would be no need to emphasize or delimit a focus on practices as particular for being 'digital'. In response to this imagined critique, I will however argue that the digital condition *is* special: first and foremost for bringing about a profound phenomenological, practical and self-referential subjective networked condition and digital culture within which artists depart their practices; secondly, for enabling the artistic expression to become generative and operative; and thirdly, for enabling art to be extended, distributed, reproduced, recycled, remixed and repeated globally and instantaneously. As proposed with the collective project of this book, these changing conditions are shaping a context for art that is profoundly different from contexts of previous paradigms – such as movements of the modern era and dominant conceptions of 'modern art' – from which we can begin to glimpse the emergence of forms, philosophies and orientations in art that will evolve toward still unimagined expressions and roles for art in future times.

The Contemporary Nordic Artistic Context

The book emerges from a concern with art as related to the conditions of being in (and belonging to) a particular context – namely that of the Nordic region. The Nordic artistic context, or *Norden*, refers to Iceland, Finland, Norway, Sweden and Denmark, as well as Greenland, the Faroe Islands and the Åland Islands. During the 1960s and early 1970s, coinciding with the early proliferation of digital computers when artists began to investigate the possibilities offered by technology, some of the avant-garde artists considered to be early pioneers in digital art emerged from the Nordic region. Among them were Swedish artist Billy Klüver, who collaborated with Jean Tinguely and Robert Rauschenberg on the Experiments in Art and Technology (E.A.T.) project in New York City; Icelandic artist Steina Vasulka, who, together with her partner and Czech artist Woody Vasulka, made media-based artworks based on video, electronic media performance and music programming in the early 1970s in the multi-use theatre The Kitchen (also in New York City); and Finnish artist Erkki Kurenniemi, popularly known for his electronic music compositions and design of electronic instruments in the early 1970s (Norberg and Engqvist 2009; Krysa and Parikka 2015) – undoubtedly together with a number of visionary female artists, who during these decades might not have been granted the appropriate attention and recognition to enter the archived art history we have available today.

We have to acknowledge the importance individual artists have played in an art historical perspective to how the field of contemporary art (and certainly in perspective of the Nordic art context) has expanded with technology; however it is not the ambition with this book to trace and promote 'new pioneers' of digital art in the Nordic art scenes. The aim is rather to examine the directions in which contemporary art is moving today – influenced by the digital – especially in consideration of the art's evolvement in response to particular conditions and challenges in the Nordic regional context and beyond. In light of our networked reality today, the book therefore examines emerging orientations in contemporary art in depictions of interconnected and collectively evolving artistic cultures, thoughts and expanding modes of agency, which the practices of individual artists may have furthered and exemplify.

To address a 'Nordic context' as a focus for artistic examination is not unproblematic. When initiating this book, the question surfaced of whether it even makes sense to speak of a regional context in relation to contemporary art, especially given our current networked, digital condition – a question echoed by several artists in their testimonials. When considering contemporary art that is symptomatic of our digital age, in which artists' inspirations and cultural boundaries are becoming more obscure, is it not just one big, interconnected and rhizomatic territory? Mindful of this challenge, the book examines how a contemporary national, regional as well as international mode of contextual existence informs artists' conditions for practicing, as well as the inquiries and expressions of their art. The term 'Nordic artists' is used in the book to refer to a broad category of artists who are working in, departing from or having strong affiliations with the Nordic art context. In that sense, the term includes artists whose origins are geographically non-Nordic, and artists who might originate from but have mainly lived and worked outside of the Nordic region.

Art in the Nordic context(s) has tendentially been characterized by a particular Nordic aesthetic canon, evoking the grand themes associated with nature and natural phenomena as portrayed in distinctly Nordic interpretations of realism, impressionism and symbolism at the turn of the nineteenth century (Jackson 2013). These periods of art history in the Nordic region offer a legacy of realist, magical, sublime and dark aesthetics, which reflect the natural environments of artists in this geographically specific context. Painters portraying nature have embraced an environment associated with rough landscapes and the characteristic Nordic light conditions (a region of stark seasonal contrast between a scarcity of light in the winter and long, luminous summer days), as well as a sense of authentic wilderness. This visual heritage from painting, together with a strong Nordic tradition of minimalism in design and architecture and a social-realist tradition in cinema, seems to have informed a certain aesthetic canon (or perception thereof) in Nordic contemporary art that still prevails today. This is sometimes portrayed by the Nordic subject as introverted, contemplative and melancholic, and examined in art through existentialist themes and a sense of intimacy between the human inner world and the surrounding natural or artificial world (themes also noted by art historian Lorella Scacco as characterizing Nordic video art in her book, *Northwave: A Survey of Video Art in Nordic Countries,* 2009). The digital however contributes to lifting the art out of the oft-repeated aesthetic narrative and into a complex, hybrid realm. With its focus on digital art this book thus seeks to avoid suggesting an extension of what might be a more or less established aesthetic or emotional canon.

Despite attempts to broaden the cultural conversation to incorporate the varied and emotionally rich identities and traditions of the Nordic region, the notion of a certain 'Nordic feel' can be said to inform an 'image of thought' in contemporary artistic practices in this context. Asked about the extent to which they believe that the themes or questions in their work reflect a Nordic context as a geographical, cultural, societal and political territory, and how they (as artists themselves) see the digital affecting art in this context and internationally, the artists' responses have brought some interesting and quite deviating reflections to the surface. We find in the testimonials a dichotomy between, on the one hand, an expressed awareness of certain Nordic aesthetic associations (for example, some of the artists – although not considering themselves as particularly 'Nordic' – acknowledge the 'Nordic themes and aesthetics' people recognise in their work, and, in some cases, even identify with a certain Nordic aesthetic discourse). On the other hand, some artists admit to distancing themselves from or plainly rejecting such a discourse while subscribing to an international artistic self-reference.

Eventually, most of the interviewed artists belong to a globalized world and work with universal, global themes. Some of the artists share in their testimonials a concern for using the Nordic term in a manner of implicit homogenization, which easily results in a sense of blindness towards the art and its diversity, especially considering how new orientations in contemporary art influenced by the digital increasingly develop in hybrid and translocal relationships. Their concerns evoke how an idea of 'the Nordic' as an aesthetic and cultural concept has been established and destabilized in continuous conflict since the 1980s; heavily criticized for romanticizing Nordic aesthetics through its use of unifying metaphors, and for eventually turning the Nordic concept into a marketing label (Ekroth 2008).

Digital Dynamics in Nordic Contemporary Art is intended to confront a tendency of homogenization in art that delimits the concepts and aesthetic foundations we use for decoding and making sense of it – for example, by reproducing a romanticist and perhaps in recent decades export-oriented aesthetic concept of the 'Nordic' as an aesthetically descriptive term. But also in terms of confronting a homogenized attitude to the forms art can take and its contexts of existence, the roles artists can enact, and how art might engage and exchange with other fields (e.g. biology, neuro science, design, architecture, urban development and innovation technology).

Jonatan Habib Engqvist evokes in his chapter the scepticism towards a Nordic concept in relation to art and suggests that the meaning of 'Nordic' as a descriptive term depends on what is attached to it at a given point in time by the individuals who make up the given context. When transported to the Nordic context, technological and global narratives seem to be taking on distinct forms reflective of the particular sociopolitical conditions in this context. The affects and resonances of artists' works, the aesthetic, cultural and social discourses they fuse into, and the politics they engage with, to some extent reflect a context in which some metaphors are more descriptive than others, where certain issues or politically informed conditions are more pressing than others, and where a certain collective awareness of the past, present and prospective future consequences of current matters enable art to have meaning and resonance. Art reflects not only what it immediately depicts or abstracts, but also the result of a complex process of interpretation and meaning making that is influenced by its cultural climate, local urgencies, perceptions and impressions of the contemporary context, as well as by the ideas and world-views of its contemporaries.

Engqvist's perspective points to how an 'image of thought' is eventually tied in with a given sociopolitical reality. Contemporary art thus reflects the challenges and changes taking place in established structures and belief systems within a given contextual society during a given period of time. In this perspective, the book's method of interviewing artists as point of departure for the authored chapters seeks to identify symptoms and patterns of adjustment and contingency in art with the specific sociopolitical context(s) of the welfare state, as found in the Nordic region.

While the Nordic context is one of aesthetic diversity and international influence, affected by globalization, internationalization, translocal exchange and hybridity, it encompasses a somewhat common social, cultural and political reality from which many of the interviewed artists depart or which conditions their practices. Some of the most deep-rooted and politically integrated common values of the Nordic region reflect a pursuit of collectivity that can be grounded in inter-Nordic cooperation on social policy in the 1930s and the post-war period (Petersen 2006: 68–69). As such, the Nordic countries share a common political history shaped by strong social democratic governments. This has formed a way of life and a general communality of values that can be summed up in a 'Nordic model' (Petersen 2006: 67). Characteristic to this model is a sense of collective upbringing in the welfare sector, in which education and healthcare are free (or have minimal fees), municipal day care for children is affordable, associations are common within both culture and sports, and labour unions are strong. All of this fuses into a contextual reality in which artists evolve their practice.

The collective upbringing in the social democratic project of the welfare state can be said to have cultivated a culture of collaboration and collectivity in the arts. This is also reflected in a tradition of support models for artist collectives, production networks, and labs providing access to technologies and equipment. As pointed out by both artists and authors in this book, the high quality equipment made available early on in shared environments within the Nordic art scene(s) may have given artists a regional advantage. In this condition, Laura Beloff for example describes how the field of bioart in the Nordic context emerged from groups of active individuals in small grass-roots organizations. Through arranging various workshops and events, artists and biohackers initiated new topics and activities before further developing them as formalized structures in the shape of small arts organizations. Still today, the sharing of equipment in autonomous artist environments is important to the development of media-based and digital art. Many artists mention their memberships in or affiliations with groups and networks, such as hacker communities, critical code studies groups, digital humanities groups, and other forms of artist associations, clubs or networks – what Jamie Allen and Bernhard Garnicnig characterize by a specific cultural tendency of 'instituting'.

The collective awareness we find in the Nordic context however also reflects a universal artistic language and culture that finds inspiration in Internet resources and networked phenomena, such as open-source software, and sharing and maker culture. As mentioned by some of the artists interviewed for this book, a logic within 'open-source' – i.e. using digital technologies as either material or method for artistic production, the integration of digital tablets, and the use of the Internet as a dissemination platform – has reshaped artistic practices by providing new conditions for participatory and collaborative art; DIT (do-it-together) replacing DIY (do-it-yourself).

It might be that a certain 'Nordic feel' is most visible in the methods artists use, or in the ways in which things are supported, as suggested by some of the interviewed artists. The Nordic context(s) for contemporary art and the proliferation of digital technology, culture and aesthetics within it has benefitted from public policy measures coinciding with the emergence and development of the welfare state in the latter half of the twentieth century. Particularly in Norway, Denmark and Sweden, public funding for art has been generous – not least in recognition of the important role that the arts and artists have been considered to play in the process of nation building and the construction of national identity. Support provided for individual artists' practices has largely reflected a policy of 'improving the preconditions for artistic creation' by granting financial support directly to individual artists – traditionally in the form of income guarantees and grants for projects or individuals (Heikkinen 2003: 7). Additionally, since the mid-1960s Nordic cultural funds made available under the Nordic Council of Ministers, an official body for inter-governmental co-operation in the Nordic region, have acted as a key component in encouraging artistic and cultural cooperation and exchange between the Nordic countries (full disclosure: also this book project has received support from Nordic funds).

While reflecting a global political climate characterized by neoliberal governance, increasing commercialism and formation of non-transparent (digitalized) modes of surveillance and control, the Nordic region nonetheless faces a current critical moment for the collective belief in the social democratic welfare project. In perspective of – but not only relevant to – the current state of this particular regional context, *Digital Dynamics in Nordic Contemporary Art* also tracks relations between artistic modes of practice and inquiry against the contours of societal protocol, endemic to the (declining) liberal, social democratic welfare state.

Digital Dynamics – Introduction to Chapters

While aiming to shed light on a recent chapter of art's history (or, histories, in consideration of how contemporary art emerges in convergence of fields with different histories of equal influence), particularly within the Nordic context, this book does not set out to announce a complete framework for all the digital dynamics that can be considered to influence contemporary art today. The aim is rather to point out some of the significant forces or tendencies of digital culture that influence momentous orientations or shifts in contemporary art.

The book contains chapters by seventeen authors who have extensive experience with the contemporary Nordic art scenes as well as international digital art environments. The chapters examine how the digital influences contemporary artistic discourse and how this digital influence has impacted the art scenes differently in the national contexts of the Nordic region. The authors draw historical lineages that characterize in particular the different Nordic contexts for contemporary art, some of which have escaped the conventional mono-Nordic art historical canon. In these lineages, they recall people, ideas, places, events, sociopolitical changes and cultural characteristics that have been pivotal in shaping what amounts to a current, expanded Nordic context of contemporary art.

Departing from the artist testimonials the authors have each identified a digital dynamic around which their chapter is structured. The depicted digital dynamics are anchored in the authors' observations of the relationship between societal technological innovation and artistic discourse. In particular, how the digital influences subjectivity construction and the agency of citizens and artists (as citizens) under the contemporary neoliberal and sociopolitical conditions of the Nordic welfare state in the latter half of the twentieth century and early twenty-first century. Each chapter thus opens up to ways of understanding connections between political dimensions in art and society today. However, as is explicated in the different chapters, each local context has different forces that dominate the historical sensorium, and therefore what these connections entail varies between the different national Nordic contexts. Moreover, the digital dynamics structuring the chapters are not unique to the Nordic context. While their concrete influence on contemporary art and society is examined in light of conditions and challenges of this specific context, they are also examined in perspective of wider global interrelations, exchanges and aesthetic encounters.

In his chapter 'Dynamic Seclusion: Nordic Noir and Digital Culture', Jonatan Habib Engqvist examines the 'Nordic' term in relation to art in detail and with thorough attention to its coming about and philosophical complexity in the Nordic cultural context. He identifies a dynamic of seclusion as a consequence of recent technological developments, namely the personalization and filtering of the Internet, causing isolation of individuals and communities. He evokes a common aesthetic notion of 'Nordique noir' – relating to artistic themes of isolation, alienation, and eventually, escapism – as an artistic effect of this dynamic and a response to the dematerializing welfare state, depression and high suicidal rates in the

Nordic region. Engqvist however points to a rise of a potentially different direction for art in the conception of 'Nordic magical realism', transfiguring in cultural modes of absurdity and humour and perhaps to be traced in a desire recently emerging for the spiritual and imagination. With this he suggests a potential politically persuasive horizon from which new meaning, relevance and a newfound intelligence for Nordic culture and contemporary art might arise.

Jens Tang Kristensen's chapter 'Concretism and Danish Digital Art: New Political Dialogues from an Avant-Garde Perspective' identifies how a dynamic of technical fetishism in contemporary art can be detected in the post-war art movement known as *concretism*, a Danish variant of the avant-garde. This movement, which he traces in a thorough historical analysis of the Danish post-WW2 avant-garde scene, considered art to be integrated into the public sphere and workplace in a self-referential form – expanding and complicating the concept of 'art' from a discreet and authentic object to a universal, non-objective form based on socialist, humanist and mathematical principles. In the contemporary continuation of the work of the historic avant-garde, Kristensen sees a potentially subversive critique of the global, neoliberal doctrine of Nordic societies today in the sociopolitical engagement of digital art. He emphasizes the need for new forms of artist collectives and calls for the artistic activist act to occur through activist-oriented modes of life-practice in sync with broader global collective movements.

In the chapter 'The Art of Instituting', Jamie Allen and Bernhard Garnicnig examine a digital dynamic within a networked sense of collectivity, and how this has influenced and enabled institutional experimental sites of thinking and production. They locate a tendency to organize oneself in collective groups as particularly evident in the Nordic context, reflecting a cultural history of 'instituting' (i.e. the formation of associations and unions) and today forming sites of hacker spaces, DIY technology groups, and artist-run project studios that hover between science, art and technology. These sites are necessary, the authors argue, as institutional forms to diversify responsibility across collectives, while simultaneously helping to equalize agencies, energies and temporal resilience, and exert post-capitalist influence.

Jøran Rudi identifies in his chapter 'Representation, Complexity and Control: Three Aspects of Technology-Based Sonic Art' a digital dynamic of data convergence into binary representation. This is a mechanism by which discrete numbers within digital media replace continuous signals in analogue media, and content becomes available for mathematical operations and 'filters' our experience. He locates this dynamic in binary representation in sound art, for example soundscape recordings combining digital, social and biological processes, and in digital art that appropriates other kinds of data, for example sensor data from the environment. Rudi stresses how the mechanization of sound as data allows for its combination with other kinds of material data, which increasingly characterizes 'sonification' (representation of data by non-musical sonic means) and which opens up new avenues of complexity, control and conceptual developments in sonic art – allowing for stronger connections to the 'real' world, which might be a prerequisite for developing new forms of 'nearness' in our landscape of make-believe and increasing behavioral adaptation to technological environments.

Budhaditya Chattopadhyay's chapter 'Uneasy Listening: Perspectives on (Nordic) Sound Art After the Digital' examines a digital dynamic of spatiotemporal disembodiment, identified in how soundscapes of everyday life have become increasingly 'unsitely' – disorienting and juxtaposing soundscapes from other places and times. Chattopadhyay examines this dynamic in the methods of contemporary sound artists who use 'unsitely' aesthetics to trigger subjective experiences that purposely disorient or disembody the sonic object. He emphasizes a potential in the art to counteract society by way of offering alternative sonic experiences to society's constructions of medial encounters.

In 'Reformulations of the "Natural" World: Jana Winderen's Sound Installation *The Wanderer*', Ulla Angkjær Jørgensen addresses the fixation and quantification of nature as scientific phenomenon. Jørgensen elaborates on how the quantification of nature tends to disconnect humans from it – and with that, disconnects us from the critical ecological conditions of our planet. In examining the aesthetic reformulations of human-nature relations in the audio works of the Norwegian artist Jana Winderen, who excavates data materialities and presents these to audiences in an accessible form, Jørgensen proposes an alternative concept of nature as a quality embedded in and dependent on human perception and sense-experience.

In 'Intertwining of the Digital and the Biological in the Artistic Practice', Laura Beloff examines a dynamic of scientification in the biological realm and the recent shift in technology-based arts towards techno-organic works and practices, which combine biological organisms and living matter with technology. She examines artistic emergences in between the biological and the technological realms as affecting the wider field of contemporary art, influencing a certain environmental aesthetic in Nordic contemporary art, while pointing towards current and future redefinitions of our human relationships with 'nature'.

Björn Norberg addresses in his chapter 'In Between Worlds' a dynamic of real and virtual fusion, a condition of digital culture by which the natural and artificially mediated environments increasingly merge together in augmented scenarios and designs of everyday life. From a personal, embedded approach, he draws on his own experiences of working with art and new media since the late 1990s – particularly in the Swedish context – to trace how the current artistic orientation in creating immersive environments grew out of the formation of art collectives in the 1990s and today manifests in practices offering real-virtual experiences on the premises of artistic inquiry. Norberg's analysis sketches a critical moment for artistic application of immersive technologies in a daunting technological climate of human infancy towards smart city visions (for Stockholm and beyond).

Elizabeth Jochum and Mads Deibjerg Lind's chapter 'Virtual Worldmaking: Cultivating Digital Art Practice' examines a dynamic of interdisciplinary fusion. In particular, the chapter explores how digital innovation traverses art, entertainment and industries, with Virtual Reality (VR) as an example of how aesthetic interventions operate within a complex network of industrial, social and cultural needs, while intertwining with political and economic imperatives. With Denmark as a contextual example, where public and private funding for arts and digital growth often explicitly call for innovation and outreach activities, they point at the far-reaching consequences of this dynamic for the contemporary art scene where art is interdependent on the larger political and cultural economy.

In the chapter 'Computational Diffusion and Art's Radical Rematerialization', I characterize a dynamic of computational diffusion that transforms all urban surfaces, materials, architectures and infrastructures of our world. I describe how this dynamic is reflected in a conceptual shift from 'dematerialization' to 'rematerialization' in digital- and media-based art. Namely in a manner I describe as *radical rematerialization*, denoting how media art implements directly and operationally into the surfaces, connections and (media) architectures that 'materialize' (or make up) our environments and life-worlds today. Within the Nordic context, in which resistance happens through sensible redistribution rather than activism and protest, radical rematerialisation enlivens a political aesthetics in art, potentially changing (by re-materializing) how the world is organized and fabricated 'materially' and sensibly.

In her chapter 'Critical Thoroughness: The Dynamics of the Artist as User and Producer of Digital Elements', Mette-Marie Zacher Sørensen examines a digital dynamic of digital material crafting by which 'users' of digital culture simultaneously become producers of digital media and aesthetic material. She identifies this dynamic in the practices of Nordic artists who produce their digital elements from scratch, from a method, approach or, perhaps rather, an attitude that she names 'critical thoroughness'. With this, she argues, artists regain a sense of human agency and independence within the frameworks, templates and tools of digital culture.

In her chapter 'Interactivity Dynamics', Lorella Scacco examines a digital dynamic of interactivity of digitally informed systems and infrastructures in contemporary artworks. She traces various modes of interaction within the artistic practices of bioart, light installations, electronic and algorithmic installations, interactive projections and sound art. She examines how, through the quality of interaction, explored through digital art, we can rediscover our relation to the world. In perspective of the practices of contemporary artists Laura Beloff, HC Gilje, Mogens Jacobsen, Egill Sæbjörnsson and Jana Winderen, she suggests that interaction entails a rediscovery of a new hybrid relationship with nature.

In the chapter 'Where the Inaction Is: The Politics of Digital Things and the Significance of the Lab… in the Practices of Laura Beloff, Kollision and Mogens Jacobsen', Morten Søndergaard examines an opposite mode to the dynamic of 'interaction' in the critical notion of 'inaction' as a cultural and political, speculative mechanism in society today. He describes how when transmitted into the physical materiality of fabrics, architecture and 'things', this mechanism effectuates ideological frameworks for our conceptual understanding of the world and affects the ways in which we operate with phenomena and perception. Søndergaard suggests that artists in their practices with the digital – as forms of laboratories – may propose inversions of the digital dynamic effect of interaction, and hence in their practices lies an opportunity for reducing imperatives of interactive aesthetics to democracy-diminishing modes of inaction.

In 'Visions and Divides in Icelandic Contemporary Art', Margrét Elísabet Ólafsdóttir depicts a digital dynamic characteristic of the adaptation of digital technology in the context of Icelandic society, located in the divide between scepticism and enthusiasm in attitude to new technology. Based on her curatorial involvement in the Icelandic art scene and historical research, she explains how this divide has translated into two coexisting discourses in the Icelandic art scene: on the one hand, technological vision and the formation of a 'media art scene'; and on the other hand, artistic evolvement in the more established scene of 'contemporary art'. She argues that this dynamic has resulted in a dominant non-media specific attitude to contemporary art, which consequently has not benefitted from experience through an experimental phase with new technology (unlike other Nordic and international art contexts). Olafsdottir's chapter evokes a concern with dichotomy and distinction between fields and phenomena that beyond her analysis located in the context of Icelandic art is critical to how knowledge evolves and results in practice in Western epistemology and co-evolution of culture and technology in society and the world at large.

Stahl Stenslie characterizes in his chapter 'Digital Dragons of the North: On Digital Dynamics and New Nature in Nordic Aesthetics' a dynamic of technological optimism in terms of a visionary and passionate relationship with new technologies, which he identifies in highly technologically developed Nordic societies and also in artists' use of advanced technology in their practices today – mainly in regards to the Norwegian context. This dynamic influences artistic methodologies today of applying scientific technologies combined with social networking tools and expressions of political activism to examine the world – and nature – as an experimental and living laboratory.

References

Amirsadeghi, Hossein (2015), *Nordic Contemporary*, London: Thames & Hudson.

Anderson, Steve F. (2007), 'Aporias of the digital avant-garde', *Digital Humanities Quarterly*, 1:2. www.digitalhumanities.org/dhq/vol/1/2/000011/000011.html. Accessed 1 March 2018.

Deleuze, Gilles (2000), *Proust and Signs: The Complete Text* (trans. R. Howard), Minneapolis: University of Minnesota Press.

Ekroth, Power (2008), 'Pissing on the Nordic miracle (2008)', *Art Map*, www.artmap.com/powerekroth/text/pissing-on-the-nordic-miracle. Accessed 1 February 2016.

Heikkinen, Merja (2003), *The Nordic Model for Supporting Artists – Public Support for Artists in Denmark, Finland, Norway and Sweden*, Helsinki: The Arts Council of Finland in cooperation with the Nordic Cultural Institute.

Jackson, David (2013), *Nordic Art: The Modern Breakthrough 1860–1920*, Munich: Hirmer Publishers.

The Kitchen Official Website (2017), '1970s', www.thekitchen.org/event/steina-and-woody-vasulka. Accessed 1 March 2018.

Krysa, Joasia and Parikka, Jussi (2015), *Writing and Unwriting (Media) Art History. Erkki Kurenniemi in 2048*, Cambridge, MA: The MIT Press.

Norberg, Björn and Engqvist, Jonatan Habib (2009), 'The Nordic pioneers of new media art', *Gama Gateway*, www.gama.hfk-bremen.de/on-media-art/the-nordic-pioneers-of-new-media-art/. Accessed 1 March 2018.

Petersen, Klaus (2006), 'Constructing Nordic welfare? Nordic social political cooperation 1919–1955', in Niels Finn Christiansen, Nils Edling, Per Haave and Klaus Petersen (eds), *The Nordic Welfare State: A Historical Reappraissal*, Copenhagen: Museum Tusculanum Press, pp. 67–98.

Scacco, Lorella (2009), *Northwave: A Survey of Video Art in Nordic Countries*, Milan: Silvana Editoriale.

Part 1

Directory

Katja Aglert
Practicing with the digital since approx. 1998
Swedish, works worldwide
Testimonial pp. 40, 59, 76, 103

Matti Aikio
Practicing with the digital since 2009
Finnish, works and exhibits mainly in Norway, Finland and Sweden
Testimonial pp. 45, 70, 109

Hrund Atladóttir
Practicing with the digital since 2004
Icelandic, works and exhibits mainly in Iceland and USA
Testimonial pp. 36, 102, 108

AUJIK (Stefan Larsson)
Practicing with the digital since 2001
Swedish and Japanese, exhibits worldwide
Testimonial pp. 38, 108, 112

Laura Beloff
Practicing with the digital since 1995-96
Finnish, works and exhibits mainly in Europe
Testimonial pp. 57, 61, 68, 73, 76, 85, 87, 98

Bombina Bombast (Emma Bexell and Stefan Stanisic)
Practicing with the digital since 2012
Swedish and Serbian, works and exhibits mainly in the Nordic countries
Testimonial pp. 43, 58, 61, 66, 77, 92, 101

Niels Bonde
Practicing with the digital since 1990
Danish, works and exhibits mainly in Denmark, Sweden, Germany and USA
Testimonial pp. 35, 99, 101, 105

Jesper Carlsen
Practicing with the digital since 2001
Danish, works and exhibits mainly in Denmark
Testimonial pp. 43, 69, 101

A K Dolven
Practicing with the digital since 1995
Norwegian, works and exhibits worldwide
Testimonial pp. 33, 38, 111

Tor Jørgen van Eijk
Practicing with the digital since 2000
Norwegian, exhibits worldwide
Testimonial pp. 44, 65, 74, 97

Alberto Frigo
Practicing with the digital since 2000
Italian, works and exhibits worldwide
Testimonial pp. 44, 47, 50, 78, 89, 105

Søren Thilo Funder
Practicing with the digital since 2002
Danish, works and exhibits mainly in Denmark and worldwide
Testimonial pp. 37, 51, 64, 79, 82, 88, 97, 102

HC Gilje
Practicing with the digital since 1995
Norwegian, works and exhibits mainly in Norway and Europe
Testimonial pp. 46, 94, 107

Goto80
Practicing with the digital since 1993
Swedish, works and exhibits mainly in Sweden
Testimonial pp. 50, 55, 79, 83, 100, 104

Marie Munk Hartwig
Practicing with the digital since 2010
Denmark, works and exhibits mainly in Denmark and England
Testimonial pp. 38, 46, 66, 68, 80, 86, 89

Bjørn Erik Haugen
Practicing with the digital since 2002

Norwegian, works and exhibits mainly in the Nordic countries and Europe
Testimonial pp. 42, 72, 102

Ilpo Heikkinen
Practicing with the digital since 2008
Finnish, works and exhibits mainly in Finland, and occasionally elsewhere
Testimonial pp. 34, 59, 64, 81, 85, 88, 110

Marianne Heske
Practicing with the digital since 1984
Norwegian, works and exhibits worldwide
Testimonial pp. 40, 107

Hanna Husberg
Practicing with the digital since approx. 2000
Finnish, works and exhibits mainly in Nordic countries and Europe
Testimonial pp. 36, 39, 70, 110

IC-98 (Patrik Söderlund and Visa Suonpää)
Practicing with the digital since 2006
Finnish, works and exhibits worldwide
Testimonial pp. 43, 82, 98, 110

Illutron (testimonials by Nicolas Padfield and Mads Høbye)
Practicing with the digital since 2003
Danish and international, works and exhibits mainly in Denmark, occasionally Sweden, Berlin and USA
Testimonial pp. 34, 57, 60, 81, 87, 93

Marie Kølbæk Iversen
Practicing with the digital since 2004
Danish, works and exhibits mainly in Denmark and Brazil
Testimonial pp. 55, 56, 91, 103

Ewa Jacobsson
Practicing with the digital since the early 1990s
Swedish, works and exhibits mainly in the Nordic countries, Central and Eastern Europe and USA
Testimonial pp. 35, 36, 39, 40, 52, 53, 63, 74, 82

Mogens Jacobsen
Practicing with the digital since 1989

Danish, works and exhibits mainly in Denmark and worldwide
Testimonial pp. 34, 49, 75, 98

Johan Knattrup Jensen
Practicing with the digital since 2013
Danish, works and exhibits mainly in Denmark and worldwide
Testimonial pp. 53, 61, 67, 73

Vibeke Jensen
Practicing with the digital since 1990
Norwegian, works and exhibits worldwide
Testimonial pp. 34, 71, 81, 94, 100, 104

Lisa Jevbratt
Practicing with the digital since 1991
Swedish, works and exhibits worldwide, mostly in USA
Testimonial pp. 49, 70, 98, 104

Erik Johansson
Practicing with the digital since 2000 and professionally since 2008
Swedish, works and exhibits mainly in Sweden and Czech Republic
Testimonial pp. 53, 108

Arijana Kajfes
Practicing with the digital since 1997
Croatian and Swedish, works and exhibits worldwide, mainly in Sweden
Testimonial pp. 42, 48, 77, 89

Tove Kjellmark
Practicing with the digital since 2007
Sweden, exhibits worldwide
Testimonial pp. 69, 94, 111

Kollision
Practicing with the digital since 2000
Danish, works and exhibits worldwide
Testimonial pp. 34, 60, 64, 73, 81, 95

Jette Gejl Kristensen
Practicing with the digital since 1999

Danish, works and exhibits mainly in Denmark and USA
Testimonial pp. 69, 75

Kristina Kvalvik
Practicing with the digital since 2008
Norwegian, works and exhibits mainly in the Nordic countries
Testimonial pp. 53, 102, 104, 107

Marita Liulia
Practicing with the digital since 1988
Finland, works and exhibits worldwide
Testimonial pp. 39, 51

Lundahl & Seitl (Christer Lundahl & Martina Seitl)
Practicing with the digital since 2005
Swedish, works and exhibits mainly in the Nordic countries, UK and Europe
Testimonial pp. 38, 56, 61, 67, 80, 95

Anastasios Logothetis
Practicing with the digital since 2005
Swedish and Greek, works and exhibits mainly in Sweden and worldwide
Testimonial pp. 48, 64, 77, 101

Dark Matters
Practicing with the digital since 2005
Danish, works and exhibits mainly in Denmark and Europe
Testimonial pp. 43, 60, 65, 107

Mia Mäkelä
Practicing with the digital since 1992
Finland,works and exhibits mainly in Finland, Europe all around the western world
Testimonial pp. 39, 40, 45, 55, 107

Teemu Mäki
Practicing with the digital since 1994
Finnish, works and exhibits mainly in Finland and Europe
Testimonial pp. 37, 52, 90

Elisabeth Molin
Practicing with the digital since 2009

Danish, works and exhibits mainly in England, Denmark and Germany
Testimonial pp. 65, 79, 95, 101

Tone Myskja
Practicing with the digital since 1990
Norwegian, works and exhibits mainly in Norway
Testimonial pp. 41, 42, 63, 108

N55
Practicing with the digital since 1994
Danish, German, Norwegian, Swedish, works and exhibits worldwide
Testimonial pp. 60, 72, 86, 93, 97

Nuleinn (Rine Rodin & Magga Ploder)
Practicing with the digital since 2013
Danish and Icelandic, works and exhibits mainly in Denmark and Europe
Testimonial pp. 54, 68, 70, 96

Marjatta Oja
Practicing with the digital since 1989
Finnish, works and exhibits internationally
Testimonial p. 109

Erik Parr
Practicing with the digital since 2001
American, Icelandic, Finnish, works and exhibits mainly in the Nordic countries
and worldwide
Testimonial pp. 48, 49

Andrew Gryf Paterson
Practicing with the digital since 1997
Scottish, UK, works and exhibits mainly in Finland and Latvia
Testimonial pp. 37, 48, 77, 84, 98

Pink Twins (Juha Vehviläinen & Vesa Vehviläinen)
Practicing with the digital since 1997
Finnish, works and exhibits in Finland and worldwide
Testimonial pp. 36, 41, 66, 76

Tuomo Rainio
Practicing with the digital since 2004

Finnish, works and exhibits mainly in Europe
Testimonial pp. 54, 56, 88

Juan Duarte Regino
Practicing with the digital since 2002
Mexican and Finnish, works and exhibits mainly in Finland, Sweden, Estonia and Germany
Testimonial pp. 57, 64, 83, 93

Jacob Remin
Practicing with the digital since approx. 2002
Danish, works and exhibits mainly in Denmark
Testimonial pp. 34, 86, 38, 100

Stian Remvik
Practicing with the digital since 2010
Norwegian, works and exhibits mainly in Norway
Testimonial pp. 57, 60

Carl-Johan Rosén
Practicing with the digital since 2006
Swedish, works and exhibits mainly in Sweden
Testimonial pp. 33, 48, 49, 50, 55, 72

Petri Ruikka
Practicing with the digital since 2002
Finnish, works and exhibits mainly in Finland and worldwide
Testimonial pp. 44, 51, 63, 67, 92, 107

Anne Katrine Senstad
Practicing with the digital since the 1990s
Norwegian, works and exhibits worldwide
Testimonial pp. 41, 53, 67, 73, 83

Joonas Siren
Practicing with the digital since the early 2000s
Finnish, works and exhibits mainly in Finland and worldwide
Testimonial pp. 34, 65, 74, 99

Mats Jørgen Sivertsen
Practicing with the digital since 1988

Norwegian, works and exhibits mainly in Norway
Testimonial pp. 35, 39, 41, 44, 62, 69

Jacek Smolicki
Practicing with the digital since 2003
Polish, works and exhibits mainly in Sweden, Poland and Europe
Testimonial pp. 46, 47, 72, 80, 86, 90, 93, 99

Lisa Strömbeck
Practicing with the digital since 1995
Swedish, works and exhibits mainly in Sweden, Denmark and Germany
Testimonial pp. 41, 75, 84, 111

Egill Sæbjörnsson
Practicing with the digital since 1994
Icelandic, works and exhibits worldwide
Testimonial pp. 35, 62, 63, 71, 92, 94

Tina Tarpgaard (recoil performance group)
Practicing with the digital since 2003
Danish, works and exhibits mainly in Denmark and worldwide
Testimonial pp. 62, 82, 110

Hanne Lise Thomsen
Practicing with the digital since 1996
Danish, works and exhibits mainly in Denmark and the Middle East
Testimonial pp. 39, 88, 96

Björk Viggósdóttir
Practicing with the digital since 2003
Icelandic, works and exhibits in Iceland and worldwide
Testimonial pp. 42, 68, 71

Magnus Wassborg
Practicing with the digital since 1995
Swedish, works and exhibits mostly in Europe
Testimonial pp. 83, 84, 99, 110

Jana Winderen
Practicing with the digital since the early 1990s

Norwegian, works and exhibits worldwide
Testimonial pp. 45, 108, 109

Kristoffer Ørum
Practicing with the digital since 2004
Danish, works and exhibits worldwide
Testimonial pp. 37, 59, 74, 82, 91, 106

Artist Testimonials

Introduction

Between 2015 and 2016, with revisions and a few additions during 2017 and 2018, artist testimonials were collected from 78 artists, practicing individually and in groups, departing from or working within the Nordic art context(s), whose practices significantly engage digital technology. The artists were asked to describe how they experience the digital as influencing and having influenced their work and the contemporary art scenes in the Nordic contexts and worldwide; to what extent the themes or questions in their art reflect their connection with any geographical, cultural, societal and/or political Nordic context; and how the digital affects the ways in which their work responds to contemporary society.

The testimonials were collected to form a point of departure for the authors of the book's chapters. Conveying diverse perspectives and positions of artists of different generations, backgrounds and orientations, the testimonials as presented here are thematically organized and form a collective whole. Together, they reveal how the digital dynamics that currently change our world simultaneously change the inquiries and forms of contemporary art, by changing the conditions, tools and imaginations of artists' practices.

On Being an Artist with the Digital

A K Dolven

The digital is just part of being a person (artist) in our time and natural to use when needed. As any other influence, it is a part of who I am in our time and therefore, of course, part of the work.

Carl-Johan Rosén

To me, the digital departs from the immaterial processes within a computer processor, a CPU (central processing unit). The digital is an active process of transformation, not so much a static storage of binary data. In extension, the digital comes to represent all technologies, structures and activities that cooperate to keep these processes alive and therefore the digital becomes a term to describe a large aspect of contemporary society where humans and machines engage in mutual transformation processes.

Ilpo Heikkinen

The digital pierces almost everything I do. The most interesting thing about the digital (as with any other term as broad as this) for me is its relation to the world, how it changes, what it shows us – and what it does not. I do not really work with bits or data as an aesthetic category. I am interested in the relationship we have to them, what kind of power and meanings they carry, and how much we trust them.

Jacob Remin

The digital is in everything we do, it is how we exist in the world.

Kollision

The digital is the DNA of most of our work; it is not so much an influence as a native language.

Illutron

The digital is not merely influencing our work; it is the source, the inspiration, the core, the input, the output, the subject, the object, the cause, the result and the description. Our work relies on the digital and is meta-digital.

Mogens Jacobsen

I have a hard time believing that the phrase 'the digital' has any meaning. Digital tools and methods are being used in most contemporary art practices: Theatre, photo, video, sculpture, dance and music. Digital technologies are so pervasive; I do not think there is any such thing as the digital anymore. My everyday life is based on the same technologies as any white-collar worker's: Email, word-processing (like answering this survey), balancing budgets, etc. The main difference is probably the pay (mine is a lot lower!).

Joonas Siren

The tools I use of course have a fundamental influence on the actual work, but in general I feel like I am a citizen of a global digital online world and that has many effects on me and my work. I feel that I am a dual person, I have a real-life persona and a digital-online persona, and none is more real than the other. I am at the point where I cannot separate if the inspiration for an artwork comes from the digital online world or the actual 'real' world.

Vibeke Jensen

The digital is contemporary. This is why I am using it and why I am often intrigued (and appalled) by it – because the digital constantly offers new tools and ways of seeing, recording, projecting and communicating. Because my work engages with the everyday, with society and the public, it also engages with the digital. However, I do not define my work as digital or seek a specialized audience. The digital has become an integral part of most contemporary artists' research, communication, promotion, networking, sharing and knowledge base. Along with the connectivity provided by the Internet comes the inherent tracking, endless storing and corporate control of all this activity – the effects of this on the art scene are currently unfolding.

Egill Sæbjörnsson

The digital has played a vital role in my art making for the last 20+ years and my work is largely based on digital media, although I have started to widen the way I work to gain more width. I started doing animations as a child and I started doing projections when I got to know and could afford a video projector. I use computers and computer programs to make animations that are usually mapped onto surfaces of objects, standing on a pedestal or hanging on a wall. Sometimes I make everything myself, but in the recent years I have involved more people in the process. Some of my earlier works might have resembled a typical object or a typical artwork that one had seen before – but a layer of animated projections and sound was always added, which changes the appearance and effect of the piece in total. The animations are often spiced with humour, although they have an underlying tone of contemplation on different topics.

Ewa Jacobsson

I entered this field early on and have followed the eroding change of technical tools, considering them as different instruments with their own languages.

Niels Bonde

My work spans several media: painting, drawing, installation, video and digital media, CCTV installation, video installation, data-controlled installation, net-based art and animation. In a Danish context, I was a really early protagonist of Internet art: my *Recovered Files* project from 1993 – picked up from art school computers around the world that I remotely hacked access to – were made only a few months after Mosaic, the first web browser, came out.

Mats Jørgen Sivertsen

I grew up programming and making computer graphics, so it has always been part of my work. Although I sometimes yearn for something more tactile than the ephemeral ones and zeroes on the hard drive, I realize my perspective and perception of the work (and the world) is shaped by the digital in such a way that it is an integral part of me.

Ewa Jacobsson

The young, who are born into the digital, combine this with crappy old equipment and make their own mechanical instruments and objects and I find this to be a fine and exciting reaction to the absence of tactility and vulnerability that some digital medias have created.

Pink Twins (Juha Vehviläinen and Vesa Vehviläinen)

We are digital natives in the sense that we probably belong to the first generation that grew up with mass produced home computers, while also having experienced life before them. Since we started, digital technology has been a natural tool for us for producing art. A great majority of our work is immaterial and exists as digital files.

Hanna Husberg

I was introduced to digital instruments, such as computers, video cameras, digital cameras as well as to the Internet quite early, but I was not born with an iPad in my cradle. I have also, from an early stage, used digital tools when making art, in several cases in ways that explicate the differences in perception between machines and humans.

Hanna Husberg

The digital space of social media has become a very real space affecting us in our everyday lives. An enormous flux of information is being spread and shared over the Internet. This affects spatial and temporal relations and also raises economical and ethical questions. For example, the digital makes it possible to produce (art) objects at a reduced price on the other side of the world. Many artists are incorporating the ambiguities and complexities of these digital and global realities into their work. The digital pace also privileges some kinds of practices at the expense of others. The mere number of artists on the Internet makes it close to impossible to have an overview of current artistic practices.

Hrund Atladóttir

The digital can be an easy way to reach a wider audience, add motion and create grand illusions with little or no money. When you do not have to rent a studio, build sets and buy materials, you also do not have to deal with real problems like gravity and such, which can be a pain to work around when getting some complex idea across. The digital enables me to show a wider range of topics (being influenced from things online), using images from all over the world and working in English – for a wider audience. The freedom and range of possibilities always pull me back into the digital.

Teemu Mäki

The Internet and current ways of receiving and transmitting content in digital, immaterial form has opened the world to me, too. It is easy to get material, knowledge, stories and also images, video clips, sounds, and so on, online. When I started my career in the late 1980s and early 1990s, it was still difficult to get one's hands on books, films etc. In other words, because of digitalization, it is easy to feed one's artistic practice. Also, if I want, I can send photos or films as files anywhere, without any costs. It is liberating.

Andrew Gryf Paterson

The digital has encouraged me to get involved in subjects, scenes and activities in ways that (practice-wise) go beyond the mainstream contemporary art scene of the Nordic region, at least if we speak of galleries, museums and exhibition spaces presenting solely artefacts. From 1998 onwards, the digital has influenced my work in the use of software tools, media disk storage, organizing principles, theories to read or platforms online to represent and narrate my activity, process or work.

Kristoffer Ørum

I think the digital affects all parts of my practice: from sketching out ideas and writing applications, to producing and disseminating works of art. The reason why the digital interests me is because the use of mobile phones or screens in public spaces affects and interferes with daily life. It is not so much the technology in itself that interests me, but the exploration of the role that digital technologies play in our understanding of the world around us, in our self-images, and in turn in our behaviour and imagination.

Søren Thilo Funder

My works are primarily video and installation. They are mash-ups of popular fictions, cultural tropes and sociopolitical situations and histories. They are narrative constructions insisting on new meanings forming in the thin membrane negotiating fictions from realities. The digital allows for a different economic and logistic range of possibilities in the actual shooting of material. The hard disc capacities of the digital allow a different accumulation (and sloppiness) of shot material. I personally work highly performatively and experimentally with the participants of my video productions and often utilize the long time-cycles that the digital format enables. My works are always highly influenced by the digital – also in ways I cannot always answer for.

Kristoffer Ørum

As I work a lot with technologies that are traditionally categorized as digital, I am often referred to as a 'technological artist'. While this might not be completely wrong, to me much digital art continues traditions that have been part of the art scene long before the rise of digital technologies.

Lundahl & Seitl (Christer Lundahl and Martina Seitl)

Unknown Cloud on Its Way to Skinnarviksberget, Stockholm (2016) is our first purely digital work with no analogue media. It uses choreography and dramaturgy in the form of movement instructions, steering awareness of body movement in relation to the positioning of celestial bodies. This work simply could not have been made without the availability of key technologies. Smartphone location services access the viewer's location and orientation as they experience the work and activate different elements of the work's content. Web-based APIs are used to feed real-time data for the experience, including the weather in the viewer's location and the position of celestial bodies in space.

AUJIK (Stefan Larsson)

The AUJIK conceptual format is basically constructed as an esoteric cult, which derives from the Yamabushi monks; practitioners of an ancient-ascetic form of Japanese Buddhism called Shugendo. It is also influenced by ideas of technological singularity, as described by Vernor Vinge and Ray Kurzweil. During the years I have discovered new aspects and technologies that I have been adapting and incorporating into this concept. I mainly use computer-generated imagery (CGI) integrated into film footage, using motion-tracking software. I have also been working with Virtual Reality, 3D printing, installations, photos, and text-based art. For some of my videos I have made the music myself, for others I have collaborated with musicians such as Scottish electronica artist Christ and British modern classic/electronic composer Mira Calix.

Marie Munk Hartwig

Technology is clearly affecting the contemporary art scene, not only by the tools and technologies artists use, but also very much in what artists are eager to illustrate or tell. Artists are not only critical analysers of the digital world, but just as much a part of the development of it.

A K Dolven

I work with mixed media – analogue and digital – first of all based on content and concept. I have explored themes of looking for balance in the world and time we live in both politically, ethically, aesthetically and personally.

Hanna Husberg

My practice has been influenced by the time I spent in Paris, especially by the immaterial practices that emerged in the French scene in the 1990s. Even so, although I have not ever studied art in Finland and have lived most of my life in other contexts, my practice easily resonates with that of many other Finnish artists. I address the human relationship to one's surroundings, a theme which has been recurrent in Finnish art history, both in relation to natural environments as well as to the technological and man-made. I am particularly interested in a feminist-materialistic approach to this.

Mats Jørgen Sivertsen

Some of my works deal with themes around gender roles, sex and masculinity. I think these works are best understood in an egalitarian Nordic context.

Mia Mäkelä

In the live cinema-scene there were only a handful of women who performed on their own. It was considered a very tech and male oriented 'boys with their toys'-scene. That was the reason I directed audio-visual workshops especially for females in 2003. Since then, the workshop participant ratio has been almost equal, but men still dominate the performance scene.

Ewa Jacobsson

Digital techniques might create a gender problem. The young men working with advanced technique, which talk among each other and exchange help and support, and who are helped further because the new and advanced technique domain is highly appreciated, can be excluding. Where are the young women? It has been important to me in my choices of combined materials to learn the different tools so I can express myself. It is a societal and political action in itself to be a grown woman working in this sphere and still be working there, since 1983 with sound, film and photography, and since 1995 with digital tools.

Hanne Lise Thomsen

As a female artist who started in the 1970s, the relatively high level of gender equality in Scandinavia has played a major role in my work. Equal rights are essential if women are to navigate freely in their own lives. My art has always had a strong focus on gender, equality and diversity.

Marita Liulia

A female artist or director can have a very strong position in the Nordic countries. Most of the internationally successful Nordic artists are women. Also, equality and middle-class ideology influences art in this region.

On Digital Tools, Methods and Research Processes

Katja Aglert

I am right now writing this on my computer. My research in practice, when I collect material as part of the process, is commonly conducted with the use of my digital camera (still and moving image) and microphone. When I do research of other sorts I use the Internet and other digital media. I communicate via mail, have meetings over Skype. I would say that 90 per cent of my practice involves the digital, in one way or the other. Perhaps 100 per cent, because today, what is not in one or the other way influenced by the digital and as such influencing our work?

Marianne Heske

A new tool came into the world. Thanks to the digital, I could create my *Mountains of the Mind* video paintings (first shown in the Nordic Pavilion at the Venice Biennale in 1986). In my practice, I use unlimited kinds of materials in order to convey the message. I could make my dolls alive in a social context. 'All the world's a stage, and all the men and women merely players; they have their exits and their entrances; and one man in his time plays many parts...' – William Shakespeare.

Ewa Jacobsson

The digital came in as a new tool, first in sound – since this was fast becoming a method that you could afford, and also which did not use that much data, power and time. I use portable field equipment, which allows me to act freely, and have been able to work in studios where digital equipment was installed early on. I worked at DIEM in Århus with one of the first samplers (used in among other things *Berula Pimpinella* (1995), part of a Nordic land art exhibition titled Moxtrot in Godbrandsdalen in Roåker, Norway). Artist Morten Carlsen and I stretched one of the first sound fragments there.

Mia Mäkelä

In my early live cinema works from the beginning of the millennium, the 'digital' was very much my aesthetics; I was having a blast with pixels. I referred to these works as desktop visuals, or visual noise, which resonated with the experimental digital scene in the early years of the 'desktop revolution'. Lately, HD-video technology has opened up new exciting possibilities and aesthetics, which seem like a never-ending road to add more and more pixels per inch. This has not only affected my work and fed the hunger for 'good quality, more precision' but also the way I see the world. However, it can be tiresome when both the technology and the skill of mastering it get outdated after just five years.

Tone Myskja
I see the digital as an important tool in my artistic practice. Some artists use paint, some wood, some words, some use sound, and these are all different kinds of material that have certain qualities of expression; materials with limits and possibilities. I think of the digital as another tool with qualities that are suitable for my artistic aims. I am not a data nerd that uses hours learning new kinds of software out of technical interest. For every work I try to do something new, to surprise myself. I teach myself new software to be able to do what I want.

Mats Jørgen Sivertsen
I think availability of tools has been a big thing – the means of production are now available to everyone (at least in the context of western art-making). Software and hardware prices are down. Computers, HD cameras, 3D printers and audio interfaces of professional quality are no longer for the select few. The Internet has also had a big impact, of course. You can sit with your laptop, edit video and download the resources you want, from all over the world. Work that could only be realized by 'bank-roll artists' before can now be done on a low budget. It opens new doors.

Anne Katrine Senstad
I use the digital as a tool. It is not the subject matter itself. My work is not about technology or digitalization of the material. The digital allows me to intersect and interfere with space, large spaces, site-specificity, transformation of spaces, the psychological space, mobility and physical displacement.

Pink Twins (Juha Vehviläinen and Vesa Vehviläinen)
We are not purists or dogmatists. We see digital technology as a potent tool that gives a lot of possibilities and options to realize our works, but it also mixes well with analogue, acoustic or physical tools. Still, to realize the work we put a lot of effort into the way it is presented. We consider the work as digital handicraft. It happens mostly in the digital realm, it involves a lot of coding and working with algorithms. Employing parametric design is a natural way to work in digital surroundings and it is a great influence on our work. We typically use commercial software and existing tools, modify them for our needs or build our own.

Lisa Strömbeck
Since I seriously started to work with video in 1995, I have benefited enormously from every step in the digital upgrade in the medium of video. When I started out, I filmed and edited

my videos on S-VHS, then after a course at the Royal Danish Academy of Fine Arts I got into the better BETA-CAM editing room. Since 1998, at the Art academy we had AVID editing equipment, which made it much easier to make fancy editing such as A-B roll and different dissolves. When I finished the Art Academy in Copenhagen in 1999, I heard about Final Cut, an editing program that was possible to have on a private computer. It took some years before I could afford a computer with capacity enough for it, but when I did – and also got a pirate Final Cut Pro from a friend – it made my work much easier. In 2001, I edited a video on my own computer for the first time, which was *I Love You – You're Mine*.

Arijana Kajfes

The digital has affected the art scene both content-wise, with more time-based and temporary work and distribution-wise, creating a completely new and widespread arena through the social media. At this point I see the digital as a tool as any other, although at times I find it to be psychically limiting and too self-explanatory. When I started working with digital tools I was interested in the shift of materiality, time and space that was enabled with the medium and also in the plasticity of data or the signal, its possibilities of translation and transformation. Now it has become integrated in my work and I don't think about it too much.

Bjørn Erik Haugen

All the artists that I know use a computer of some sort as a tool in their art-practice, even painters. The digital is my main influence, my base for research and my main tool for creating art. All I do is work through a computer, and the result of my digital working method is central to the aesthetics of my work.

Tone Myskja

In my work I use a type of collage editing technique combining filmed natural material with digital developed material, building up a layered and complex imagery referring both to a natural and a digital world. I think this reflects the complexities and fluent character of contemporary social life. We live in a world characterized by transitions and rapid change, which has been a recurrent theme in my work.

Björk Viggósdóttir

Technology and technological advances in our contemporary society are simply astounding; every day there are new methods for the creation process and mediation of art. It is important for me to continuously keep up to date with the new technology and find ways to convey my ideas through my artwork. I work a lot with installations, very technologically complex installations that often entail research into some new technical aspects that might be the optimal method to create my art.

Bombina Bombast (Emma Bexell and Stefan Stanisic)
Today our work is based on many digital tools. We make VR films but additionally use video walks, live-streaming technology and apps as integral parts of our performances. Of course we document, archive and spread information about our work digitally, so in that sense now and in the future we will be influenced by the digital. By allowing senses to oppose or enhance each other in narratives in both our VR performances and Walks, you might say that the digital in a way has influenced our work to become more tactile and physically bold. Most definitely the digital has made us look out from our black box and search for other spaces than the given. For us, the digital has meant a higher level of interaction and mobility. For us the word *interaction* is synonymous with *negotiation*, and if anything, the digital has had such an impact on our world that what we are negotiating is not just the amount of influence it has had on art but also how we answer questions about what is real, what is close, what is yours and what is mine.

Dark Matters
We approach the digital as a tool for our work. As an artist, you have the mission to control the tool and not the opposite, which is the big pit trap of modern technology, in our humble opinion. We do Virtual Reality installations, but the VR goggles is just a tool to experience another universe. When the wow effect of the 360 degrees view is gone, you are in charge of making the story, concept and idea for the piece significant for the audience.

IC-98 (Patrik Söderlund and Visa Suonpää)
We are interested in society, not in the medium. The digital is just a tool for us. As heavy users of digital imagining products, we rely on these tools to realize our vision, especially when working on our animated films. Though the animations start with traditional pencil drawings, from that point on everything is made digitally. Then again, it is a question of what you are used to: we would work analogically if that happened to be a more familiar method for us. Ethically and politically, another important level of the digital is its infinite reproducibility, the lack of the auratic original and the ease and lightness of only having to deal with files.

Jesper Carlsen
I see the digital present as a constant stream of information and access to new tools to create content, so the process of actually creating the work becomes a form of sensory deprivation,

cutting the cord in a way and focusing on a single detail. Digital tools for communicating, spelling and translating enable me as a dyslexic, to communicate almost on equal basis, beyond the pure visual. Language, both text and visual, has become more democratized with the digital. Old monopolies, with perfectly pronounced or produced content, are only one voice among the many. I think that is really important, especially for people outside of the western world.

Petri Ruikka

Digital methods and tools are the foundation for many of my moving image works. Without certain digital processes many works would not have been made at all. The digital domain has created whole new areas to explore and while many things could be replicated through analogue methods, the speed and ability afforded by the digital allow for creating variations that are not possible to make in any other way.

Mats Jørgen Sivertsen

In a project I did some old-fashioned pencil drawings on paper. I soon started planning them on the computer, using software such as DAZStudio to pose the anatomical figures, rather than work from a live model or a photograph. At one point I even took photos of the unfinished drawing with my phone so I could try out some changes in Photoshop, before committing them to paper – where there is, of course, no possibility of undoing.

Tor Jørgen van Eijk

During three residencies at the former Experimental Television Center situated in Owego, upstate New York, I was among artists who work with a purely analogue video system. The work is, for the most part, done in real-time, for example including pre-recorded video through different patches. I have come to strongly appreciate the accuracy of a digital method of working – as opposed to the analogue workflow. The artist's digital control over the video-image can be manipulated down to its most minute detail. At my studio in Oslo, I work with a program called Jaleo. This is an obscure format running on Silicon Graphic computers from the late 1990s. An updated version of the program exists under the name Mistika. In the Jaleo program, the possibilities for processed manipulation of the video image are limitless. I utilize this possibility to its fullest potential with the ambition of composing fresh and new video images.

Alberto Frigo

The digital has become a tool for me to practice my art proactively and without so much post-editing. It is a method to deal with my mental proliferation, as much as the art of memory was for humanists prior to the enlightenment. The digital media I use are extensions of my programmed artistic willing and yet it is not the message, but the medium. When my right hand uses an object, my left hand picks the camera from a pouch on my belt to photograph it. I do not have to think about it; my life goes on unobstructed. In this respect, while the digital of my own art practice is literally part of me and has very little influence, the digital that has grown around me – like social media as well as traditional mass media – is the great source of influence. If I write down a dream about having sex with a top model I can trace back the movie or the newspaper commercial that has provoked such a dream. I therefore feel that, through my digital art practice, I am simply filtering the overflow of the big digital mediascape surrounding me as well as others. My practice with the digital is therefore a way to deal with the digital mainstream and stay human, like a Chinese farmer refuses to automate the irrigation of his field and instead gets the water manually.

Mia Mäkelä

I work with digital video, audio recording and editing, live cinema, live audio-visual art, visual composition, video effects, image manipulation and digital alchemy. The digital has allowed me to do artworks on my own and move around with lightweight equipment. My whole art production can be fitted into a two square centimetre physical space (SD card). That has allowed for a nomadic lifestyle.

Matti Aikio

Working with digital tools makes it easier for me to work very lightly among indigenous communities. I can work on the road without a large team and gather a lot of material relatively modest budget. But on the other hand, I feel that digital tools are taking something away from the artistic process, like your brain also needs more hands-on, practical practice to be able to develop the work, so I am always trying to find ways to include more manual practices in my process as well.

Jana Winderen

I use the digital realm to obtain knowledge. It is convenient that I can access papers online, for example, about how fish hear or the sounds made by crustaceans. Through these papers, links and websites I can find professors and others working with similar interests. Research is more accessible now through digital media than it used to be when I had to go to the university library, searching through books to find a fraction of the information I can now find in almost an instant.

I used to love making things and the physicality of the world surrounding us – especially localities with less interference by humans. I go to these wilder places, bring my recording gear for audio and images, and bring the digital recordings back to the studio. In some ways my studio is more outside than in. I hope, through using sound as my main medium, that at least I make smaller objects. Storage takes less space than it would have if I had continued with making large sculptures, as I started to do in the beginning of my art education. I am interested in highlighting places and issues through the medium of sound and to make what we do not necessarily think of – in terms of sound – audible, from animals operating in inaccessible places or frequency ranges not audible to humans.

HC Gilje

When I make my work, in the back of my head I always work with the idea of improvisation. My custom tools allow me to work like this also when involving hardware and software, making it possible to do projects in a park in Rabat, Morocco, in an abandoned industrial site in Russia or in a forest outside of Oslo.

Marie Munk Hartwig

I am interested in trying to illustrate the effects of the digital world and translate the digital tools into something else, rather than literally using the tools. When responding to technology, it can be a dilemma to use it. If I wish to illustrate a future scenario, technology restricts me with the state of development it is currently in. If I imagine a new future technology, it is important to think of other ways to picture the idea. The same goes for the situation with materials and materiality in general. Technology has developed its own aesthetics. Literal technological references are no longer only futuristic symbols; they can also be nostalgic. Technology is becoming less and less foreign to us, almost more natural and reliable than nature itself. What both challenges me and drives me in my work is to imagine these future perceptions in society and use those, rather than the current ones.

Jacek Smolicki

I perceive my artistic practice as being divided into two major streams: exhaling and inhaling. Exhaling happens through various projects, international collaborations and initiatives that take forms as self-enclosed, temporary projects (e.g. installations, sound-walks, performance), which is to say a rather conventional means of participation within the realm of art. The inhaling stream is my *On-Going Project*, which perhaps lends itself to be described as durational art or personal, experimental archivization, or what I came to call para-archiving. This initiative is tightly embedded into my everyday life and, in contrast to the first stream, is not constrained by time, space or any other external mechanisms of the art world. This initiative, performed ever since 2008, is a consistently woven, multi-modal archive aided by a reflectively and subversively deployed set of recording and tracking technologies.

Stemming from a project aimed at mapping and archiving sounds of everyday life, *On-Going Project* consists of several practices carried out, as the very title suggests, in an on-going, open-ended, yet regular and consistent way. These practices include, for instance, documenting patterns of my daily walks by the means of a wearable GPS device, recording at least one minute of soundscape every day, making one collage every week out of freely distributed newspapers and recording ten seconds video each time when stumbling upon a particular and thought-inspiring configuration of various elements of the public space. During the last several years of executing the project, due to the stability of its principles and its long-term, durational character, *On-Going Project* became a type of a lens aiding me to better spot, address and reflect on various techno-cultural transformations and evermore dynamically changing, archiving, recording and storing technologies, as well as digital practices they give rise to. This is why I also use *On-Going Project* and its constituent practices as a methodology in researching the ways of living with complex implications of our contemporary technological condition, which I describe in terms of 'capture culture'.

Alberto Frigo

My work in progress has often been seen as retaining two negative connotations: on the one hand, critics have looked upon it as a form of archiving and more recently as a form of hoarding. I understand the quick associations of these theoretically grounded critics, however, having myself investigated in their theories, I have come to the conclusion that the method or drive behind my practice relates to a sense of digital 'stowing'. Therefore, if hoarding is an exuberant collection, and archiving is a dictatorial act, I see my practice, and that of other more or less known practitioners, as a precarious sampling of chosen elements in life within a predetermined structure meant one day to be transmitted to a different temporal and/or spatial dimension and there scavenged of its potential. Technology enthusiasts have quickly labelled my practice as 'life logging'. While life logging makes use of sensors and algorithms to record the lives of their users effortlessly, my artistic operation is 'effort-full'. I am, therefore, up to some kind of digital life-stowing practice. This implies that I do not use any automation but manually pick what in my scheme ought to be stowed. Coming perhaps close to the realm of Database Aesthetics, I sample different aspects of reality while using a broad palette of different techniques to do so.

Jacek Smolicki

Archiving, especially personal archiving, is the main domain of my artistic and scholarly interest. Both through my own practice and by pointing at others' meaningful practices I am trying to inspire possible directions that one might take in order not to feel subjugated by the increasing automation and standardization of the means we use – or are used by – to document our lives. By these standardized means I mean not only mainstream frameworks for personal data aggregation, like Facebook, or more generally practices of obsessive data capturing, but also network media at large, which can be looked at as to some extent enrolled in an involuntary, ubiquitous archivization of our everyday lives.

Erik Parr

I see my practice as a continual research process. I often find a question that interests or provokes me in some way and I then approach that in different ways, using different strategies and media. The work emerges out of that process through many different experiments. The work is simply a response and often part of a larger process of inquiry.

Arijana Kajfes

My artistic practice is often process-oriented and time-based. I come out of a sculptural tradition and I always work in the context of real space and physical presence, whether it is with more immaterial media such as light or sound, or with objects.

Andrew Gryf Paterson

My artistic practice is strongly process-oriented. I often like to say the process involves 'outcomes and -goings', to emphasize that what might be presented as results are more often just the marks and traces in the process of development. I started out with very material and physical workshop processes, then the increasingly immaterial and ephemeral ones.

Carl-Johan Rosén

My practice has gradually come to involve more long-term investigations into specific aspects of the digital process itself. Since 2008, my main question has been: What is it like to be a digital process? Or, what is it like to be 'a running software'? In order to communicate with this sort of digital actor/object that I believe the process to be, through several investigatory art projects I have increasingly focused on the details of digital materiality and digital processes.

Anastasios Logothetis

One could argue that my practice is about subverting the way in which artists are required to work in a research-like manner towards a uniform goal (whatever that may be); moving freely between a diverse multitude of themes, materials and methods. Like a fluid, or as a digital nomad, I transpose between a set of ideas and personalities to allow for (only) seemingly paradoxical entities to materialize in a unity so as to display the confused period of our times as time-sculptures of terrifying ambiguity and vulnerability.

Carl-Johan Rosén

Through the de-digitization of digital processes or digital material (code on paper, video as object, etc.), I try to extract key concepts of the digital. This can be compared to a sort of *Verfremdung* of objects permeated with the digital, in order to begin forming a new language through which we can critically discuss what it is to be 'a digital process'.

In my practice I have been working with the concept of 'code', starting with the publication of the book *I speak myself into an object* (2013), which is an attempt to turn a digital process inside out and investigate code as a common language of humans and digital others. As an example, my work *At the Catastrophy-Point* (2016) is based on an early, programmed video (film) artwork (Manfred Mohr's *Complementary Cubes* (1973–74)), where through video analysis I am trying to recreate or find the code that preceded the video. Connecting video surface and video code by micro-narratives – or via paths through the digital video material – will hopefully enable a different understanding of, or at least a different perspective on, code; and, of the particular digital actor that Mohr created.

Lisa Jevbratt

The German media theorist Friedrich Kittler said in an interview in the Swedish newspaper *Dagens Nyheter* in the mid-1990s that to understand contemporary culture, one needs to know at least one natural and one artificial (computer) language. This still holds true in my mind – I think it is important to engage in technology on a really basic level, to actually use and write those language that generates the networked world we live in. My work is referencing our contemporary culture on that fundamental level by exploring the networks (from social media, the web and the Internet to genetics and genealogy) we create and exist in.

Erik Parr

Ten years ago, artists working primarily in digital media were still grouped into a kind of subgenre called new media, but now they are just called artists, which I think is a good thing. However, many artists are still afraid to learn how to program, which is a fundamental aspect of digital media. This has created a situation where technicians are often hired to produce the artwork. I find the division of labour into artists who come up with an idea and technicians who produce the work to be double edged. On the one hand, it presents an opportunity for exciting interdisciplinary collaboration; on the other hand, it can reproduce all of the problems regarding production that are found in industry. Such issues manifest themselves in the work and cannot be separated from it.

Mogens Jacobsen

I consider programming-languages and code as my main materials. Since 2000 I have tried to avoid doing screen-based pieces. I work with critical systems and critical interfaces, often artefacts in the form of machines or apparatuses. I feel very connected to speculative or critical design. My pieces are functioning devices or systems rather than conceptual artefacts. My practice is based on things that could be possible (but not always preferable). I see it as my personal take on constructive research. At the present I feel very explorative and am working in unknown territories when working with physical materials. I think this is contrary to some other artists working with material practices and beginning to add to their practice the interaction, behaviour and responsiveness of algorithms running on a computer.

Carl-Johan Rosén

In my art practice, my main activity is programming. Programming is a very direct method of engaging with the digital process: by creating it and communicating with it iteratively. In such terms, the digital is not only influencing my work but also co-creating the works with me.

Goto80 (Anders Carlsson)

A computer is, to the best of its ability, a universal machine that can do anything, regardless of the intentions of the designers or user expectations. I try to be humble about my knowledge of what computers are and not give in to dominant ideas about what it is supposed to be. For my art-oriented performances, I try to be less of an artist and more of a worker. Instead of using pre-made music and algorithms, I use software that forces me to do most things by hand. I often play with the idea of ownership and copyright, especially in relation to the political economy of music. I program sounds and compose music from scratch, live, in front of the audience. They tell me what the music should sound like, so I am there to fulfil someone else's ideas as best as I can.

Alberto Frigo

I believe my practice is a continuation of, on the one hand, constraints – based on experimental literature – and on the other hand, body art. Particularly relating to the latter, I see my practice as a step forward in using myself as the material of the work. No longer constrained by the spatial and temporal framework of cultural institutions, I have come to develop a whole encompassing practice, which, through a constant engagement with several aspects of my life, provides me with a new framework of artistic operation. I do not so much play around with algorithms but *perform* as an algorithm, for example by photographing every object my right hand uses. In a mode of evolutionary thinking, I see my work not so much as a physical endurance but rather as a psychological one and therefore more related to something I would call mental art.

Goto80 (Anders Carlsson)

I use the sounds of low-tech computers to perform, record and release music. I give much importance to developing skills in relation to the specific materiality (platform and interface) of the machine. In that sense, my music making is a form of hacker craft. I put myself in a position of power to make the machine do unexpected things. On the other hand, I am also submissive to the traits and glitches of the platforms and interfaces that I use. As such, the dialectic of object and subject is omnipresent in my work.

Petri Ruikka

My exploration has risen from a desire to look for a new form of moving image language, one that traces the interactions between our movement and our surrounding environment. This is to think about the visible and invisible traces we leave behind. I have been exploring this through purely analogue methods as well, for example through underwater-costume-dance combinations. I am interested in elements that produce results that I sometimes cannot control completely, to introduce variables in equation that randomize some of the elements in the final output. While my method is not programming, and thus may be not the classical generative process, I see that by combining several elements – that have fairly simple variables – the end results end up being generative.

Marita Liulia

Since early computing, I have been waiting for the technology to be available for my content. I have worked all my life with engineers. I immediately started to work with film when it turned digital and when the first Canon 5D cameras and virtual software arrived at the market. I also studied film production in order to be free as an artist to do these productions myself. I experiment with how certain kinds of videos could be used in different contexts and displayed simultaneously in different platforms (theatre stage, Internet, mobile devices).

Laura Beloff

My initial early interest was formed with a realization that one can imitate behaviours and responsiveness of a system in real-time. Later, this shifted to ideas on and explorations of the divide between the digital and the physical world (an example of this is the project *Seven Mile Boots*, 2004). And further, towards explorations of what it means to be a human that is enhanced with technological possibilities – specifically investigating ideas about a networked human and his or her presence in the world. Today, my interest is focused on the merger of digital/technological and biological matter with a development of ideas that explore technologically formed relations to physical/biological environments and also to non-human organisms. This interest also includes biotechnologies, which I see strongly related to digital technologies in their structure, methods and the underlying mindset.

Søren Thilo Funder

The digital offers processes that go far beyond my own capacity of technical understanding – and I frequently use these digital techniques, be it the use of filters, engines, codecs, transfers, tools, layers or compressions. In one part of my work I rely highly on the digital to mimic (and paraphrase) the technical (and magical) mechanics of classic cinema – the production here mirrors the classical film production with large crews, pre-conceptualized framing and production schedules. In a different, yet much related, part of my work, I use pure computer-generated images in building full environments from collected research material as well as imagined settings. Working in a very close relationship to the realm of cinema, the digital acts the part of mediator for me, between the classic language and mechanics of the cinematic apparatus (the continued succession of exposed film frames creating the illusion of movement), as well as its (historical and present) influence on the societal and the fluid screens, hovering eye cameras and information clouds (of the visual, indexical and chronological) that envelop our contemporary reality.

On Materiality and Behaviour in Digital Art

Ewa Jacobsson

From 1984, I worked analogously with colour photo and also used film in my live performances and installations. I made sound and visual programs with moving slides and sound, text and vocal. I chose not to go into video since the difference between the clearness in analogue photo and the processes that are used in manipulating black and white photos or positive colour slides, and the processing of film, are totally different from electronic colouring in video. Especially in the beginning the instrument did not like natural light. Sun and fire were too strong. With video, the pureness in the old photo and film formats was gone. I did not begin using the digital in film and photo until lately, when the digital film format, Photoshop and Final Cut made it possible for me to connect to these areas of exploring again. Of course, it also changes your way of working when you can no longer get help from laboratories because the method is not in use anymore. I turn to what is available in the time that I live in and this interests me as a statement in itself.

Teemu Mäki

I used to work with analogue photography, film and video. The big difference in moving images now is that I can make Full HD or 4K content with relatively cheap equipment. The difference between budget-less productions and rich productions has in this sense disappeared. The equipment is available for all. The difference is more on what you aim your camera at, what you do with it. In photography, I still use analogue film (dia / nega) and a big format camera because I can get better resolution with it than with any available digital camera. However, after taking the shots, I scan the images and work in digital all the way after that. The major jump from an artist's viewpoint to a craftsman's viewpoint here is that now there is no original, which is a good thing. I can have digital safety copies of all of my finished photo artworks and films in multiple locations.

Johan Knattrup Jensen

I still feel that there is a need for balance between the analogue and the digital. I am trying to express myself through stories, characters and ultimately emotions. I cannot get lost in mimicking something in a digital way when there is no need for it. So in my daily work I am very critical on which tools, methods or techniques I am using.

Erik Johansson

Although I work a lot with a computer to put together my images, I always try to capture as much as possible on camera. The digital world has given me possibilities to create these images, but I would not say that I am really a digital artist. I create surreal scenes in a realistic way with the help of my camera; a kind of surreal realism. I do not capture moments, I capture ideas. I use a sketchbook to come up with ideas, a camera (Hasselblad H6D-50c), and the computer and Photoshop to put together the photographs I shoot. If there are new better features in a new version, I take advantage of that to twist the images even more. I do not create anything digitally. All the material and parts that make up a picture are real, something that exists; I just put the pieces of the puzzle together in the computer. I want to create the ideas that come to my mind. It is just ideas and people can interpret them as they like. My goal with my work is to make people think, to make them feel like they are part of another world for a second.

Kristina Kvalvik

I work with both the analogue and the digital, often mixing these two components together in a project. Sometimes I work with both still and moving images, using the still images to create a moving image. This gives me a lot of flexibility as I can work with a medium that later on is digitalized. My work investigates the relationship between film and video and I use elements from classic cinema. I deconstruct these elements and use strategies of repetition to present viewers with something familiar yet disorienting at the same time.

Anne Katrine Senstad

As my practice originates in analogue photography and 16mm film, I work in a hybridity of the analogue and the digital. My source material is often film, which is then transferred to digital media for further manipulation with a digital output yet maintaining a sense of materiality.

Ewa Jacobsson

The difference between what the digital does and what the analogue does to sound, sound fragments and processing is in how it functions as instrument. The digital is not 'new things' for replacing 'old tools'. There was some conflict about this in the beginning, since new techniques always create hierarchies and tension. I have had some heated discussions with sound technicians who could not understand my wish to keep old sound machines and methods parallel with new methods. I experience that my knowledge of both sound and visuals in the old techniques makes it easy for me to navigate in between new mixing and processing tools, because the aesthetics they use are in some ways based on old forms. It is the same with my knowledge in drawing and especially oil painting. Photoshop and Final Cut uses experience and language that I know. It also makes it easier for me to *not* choose some effects and easy solutions.

An evaluation of good and bad in comparison of analogue techniques, digital tools and software makes no sense, but with each comes an aesthetic that is formed by the tools. You have to work across those paths. I have never been interested in exploring how to develop new programs, but I use what comes my way. I have learned the different tools and instruments through the years, from simple mono tape-recorders, to advanced stereo tape recorders, mono-mic, stereo-mic, surround mic-recording, a DAT recorder, digital sound devices and in different studio programmes. For many years, I have been working mostly with Pro Tools with all kinds of attached software, in the big studio at NOTAM in Oslo. I still use materials from old tape recorders. I use those old methods in mixing and processing when preparing materials that end up in advanced digital methods. The clear 'hard edge' (that I use and make even harder sometimes), as well as the cuts and pulverization of understanding you can create with the digital, are different from the softness in other medias, such as live acoustic objects or voice/text or analogue methods. Also, the noise that digital tools create is the language of the technique and it is different from others.

Nuleinn (Rine Rodin and Magga Ploder)

The digital influences our works on different levels – working in the aspect of social experiences, sci-fi literature, pop culture and feminism, online and offline. We are focused on working with mixed medias where the digital and analogue intertwine. The digital is turned into a material, which transforms its forms consisting of impulses to becoming physical bodies of work. We are therefore highly dependent on the digital in our work.

Tuomo Rainio

Since 2004, my work has combined photography and the moving image with computer programming. My works explore the construction and deconstruction of pictures (the moving image). With the experimental use of computational photography I emphasize the conditions of the digital image itself and the dialogue between the material and abstract dimensions of the image. When looking at the image, the questions of what is being depicted are overridden by how the image is constructed. This construction functions as a route beyond the surface of the image towards the logic of the digital image. The question of space is at the heart of the photographic apparatus; the camera obscura is a room where the space of images opens and also the space of translations. Instead of looking at what comes out of it, I try to examine what happens inside it.

Carl-Johan Rosén

I am interested in bringing the digital out of its context, as I have done in *I speak myself into an object* (2013) by printing code on paper, or in *At the Catastrophy-Point* (2016) by creating small sculptures from the digital video material. By transposing the material or information to a non-digital medium, I believe we can discover aspects of the digital that are impossible to identify within the digital medium.

Goto80 (Anders Carlsson)

Digital electronics set the material boundaries of the craft of my music, but I do not see a digital platform as fixed. The Commodore 64 is still revealing new secrets after 30 years of intense exploration from thousands of hackers. We change what we think of it, which influences its materiality (which, as N. Katherine Hayles points out, is not only physical). Digital electronics are both objects and subjects, especially in these cyborg times.

Marie Kølbæk Iversen

To me, digital materiality is one among other materials that each have distinct sets of properties to be played out in relation to idea and form. I apply coding and genetics to generate redistributive processes of the material and the conceptual that cause them to touch and exceed their inherent boundaries, making them resonate beyond themselves. I have done this with both digital and natural, discrete and continuous matter, from a desire to cross or blur the imagined nature/culture-divide by calling forth so-called natural forces in the explicitly digital, as well as virtuality in minerals. My distinctly digital works are digital to the core. They do not represent or signify anything else than themselves and their autopoietic processes. Yet they trigger the human imagination that sees rabbits and elephants in (digital) clouds and they play with the intentionality that reads nature as scripture. When I work with digital technologies, 'digitality' is at the same time the ontology and the nothingness of the work.

Mia Mäkelä

Let me give you an example of how the digital has affected my artwork, process-wise: I processed and mixed the video clips for the *Kaamos Trilogy* (2007–09) using Max/Jitter software. As a result, the original footage adopted a more synthetic and symbolic appearance. These modes of processing – which are mathematical calculations operated in the software – invite for infinite experimentation. This kind of experimentation also offers surprises: The fire at the end of the journey in *Kaamos Trilogy* is a mix between the footage of the sand from the bottom of 'the Sacrifice spring' and the forest. The sand metamorphoses into a different element: from earth to fire. I call this process 'digital alchemy'. This kind of experience might resemble the experiences of the early video makers in the 1970s who got enlightened by the amazing effects of the first video synthesizers, such as the feedback effect, which they had never seen before. They were blown away by the possibilities of electricity and some even believed that they had found a key to some sort of a mystical universal system. It is interesting that the latest scientific discoveries have proved them right – the feedback loop seems to be one of the core concepts of life.

Tuomo Rainio
My work with the digital started when I began to develop and use my own programs for post-production in 2004. In the same way as photographs are created within the conditions of light, I was interested in finding something as elementary to start with. In my early works, I started to analyse movement and change through difference. I discovered that the mathematical difference between two images actually created a new image. For me this pointed out the fundamental change that the digital revolution had made to the way we think about images – that all digital information is related through a common structure. For an artist working in the post-conceptual era of image-making it is fascinating to find an underlying digital structure where ideas and concepts can be turned into codes, and further, into images. Not only images relate to each other, but the whole realm of digital information.

Marie Kølbæk Iversen
I do not think of materials as media or mediators for me or my artistic intention, but rather as a kind of collaborators, for lack of a better word. The mediation that takes place is mutual: the material mediates me, and I mediate the material.

Lundahl & Seitl (Christer Lundahl and Martina Seitl)
Around 2003, we started using digital sound recordings of voices that instructed and synchronized the touch of an unseen guide on a single visitor wearing headphones and sightless goggles. Technically, it was a way to activate a sense of liveness in simple digital media playing on Mp3, making it a catalyst in a multisensory binding process. Though very simple, it convincingly changed the visitor's own interface to the world by triggering memory and imagination, a technique future VR is likely to use. Since then, our work has been increasingly influenced by digital technologies. Today we use a Neumann KU100 dummy head and a Sennheiser Ambeo VR mic, which allows us to record high quality, interactive, three-dimensional sound, as well as to control the placement of sounds around a viewer's body. Our project *Unknown Cloud on Its Way to* (2016) intersects different interfaces from everyday life: smartphone AR technology, fiction and perceptual illusions evoke a global secular ritual of our time, allowing for large scale participation.

Laura Beloff

One of the aspects that I have worked with for a long time is data and communications networks and its relation to how we sense our place, space (and existence) in the world. Before this interest in network aspects I started working with ideas of, and experiments with, creating behaviour with technology. This was what drew me towards working with digital media and technology: that one can imitate behaviours and trigger immediate responses. In some sense, instead of representing the surrounding world, the shift concerned the construction of new worlds, ideas and unexpected behaviours. My first experiments were interactive installations, which I think is quite a typical starting point for this kind of art. I started to think about 'systems' rather than 'reactions', which I saw as limitations in interactive/reactive works. There always was, and still is, this very strong expectation from the audience that something should happen, something that reacts to their actions. It was somehow obvious to me to move towards systems and system thinking, where a technological thing would have a life of its own and would evolve based on its environment, less dependent on the user's actions. Even in the large body of wearable works that I have produced, where the user plays a crucial role, these are designed more as novel potentialities for users to engage with the work long term, instead of depending on quick reactions of responses to users' immediate actions.

Juan Duarte Regino

I rely on digital platforms mostly to deal with interactive media development. In sound, the aesthetic is based on algorithmic processing and automation to link visual and sonic stimuli. There are many open-source hardware digital platforms that enable bridging of digital with analogue supports. The digital works as a bridge to 'listen' and manipulate other traditional forms of art, such as those based on analogue media. These possibilities enable a dialog to investigate broader topics as generative art and Augmented Reality introspections.

Illutron

All our art is interactive. While some is extremely low-tech, most is digital, programmed, computer or microprocessor controlled. Much is digital art about the digital world: robots, digital displays, game boys playing music, extracting music from the barcodes on every item in the supermarket. Interactive installations typically include sensors, digital control, digital effects processing and outputs in the form of light. Oftentimes our work is using the digital to comment on the digital.

Stian Remvik

Apart from the obvious use of computers and smartphones for everyday tasks, like watching news, e-mailing, paying bills and so on, my digital influence comes from video games. Since I also design and develop video games, I obviously play a lot of games. For me, the interactive and creative part of video games makes it the most interesting medium today. As said by James Portnow, the magic of video games is our ability to let a person walk a mile in someone else's shoes; to let the player explore a space of possibility and discover for themselves rather than be told, our ability to educate without teaching.

When playing video games, you can choose as you will. You can experience the life that someone else may have lived and through doing so arrive at a state of compassion and understanding, of sympathy and empathy. Or, you can experience a life that you always wanted, for example that of a rock star or a magician. You can even explore the chance to escape the real world and experience a fantasy world. No other medium can better put us in the shoes of other people, face their struggles and wrestle with the problems that challenge them. Through doing so we come to better understand how we face the world and wrestle those challenges ourselves. Video games are the first medium in history where you do not just sit back and receive. It is the first mass medium where you interact and are a part of it. As a designer, your role is to let the player explore a space of possibility and discover for themselves, rather than be told. I lay out a space of possibility. You make your own choices. And through that you come to better understand who you are. You learn to think creatively – and that is a powerful ability when you face challenges in life.

Bombina Bombast (Emma Bexell and Stefan Stanisic)

The booming game industry has been a big influence on our work. Nordic artists around us work with the big game companies or develop their own indie games. Game developers are showing an interest in our theatre works. This is a cultural development that has already had an effect aesthetically, cultural politically and economically on the Nordic art scene. Coming from a theatre background, we got competences that game makers usually do not have – handling a live audience or discussing representation. We have seen immersive theatre and open world gaming develop side-by-side, oddly unaware of each other. We think we are seeing more human-specific performances, like our own, in the Nordic art scene, and sometimes we link this to our society that is increasingly shaped by individual smart devices, avatars, profiles and a generation growing up with the Internet being portable and personal.

We directed students at Stockholm Academy of Dramatic Arts in a performance responding to the reality TV series *Paradise Hotel*. The performance *Paradise Activity* (2015) is just as much theatre as game show and immersive installation. We addressed the different types of viewing positions by offering different modes of participation. Through live-broadcasting, gaming, Virtual Reality-scenes, video walks and monologue karaoke we asked questions about the line between acting and spectating, about how we construct ourselves depending on who is watching, and about how we want it to be 'a paradise'; a pool in the sun, drinking and having sex without thinking about tomorrow – is this not an ultimate being together? We are definitely not alone in addressing these questions about voyeurism and the arbitrary rules of virality. We see and appreciate how these themes make artists question their own standpoint and look to new modes of performing, of interaction and negotiation.

Our series of video walks, simply titled *Walks*, started out as a series of tests that eventually grew into a travelling concept that we create site-specifically out of a set of knowledge and rules, wherever we are invited – so far in Sweden, Denmark and Norway. Our *Walks* is a way to perform the virtual and the real in order for you to play with the dividing lines. It is a gamified experience with limited options with which we create a small-scale language that performs the real and the illusion.

Games and simultaneous dramaturgies are tools we use to respond to today's societies in our work. We quote Eric Zimmerman's Manifesto for a Ludic Century: '…computers did not create games; games created computers'. Having in our hands technology that has not yet reached the commercial buyer, we consider that our art has to take into account the ethics of this new media. What we make of it will help define it and we cannot let the radical potential we see in Virtual Reality get lost in a profit-driven entertainment industry (no, we have to take risks with it).

On Art Between Forms and Fields

Ilpo Heikkinen

I value interdisciplinarity, which in many ways is natural in the Nordic context. One easily ends up working with different kinds of people and mediums.

Kristoffer Ørum

I am an interdisciplinary artist, researcher and organizer based in Copenhagen, Denmark. Through presentations, Internet projects, exhibitions, interventions and teaching, I explore complex narratives of the everyday. I hope to challenge existing systems of knowledge and technology through deliberate misunderstanding and misreading of these narratives. To this end I draw equally on sources of pseudo-scientific knowledge and established critical theory in an attempt to create new associations and narratives about familiar objects and phenomena, ranging from the complexity of the Internet, or economic terms, to the labels of store-bought products. I work both inside the more established parts of the art world and in the grey zones that surround them.

Katja Aglert

My practice is transdisciplinary in nature and includes both individual and collaborative projects. It is situated in the liminal field, for example questioning how research can be imagined and performed without reproducing the static order it attempts to critically reflect. I work with concepts and research rooted in a wider interest related to critical examinations of dominant tendencies and orders in society. The medium I work with is chosen for the context, site and research of each specific project. With the temporal manifestations of my work I attempt to align considerations of the research and the trajectory of the medium of choice.

Illutron

Illutron is a space for adventures and experiments where artistic and technological frontiers are challenged and experiments can be based on intuition instead of reason. We create collective illusions, fascinating illustrations and blinding illuminations, embracing new inspirational stories in and about the world. We started with very industrial connotations: iron, steel, rust, antique machines, and upcycled industrial relics, and we are now moving towards a more minimalistic technology representation. Technological progress happens in dialogue with the surrounding society and refers to both the past and the future.

Kollision

Kollision is hard to define within a traditional framework of contemporary art. We believe that the line between radical design and contemporary art is somewhat blurred. We are navigating somewhere at the intersection of research, business and art. Our approach is design-based: We are working as a team and in close collaboration with clients and/or directly with users to develop solutions, rather than art.

N55

We have worked in the cross fields of fine art, design and architecture for the past 20 years. The Internet and digital methods of designing are crucial to our practice. N55 works with art as a part of everyday life. Our working method is basically to produce significance in concrete situations, using things and basic functions that we all can relate to in our everyday life.

Dark Matters

Working with video projection, light and installations, Dark Matters operates at the intersection of architecture, scenography, design and art. We collect ideas, concepts and messages, and transform them into minimalist and abstract visual concepts. By embracing the audience's imagination, we bring about personal experiences, engaging narratives and unique spaces that make you think and feel in equal measure.

Stian Remvik

My background is in design and visual communication and I work in the cross-line between art and design. Design is about creating a user experience and for this it is important to understand the user, most importantly to listen to what the user tells you, and what the application tells you about the experience.

I use computers and programming in my artwork to explore how visuals, music and motion affect emotion. I was initially inspired by the theories of John Whitney about how harmonic resonance in motion graphics echoes the harmonic resonance in music and how that affects feelings; how order in patterns with elements in motion appear when they meet and achieve resonance.

Laura Beloff

My art practice belongs to the domains of experimental art titled art&science – in the nexus of art-science-technology. My work challenges the borders of traditional art genres but also explores methods, mediums and technologies that are sometimes developed within sciences. I believe it is utmost important for artists to work with technology and science because these developments need to be tested, scrutinized, experimented and further developed, also, by other people than engineers. I believe that posing different questions will reveal new insights, problematics, ethics questions, etc., as well as potentially uncover novel possibilities.

Lundahl & Seitl (Christer Lundahl and Martina Seitl)

Our works are specific to a particular place and situation, while also investigating history, time, space and human perception. We aim to exceed the limits of science, performance and art by connecting these disciplines and creating new spaces for joint enquiry.

Bombina Bombast (Emma Bexell and Stefan Stanisic)

As Bombina Bombast, we work in the field of performing arts, especially bringing together Virtual Reality and theatre. We create immersive films and performances that merge human-specific live art, game culture and video, along with developing methodologies for this kind of work. Our focus is on the digital and virtual spaces in life today: possibilities and absurdities concerning reality, fiction and agency.

We come from a theatre background but want to explore audience relations in different contexts, so we often find ourselves crisscrossing disciplines and domains. We scrounge around and steal from popular culture and cult classics and we defy expectations by playing with genre. Sometimes we call ourselves author-directors and sometimes curators. We are regular guest teachers at Malmö Theatre Academy and we are rooted in the theoretical practice discourse of the city's independent art scene.

Johan Knattrup Jensen

I come from a background as a filmmaker and dramatic writer and have been working with conventional film, theatre plays and performances professionally since 2003. In 2013, I started to engage in the digital world by using Virtual Reality as a medium for my films. In 2014, I presented the film installation *The Doghouse* (*Skammekrogen*), which allows five audience members at a time to experience the same dinner, from each of the character's subjective perspective, through the use of VR. VR gave me the opportunity to put the audience inside my film, even inside my characters, which is close to my own artistic method of embodying a character when writing. I discovered the potential for films to become physical, and actually 'being an installation' that people could touch and interact with. Being able to touch the film creates a unique bond or relation between the audience and the experience. It becomes a memory. The film is no longer only a vivid imagination, it's a memory machine.

Egill Sæbjörnsson

When I was studying painting, I always wanted to make the paintings move, or I wanted to be able to go into the painting and walk around. In the 1990s, I was very much into VR, played with QTVR and the Internet. Some of my works are quite cartoony, whereas others are minimalistic and simple in look. Some works make a narrative, whereas others are just forms and lines floating around. I use 3D animation, 2D animation, VR, self-generative video based on computer game engines, technologic parts like Arduino boards, motors, computers, wood, plaster, steal, concrete, paper, paint and other plastic materials, and I am into Augmented Reality, since a few years ago. I either set up the work in full scale in my studio or build a Marquette, if the piece is large.

Mats Jørgen Sivertsen

I started out making underground comics, but since finishing my Master of Arts in Digital Art I have focused on more gallery-oriented art. When it comes to choosing methods and materials I work very project-based and am quite open to whichever direction that fits best with my intent – that way the concept and the theme will usually dictate if a work will be photography, CGI, installation, writing, video, drawing, performance, animation or sound art. My main theme has long been man's relationship with technology and transhumanism. Because of this, most of my work has had a strong technological component.

recoil (Tina Tarpgaard)

I work with an extended understanding of dance and choreography. By 'extension' I mean that I have dealt with choreographing both dancing bodies and various materials: paper, cloth, light, sound and even microbes. I am interested in decentring the human performer and the interdependencies between all elements on stage. My experience is that the rapid development in how a computer can analyse and respond to a three-dimensional space fit for human presence has encouraged a large number of cross-disciplinary works, namely in the performing arts.

Petri Ruikka

I work mainly with the moving image through the so-called classical 2D presentation format, but also through installation and live performance. Aesthetically, I have been interested in combining abstract animation and the movement of dance through digital (various post-production techniques) and analogue methods (such as projections on the body).

Tone Myskja

I work with video as a visual and sculptural element in relation to exhibitions, concerts and stage performances. I have a sculptural and musical approach to working with art and video and compose complex and compound videos and installations. My work takes place at the intersection of different artistic disciplines, drawing on my interest in music, dance, theatre, literature, painting and sculpture. Thematically, my work relates primarily to the complexity of language, identity and perception.

Egill Sæbjörnsson

I have been making music since I was a child and it plays an important role in my practice. I usually write songs on a guitar when it comes to chords and melodies, or I use a keyboard. In music making, I have also made instruments and mixed that with my video projection works. There are many different dimensions to my technical art practice.

Ewa Jacobsson

I am a visual artist and composer. I have made field recordings since the early 1980s. I use visual castaway elements from the actual sites, combined with materials such as marzipan, oil, steel, wire, photo, film and drawing. I work with site-specific installations with visual elements, sound and preparation of spaces, pure sound composition, physical sounding objects and live performance. The works are presented at exhibitions, museums, and concert spaces, and my practice also includes works for the street and works that directly involve the audience.

My combination of advanced and low-tech techniques reflects my interest in the transportation of importance and meaning, existentially or politically, through different medias, ignoring the hierarchy commonly used. In my work with sound, I use the 'faults' that different techniques make and analogously I use spaces and materials that are considered as waste. My themes are often concerned with what may be forgotten and not seen.

Anastasios Logothetis
It might be that a hyper-movement between different social environments aided by the Internet artists has been loosening the divide between the Self and the Other. By giving rise to a more open-source kind of mind we might find ourselves in a future art scene that is increasingly dependent on the collaborative effort. This development, on the other hand, is not going down well with the current market model. And so (amongst other reasons) we see the subsequent re-rise of the old-school artist-as-sole-genius (revamped as the cool zombie painter) that is so beautifully marketable.

Juan Duarte Regino
The pervasive use of digital media in the international and Nordic region benefits networking and platform development and enables a dialogue between other contemporary practices, in order to articulate works into multidisciplinary contexts.

Søren Thilo Funder
In the postproduction and installation of my work, the digital enables a complex reworking of the shot material, and I often introduce other visual layers derived directly from the digital world. Here graphical text fields, animation and sampled audio-visual material form a new layer onto the cinematic image – often in collaboration with professionals more closely related to the sphere of digital production. In this part of the process, questions of resolution, source, layering and extra-physicality come into play.

Ilpo Heikkinen
I would describe my artistic orientation more in terms of social interaction than working with any specific media. I work with contemporary theatre and performance, but also closely with experimental research and cultural activism, as well as with noise music. I usually see myself as a performer and always try to work from a bodily, performative perspective to bring a performing social subject into the picture. The dramaturgy that I am interested in is created through a widespread of media and topics, through co-poiesis and participation. I value working together, collaborating and sharing our ideas and methods – the ethos of Do-It-Yourself turning into Do-It-With-Others, and I do not mean just human beings. My practice is most often based on interdisciplinary methods.

Kollision
In a contemporary artistic practice, a facilitator replaces the artist. This allows for a much more severe and literal interpretation of a given installation (we deliberately will not call it a

'work of art') by the user than what we are used to in more traditional art forms where all interpretation in reality leaves the original untouched. It might get ugly, it might not work as intended, but it is always interesting to see how users 'hack' the stuff we make. In an age of sharing economies, maker movements and user participation, we think this artistic practice reflects the world around us.

On Perception and Art's Experience

Dark Matters

We always try to make projects that push people to experience something 'again for the first time'. Old concepts in new contexts or cliché effects turned upside down and re-used in a completely new way. In a social way we try to unite people through a personal experience they would like to talk about with other people in the audience. Sometimes this is about the aesthetics; sometimes it is the concept of the work or just a bloody good concert experience. In the end, we try to create experiences for the audience, not for the sake of art.

Tor Jørgen van Eijk

I work solely with video, mainly digital, single channel works, but occasionally with more environment and installation-oriented works. I do not have a general theme as a point of departure, except from a meta-point of view within the video itself. Once an interesting composition of abstract images has been established, I exchange and mix those purely abstract patterns with video-recordings of whatever is of interest to me at the time.

Joonas Siren

I am influenced by the French philosopher Jean Baudrillard who described how media alters the way we perceive reality. Also, I am interested in Baudrillard's concept of the hyperreal, how media has pierced through our everyday existence and transformed how we perceive the world and ourselves.

Elisabeth Molin

The digital world has made me want to engage more directly with reality. My work has become more performative, alive and context-sensitive. I have made works that are situated in the peripheries and that are only shown at night; and performances that blur and leak into reality. The digital has made me more interested in chance and entropy and in asking questions around how we navigate.

I think the way the digital transforms, informs and blurs perceptions of reality and society is something that I respond to in my work. Here is an example: In summer 2015, I was in Athens, during capital control and the economic crisis. I was surprised to see how western newspapers covered the situation; the images and stories they showed were violent and seemed to further alienate and detach from the reality in Greece. This made me think about the power of storytelling in the digital age and how politics and technology go hand in hand in deciding what is visible and what is invisible in the world. On 5 July 2015, I filmed the night of the referendum in Athens, where the majority of the people had voted no to more austerity measures. There was a celebratory demonstration by parliament and everyone was ecstatic and hopeful about the future. The week after, the Greek people got an even worse deal than they had voted for, and my footage of the demonstration all of a sudden seemed like a dream. When I did an exhibition in Germany a month later, I decided to project this footage of the demonstration on the opposite site of the exhibition space, where a house coincidentally had burned down. Greece and Germany were two main players in the crisis and this act was an attempt to bring awareness to this already forgotten moment in Greece, by linking it to a physical space in Germany.

Bombina Bombast (Emma Bexell and Stefan Stanisic)
As artists concerned with contemporary life and popular culture, the digital and virtual is so much a part of our everyday that it trickles into most of the material for our performances. We are deeply influenced by the oscillation between what we perceive as virtual and what we perceive as real. We work in the intermediate areas with the confusion or friction that happens when you as an audience or participant become immersed in for example a Virtual Reality fiction. We also add other physical stimulus to the experience, such as touch or smell. In our *Walks* – which are video guides in tablets that take you on a journey through urban environments with different things happening in the film, contradicting or supporting the scene around you – we activate many modes of perception and make them operate simultaneously.

Marie Munk Hartwig
I study how technology influences the way people behave and communicate with each other. As technology becomes increasingly immersed with both our bodies and our lives, the way in which we are present changes, both physically and mentally. Our bodies are no longer sacred or honest, but highly manipulated – just as any other aspect of our lives. Even nature, which used to be understood as pure, is no longer reliable.

Pink Twins (Juha Vehviläinen and Vesa Vehviläinen)
Pink Twins mainly work with computer-generated moving image and electronic music. Our works usually take the form of video installations, audio-visual live performances, concerts

and screenings at film festivals. Also, sound installations and CD or vinyl releases. Both audio and visual works have a spatial and immersive quality and present a flow of sensory overload. Our works are seemingly abstract with a focus on human perception and its limits. We aim to create a physical, overwhelming experience.

Anne Katrine Senstad

A large part of my practice is focused on moving image art and unstable media; embracing and integrating new media platforms for installation and context-based installations and defining subjective and sensorial experiences through the digital and technological realm. I create installations and objectless art, so to speak. The content of my work lies in the realm of the perceptive, the sensorial and the abstract, with a focus on the phenomena of light, sound and colour as subject matter. I include an awareness of space, site and architecture as a major part of the practice and installation considerations, working with potentials of the psychological, intellectual, physical and sensorial space. I like to refer my work to Kazimir Malevich's ideas of the Supermatist faktura. In Malevich's teaching, faktura was explored as an idea; as formless phenomenon, a technological or scientific development, and a focus on future discoveries. The faktura fused the material and immaterial, challenging preconceptions about its meaning, practice, purpose, matter and use. Malevich writes about the non-object and the perception of an object, which can also relate to Plato's ideas of perception.

Johan Knattrup Jensen

The digital tools and methods create a pathway for my audience to move inside my work. I want them to experience my films as if they were inside them, not standing on the outside looking through a window into another world.

Lundahl & Seitl (Christer Lundahl and Martina Seitl)

Our work focuses on making the viewer's perception the central medium of the work. The artwork is intangible, pending its own creation inside the conscious experience of the viewer. In all our works we use a mixture of material and immaterial media in a multi-sensory binding process. This includes voice instruction, touch, movement and positioned three-dimensional audio – alternating between sensory deprivation and sensory stimulation. The viewer's imagination and body memory are important transmitters for the work.

Petri Ruikka

I am interested in the contemporary notion of our body not having a clear border between itself and its surroundings. I am fascinated by the partial fallacy of the way we construct ego, partially around an individual body, when in many ways we are completely interdependent of other living and non-living systems. We do not seem to be aware of the complexity of co-existence and think of our body as the limit to what we are. I have explored this in various short films and other works by extending the body beyond its normal limits. I could not have achieved this without the use of multiple various digital tools and processes.

Marie Munk Hartwig

Digitalization of both our society and our body has had a strong influence on my artwork, as this highly affects our understanding of our physicality and the way we behave. The body and how we try to control, design and manipulate it, not only physically but also very much mentally, is the turning point in most of my artwork. At the core is this tension, even power struggle, between our mind and our body. It seems like a constant struggle against nature, like an urge to turn ourselves into a design of our own.

Björk Viggósdóttir

I often assemble multiple and diverse digital media that become an installation with an uncanny aspect, where imagination is given free rein. Conceptually, the purpose of my art is to stimulate all the senses of the viewer. That is how digital tools become an invaluable element in my art. In my installations I aim to capture and activate the viewer's imagination, hoping to encourage people to participate in my artwork through their senses and consciousness in the space I create. I bring everyday concepts to other dimensions by creating new perspectives and settings for them. When working with multiple media, it is the fine-tuning of the harmony between the various media that matters, so the installation captures a life of its own. I compose visually and digitally, and in my music I try to allow the sound of the installation to become the image or concept I am working with each time, by capturing the spirits of the installations in sound and visualizing the concepts in video installations. In order to enhance the sensory experience of the audience I usually use multiple media to create harmony in my art, which creates an experience of illusion where the audience must use all their senses to reach for the concepts behind the art.

Nuleinn (Rine Rodin and Magga Ploder)

We use technology and the body as a tool in an inquiry into the modern, future global and local society, looking for the possibilities and boundaries of body and technology. This constellation manifests in different materials; performance art, video, larger digital installations etc. We are especially inspired by post-Internet art and cyberfeminism where we strive to question our own presence in a digital-physical world. We do so by placing the audience and ourselves in different scenarios, where boundaries are pushed and thoughts are provoked. We use digital devices, such as Arduino sensors, Kinect sensors, online forums, video projections and surveillance cameras to activate our installations and the audience.

The way we use our bodies in collaboration with technology is a way for us to place ourselves in the context and explore the themes we work within. This way we are able to get closer to the work, become one with it, and even give the audience the possibility to do so as well. In our video work *Gefilterte Realität* from 2017 we used everyday life as a focal point, removing the boundaries between games and social conditions. We are all biological robots in a social system surrounded by rules and codes to follow. We all play the game of everyday life, where all our actions are codified and scored in the game. We receive points for complying with socially established norms, but with a single meltdown or error, our whole life can change: If we lose our job, partner or home, the possibility to win the game is minimized. We combined a reality from computer games and real life, where elements from the game dictate the results.

Mats Jørgen Sivertsen

My installation titled *subConch* (2013) is about cyborg existence. It shows you what it feels like to interact profoundly with technology – what it is like to be a cyborg – by using EEG sensors and advanced Machine-Learning algorithms, to let you cognitively control sound and light. The context is the continued extension of our bodies and abilities through digital technology, such as smartphones. Here, the digital is both in the theme, the social context and the work itself.

Tove Kjellmark

In general, my works circle around the human body. I feel free using and combining traditional media, digital media as well as the latest technology, investigating new materials, working methods and aesthetics. My empathy-provoking aesthetics combined with dark humour explores what we perceive as mechanical life.

Jette Gejl

I work with the excesses and expanding of reality and very often with audience interaction. Working in the phenomenological realm, I consider the virtual as a materiality of resistance in perception between what we experience through the mind in contradiction to what we sense through the body. Therefore, I believe my work directly influences the ways in which we organize and negotiate the social space collectively as well as in private.

Jesper Carlsen

I mainly work with computer animation, sometimes used as a model for a physical object. I have a reductive approach to perceptual phenomena. I reduce and isolate until the meaning is distorted or somehow becomes fragile. It is probably a form of technical/mechanical view of the world where I try to test and push until an uncertainty arises. I also see my work as a form of logical manifestation of a cognitive phenomenon, or as a tool to visualize a perceptual detail.

Hanna Husberg

We increasingly perceive our surroundings through extensions of our senses, often through technologies we do not fully understand. We are also more and more dependent on computer-generated images and models. This shapes our perception of reality. I inquire into the difficulty of perceiving hyper objects such as climate change, a phenomenon generally considered the domain of natural sciences, which, however, needs to be addressed from a number of other alternative perspectives. One of them is to ask what tools do to our perception, rather than what we do with them.

Laura Beloff

Technologies impact how we perceive and experience biological environments. Is nature today what it used to be? And how does that relation change if biological organisms, such as plants, are no longer just biologically evolved but designed by humans? Can we experience nature via technology?

On Nordic Aesthetic Conditions and Identification

Matti Aikio

The themes and questions I work with, concerning nomadic and indigenous concept relationships to space, time and nature, are definitely reflecting my background – being a Sámi having grown up in traditional Sámi reindeer herding culture. Indigenous thinking is essentially part of me and influences my work. The political situation of my people is also something that influences me.

Nuleinn (Rine Rodin and Magga Ploder)

Being Danish and Icelandic certainly affect our works. We have been inspired by the culture and the way art is perceived in our countries.

Lisa Jevbratt

In some way I feel extremely Swedish, even though I have been living in the United States for 22 years. That deeply sensed belonging must influence my work. If I would guess how, I think my work tends to be (too?) understated.

Egill Sæbjörnsson

I think I am very Icelandic, whatever that means, growing up in Iceland during the Cold War, when it felt like Iceland was a thousand times more isolated from the world than it is today. It was a whole different experience from visiting the tourist-loved Iceland of today. Both the ending of the Cold War and the Internet changed very much for Icelanders who are born after that time. As Iceland had almost no visual arts tradition when I was growing up, my eyes were always looking outside of Iceland. I also lived for twenty years in Berlin and Paris and have quite some central-European influence in me.

Björk Viggósdóttir

As I come from the Nordic region, the Nordic culture has inevitably influenced my artwork, from social, emotional and visual perspectives. My creative process is based on research and experiences. As an artist, I have travelled to many different countries and experienced different cultures, yet despite that you can always find considerable Nordic influence in my work. I think it is unthinkable to separate me and my artwork from my cultural background and my work will always be influenced by my experiences as an Icelandic individual. My ideas will always be based on my native culture. I have done work that is inspired by sociology, natural science, physics and psychology, which is based on research and my own cultural values and experiences. You can detect Nordic and western influences in my work, for example in how I use colour, technique and various materials – despite that my art stands independently of my own origin and the audience should be able to experience it based on their own perceptions, values and cultural origin. With the emergence of digital methods in art, the world has however become smaller, and this influences art in general. The artist's inspirations and cultural boundaries are becoming more obscure.

Vibeke Jensen

The context I work in is international, urban and mostly site-specific and I believe these influences are more immediately readable in my artwork than my Nordic background. That said, I think that the state of constantly moving away from and re-entering the Nordic context has influenced my interest in looking from all directions, outside-in and inside-out. Being a stranger at home and abroad generates advantages and questions. Moving to new places teaches you a lot about where you come from, and what you used to take for granted becomes highly visible. Being brought up with Scandinavian traits, like a developed, naive sense of equality and a strong relationship to light and nature, have definitely formed me and my work. My social engagement with freedom and democracy might be rooted in a Scandinavian sensibility, but also a more universal aversion against false authority and abuse of power. Reflection and seeing are two main recurring themes in my work, which depend on light, both external and internal. Also, I am drawn to contrasts and the unknown. My strong relation to nature stays with me in the cities where I live and work. I do not attempt any literal translations of my background in my work, but it is part of who I am and what I create.

N55

It is quite obvious that the Nordic design tradition, as well as the Nordic societal model, have had a major influence on N55's aesthetical practice.

Carl-Johan Rosén

As a renowned region of early adopters of digital technology, I figure it is not so surprising that the Nordic context has led me to investigate the digital. This is a pervasive society of procedural others that co-create my environment and me. My critique of the dominant view of technology as a tool of progress is also connected to the uncritical adaptation of whatever technology that is put on the market, both on the personal and political level.

Jacek Smolicki

Over time I have become increasingly sceptical toward the digital. I have been questioning our proliferating reliance on digital technologies and particularly networked technologies and services as places for constructing and depositing our digital legacies. This is why, triggered by the concept of the post-digital as well as mixed reality media or hybrid media, I have decided to dedicate a period of time to delve into materializing a selection of my digital inventory. It can be seen as an attempt to step out from being fully immersed in the digital and, at least for some time, slow down, perhaps even look back to find or rediscover other ways of constructing while taking care of one's heritage.

For this reason I am building a cabinet, which is inspired by pre-digital technologies of storing and categorizing information, such as file cabinets used in the nineteenth century. However, this cabinet ought not to be seen as a full rejection of the digital. I see it rather as a particular remediation of the digital archive; a remediation that does not necessarily attempt to resettle one medium in a new form but rather revisits the old medium with a renewed capacity to regenerate its role. The cabinet will accommodate an offline network, enabling access to the content archive – but only within its close vicinity. The digital dimension will function not as the essence of the archive but rather as its ambiguous aura, an extra layer to be consulted if necessary.

Bjørn Erik Haugen

I see myself as a conceptual artist. Conceptualism is a central mode of expression in the Nordic art discourse. I think you can tell by looking at my projects that I come from Norway, or at least Scandinavia. I am educated in Norway, which has probably impacted my work and what I make. Biopolitics has been a central theme both in my works and in Nordic art.

Anne Katrine Senstad

The Nordic digital art scene is more involved in science and research, and in archiving material. There is a strong art practice of traditional narrative video still happening with artists coming from photography and film, as there has been a long and strong Nordic style in photography. The Nordic style in video art is quite specific, mostly narrative and performative. It has been pointed out that my themes of light and colour in a minimal visual language have a Nordic feel to them, with a reference to the influence of nature and light conditions in the Nordic context. However, I feel that my minimalism reference and aesthetics might be closer to the generation of artists in the land art and minimalism generation, such as James Turell, Robert Irwin, Dan Flavin, Robert Smithson and so on.

Johan Knattrup Jensen

My work is extremely affected by the 'Nordic feeling'. I feel very connected to the Nordic storytelling tradition, and to the themes of the North, and I will always turn to the great artists of the Nordic countries when I look for inspiration and knowledge. You can find a certain longing for a certain light in my work, and there is a certain display of the darker sides of the human nature, which is deeply rooted in the Nordic tradition. But beyond this tradition I do not feel attached to the Nordic context. My themes are universal, and I do not facilitate a discussion of the current political, societal or cultural situation of Denmark or Scandinavia. What I am discussing is the circumstances of being human, the definition of being human and the consequences of being human.

Laura Beloff

The work *Midnight Sun* (2009) definitely had a Nordic element, as it transported the northern midnight sun in real-time via the network to central Europe. So, when the sun set in Linz in the evening, the northern midnight sun (from Kilpisjärvi, Finland) went up on the façade of the Ars Electronica Center and lit up the building and its surroundings. This project was made within the framework of the just established Bioart Society (2008) in which I was actively involved.

Kollision

Darkness falls early in winter in Scandinavia, so working with light as an artistic medium is just plain, common sense.

Tor Jørgen van Eijk

I make most of my art In Oslo, Norway. I am Norwegian. I speak Norwegian. When I use samples or pre-recorded material, they are often recorded in Norway. My video *Immediate Thereafter* (2012) I recorded in the hours after the right-wing extremist terror in Oslo, 22th July 2011. I guess you can never really escape context.

Ewa Jacobsson

Abroad, Norway is considered culturally exotic, harsh, stony and cold, and, nowadays, too rich. Of course, this colours my artistic practice. My works and processes to find materials and themes are based on the sites I come to, what people there can experience or not. My Nordic origin is a statement in itself. I have an artistic lyrical language, a form, but the place I travel to, the place something shall be shown, set up, played – and my origin – are all components in the process forming the project.

There is a seducing component in being 'very Nordic' that I try to avoid, but I do not avoid, for example, words in Swedish that might not be understood, since they may still be strong as statements. Your origin is a gift, but also something that can be used as an exploiting frame. This is clearly seen in the big biennials when certain areas of our mutual life as humans become exotic themes for a few years and then disappear.

Joonas Siren

I usually work with sound and different installations that have digital or programmed visual elements. I am interested in how you can use sound as a meaningful art material and in what kind of discourses you can build with sound that are not only about the sound itself. Still, sound is not by any means the only artistic material I use. I am drawn to existentialist themes: death, identity and the concept of a religion. The scientific world also inspires my artistic works. I am not too concerned with aesthetics, more with spatiality and with how people perceive or experience the work. Although my corporeal presence dwells in a capital of a Nordic country, I do not feel any affinity to a specific Nordic context. The online world transforms artists of the present day; it breaks down geographical and national borders. I do not feel that I should be classified as a Nordic artist – just an artist.

Kristoffer Ørum

I orient myself as globally as I can. I would be foolish to claim that I have not been affected by growing up in the 1970s and 1980s in suburbs of a non-English-speaking welfare state, but I do not feel any sense of belonging to the ways in which the Nordic in general, and Nordic art in particular, has been branded and identified during the last couple of decades, i.e. as melancholic, romantic, wild and bound to nature. Rather, I think that I share experiences with many kids of the 1970s and 1980s who grew up in welfare states, with computers and subcultures. To grow up as a non-native speaker during the rise in use of the English language and popular culture is to become conscious of being marginal in both a linguistic and cultural sense. To make a long story short, the art scene in Copenhagen, where I live, is in effect bilingual. In spite of the fact that Danes still regard English as a second language, most artists work, research and write primarily in English, while they conduct their everyday lives in Danish.

The post-war Danish welfare state enabled a not too well-off middle-class family, such as the one I grew up in, to buy me a computer fairly early on – something that made me part of the first generation of digital natives who grew up while the digital infrastructures and modes of circulation were in the process of being built. This left me with the strong impression that structures such as the Internet are the malleable results of cultural, political and economic negotiation, rather than forces of nature beyond human control. The homogeneity of over-planned, wind-swept suburbs probably also played a role in my interest in how subcultures can act as forms of resistance against democratic society's tendency to institutionalize and homogenize non-conformist behaviour. I put my faith in small groups of mutually committed individuals rather than trusting in abstract narratives of nationhood or citizenship.

These are a couple of fairly simplistic propositions picked at random that might point to how a context – that might be identified as Nordic – could have affected my worldviews and practice as an artist today. I could also highlight the egalitarian traditions of the Nordic region, and the less commercialized and class stratified conditions that have resulted hereof.

Jette Gejl

Context is a big part of my production and way of working. The Nordic is connected politically, culturally, socially and geographically with the rest of the world, and I think the specificity of 'the Nordic' is a postulate difficult to isolate from the rest of the word.

Lisa Strömbeck

It is clear in my themes and questions that I work in a western culture, but I do not think it is particularly Nordic.

Mogens Jacobsen

Personally I have never felt specifically Nordic. Most of my shows have been outside of Scandinavia but of course I recognize my Nordic culture, morals and values in my work.

Katja Aglert

I am slightly hesitant about the notion 'the Nordic context', what is it? The way I see it, it cannot be perceived as 'a' context but rather as a set of micro contexts, a mix of influences and events in constant flux throughout history and in the now. In my project *On Invasive Ground* (2012) I worked around questions related to this, with the starting point of the context of the UNESCO world heritage of Suomnelinna in Finland. Through the micro-histories of the diverse international flora of this island, the narrative of the work challenges what notions like the Finnish, or the Nordic, can mean.

Laura Beloff

Firstly, I think the art scene in each Nordic country differs from the others. Obviously, as many of my activities (and life) are currently located in the Nordic region – from north to south – this definitely has an impact on my works. The ways are more difficult to pinpoint. Let me give you a few examples.

I often reference something Finnish in my artworks, however it may be quite hidden. Currently, my interest in merging the biological and the technological – and specifically investigations into our (human) relation to nature/biological environments – is fuelled by the strong myth-like idea that we (Finns) would have stronger human-nature relations in comparison to other people or nationalities. I am purposely speculating on this with my following hypothesis: If humans are increasingly enhanced with technology, and if our biological environment (nature) is increasingly enhanced as well (with technologies and biotechnologies), this must impact also the human-nature relation. My viewpoint to this issue is often ironic.

My installation *The Condition* (2016), created in collaboration with Jonas Jørgensen and a part of the *Hybrid Matters* project, was partly triggered by the fact that Denmark is the largest producer of Christmas trees in Europe, with a fairly large economic value. The trees in the installation were part of a research project on cloning of Christmas trees for economic benefits pursued by the University of Copenhagen. In the installation, the trees were placed in a micro-gravity condition with rotating boxes. This formed a small-scale forest with 12 rotating boxes, which was controlled by a space-weather satellite and self-organizing algorithm for rotation speeds.

So definitely, my art has influences from the Nordic region and the location where I live and where I am active. I think this is almost always the case with artists; one observes one's immediate surroundings. My current work environment at the IT University of Copenhagen and people I work with here also influence me. For example, my interests in artificial life and robotics have gotten a new boost as I am surrounded by experts on these matters.

Pink Twins (Juha Vehviläinen and Vesa Vehviläinen)

We do not necessarily see our work as specifically Nordic (or Finnish). However, the fact that we have lived and worked in a relatively stable and wealthy society probably makes it possible for us to create art that focuses on aesthetic and formal issues, ways of seeing, conventions of a narrative, etc., rather than on the current political climate.

Bombina Bombast (Emma Bexell and Stefan Stanisic)
It takes 20 minutes for us to go from our home in Malmö, Sweden, to Copenhagen Central Station. This geographical proximity reflects in collaborations as well as talks over beer. A common denominator in these talks is the Nordic in the context of urgent political discussions about borders, hospitality and belonging; those convinced that if a Nordic identity cannot hold cultural diversity it is completely disposable; and those who feel a need to 'protect' the Nordic from any kind of cultural influence. Malmö is an arrival city whose identity is made up of a multiplicity of cultures, proud to co-exist. This pride is a threat to some.

Anastasios Logothetis
Having a nomadic outlook by virtue of a dual citizenship has allowed me to deal with breaking national and regional contexts and heritage, rather than propping it up; using the Greek to see the Swede better and the other way around. Nations and flags feel out-dated to me.

Arijana Kajfes
As an immigrant, I have never felt completely in tune with or representative of the Nordic context.

Andrew Gryf Paterson
I am an immigrant and guest in and among the Nordic and Baltic people. However, I have now been based in Helsinki, Finland, for longer than in my childhood-memory home in the central Scottish rural countryside, as well as in Glasgow, the place in which I have spent the second longest period of time. I am originally from Scotland, but now I am also from Helsinki and the Baltic Sea region. I have visited Latvia, Estonia and Lithuania often, since I have been based in Helsinki. Due to this I have re-inscribed a locative group-identity for myself. I am a Baltic-Scot. My particular cultural identity background straddles an islander, internationally networked, solidly European, left field, autonomous-spirited and outward-minded orientation, with a peripheral Northern perspective. This is not so dissimilar from a Nordic one.

For my bachelor of honours degree thesis of 1996–1997, I made a historical and political research into modern identity politics, with the title *Raising Flags of Difference*. My original inspiration and motivation for visiting Finland for the first time, in 1998 thanks to a Peter Kirk Memorial Scholarship, was with hopes to visit the crossroads between East and West and also visit a 'dream-centre' of Europe. After several months in Helsinki, I realized my interest was in between an axis of Isolation – Integration, and an axis of Nature – Technology. In some ways, being an immigrant in North Eastern Europe was not so hard, due to my very privileged entry point of arriving and being of Scottish/UK-origin and a well-educated doctoral candidate at the University of (applied) Art and Design in Helsinki. I thus had an ideal and smooth start or route towards being a *Stadilainen* (Helsinki-resident). My artistic and research practice in the Nordic context ever since has arguably been an engagement with that reality, including the accompanying privileges, challenges and difficulties, with my personal social, economic and technological utopia breaking down several times. I recognize that after the economic recession and due to the current contemporary context, the way into the Nordic-Baltic culture and society is maybe not as easy as it was for me then in the early 2000s as a privileged EU citizen, although there has been an increased presence and influence of immigrants in the Helsinki cultural scene since.

Alberto Frigo

When I started my 'life-stowing operation' I had the great opportunity to work on a farm in Uppsala, not so far from Carl von Linné's old dwelling. Having grown up in a rather bourgeoisie and middle-class context, the Swedish countryside offered me a great opportunity to learn the processes of a sustainable life. Coming to Sweden was for me like the starting of my first website in a time in which it was not yet colonized by the social media industry. I have learned very much, however, with the years. I had to face quite some challenges in the more traditional cultural context – not yet acquainted with the kind of artistic operation I was undertaking. I guess that what I have experienced overall is a rather natural context, which has allowed me to mature my own artistic framework.

Things have changed though, and in recent years I began to worry about the increasing xenophobia, particularly in the countryside context where I have dreamed of one day physically depositing my work. On the other hand, I began to feel an emerging political attitude in the art and intellectual community. At the moment I therefore feel quite oppressed by an unhealthy climate, which was not in the least present when I first came to Sweden to attend a Master in Art and Technology at Gothenburg University. Unfortunately, the expat community that these international and artistic oriented courses generated has suffered in recent years from new laws, whereby for example international students from outside the European Union have to pay excessively high tuition fees.

The continuous focus on ideology and power proposed by my colleagues at Södertörn University in Stockholm is slowly deteriorating me, as I feel it leaves no space for more poetic undertakings. Hopefully, in the coming years, a fresh look into digital aesthetics and their more uncanny meaning will be brought forward. I acknowledge that the Nordic context has influenced much of my work, providing me with both the space to mature it and present it. However, given the change of attitude of the social and cultural mass, I, after all, do not belong here and I am not so welcome.

Søren Thilo Funder

I guess there is a certain tone in many of my works that I can hardly dismiss derive from my Nordic background. In my work, I am very interested in the role of citizenship and the individual citizen's relationship to the common, the commune and the collective. Many of my ideas of a sociopolitical subject, regarded as citizen, come from a Nordic point of view and takes off from the idea of a Nordic welfare state. My works are invested in the question of possible alternative societal forms, and the society that I am a part of in my everyday life is always at least one of the societies I measure this alternative up against.

My personal position, from where my observations and works derive, is deeply rooted in the countercultural and in a critical approach to the political situation and environment of the Nordic region. A major concern of mine is the ever-blossoming fear and xenophobia of this part of the world. Hopefully, the Nordic tone in my works vibrates with the melancholic position of being of the scared, ignorant and paranoiacally secured.

This being said, I have also found myself in numerous international contexts where my work has been shaped by very different collective and societal logics than the one in which I normally reside. These works often contain different divert energies and tones directly shaped by shifting circumstances and local participants. But yet here the works still somehow reflect a certain being from the outside looking in. My position in these works is one of constant contemplation and I always attempt to introduce gaps, spaces, tools, errors, loopholes or dead ends – directly highlighting this uneven relationship. Again, the essence is the paradoxical situation.

Elisabeth Molin

I think it is fascinating how the everyday is often a reoccurring theme in the Nordic. There is a sense of de-familiarizing the familiar, both in terms of materials and storytelling, for instance in the works of Elmgreen and Dragset, Superflex and Third Ear. I think equality and the rather socialist upbringing – that the Nordic stands for – has had an effect on how I engage with and look at the world. I am interested in a language, which can reach out to all sorts of audiences and be 'democratic'.

Goto80 (Anders Carlsson)

Today, function and perfection are centre stage, and as artists we sometimes confirm this, sometimes rebel against it. Personally, I like to rebel against Nordic conformism in general.

Marie Munk Hartwig

I see myself generally reacting contradictory to my surroundings in my artwork. Coming from a minimalistic, control-obsessed, neat and cold Nordic country, I guess you can trace a reaction towards this in the aesthetics of my artwork. Control is an important theme for me. In my work I am concerned with both the obsession and struggle we have with the control of our lives and our bodies. I am eager to illustrate the absurdity in this.

In Denmark, I guess the Jantelov (the idea that there is a pattern of group behaviour towards individuals within Scandinavian communities that negatively portrays and criticizes individual success and achievement as unworthy and inappropriate) has made Danes very modest and neat. We want to fit in and if you are too extravagant you are too much. I reckon this has influenced the development of our minimalistic and strict Nordic signature aesthetics. I guess I unconsciously try to break with this in my artwork where I am usually seeking a happy, playful, imaginary, almost childishly naïve and untamed, free universe in which unwritten rules are forgotten or ignored. I create a parallel world where I am not restricted by my culture but allowed to use it freely and creatively. I never use black, grey, white or any dark colours in my work, which probably reflects my urge to escape the grey and cold reality of the Nordic climate and mood. This probably reflects both a personal need and an urge to shake up and loosen up the tamed Nordic mind.

Jacek Smolicki

When it comes to my *On-Going Project*, the bare fact that I live, reside and spend a vast amount of time here certainly makes a significant imprint on its continuously expanding content. For instance, one practice is based on photographing seven objects found in public spaces every week, while taking a walk. It results in a para-archive of an urban refuse as an important signifier of material culture. After six years of its consistent realization, I can tell that sequences of objects photographed in Sweden certainly differ from sequences taken in other countries. There is an interesting recurrence of particular objects that to some extent reveal a bigger picture of that society. Here, for example, I have in mind pacifiers that might represent the advancement of Swedish child care and maternity policy, letting parents with their infants be actively present in the public zone.

Lundahl & Seitl (Christer Lundahl and Martina Seitl)

We work within the broader idea of inclusion or democracy. Our work is constructed in the minds and active movements of the visitors, as much as it is determined by us. Life today is continuously affected by the hidden technologies we use to search information, network communication and orientate ourselves. It has been suggested that social media use has reduced empathy levels in its users, perhaps because it lifts lived experience out of context. Reduced to information and image, experience loses its body. In Jean Baudrillard's world, our world, a longing to connect with the present tense is a counter-trend that seeks to find something that is true in our postmodern hyper-reality.

Technology shapes our perception, which in turn shapes our environment and our relations with others, in a feedback loop. Questions we are concerned with in our art are: how can the use of technology enhance emotional qualities, like empathy, rather than deplete them? Could technology train us to be aware of mental reaction patterns and addictions?

Ilpo Heikkinen

Personally, I would guess the Nordic feel is most visible in the methods and in the way things are supported, not so much in the themes themselves (as I find the themes I mostly work with to be quite global).

Illutron

We are of course a product of our society and the possibilities we have, and the issues we take up are defined by a contemporary Nordic society. Our most explicit inspiration is however participatory art, as found at Burning Man in San Francisco, USA. Scandinavian reticence is a particular challenge for us. The purpose of much of our art is to encourage participants to interact with each other, to play. We are interested in the social outcome around the technology, not the technology in and of itself.

Kollision

Most of our projects take the users or the citizens into account or aims at directly engaging them. Our research has in many ways circled around this notion of democratic or participatory design. Perhaps this immanent interest originates from a regional socio-cultural practice of grassroots democracy and a Scandinavian design tradition, perhaps not.

Vibeke Jensen

I think the relationship between the digital and the contemporary art scene in the Nordic region can be understood by looking at funding structures and who influences these. In the 1970s, strong artist unions fought for and helped to establish many grant and support structures for visual arts in Scandinavia. These structures enabled many artists to develop their praxis without depending on commercial galleries (of which there were very few). Some of these artists were very interested in new media in the mid-1990s and started inter-media departments at the art academies, set up hubs for electronic art in the biggest cities, initiated exhibitions and conferences and took initiative to establish state financed grant programs for art and new technology. Many times my work has been supported and enabled by these initiatives and I have also contributed to forming them through my work and practice. *Screens* (1997) at Trondheim Art Museum was the first major international digital art exhibition in Norway where my work was presented as part of the collective individual electric, a collaboration between Norman Douglas and me. Decades later, the media departments still exist and some artists are dedicated to venues for digital art like Ars Electronica, Meta.Morf, Piksel, etc.

IC-98 (Patrik Söderlund and Visa Suonpää)

We do not identify ourselves primarily as Nordic artists. Institutionally, though, our practice relies largely on Finland's public funding of the arts. This funding enables us to concentrate on our often very work intensive projects.

Søren Thilo Funder

Coming from the Nordic region, my possibilities for public funding are (still) rather privileged compared to most parts of the world and my nationality in itself enables at least some sort of economic advantage point.

recoil (Tina Tarpgaard)

I experience that working in a Nordic context makes a difference in terms of the possibilities for independent artists to work with relatively large-scale productions, in the Nordic countries. This I believe has a very positive influence on the dynamics of the arts.

Ewa Jacobsson

There has been a growing feeling of detachment and shame because of the distance between what fellow artists in other countries can afford and/or are allowed to do and the situations of prosperity and non-conflict that the Nordic countries have been in for a long period of time. The digital change and artistic tools are also pushed by gigantic economical structures, where rich cultures, as the Nordic, are the winners.

Kristoffer Ørum

With the on-going neoliberal turn in society, the Internet in general is in a process of becoming more domesticized, commercialized and mainstreamed. In Denmark, as compared to the rest of the Nordic countries, both political and private support as well as general public support for funding of the arts seems to be rapidly disappearing. Once the ideals of public education through art, which have underpinned the Danish state support for the arts at least since the Second World War, crumble, we will be left at the mercy of a very limited market and tradition of patronage. I cannot help hoping that at least a less state reliant art sector might provide fertile ground for a rediscovery of the traditions of the historical avant-gardes: A rediscovery of traditions of collective authorship, networked solidarity, non-conformist aesthetics and institutional unease that could also be said to characterize early Internet art. While these traditions might have become relegated to the canon of art history, from where they are called upon to legitimize the current institutional and economic hegemony of the art world, they are rarely put into action.

On Participatory Practices and Collaboration

Anne Katrine Senstad
Especially in the practice of sound art, the Nordic region was early in streaming and file sharing when composing or collaborating across borders.

Juan Duarte Regino
I work in the field of sonic and ludic interaction, merging performance and installation with participatory art practices. I am interested in the development of tools that follow the 'do it yourself' and open-source platforms-perspective, in interfaces that can enable audiences or users to participate on the final outcome of an artwork.

Goto80 (Anders Carlsson)
In the Nordic countries there is a long tradition of organizing in groups to work with what Daniel Botz calls hacker aesthetics: the demoscene. It was and is unusually big in the north, and since I grew up in this context (and have published papers about it) it has influenced my view on creative digital work in a way that seems to be quite Nordic. Piratbyrån influenced the public discussion about file sharing, but more importantly what affluenza and digital networks do to art and culture. Swedish (and perhaps Nordic) media debated these questions very early on compared to other countries, and it contributed to a new tension between the state's protection of the music industry and professional authors vis-à-vis the ideas of a non-owned culture of commons. This tension I think was an important inspiration for me to work with concepts such as authorship, distribution, performance, work, art and money. It could be argued that these are typical themes for the social democracy that shaped the Nordic countries.

Magnus Wassborg
The first wave of Swedish artists working with digital art was in the 1960s where artists used 'supercomputing' to create graphical forms or EAM music. Today we have the second wave,

which started in the 1990s when computers became common in universities and had a good working capacity and interfaces.

Lisa Strömbeck

The Nordic art academies had better digital equipment than most other countries in the 1990s. I started at Freie Kunst at Hochschule für Bildende Künste in Hamburg but applied to study in Copenhagen instead – because in Hamburg the video editing room was only for those who studied *Visuelle Kommunikation*. In the subject of Visual Arts, we were early in the Nordic art academies to have good computers and video editing equipment. I had international success with my videos in the late 1990s, maybe because there were not many young artists working professionally with video at that time. We were blessed with good video equipment up here in North.

Magnus Wassborg

My biggest contribution was probably in the early 2000s when I was a supervisor at CRAC Stockholm (Creative Room for Art and Computing), a digital platform that developed and provided modern digital tools for artists. We were one of the most advanced digital platforms and had artists from all over Europe as members. As a supervisor, I was responsible for teaching and for the content of CRAC.

Andrew Gryf Paterson

The digital enabled, empowered and facilitated collaboration and communities of association, both locally where I have lived and been in residence (i.e. Scotland, England, Germany, Finland, Latvia, USA) but also internationally through travels. My practice(s) and aesthetics lie in hybridity, communications, organization and network arts: the ability to bring together and involve people in creative, collaborative exploration, developing temporary communities, and gathering unexpected elements and components as new spaces for everyday and sustainable cultural activity in relation to life.

During my practice, I have become increasingly focused on social (human) interactions, which influenced the community arts context in the United Kingdom in the late 1990s, socially engaged arts (or what is now often called social practice) from the United Kingdom, the United States and the Nordic countries in the 2000s, and then, within the Northern European cultural and media activism(s) that has included open-source culture, network arts from 2003 onwards; and sustainability issues, art and ecology, environmental issues, art&science, and bio arts from 2009 onwards. Since around 2010, practices of everyday life, connecting cultural heritage and traditions with knowledge-sharing, peer-learning and production and appropriate networking – as well as giving and taking care – have become priorities for me. The result of this combination of approaches means that nowadays I am putting the aesthetics of living a good, ethical, sustainable and appropriate life well before those of media, art or technology.

The over-abundance and proliferation of technology in the wealthy Nordic context, as well as experience of prototyping new media or digital imaginaries – in particular mobile and locative media – led me deeper into the local new media culture and art-science communities of Pixelache Helsinki, Finnish Bioart Society and RIXC Riga (including their related local, regional and international networks). This was a very enriching experience, however I also witnessed several churns of those early artist-led experiments becoming mainstream practice by people other than artists, innovative designers or early adopters. In other words, experiments developed further by start-up enterprises, university research groups, and eventually corporate entities getting fully – and sometimes lucratively – involved in the digital influences, which previously I was keenly interested in exploring.

This digital industrial and capitalizing process encouraged me to go further and further with associative, and consciously non-profit, peer-to-peer, activist and Commons-oriented processes. This included developing increasingly *less* mediated activity for and with my peers. Among people in my network I was leaning more towards the Ache than the Pixel. From that point onwards, around 2009, I decided to focus on alternative economy cultures, intangible cultural heritage subjects, 'cooperativism', growing food and foraging wild plants and fungi – for example the *Herbologies/Foraging Networks* project (2010) about plant and berries – and presence-based, socially orientated cultural events such as with the *Clip Kino* project (2008–11). Throughout I saw relationships and overlaps with online, networked cultural practices and knowledge-sharing, but I was interested in how it manifested in relation to our corporeal material and unmediated realities, at physical – not virtual – sites. Hence, I got more and more involved in direct engagement with people, places, plant-life, nature-culture and food. A recent example which illustrated these issues combined was the *Gourmet Geophagia.lv* artefacts made during the *Soil Presents, Pasts and Futures* workshop at Art Research Lab in Liepaja, Latvia, in 2015. I continue to advocate applying D.I.Y. (do it yourself) to D.I.W.O. (do it with others), peer-to-peer, sharing is caring, Commons, CopyLove offline as much as possible.

Ilpo Heikkinen

The Pixelache Network has been active in most of the Nordic countries. There is a lot of work being done focusing on themes such as open-source, environmental crisis, the Anthropocene, commons, experimental money, hacking and recycling, Internet, data and so on. I guess that is because in the Nordics we have systems that have been supporting these kinds of things. They have been seen as valuable fields of art and culture, although in the contemporary art scene they make a small fraction. I feel that the so-defined 'digital' used to be a bigger topic in art scene of the early 2000's.

Jacob Remin

I am a Nordic person, so I guess I carry some cultural heritage from this. My art practice is not focused on the Danish or Nordic art scene or practice as such, but I have facilitated local digital communities such as 8bit Klubben, Science Friction and CLICK Festival throughout my practice.

Jacek Smolicki

Certainly, some small media art-concerned initiatives and communities have been around for some time. But they have always operated mostly thanks to their own, inner effort. And that is perhaps how it should remain. The art scene in Sweden, for example, is very much divided into a highly established one and an informal, activist-like art culture. There seems to be no middle ground or place for cross-pollination.

Marie Munk Hartwig

You see many artists starting to collaborate with scientists or computer programmers and art and science merging again.

Laura Beloff

I am a strong proponent of collaborations between various disciplines and specifically of stepping out of one's comfort zone and reaching beyond one's peer-community, even if it means hard work and failures. However, enabling these kinds of work situations, which afford exploration and experimentation, requires support from surrounding infrastructures, institutions – both academic and non-academic, museums, companies and also state funding.

N55

N55 is a platform for people who want to work together, share places for living, economy and means of production. N55 is based both in Copenhagen and in *LAND* (ongoing land art project initiated in 2000). N55 has its own means of production and distribution. Manuals for N55 things are published at www.N55.dk and in the N55 periodical. All N55 works are open-source provided under the rules of Creative Commons. N55 is financed by selling durable, environmentally and socially sustainable products based on homemade open-source systems and by exhibitions, grants and educational work. We have built up a non-institutional praxis financed by the production and distribution of things, like cargo bicycles. N55-things are implemented in various situations around the world, initiated by N55 or in collaboration with different people and institutions.

Illutron

Our art is a joint creative process in a group; a dialogue between the group members and with cultural undercurrents in society. Art involves the audiences who become actors in dialog with the work of art and its story. In our projects, people are creators, not consumers. Audiences are participants, not passive observers. Our work fosters interaction with the audience and is a living process, not a static product. We make the works of art and source code available under Creative Commons and encourage others to expand on our work, as long as Illutron is given credit.

Laura Beloff

I think the official art scene of museums, galleries, etc. in the Nordic countries has been late in showing any interest in artworks with technological components, or perhaps found it difficult to exhibit. I see very little impact of the digital in the 'official' Nordic art scene. More is present in the subcultural art scene – and typically initiated with small-scale associations and organizations. Norway has been the first country to get these small organizations somehow present and organized, especially with their umbrella organization PNEK (Production Network for Electronic Art) during the first decade of the twenty-first century, which covered all the small organizations. I believe it helped to get the digital/technological art scene a stronger presence in the general art scene. Later on, PNEK shifted its direction and focus. Finland has something similar; an umbrella organization connecting several small organizations. However, recently the Cultural Ministry of Finland has been aiming at abolishing small organizations. This is very sad for the art and cultural scene, as it basically declares that only the mainstream art scene will be supported, whereas most novel ideas are often 'cooked' within these grassroots organizations with many enthusiastic (and unfortunately often unpaid) artists. Among the most active ones in Finland are Bioart Society, m-cult and Pixelache, which have the longest history. One can also see a trend (at least in Finland) of media theorists leaving to work in other countries. Just to mention two big names: Erkki Huhtamo and Jussi Parikka, who both now work abroad. I wonder if this has something to do with the official art and culture scene not being very supportive of media and technology art?

Living in Denmark, I find it interesting that there are very few organized activities in the digital/technological art scene. Of course, there are some occasional exhibitions or events, but nothing regular or officially organized. Cultural activities around the DIY-bio and citizen science are currently more active in Denmark. I also think that arts education in Denmark is lacking in these areas (as in other Nordic countries). Sweden had a good start with the establishment of the Interactive Institutes in the beginning of the 2000s and Electrohype Festival in Malmö. But strangely, there is currently very little coming to public visibility. Few of the Interactive Institutes still exist, but they seem to be more focused on research, design and technology development than art. I assume one of the reasons for the negligence of digital arts in the Nordic region has to do with not having educated experts in museums and galleries – leaders, curators, theorists, historians, etc.

On Art and Society

Jacob Remin

In a specific societal context I would say that the digital is transforming the political, stretching and subverting known structures. This creates many situations to respond to.

Tuomo Rainio

I am interested in the points of access where the borderline between the autonomous field of art and the societal context breaks and creates a new energy flow that benefits both the art world and the world outside it. Digitalization brings forth one of these access points, since images that did not earlier (before digitalization) have any connections with each other are now relatives and originate from the same mathematical foundation. The fact that we measure, analyse and prognosticate the world is paradoxically revealing the chaotic basis of nature and its processes.

Ilpo Heikkinen

The digital is some sort of a starting point, or something that is inevitably part of almost everything I do, as related to the contemporary societal context. The focus on structural things, the themes of works and how we work together are all intertwined with societal and digital culture.

Hanne Lise Thomsen

In my work as an artist I focus on social and political issues and in that context digital media are an invaluable frame of reference. The images montages I use are often based on personal stories that function as an eye-opener to broader social themes. Take the video installation *Inside Out Istedgade* (2015) presented in Copenhagen. In this, the starting point was the personal stories and homes of people living on the same street in Copenhagen. I gathered the images and stories by choosing and visiting 40 apartments on the street. The concept was to turn the apartments 'inside out' and show the different but often parallel lives that are lived behind the façade. A key part of the project was that all the people involved contributed to creating a communal, visual narrative, creating new experiences and challenging our perceptions of public space. As the most important premise throughout, the project was based on real-life meetings with the people living in the apartments.

Søren Thilo Funder

My works are formal investigations of the power relations of modern day society. Through the use of cinematic narratives, mise-en-scène and non-fiction material, the works aspire to propose new connections between cultural and political matter and generate new potential spaces, third places, for political contemplation and counter-memory. Through small fictions entangled in real life I examine and test the link between rituals of citizenship and the psychology of the individual citizen, as well as the mechanisms and paradoxes of engaging in the societal, the communal and the relational. The works slowly and carefully circle in on an ambiguous, weirdly animated image of the detached modern subject and its relentless pursuit of collectivity. They are caught in between re-enactment, performance and pure fictional cinema, driven by a methodical and experimental research in visual language. My works aim to reflect both the surrounding society and the inner construction of the works themselves in an attempt to challenge the truisms of both.

Arijana Kajfes

I suppose the digital medium is inevitable in the contemporary societal context, but maybe it is more interesting to ask oneself how it does not influence, or what the problems of the digital are in my contemporary society. I find that a disembodiment and disenchantment has evolved with the digital era, which affects young people and their behaviour, as well as the role of the viewer. For sure, embedded digital media have become more sophisticated. Evolutionary systems have become more unpredictable and human-like. But there is a coldness and sterility in the digital medium that I have always had issues with and tried to come around by mixing media, both digital and analogue, and by trying to create awareness about perception and creation of meaning.

Marie Munk Hartwig

I read the tendencies in society to picture a possible future for people to reflect on where they wish to go. Artist Susan Hiller has proclaimed: '…by definition art is an anthropological practice… the role of the artist is to unveil codes not yet articulated within a culture… to look for new forms known but as yet not understood' (*Thinking about Art: Conversations with Susan Hillier*, 1996). I find this very much to be the case with the influence of technology, synthetic biology and the Internet. All well-known forms are highly developed and in constant improvement, but to me it is clear that we still have not developed a good understanding or responsible use of these inventions. They have manipulated us to think we need them and they have improved our lives in many ways, or at least made some things easier. But I am sure that in 50 years looking back, we would laugh at how naïvely we were willing to indulge into the world of technology and hopefully have a healthier understanding of it. As an artist, I am not trying to give answers but simply taking part in a healthy development of our society and the future.

Alberto Frigo

I have often reflected on the societal implications that my art practice might or might not have. It looks like I am the impersonation of Narcissus, constantly with his head down looking at his reflection. In the course of twelve years of dedicated work it is now clear to me that when I started photographing every object my right hand uses, with the first digital cameras back in 2003, I was part of a cultural symptom of a new paradigm to come. To be more specific, and with the help of heretic theorists like Slavoj Žižek and Marshal McLuhan, I have recognized that the operation I started, before the era of social media, was just a premonition of what society is nowadays experiencing. According to McLuhan, the work of marginal media artists can in fact help society to identify in time the crises that are often associated to new paradigm shifts, such as perhaps the wars and economic crisis that are more or less linked to the advent of digital technologies. One could go as far as to see my digital practice as a technology of magic versus the destructive technology of the homo faber. With reference to Jacques Ellul, society should be more aware of the repetitive and formula-based technology of magic, which shaman-like individuals, like media artists, intuitively develop.

If we are not to believe these theories, I guess we can content ourselves with one of the last writings of Michel Foucault in which he emphasizes the shift from a technology of power to a technology of the self, considered not so much as a way to know ourselves better (as for example the idea of the 'quantified self' advocates) but rather as a means of taking care of ourselves. These theorists and my own reflections have made me consider that in fact my own work does not loudly respond to a contemporary societal context. Rather, it is a subtle manifestation, an alternative for the people I meet down the road to be inspired from. Moreover, it is a moment of escape from the heavy political and economical dimensions. It is, as the Greeks would call it, a *katharsis*.

Teemu Mäki
Nordicness is an important political theme in my work. On the one hand, the Nordic welfare society is the closest mankind has gotten to communist/socialist goals. It is worth defending and improving still. On the other hand, through globalization the Nordic countries have been actively participating in the exploitation of the poor on the other side of the world; the poor who sell us raw materials. The poor, who do not get properly paid for manufacturing most of the objects we consume, just properly polluted. I am also considering the people in Iraq who were not very poor, but who we made poor or killed by participating in the US-led war on terror (1.7 million dead Iraqis so far).

Jacek Smolicki
I worked on several sound walks and site-specific installations of which subjects were tightly bound to their local context. Here, I have in mind the sound walk *Last Walk of Olof Palme* (2011), initiated to commemorate the 25th anniversary of the assassination of Olof Palme, which was performed at the very day of the anniversary and at the very spot where this tragic act took place. Another project of mine, *Hökarängen Project* (2013), was a performative installation based on field recordings from a neighbourhood of Hökarängen in Stockholm

that at the time was undergoing a process of gentrification, representing a somewhat larger phenomenon, which has been affecting not only Sweden but also other Nordic countries.

Kristoffer Ørum

Since political arguments in Danish media have to a large extent been supplanted by statistical data, and since neoliberal ideology is increasingly camouflaged as rational by way of proprietary algorithmic systems, it seems increasingly important to educate oneself as an artist and to formulate alternatives based on a combination of real insight into digital infrastructures and methodology combined with the traditions of avant-garde movements such as Fluxus and Mail Art that resisted the siren call of the commercial mainstream. Through projects such as *Captive Portal* (2014, ongoing) I have examined the viability of open Wi-Fi networks as a parallel to existing channels of distribution, such as bookstores, galleries and museums. Captive Portal projects are always site-specific and durational, so the only chance to see these projects will be at their respective physical sites. Bring a smartphone, a tablet or laptop along to the location and log on to the open Wi-Fi network Captive Portal to enter. If you attempt to access any website, you will get to see an art project.

Marie Kølbæk Iversen

Scandinavian societies are characterized by highly advanced technological solutions and high service levels in the public sector (or at least an idea thereof). These are factors that may contribute to a kind of virtualization of the ideas of care, human interaction and mutual aid. For all its cultural benefits and institutionalized social care, the welfare state has the potential to flip into a mediated state in which it distances human responsibility or cancels the meeting with the Other. This describes a certain de-humanizing effect: 'I am not personally responsible, but I realize my humanity and fulfil my civic duties through taxes'. Personally, I am all for welfare and universal social safety. However, to facilitate such security, a kind of generalization is bound to take place: Scandinavian civitas places a high degree of trust in the system, trust in the State, which cares for us like a mother and teaches us to think of ourselves as givers and receivers to and of the system. But maybe the relation to our societal mother has grown incestuous in the pairing of such high levels of institutionalized intimacy with capitalism, another system based on generalization, equivalence and recursive dependency.

My thought is that an uncritical and trusting upbringing within the welfare state makes you structurally prone to 'capitalist capture' – to use a phrase coined by Isabelle Stengers and Philippe Pignarre in *Capitalist Sorcery* (2011). Here they advocate for the singular as a guard against such capture and speak of the inherent danger of scientific-capitalist generalization. At any rate, the effects of capitalist capture have in recent decades hit the welfare type of governance hard, because of the latter's psycho-institutional readiness to trust social authority. The welfare state prepared the cannula, and capitalism was the drug. In this circuit, digitality is not necessarily a friend, but rather a kind of doctor-pusher preparing and sustaining your body for the load; or, an antibiotic keeping the wound clean and the substance flowing, even if inflammation and irritation might be the better responses.

Petri Ruikka

Politically, the Nordic countries have been considered champions of the welfare state, but at the same time our societies are quite closed, especially in Finland. Maybe in some ways I have wanted to fight against the false notion of 'the other' by creating sort of mash-up characters that defy definitions and also sometimes clearly mix cultural influences.

Bombina Bombast (Emma Bexell and Stefan Stanisic)

How do we artistically oppose the fear of a 'watered down' Nordic culture? How do we debate this when we have such diametrically different views on what the Nordic is? In the summer of 2015 we made an immersive piece dealing with the Swedish eugenics, the institute for racial biology that closed down in the 1950s in Sweden and is not talked about very often. In that performance we used video walks and virtual realities to embody memories of people abused in the name of eugenic research. The piece was overloaded with perspectives in a format that sometimes came close to a gallery setting where the audience walked freely among different installations, although submerged in darkness, borrowing from horror films and Swedish folklore. It was performed in the Dalarna province – home to what by many is perceived as essentially Swedish and one of the more hard-core nationalist parties in Sweden. We found this to be the right place to be geographically remote to the larger cities but deep-set in the core of what is considered to be 'Swedish'. A lot of those who came to see it had never been to the theatre before. We do know that fragments of that performance are disseminating into other projects around us and we hope it inspires a more daring attitude towards political correctness.

Egill Sæbjörnsson

Among my topics or themes are 'the artwork as a living being' and 'art as species'. What I also see re-occurring in my work is the contemplation of a place as a living force or something we can be in a relationship with. In my video installations, a place with some sort of life is created or an object is made alive in some way. In my work with refugees in Sweden, we are making a restaurant, which is very much about making a place. Making a place is also what I did as a kid when I was playing at home, making landscapes and cities with Playmobile or Lego. I am interested in play and how it is represented in Modern society versus nomadic societies. Play is being pushed out of society and that is very repressive for the human being. That is why my work very often so childish- it is because I like playing.

Illutron

Artists hold up a mirror to society and often use the most modern technology, to an extent not credited. Oil painters were quick to adopt new possibilities. We see much digital art – most of it cleverly – telling a story about some new aspect of society: The Internet, surveillance, throwaway culture, open source or big data. Our additions to the scene have especially been fire (we are pretty much the only artists in Denmark who regularly work with large scale fire) and the post-industrial.

Juan Duarte Regino

The digital platforms have an intrinsic load of cultural meanings rooted in social interactions. Societies with a deep connection with digital technologies might require finding new ways to adapt to technological developments, as artistic practices can provide interpretations and reflections on how to negotiate between human and artificial realms, if there is still a clear distinction between them.

Jacek Smolicki

Both through my practical and theoretical work I address a problem of information overflow and the ubiquity of technologies capturing our attention, experience and personal memory. I advocate for a moderation in the way we speak of digital technology and subsequently the way we incorporate it into our lives. Here I second Bernard Stiegler's idea that we have always been technological and that we cannot simply disable its role and eliminate its presence from our lives. Capturing devices of today are remediations of early forms of technologies of the self (Foucault's term), including meditation practices, techniques known as memory palaces or writing in notebooks. The key is to be able to perceive them as not merely objects that do things for us, or with us, but to actively and critically adopt them towards some meaningful ends.

N55

N55 suggests respecting the 'conditions for description' (the general rules to which language must conform if it is to serve descriptive purposes), such as logical relations and facts, as a basis for politics. Ideologies, religions, subjective opinions, social conventions and habitual conceptions do not necessarily respect conditions for description. Our society is characterized by concentrations of power. Concentrations of power do not necessarily respect people's rights. Concentrations of power force people to concentrate on participating in competitions and power games in order to create a social position for themselves. Concurrently, with the concentrations of power dominating our conscious minds and being decisive to our situations, the significance of our fellow humans is diminishing. And, our own significance becomes the significance we have for the growth and the conflicts of concentrations of power. It is decisive that people try to find ways of existing with as small concentration of power as possible.

Egill Sæbjörnsson

One theme I have been interested in is the power of art, how art has a healing power and stands close to the core of humans. Perhaps the creative force is older than religion or art itself. The creative force is related to survival, in a broad sense. Art has created a commercial crust. It is a crust of professionalism that is opposite to the core of art, which is soft and belongs to every single person on earth, the ability to survive and to move thought and feeling, in relationship to the environment and society towards new directions.

On (Alternative, Urban and Public) Spaces for Digital Art

Tove Kjellmark

The digital is a perfect tool to create life. Take my work *Alone Together* (2013) as an example, a handmade, mechanical, speaking bronze sculpture whose movements and words are controlled by the public via social media, live. The sculpture is something of a digital exorcism of the traditional sculpture. It was unveiled in January 2015 in the large hall of the Stockholm Central Station where thousands of people pass by every day on their way to their destinations. Through the sculpture, the digital public space got a body and a voice in a physical public space.

Vibeke Jensen

As digital media has become omnipresent and has taken over almost every part of life I have become less intrigued by it and more drawn to the tactility of physical materials, hands-on situations and processes. My work *1:1 CONNECT_DiamondScope* (Brugge Triennale 2015) does not contain any digital components in itself (it is a glass-mirror sculpture with a wooden frame) but engages digital technology by confronting people's use of digital cameras and social media. Outside, the piece multiplies and mirrors the medieval square where it is inserted, while inside it offers a secret viewing chamber. It thereby exists in the gap between the digital visual consumption and the mental reflection/social meetings that can take place.

HC Gilje

On a general level I am interested in the manifestation of digital systems in physical reality, moving from the general digital to the specific physical. For many years I have been working with an over-arching concept I call Conversations with Spaces where I look at different ways of transforming and activating spaces using light, projection, sound and motion; ephemeral media that create temporary transformations of physical spaces, which again influence how we experience these spaces. I am interested in how motion passes through spaces, objects, bodies and landscapes. I am not particularly interested in the light source itself but in how light interacts with physical structures. Light is only visible as manifestations in materials through reflection, refraction and shadows.

Kollision

In recent years, artistic, digital installations have become more widespread in urban spaces. Using the digital to augment physical spaces and infiltrate artistic domains is to us an almost evolutionary step to take. Digital stuff is all around us. It is only natural that it also pervades artistic practices – and that those practices in turn trickle into society, as art has always had a way of doing. Digital tools allow for constant reconfiguration and interactivity, which is much more in tune with the pace of our society than having urban spaces, buildings or artworks remain unchanged and almost sacrosanct for millennia.

We are moving away from large, commercial screens or classic on/off-lighting toward a place where different media and new technologies collide, bringing new opportunities for artistic expression. At the same time, companies and organizations are willing to let their buildings and urban spaces be utilized for new and exciting projects. For example, *Urban Canvas* (2013), a project on the façade of the headquarters of the Foundation of Danish Industry in Copenhagen, has equipped a rather conservative and highly commercial organization with a much more subtle and contemporary voice through a digital language of light, both directly and ambiently engaging the city surrounding it. In general, we think that the most interesting digital installations work somewhere in the space between ambient experience and direct engagement.

Elisabeth Molin

My work often stems from chance encounters with objects, characters or everyday stories that spur a curiosity about the appearance of reality. In my recent work I explore the blurry line between real and artificial rhythms. I am looking at natural rhythms in the urban context, such as night-time, the tide and animals. I am curious about the role of labour in the neoliberal world and have interviewed and made works about people who live on the peripheries of societies. These themes are a way for me to further investigate visibility and invisibilities, and the relation between perceptions and politics. Whether installed in a public space or in a gallery, my work relates and subtly engages with the architecture and the context. As site-specific interventions, they function at the edge of awareness, implicitly questioning the scope of perception.

Lundahl & Seitl (Christer Lundahl and Martina Seitl)

Our piece *Unknown Cloud on Its Way to* (2016) is available to download on smartphones and is our first work to appear outside of an art context, available to be experienced and organized by viewers independently over the social media. We use geofencing to track the Cloud over the globe and to define locations in which the artwork can be experienced within a certain timeframe. In this way the work can be experienced in diverse locations, such as a residential area, a park, a village in Ukraine, a hospital, an art gallery, a museum, an observatory, a university, a fishing boat in the Baltic Sea – to name just a few examples. The narrative proposed by *Unknown Cloud* is that our culture produces a reality in which abstract fictional creations – money, contracts, corporations, religions, politics, borders etc. – are understood as more real than the physical reality around us. We would like to use this work to reconnect people with their senses and at the same time employ the power of fiction and imagination to co-create the future.

Benedict Anderson argues that communities can be distinguished not by their relative authenticity, but instead 'by the style in which they are imagined'. If nationalism can arouse deep attachment, can a nomadic imagined community do so too? In the current geopolitical context it seems wholly appropriate for us to create a participatory artwork that builds on intersubjectivity; that transcends national boundaries and heightens viewers' feelings of connectivity between the immediate environment and the life-worlds of distant strangers. *Unknown Cloud* wants to evoke in us that which is beyond our perceptual horizon. An example is what some astronauts reported experiencing during space travel. Looking at Earth from space, these astronauts see the planet as a whole system where everything is connected and interdependent: the overview effect.

Nuleinn (Rine Rodin and Magga Ploder)
Working with the digital, the artist is able to remove herself and the art from the boundaries of the typical art institution and out into public space. We have used this as an agenda in our work, creating installations for public transit spaces. With the performance *Parasite* from 2017, for example, we used the Copenhagen Metro as a host for an interactive performance. By using these different contexts, the art is exposed to different audiences and reactions, as well as the digital, activating the audience in a completely new way.

Hanne Lise Thomsen
My work as an artist focuses on dialogue with the surrounding society, using urban spaces as a platform for site-specific, temporary projects, commenting on contemporary issues – both social and political. My primary approach is processual, with a lot of co-creators along the way. My site-specific projects appear in carefully chosen places where people come and go and they are accessible to everyone regardless of background, age, etc. A central catalyst for my work is the complexity of cities with their constantly shifting atmospheres and multitude of architectural spaces, which guide the overall choreography of each individual project.

My projects are all site-specific and in public space, so it is crucial that they also exist on social platforms and that people can visit the project's website. Digital media are also crucial to the creation of projects involving a lot of collaborators, like the billboard projects *Women2003* in Copenhagen, *We are from here* (2012) in Palestine and *Billboard Festival Casablanca* (2015) where the agenda is to encourage public debate on gender issues, as well as to bring contemporary art to a wider audience of all genders and ages. All communication with the many people I work with is digital, both in the initial research phase and during the actual production.

Tor Jørgen van Eijk

With the democratization of video-tools since the mid-1990s I find it extremely strange when I meet video artists with reservations for embracing social media with their works. Most video artists that I know of in the Nordic region put out their art mainly in gallery spaces. If they share their work via the Net, it will be as private videos, secured with passwords. I do not have a personal website but rely solely on digital participation through YouTube. For single channel works, a three-dimensional space such as a gallery is not an absolute necessity. All you really need is a screen. I consider a computer screen displaying video streams from the Internet to be just as relevant or authentic as the CRT-monitor and VHS deck were in previous times. This gives contemporary video art a huge democratic potential.

Søren Thilo Funder

There is something to be said about the representation of artworks on social media platforms and digital art platforms; the polishing up and sameness of all these images of photo-shopped, whitewashed walls and perfect alignments of art objects; the endless scroll of digital representations of artworks and exhibitions, all creating a radical sameness and threat of eliminating all forms of social impact. This is not often a problem to me, since video art is more difficult to document in this fashion, but yes, the video still or the digital version of a work online does differ from the actual experience of spending time in a darkened space together with other real people. Furthermore, it seems that exhibition installations recently, globally but in the Nordic region especially, have tendentially looked somewhat cleaned up – like the real physical installation was ordered in a way that it would fit later digital representations of it. This might just be my paranoia.

N55

The so-called art world and the current system of distribution of art is a leftover from before the Internet. The main reason why this system of galleries, museums etc. exists is that it administrates the flow of public and private money invested in art. This should be changed. And it will be. We do not need the current system in order to be able to communicate with other people. N55 has an average of 10,000 unique visitors at our website every month. In time, artists would want to be independent of the old system and the Internet and digital ways of manufacturing will facilitate this process.

Andrew Gryf Paterson

I have felt closest to the creative practices that have an aesthetic outside the mainstream gallery, Kunsthalle and contemporary art centre spaces; those which emerge and are presented in temporary and often self-institutionalizing festival gatherings, public and urban spaces in city or small-town environments, as well as what you might call nature-culture-spaces ('out in the Nature').

Laura Beloff

Since the mid-2000s, most of my work has been made for public space, not necessarily a gallery or museum, which is however the place where my work is often exhibited. My aim is that my (wearable) works should be used by the public and integrated into their lives, rather than hanging in a museum.

IC-98 (Patrik Söderlund and Visa Suonpää)

We do not follow the art scene much.

Mogens Jacobsen

The hard-core digital scene is something I hope to avoid. It is a ghetto where you see the same concept and same people again and again. In this ghetto, it seems as if the electronic arts started twenty years ago – a genre without any history. Of course, this is not true. When I lecture, I spend a lot of time showing works by pioneers such as for example E.A.T., Ant Farm or Myron Krueger. Personally, I try to be more connected to the general contemporary art scene than the digital art community. The digital scene sometimes tends to be very conservative with an old modernist view on aesthetics.

Lisa Jevbratt

I cannot really talk specifically about the Nordic region, but in general I still see a gap between work informed by, or investigating, new technologies and the traditional contemporary art world. I moved from Sweden in 1994 to study computer in fine arts in Silicon Valley because I did not see any interest in computer technology and networks in the Swedish art scene at that point in time. When I arrived in the United States, I found that there are many different art worlds here and there was one I could easily fit into. Since then, technologically informed art has by necessity merged somewhat with the traditional contemporary art scene in Sweden and internationally. We live in and through computer technologies, whether we want it or not, so it should be impossible to make contemporary art that does not acknowledge that on some level. Still, there are many museums, curators, critics and artists that seem oblivious to that.

Jacek Smolicki

My feeling is that while the Nordic region has always been at the forefront when it comes to innovation and commercial application of digital technologies and methods, their presence and creative incorporation into art practices have always been somewhat limited, or perhaps present but scarcely attended.

Joonas Siren

Art institutions are largely lacking behind the rapid speed of the online world. Even contemporary art museums seem to be content with recycling the past art heroes of the 1960s and 1970s, leaving the new generations behind. Artists of the present day might be content with only presenting their work online, without any support of typical art institutions.

On Art and Representation

Magnus Wassborg

In the generation of the second wave of digital artists in the 1990s, almost all Nordic artists working with digital sculptures had a master's degree from the fine art program at an academy in Sweden, Norway, Finland, Denmark or Iceland. Many of our colleagues from Europe had different backgrounds, for example a Master of Science or similar. They did not have the same critical approach to digital sculptures or other types of digital art. This created an interesting curiosity that was bi-directional.

Niels Bonde

In the 1990s, new media were very new as artistic tools. When I in 1993 hacked access to computers on the net and used the result as art, the description of the project sounded as science fiction to most people (as well as to my gallerist, Nicolai Wallner). It demanded a technical explanation. I hacked into other art school computers and recovered the deleted image files. Then, I downloaded the files with the most interesting names to my own computer, before transferring them to Duratrans and mounting them in light boxes. In another project, *Market Economy for Beginners* (1994), a computer-controlled credit card reader reads the visitors' own credit cards and displays the data on the cards in its binary form on a Dan Flavin light organ. I modified and rewrote software and produced the hardware (print board and controllers) from scratch. In these early works, I worked with hacking in the context of surveillance paranoia in an early 1990s mix of dystopia and exhilaration over the possibilities of new technology. Inspiration for the work came from lectures at Städelschule as well as Burroughs' *Electronic Revolution* and *Terminator 2*. Ever since then, my work has had its base in questions regarding media art.

In the 1990s I also developed my paranoia- and voyeurism-theme with surveillance video installations, which I showed at the MIT List Visual Arts Center, Stedelijk and ZKM. The installation *I never had hair on my body or head* (1995) (first showed at Gallerie Voges + Deisen in Frankfurt) is basically a furnished apartment filled with surveillance cameras. This was incidentally exhibited in Stedelijk Museum, concurrently with the world premiere of the reality-series *Big Brother* in Holland, on September 4, 1997. My inspiration came from a mix of sources, partly that some of my friends were committed to the closed psychiatric ward because of intensive use of LSD, partly Philip K. Dick's *A Scanner Darkly*. Back then there was no theoretical discourse or analysis that fully covered the new technological developments and their ramifications in society. Seen from today's perspective, the projects have lost their science-fiction feel but have kept their relevance as critique of a widespread surveillance in society.

Vibeke Jensen

When I first started out as an artist I was not interested in new technology or the digital per se, but as something part of the contemporary everyday environment. Having developed a strong interest in acts, propositions and ways of looking meant that the use and origin of vision technologies became central to my work. I mixed digital devises including night-vision (infrared), video and surveillance cameras, sensors, sound and light sources, with mirrors, glass, auto-destructive materials and a careful selection of whatever I found most relevant to each context.

Goto80 (Anders Carlsson)

I have learned to enjoy what others see as limitations in the old platforms I use. Learning how to live with less seems like a relevant future vision of society. This has also taught me how to see so-called limitations in technologies and social structures that are often described as being non-limited. Using old computers in general gives me a feeling of being outside of capitalism, if just for a moment. It is a way to show that you can use digital tools without playing into the hands of consumerism. We do not need as much as we think.

I think the 'low-level' hacker cultures and aesthetics that I have grown up with, the tools I use and the work that I do, have driven me to work against a pre-set readymade remix culture where anything goes. My view on creativity is sort of conservative and that is in large part due to the technology that I use. It requires a lot of human effort.

Jacob Remin

My practice is a critical and poetic meditation over technology as material, which often manifests as physical works in the meeting between light, space, composition and interaction.

Bombina Bombast (Emma Bexell and Stefan Stanisic)
In the Nordic performing arts contexts there is much talk about representation. There is a great will to change reiterating patterns regarding how and whom we represent on stage or in film. There is a strong will to do things right. Unfortunately, this ends up in confrontational and negative patterns in far too many cases. We believe Virtual Reality has the potential to disregard this stasis of representation simply because it is a media where there are no established rules or methods.

Niels Bonde
My key artistic ideas can be condensed to thoughts on what media means to our culture, especially with regards to control, surveillance, voyeurism, exhibitionism and paranoia, and how these topics are core elements in our society rather than kinky fringe phenomena. Images today are used as currency, and over the last ten years they have become increasingly dominant in communication. The hierarchy of mass communication, which had the printed word as the most important media ever since Gutenberg invented the printing press, has been upended.

Anastasios Logothetis
One of the main issues I am dealing with is the impact of the superfluity of digital imagery. We view everything as images and our mind is being retrained to do so – even when we are subjected with the real, the physical. Everything is constantly translated into an image. Where is our own body in this? But I am not interested in negating the digital its power either. Instead, I try to use it in synergy with sculptures and painting as to enable the physicality of objects and our own body-minds to be re-energized.

Jesper Carlsen
I see my work with computer animation as an analytical and sometimes poetic counterpoint to the huge forces that use the same medium in advertising, film and architecture visualization. I think the power of the media is often problematically masked as being just visual, but it has the potential to create cities and change policies, so it is far from only visual.

Elisabeth Molin
My project *Notes on Darkness* (2017) is about invisibilities, blindness and darkness, an implicit response to navigating in an increasingly lit and informed world. The project is about people who see differently, who do not see or who see things that are not there. It is an exploration of the relationship between seeing and imagining, visions and perceptions. As part of the project I have looked at the camera in relation to the eye and imagination. In the book *Techniques of the Observer* Jonathan Crary explains that the camera became a metaphor

for a standard way or looking, and in *24/7* he asks if the Internet is standardizing our perceptions. I find it fascinating that much of what we see is subjective and always an interplay between vision and memory. I am wondering how the digital might be affecting this.

Bjørn Erik Haugen

I work mainly with sculpture, sound and video installations. I work from a conceptual platform where the idea for the work comes before the material, media or way of expression. I am concerned with how TV and other screen-based media impact our lives and the influence this has on our perception of reality. This is something I think is problematic and fascinating. It is my intention that my work shall make the viewer react and discuss the speculative and spectacular of what we see on the screens that surround us in our daily lives, meaning everything from Internet and computer games to TV, films, commercials, banners and video.

Hrund Atladóttir

I create animated works mostly using video as my medium, recently transforming from the second dimension into the third towards sculptural objects and Virtual Reality. My work points to the increased screen time and sense of reality, or lack of this, that we are all experiencing during this major shift in having online-offline attention spans and existence.

Kristina Kvalvik

I am interested in the seductive abilities of cinema, what it does with the audience and how these narratives affect our culture. I think film shapes us as human beings and creates expectation and hope in our own lives. In this way, fiction becomes part of our own reality. The fictional world that we watch we also want to transfer to our own lives. My videos encounter the closed perspective of mainstream film by presenting a narrative structure that is open to the interpretation of the spectator. Through these means I seek to abstract film to the basic elements of storytelling. I want to disturb the perception of reality and point to the fluid boundaries between fiction and reality.

Søren Thilo Funder

I have been very alert to a rising access to very aestheticized, high definition video productions, as well as programs for creating 3D animation. As an example, I have noticed the use of the Canon D5 and it is combination of mirror reflex still camera and HD video recording. The camera enables an immediate access to a kind of cinematic imagery that was formerly restricted to high-value production and use of a more professional apparatus. As positive as this new access has been, the use of it has proven to not always live up to the responsibilities of shooting subjects with cameras. Due to the new accessible aesthetics of the photographic lens, as well as the convenient size of the camera, compared to bigger professional HD video cameras, a new way of engaging with the subject within video art productions has seemed to be getting popular, seemingly unconcerned with the psychological effect and the oppressive power of the camera lens. With this new hand-size HD camera and its possibility for short depth of field, a collective fetish followed in which the subjects of art films and documentaries always had to be filmed in close-ups, revealing every crummy detail of the facial skin; an often-careless moving into the personal, most often intimate, space of the filmed subject, before any formal or proper introduction – before becoming acquainted with this subject. I see an ethical as well as an aesthetic issue at play here and find it difficult to grasp the full consequences of this.

I am curious how the rise and accessibility of the digital might devalue an art form as well as set new demands for critical self-reflection and responsibility within the field of video art and digital art. I am myself very concerned with this paradoxical situation of on the one hand utilizing the digital aesthetic imagery to engage critically and experimentally with subject matter, and on the other hand fall into the trap of fetish, subjugation, immateriality and deceit. And in the full-on CGI built environments, I personally feel disconcerted, as a video artist invested in time-based issues, by the way that the frame becomes redundant in the omnipresent image field and timelines convert to architectural constructions. A logical approach to this problem could be to discard the use of the digital in favour of real exposed film. But my insistence of working within the digital becomes a critical field wherein my own position is always in debate. I find this an interesting field of tension that I am always challenged and ethically affected by.

Marie Kølbæk Iversen

While studying at the Media Arts Department at the Royal Danish Academy of Fine Arts, I was drawn to the ephemerality and contingency of film and digital technologies. Even so, I felt a sense of loss when exporting my project as .mov-film. It was as if the flattening of the many layers and timelines killed the potentiality I had been drawn towards in the first place and left only the ghost of a representation behind. As a result, the artistic material is always a double agent in my work. It provides the aesthetic appearance as well as the work's genetics. As artistic material implements my conceptual take into its physical body, it opens up the artwork as a kind of cyborg condition that fluctuates, or exacerbates, the relation between artistic intention – the 'idea-body' – and an intractable material reality.

Katja Aglert

I have for quite some time been exploring how the digitally mediated world has been affecting our perceptions and experiences in the so-called 'real' world. My tropes in this research have been night sky phenomena and the universe. Planetariums, YouTube and other digital contexts provide us with mediations of the milky way, stars, northern lights and so on, as we, due to light pollution, habits of a mediated world developed through the screen and more, no longer experience these live. The other day I came across an anecdote about a man who decided to stop using his iPhone when he caught himself standing outside and looking up the current weather on his smartphone – rather than just looking up from the screen. My aurora series (2009–14) are examples of artworks that in diverse ways respond to this contemporary western society phenomenon.

Goto80 (Anders Carlsson)

I try to use the term 'digital' in a broad sense, meaning discrete units. Digitalization takes a continuous analogue flow and chunks up into bits as we do with numbers and letters, but also with sexual orientations, genders, psychological diagnoses and politics in general. As Alexander Galloway argues in his book about Laurelle (*Laurelle: Against the Digital (Posthumanities)*), this digital way of thinking has been (too) popular in western philosophy for a very long time. Therefore, I think humans are often worse than computers at thinking without using predefined concepts and prejudice.

Lisa Jevbratt

I use technology to make things visible that we do not typically see, in order to bring awareness to issues. For example, my iOS app *Zoomorph* (2013, ongoing) simulates the colour vision of non-human animals in order to make us more aware of the plight of these animals in a world dominated by us humans.

Kristina Kvalvik

My work deals with matter relating to surveillance, the inexplicable and the threatening. In my video installations I examine the limitations of sight and our ability to interpret what we see. I create characters that take their form from the perspective of looking, rather than the position of being looked at. My goal is to enrich the position of the subject by creating subjects in film that are whole and integral, even when they explore and expose the private space of their innermost fantasies. My work seeks to emphasize that one always looks from one's own point of view and that there is no natural form of looking – let alone of representation. Just as narrative is visually rich, so the visual is rich in narrative.

Vibeke Jensen

I have a particular interest in different points of view and positions of looking. In particular, I investigate the practice of surveillance, recognizing this as a central structural element of advanced urban cultures. I construct situations, images and sculptures that provoke a rupture in daily life perception and facilitate the meeting of strangers. Spyglass, mirrors, lenses and auto-destructing materials, close-up photography, night vision and secretly recorded video are among the materials and devices I use. My main works take place in museums and public space in the form of interventions, video installations and (light) sculptures.

In *Night_Watch* (Zendai MOMA Intrude Project 2008), recorded with a digital night-vision camera, an oval video projection of my vigilant observing eye looks down at passers-by on People's Square from top of the entrance to the Shanghai Museum. This digital female eye asks questions about who is looking at whom in the public space. By using a recognizable military aesthetic, rupture and ambiguity is introduced into the public perception. The piece explores the merging of the digital and the human, the male technology and the female gaze, presence and absence, materiality and immateriality, power and participation.

The video projection *SleeperCell* (Nordic Outbreak 2013) is based on footage secretly recorded with a nightvision camera. Details of New York City's street life not visible to the human eye becomes intriguing surveillance material where the viewer anticipates a criminal or terrorist act while nothing much is going on. This is a response to the post 9/11-climate in New York City characterized by the NYPD/MTA campaign 'If you see something, say something'.

Every time I do a piece on surveillance I think it will be my last, but then, another intriguing or disturbing new vision or tracking technology or strategy emerge and get implemented and imposed by state control or market forces and my mind starts ticking.

Niels Bonde

We live in societies that have had a tradition of strong social control for a long period of time. My work has been and still is an investigation of surveillance as phenomena, both in relation to tracking systems and big data, and its political and psychological undercurrents. Our world today is infatuated by images and the double role as exhibitionist and voyeur is an integral part of social networks Andy Warhol's fifteen minutes of fame is not enough, we need attention 24 hours a day. As a commercial for his fashion company, Kenneth Cole in 1998 polemically asked: 'Every day you are on 32 different surveillance cameras, wouldn't you like to look your best?'

Alberto Frigo

If on the one hand artists are fed with the idea that, for example, social media is a form of evil surveillance, that media and therefore power shapes us and so forth, their work cannot be but a manifestation of their disappointment towards the learned notions. In this circuit of critical theory shaping young artists, I think something is lacking. That is namely an art scene genuine and intuitive enough to show society an alternative future, producing imaginary escapes, glimpses of utopias, in which the talent of artists are dedicated to the mastering of the new digital technologies. My scepticism concerns that the vociferous context that the political engagement of artists generate brings only more smoke and no clear direction. I am speaking from my own standpoint, having committed myself to a work long before politics broke into the art world again. I am also speaking as perhaps one of the most ubiquitous figures in the Swedish digital art scene, having been a teacher of interactive art since 2004 in the main art schools, having been part of the Interactive Institute initiative and having promoted a network for digital artists in the city of Stockholm.

What I am experiencing now is a change in prospective. While initially the digital was taken with enthusiasm, and these rooms for experimentation proliferated around the country, very little of it is left today and the digital has acquired, in my opinion, an increasingly more negative connotation – or it is simply no longer the matter of artists. I am perhaps among the few who have not resigned from my exploration of digital media and I guess that has to do with the fact that I am not interested in the media per se. I believe it is the ever-changing technologies that do not allow for the maturation of any craftsmanship. Artists can counter-react this without having to undergo digital iconoclastic indoctrination.

Kristoffer Ørum

The Internet, no matter what device it might appear on, seems to be the driving force behind the increasing digital influence on the production and circulation of art. However, in spite of the Internet having become the dominating distribution channel for art, there seems to be a diminishing awareness of the structures and systems that govern digital infrastructures and the content that flows through them. The ubiquitous digital infrastructures have primarily been adopted as channels of communication and advertising by the art world, leaving both the content and the visual structures up to the dubious dictates of the communication industry. Thus many of the same visual and rhetorical strategies that are used to promote or sell commercial products, or party politics, have unwittingly come to dominate the dissemination of contemporary art, to the point where this 'grammar of sale' has become so ubiquitous and naturalized that even the web presence of most individual artists or so called alternative art venues serve mostly as excises in Public Relations.

There are many causes to which one might attribute this development, from the Slovenian philosopher Slavoj Žižek's ideas of a broader cultural loss of symbolic efficiency to the ever-increasing pressure from private and state funding for more visitors, inclusion and mediation. However, no matter what the cause might be, we seem to be in a situation where the most conservative artistic myths are unabashedly reproduced in the shape of artist or mission statements; where the images that supposedly document physical objects or situations appear increasingly standardized and removed from the way we live our lives. As a result, the art audience tends to increasingly turn to the accompanying pedagogical text, in an to attempt to glean some knowledge beyond the slick surface. Rather than conveying any real insight or challenge, this ever-growing mass of text works to deflect criticism and obscure anything that is deemed inappropriate or difficult for a given target audience.

Marianne Heske
Technology is a tool for humanity but will forever be a pale reproduction of the human mind.

On Art, Nature and Environment

Dark Matters
I guess everybody uses some forms of memories from their past and present in their artwork. Growing up close to extreme nature with harsh winter and big mountains (Norway and Greenland) you take some of this with you – it might be the simplicity of time in nature or the brutal force of destructive nature. It all depends on what memories and emotions stick in our mind and affects our later expressions.

Kristina Kvalvik
Landscapes and cityscapes of the Nordic countries are visible in my work as much of the scenery in my films is taken from my surroundings. Growing up by the west coast of Norway, I am deeply connected to this raw and wild nature. At the same time, the urban landscape also takes up a big part of my work. Different locations are an important backdrop in all of my films.

HC Gilje
I am quite influenced by the changing seasons with the different light and weather conditions, how the same place is continually transformed by light and weather.

Petri Ruikka
I suppose I could say that there is something in the Finnish landscape that has influenced my work, as maybe I try to fight against the grey dullness of our long winters, but also at the same time as I try to embrace some of the more minimal elements.

Mia Mäkelä
Nordic landscapes and nature have been central in minimum five of my live-cinema works: *Kaaamos Trilogy* (2007–09), *X* (2008), *Suonombra* (2011), *Green Matters* (2011) and *Figure de la Terre* (2013).

Hrund Atladóttir

My subjects have much to do with nature. I like to transfer things between the natural world and the digital one, back and forth. As an Icelandic artist, it took me years to accept that nature plays a big role in my work. I tried to avoid that the best I could, but it is a big part of me. I am always stepping between the digital world and the natural one. I lived in New York City for a few years, which added the feeling of city living in my work. So there is this contrast between being online- in a lava field or in Manhattan – in how time passes differently in these different places. I feel that time travels fastest online and slowest in nature. So perhaps the tempo in Nordic art is changing with the Internet.

Erik Johansson

I have always been fascinated by the Swedish and north European landscapes, they have some kind of attraction to me. It is hard to explain, but even now when I live in Prague, I still come back to those places in the north.

Tone Myskja

I am not sure if my work is especially Nordic, but I have a strong relationship to the landscapes in my life. Having been brought up spending most of my holidays in the mountains or by the sea, I guess it is just a part of me. But then again, I am interested in the complexity of identities. I think having lived in European cities where the non-urban landscape is more or less absent, this has made me long for nature, and this longing has probably influenced my work.

Jana Winderen

Because of my upbringing by the sea, first in the north of Norway, then further south, and also next to the largest lake in Norway, I have always been curious and concerned with the underwater world. In the 1970s, Lake Mjøsa was dying from algae infestation. In my lifetime, I have seen a decrease in fish population in the south of Norway – it has been drastic. These issues, and the closeness to the sea and mountains and open, undeveloped areas, have influenced how I think and what concerns me. Also, my upbringing with my grandparents – picking berries and mushrooms in the autumn and skiing on the open tundra in the winter – has of course influenced how I think and work. The social and political conditions in Norway have given me freedom of speech and I have been able to choose where and how I work.

AUJIK (Stefan Larsson)

Even though I have not been living in Sweden for nearly a decade, the geographical, sociocultural and political environment obviously had an inevitable impact on my art. Since I grew up close to nature I suppose there is a distinct nuance of that approach in most of my stuff. I guess there are also elements of political fragrances, which I absorbed growing up in the Nordic hemisphere. My themes however are more universal and not exactly pronounced in a Nordic context, even though they may contain some of these influences, deliberately or not.

Jana Winderen

I use the digital to obtain knowledge that could otherwise not be collected. I work with sound as the main material in my artistic practice. For example, using sounds from hidden creatures we cannot hear and frequencies we cannot perceive, such as ultrasound and infrasound. I am interested in focused listening, through sound, issues and concerns that are not normally understood or revealed become highlighted. In the sound compositions I always consider the format, space or surroundings it will be presented in. If I work with a radio commission I work accordingly and differently from an 80-channel installation or work for a vinyl release.

Marjatta Oja

My geographical and cultural background shows in the movements and intensity of light that I use in my works. Connections to Nordic society or politics are hazier. The only thing that is clear is the relationship with energy issues. Energy technology has become a crucial, visible part of my work, meaning wires and cables – that are normally hidden behind the walls in people's homes – are visible.

Matti Aikio

Perhaps at the core of my work, I try to understand nomadic and indigenous concept relationships to space, time and nature, in contrary to modern, urban, agriculture and state concept relationships. In my experience, most native people do not differentiate themselves or their habitat from nature, they do not try to manage nature or exploit it but rather try to create some kind of symbiotic relationship with it. This has a lot to do with the concept of time. In the western/modern/state relationship with time, you believe in something like possibility of endless economic growth by exploiting your resources. Indigenous cultures that have a cyclic relationship to time always understood that that is a mistake. Rather, you should use nature in a way that you will not use more of what nature offers than what it can sustainably provide. Or, like my grandfather always said, you can never harvest more than the annual growth, and this rule applies to trees, animals, fish etc. The nation states are not that much concerned about nature in the big picture, like how our biodiversity is really doing, but they focus on protecting some symbolically important species, like wolves. For indigenous peoples it is hard to understand these kinds of nature politics where you can destroy entire forests and rivers and lakes legally but will be put in prison for killing a wolf. I use a lot of storytelling in my work as a method of approaching these kinds of questions.

Magnus Wassborg

My art is always based on the ability to create disasters. I work with autonomous sculptures with nature as a primary element and sculptures for disasters. I started with interceptions from natural materials in 1994 and developed in parallel with these sculptures autonomous sculptures powered by solar-cells, bi-metals and thermoelectric functions to perform different processes that can interfere with nature. The overall research is then and now nature, disaster and the process of human beings as an interpreter.

IC-98 (Patrik Söderlund and Visa Suonpää)

Our animations are most definitely seen in the traditional context of Nordic art: something romantic, having to do with nature and darkness; lots of trees everywhere. Then again, the Finnish landscape is almost completely man-made – the forests are not primeval but thoroughly managed. We are surrounded by this combination of the cultural and the natural, which gives us an insight into questions about the Anthropocene.

Ilpo Heikkinen

My background is in geography, and the main themes in my work include the Anthropocene, ecological crisis, the changing definition and nature of work and its structures, societal influences on our sonic cultures and participative modes of working together in changing our society's structures. I am influenced by post-humanism and new materialism, post-Keynesian economics and the idea of the Commons. I often work with or through sound as a carrier of cultural meanings, as a kind of subject or as a material itself.

recoil (Tina Tarpgaard)

In my work with decentring the performer I have found a lot of resonance in the present post-humanistic approach to both ethical and political questions. The digital tools that are present in my work have been part of exploring this path through questions of interdependency, sustainability and open-source sharing.

Hanna Husberg

Through a practice of video and installation projects, my artistic work explores how we humans perceive and relate to our environment in times of anthropogenic climate change. In recent projects I seek to emphasize and substantiate the presence of air and atmosphere and to investigate their relational materiality; how in weather we perceive through the experience of awareness produced by light, sound and touch. My practice has always been inclined towards an exploration of (in)visibility and (im)materiality, process and change, the ephemeral and the vanishing. These phenomena are to some extent in line with a certain phenomenological definition. I attempt to incite a self-awareness of perception by making how we see perceptible, consciously or bodily.

A K Dolven

The piece *moving mountain* was filmed in 2003 on an island solely inhabited by seabirds in Røst in Norway, 68.2° North. The soundtrack, loud and distressing, is that of a cacophony of screaming birds. The camera is fixed on two young women that stand facing a foreboding landscape. As the fog gradually lifts, more and more birds are revealed flying in and out of the cleft of the rock face. Now, in 2018 – fifteen years later – the number of birds has declined drastically. The sound from the birds screaming and the worry in the girls' movements is now facing us with the global change in nature. The work captures a moment in the arctic for the future.

Tove Kjellmark

The technical side of robotics and other technology does not interest me significantly, more the existential side. It reveals something essential about our anthropocentric outlook on the world. In my current work, I use – or rather, misuse – scanners and 3D-printers, which allow me to explore the glitches in transformations between the digital and the organic; gaps in the experience when you move from one world to another. I look into the sublime gaps around the edges where technology fails to freeze time. I explore new ways to depict and portray human bodies in motion and the movement of bodies in relation to space.

Lisa Strömbeck

I work with video, photography and collage in a kind of clean aesthetic, far from minimalism though. For many years, my subject has been the bond between humans and other animals.

Tove Kjellmark

In my work, I search for another nature: a nature that refuses to accept a difference between technological and natural forces, between human life and animal life, between mechanics and organics. I explore artistic methods to trigger unsettling encounters between non-living artefacts and living agencies. My art embodies a continuous and earnest play with the mechanisms behind our thinking. Over a longer period of time I have dealt with technoanimalism, giving rise to another type of animality, another type of nature that above all very delicately plays with affecting the involved audience.

AUJIK (Stefan Larsson)

When I started working with AUJIK, I was heavily influenced by electronic music and the potential future of Artificial Intelligence. I am interested in how theories and visions regarding artificial general intelligence relates to nature and human consciousness. The ideas of Artificial Intelligence and a synthetically computational conscious mind have gained much focus in the media, because some influential profiles declared them the most crucial threats to mankind since the A-bomb. Meanwhile we have seen a lot of uplifting projects, such as the Brain Initiative by the Obama administration and the EU commissioned Human Brain Project. By mapping the brain and reverse-engineering it, the most staggering things about our own mind will be revealed and in the long run render higher insights and understanding towards all living things and our planet. As I see it, all forms of digital tools point toward an extension of the human mind and a more complex form of reality in which virtually everything will be possible.

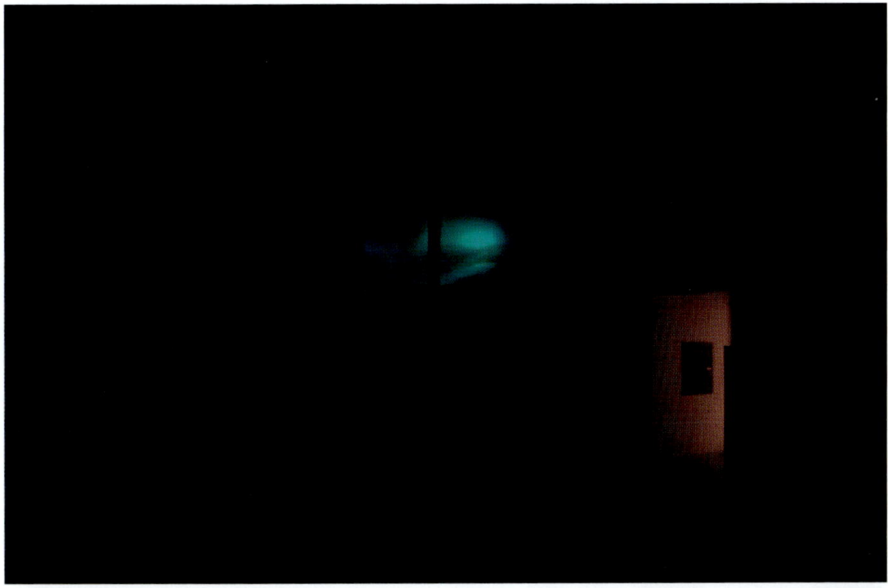

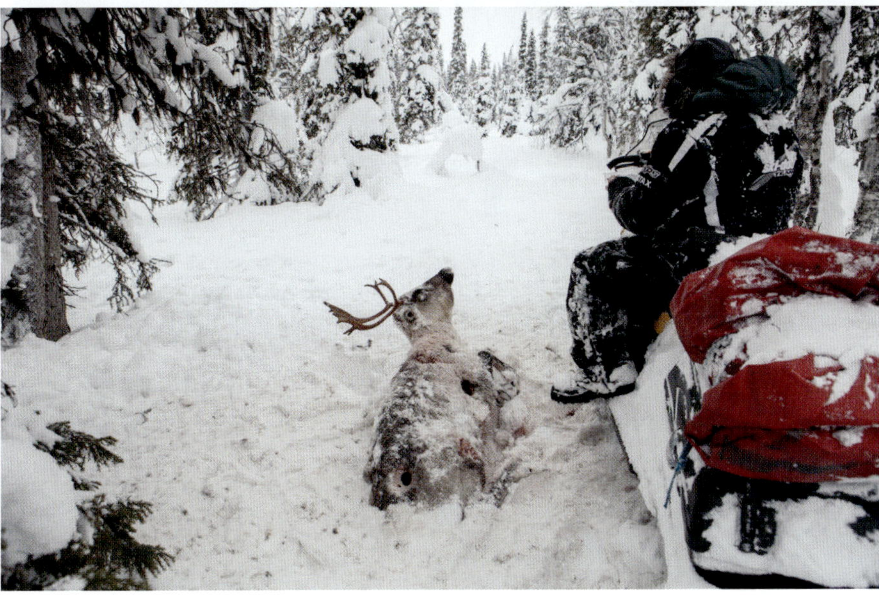

Figure 1. Katja Aglert, *32013 Years of Aurora Evolution* (2013), mixed media sculpture, 120 cm x 120 cm x 184 cm. Photo by Katja Aglert. Courtesy of the artist.

Figure 2. Matti Aikio, no title (2013), illustration image of a video art project with the working title *Crime Scene*. Courtesy of the artist.

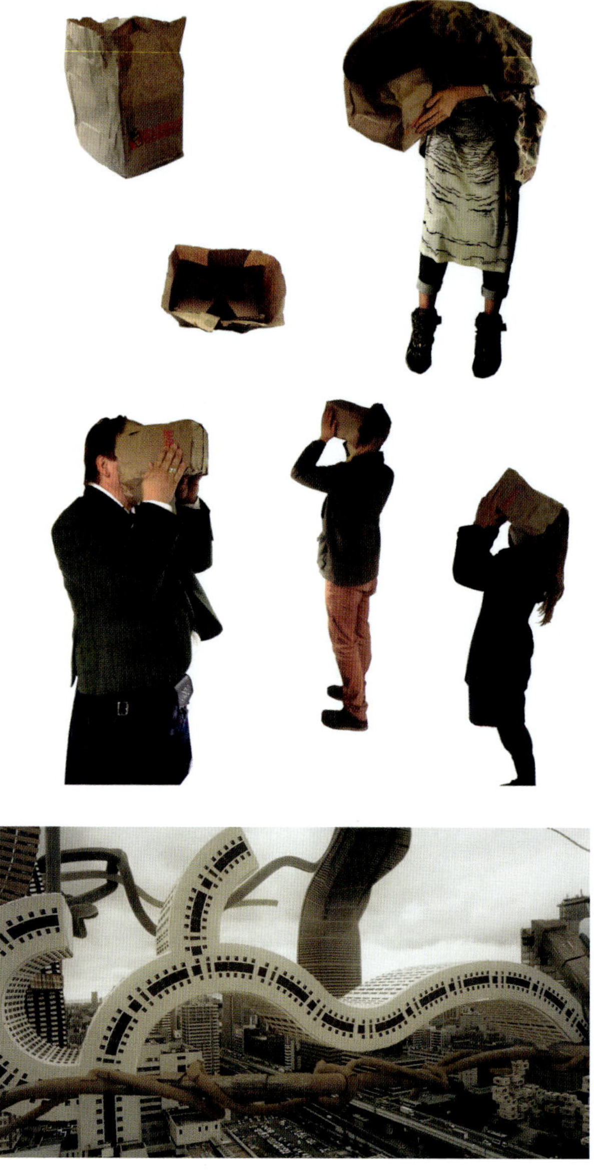

Figure 3. Hrund Atladóttir, *Digital Doughnuts* (2016), virtual reality, Google Cardboard. Courtesy of the artist.

Figure 4. AUJIK (Stefan Larsson) (in collaboration with Daisuke Tanabe), *Spatial Bodies* (2016), 1920 px x 1080 px, HD NTSC. Courtesy of the artist.

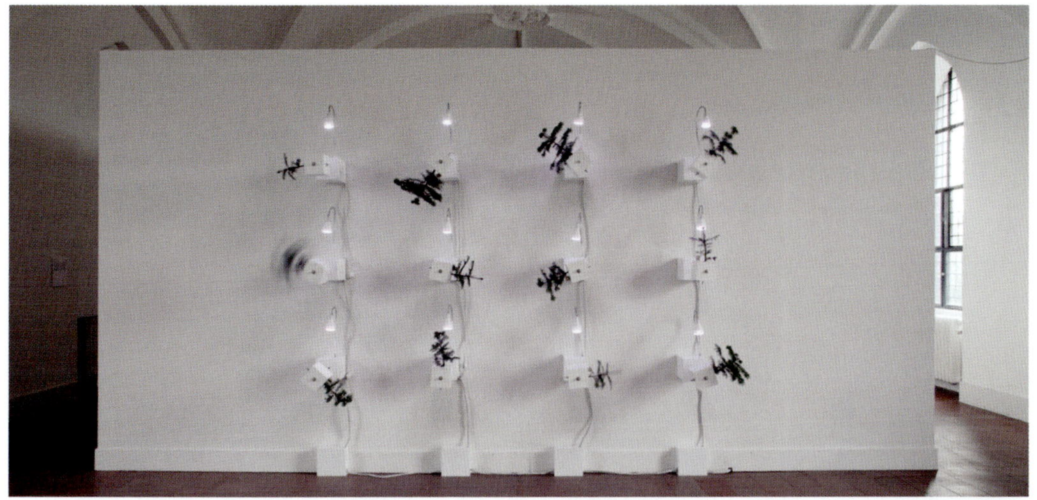

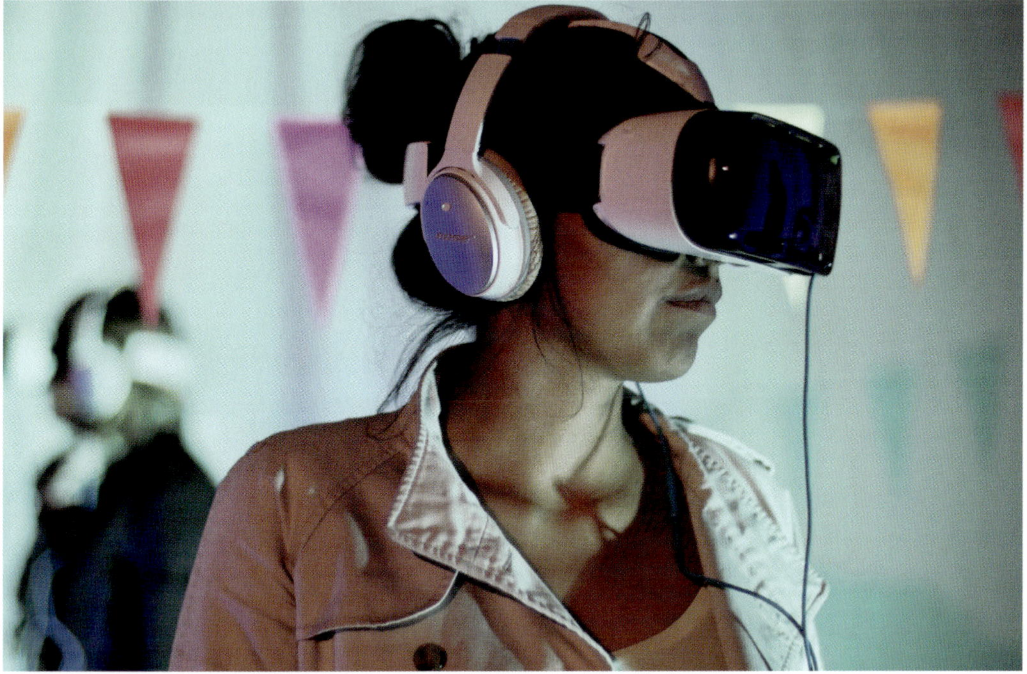

Figure 5. Laura Beloff, *The Condition* (2016), installation view. Nikolaj Kunsthall. Courtesy of the artist.

Figure 6. Bombina Bombast (Emma Bexell and Stefan Stanisic), *Strange Days* (13th June 2016), virtual reality performance. Photo by Emma Bexell. Courtesy of the artists.

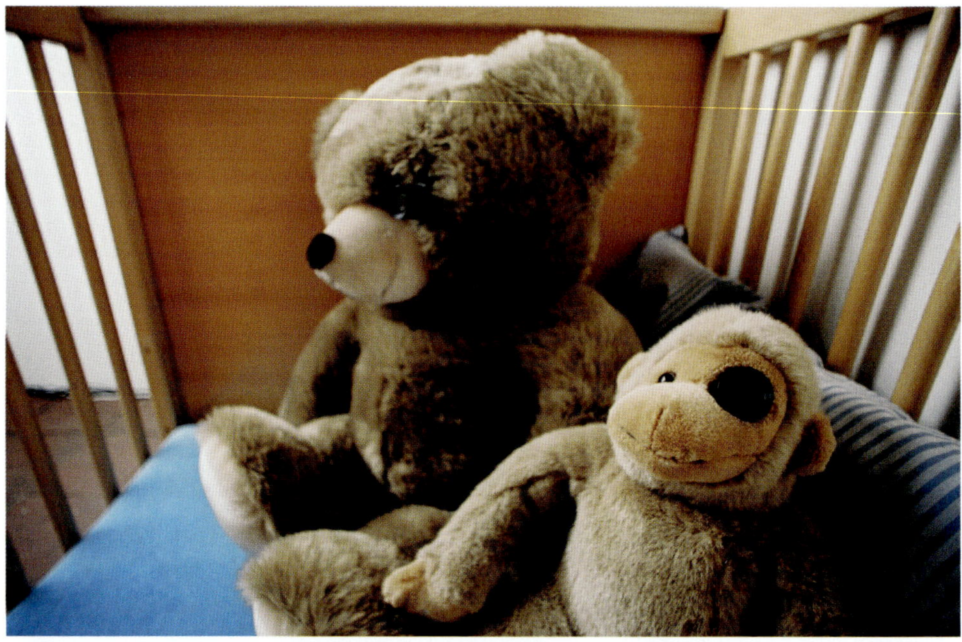

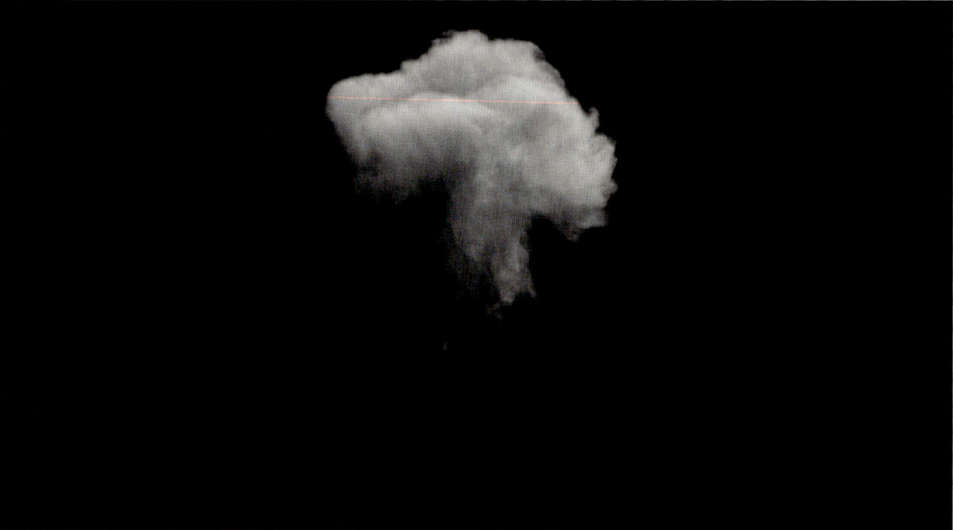

Figure 7. Niels Bonde, *I Never Had Hair on My Body or Head* (1995-2004), installation view. Photo by Niels Bonde. Courtesy of the artist.

Figure 8. Jesper Carlsen, *Substance* (2017), 8-piece animation, 3D Computer rendering. Courtesy of the artist.

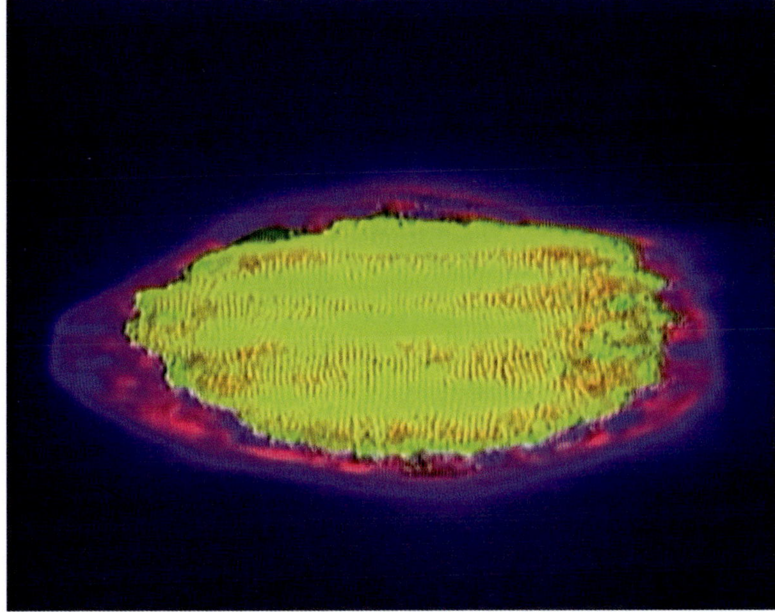

Figure 9. A K Dolven, *moving mountain* (2004), 35 mm film into digital video, 4 m x 3 m installation with sound. Røst, Lofoten, Norway. Camera: Vegar Moen. OSLcontemporary, Wilkinson Gallery, Galleri Bo Bjerggard. Courtesy of the artist.

Figure 10. Tor Jørgen van Eijk, *INFINI* (2015), analogue video from the series Infinite Monolouge. Courtesy of the artist.

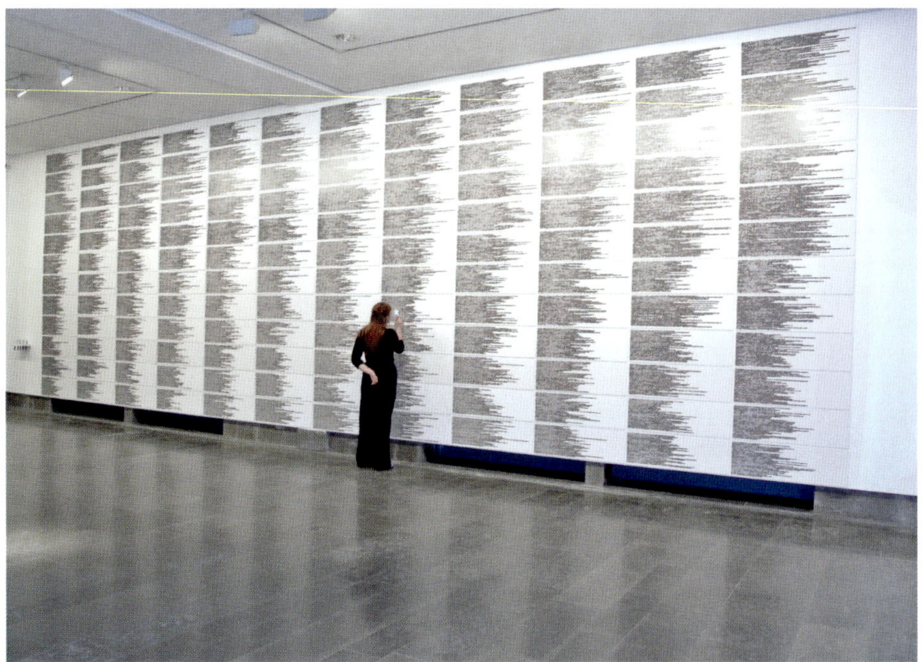

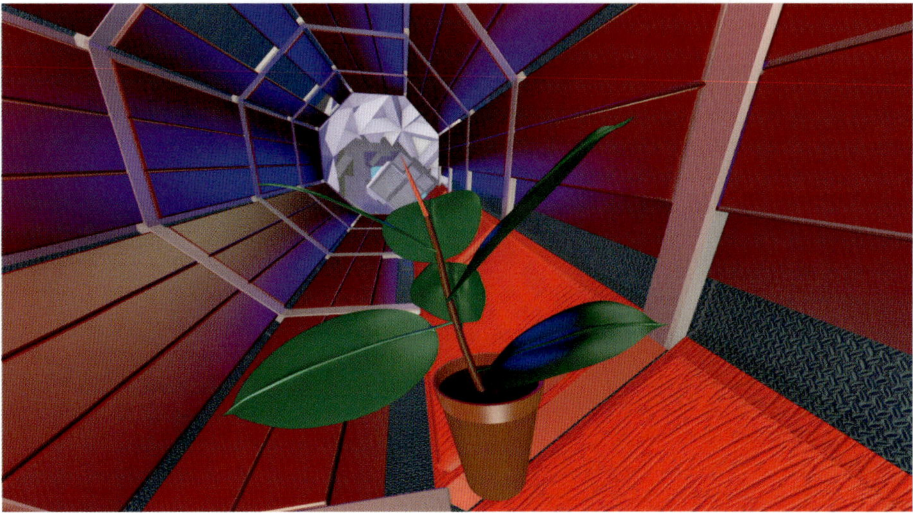

Figure 11. Alberto Frigo, *Images of the artifacts used by the main hand* (27 May 2016), 144 C-prints, 12 m x 4 m, installation view. Hasselblad Foundation, Gothenburg. Photo by Alberto Frigo. Courtesy of the artist.

Figure 12. Søren Thilo Funder, *DOWN WITH DOMESTIC TRASH* (Rubber Plant) (2016), HD video, 7' 45", 16:9 version. Courtesy of the artist.

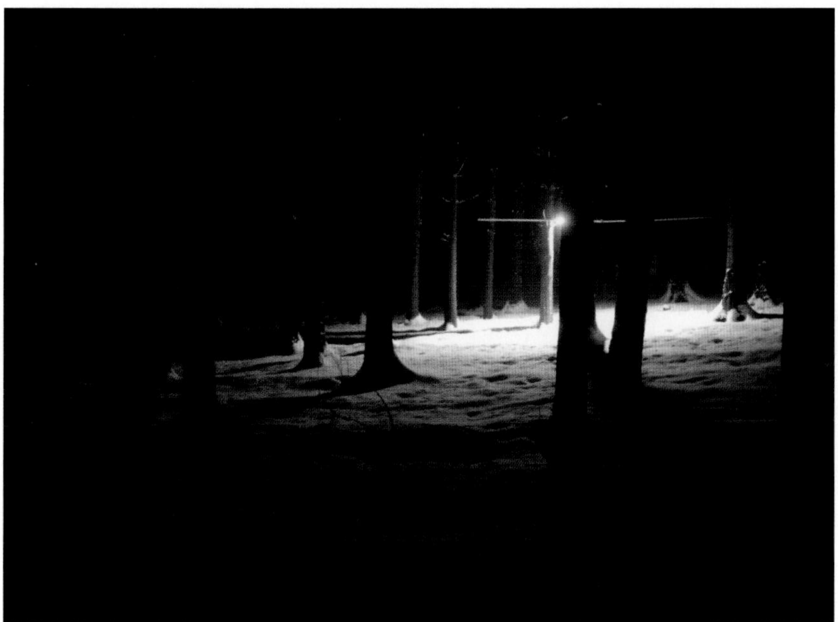

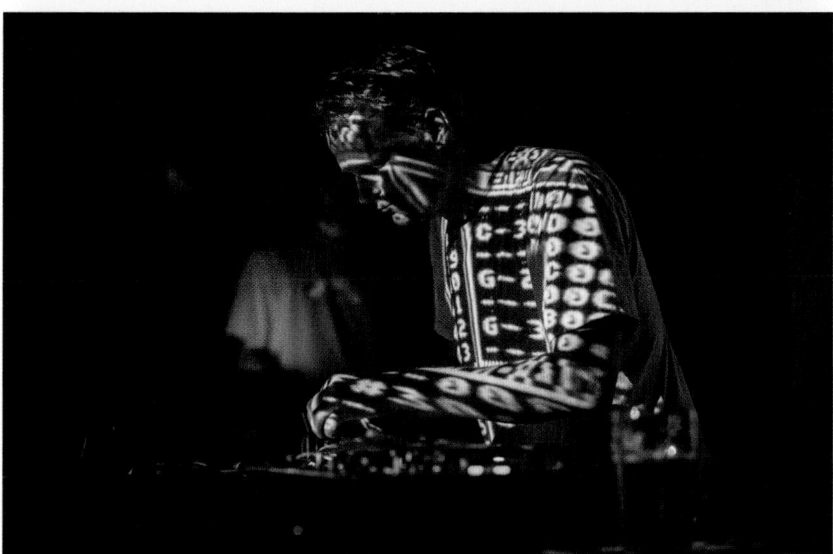

Figure 13. HC Gilje, *lightspan forest flares* (March 2014), light installation in forest outside Oslo, Norway. Photo by HC Gilje. Courtesy of the artist.

Figure 14. Goto80, *goto80 at Square Sounds – Melbourne* (21 March, 2015). Photo by Brendan Tonkin. Courtesy of the artist.

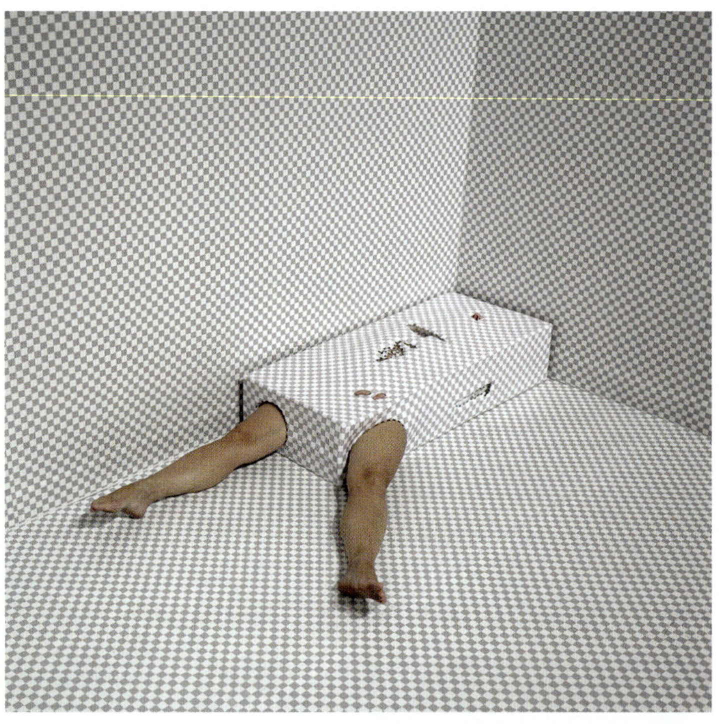

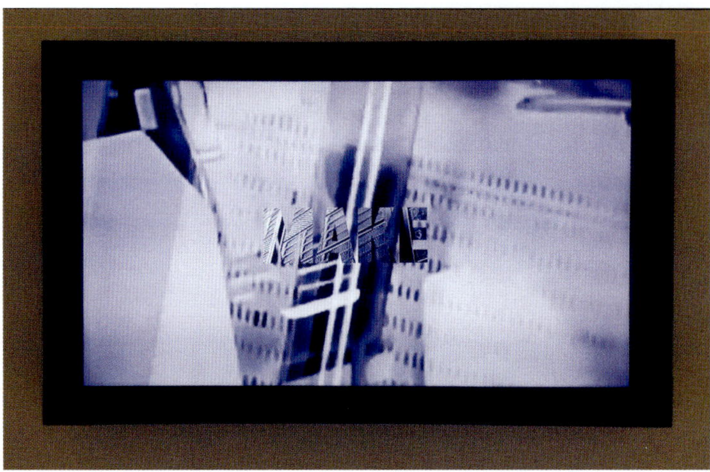

Figure 15. Marie Munk Hartwig, *Magic Wand* (2017), performance installation, 300 cm x 400 cm x 300 cm. Annika Kultys Gallery at Code Art Fair 2017. Funded by Statens Kunstfond and Aarhus 2017. Photo by Stine Deja. Courtesy of Stine Deja.

Figure 16. Bjørn Erik Haugen, *The Pen is mightier than the Word* (2017), video. Courtesy of the artist.

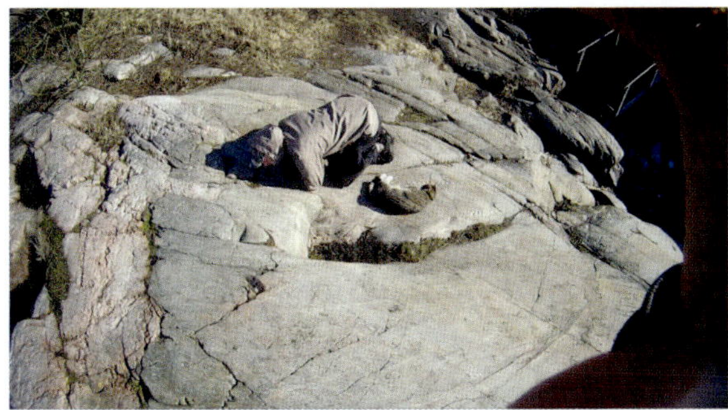

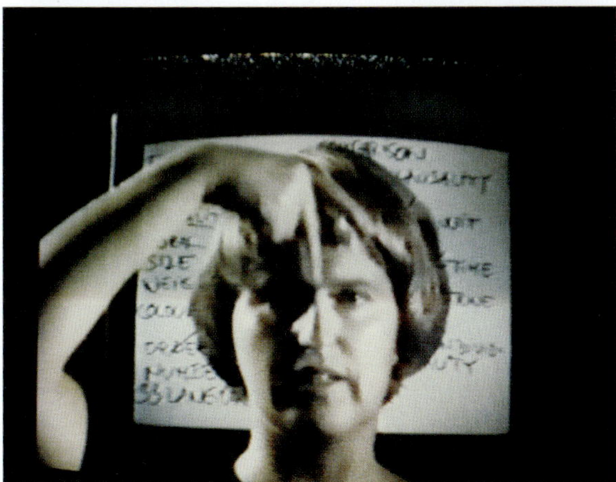

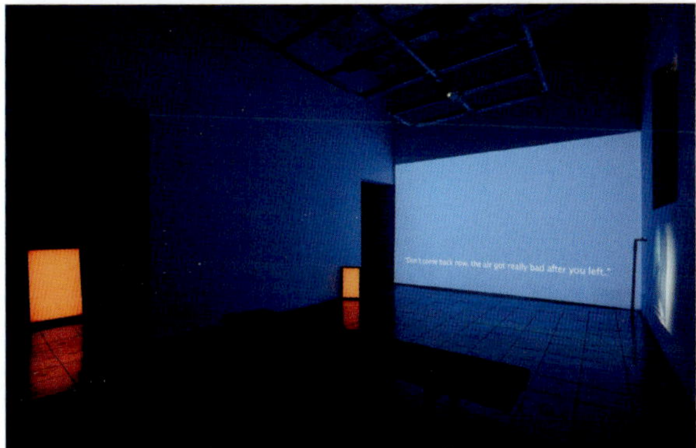

Figure 17. Ilpo Heikkinen, *Working with a random cat in a Bodybuilding Project session in HIAP Soumenlinna, Helsinki, Finland* (30 September 2015). Photo by Tommi Vasko. Courtesy of the artist.

Figure 18. Marianne Heske, *A Phrenological Self Portrait* (1977), video, one motion screen. Mukha, Antwerpen, Belgium. Photo by Marianne Heske. Courtesy of the artist.

Figure 19. Hanna Husberg, *Often people ask how birds are affected by the air* (November 2017), installation view. Institute for Provocation, Beijing, China. Photo by Sun Shi. Courtesy of the artist.

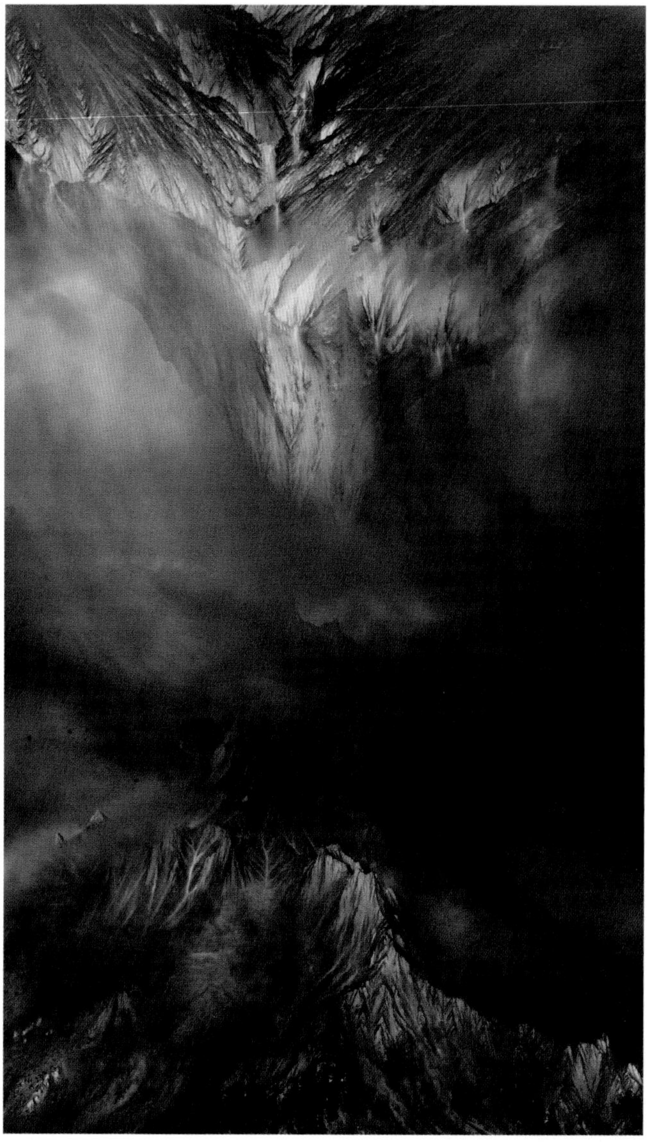

Figure 20. IC-98 (Patrik Söderlund and Visa Suonpää), *IC-98: Epokhe (The Last Sixth of the Final Hour)* (2017), 4K animation, 10 min seamless loop, stereo sound. Concept, Script, Directors: IC-98 (Patrik Söderlund and Visa Suonpää). Animators: Markus Lepistö, Santeri Holm. 3D Artist: Karj Kuusela. Music: Marko Laine. Courtesy of the artists.

Figure 21. Illutron (Nicolas Padfield & Mads Høbye), *Rite of Fire / Explosion Village* (4 July, 2008), Roskilde Festival. Photo by Shack Lindemann. Picture is licensed under Creative Commons (CC-BY-NC-SA).

Figure 22. Marie Kølbæk Iversen, *Mirror Therapy* (September – November 2016), stone slide installation, 12,5 m x 2,7 m, installation view. 11th Gwangju Biennial 'The Eigth Climate: What Does Art Do?', Gwangju, South Korea. Photo by Doyun Kim. Courtesy of Gwangju Biennale Foundation.

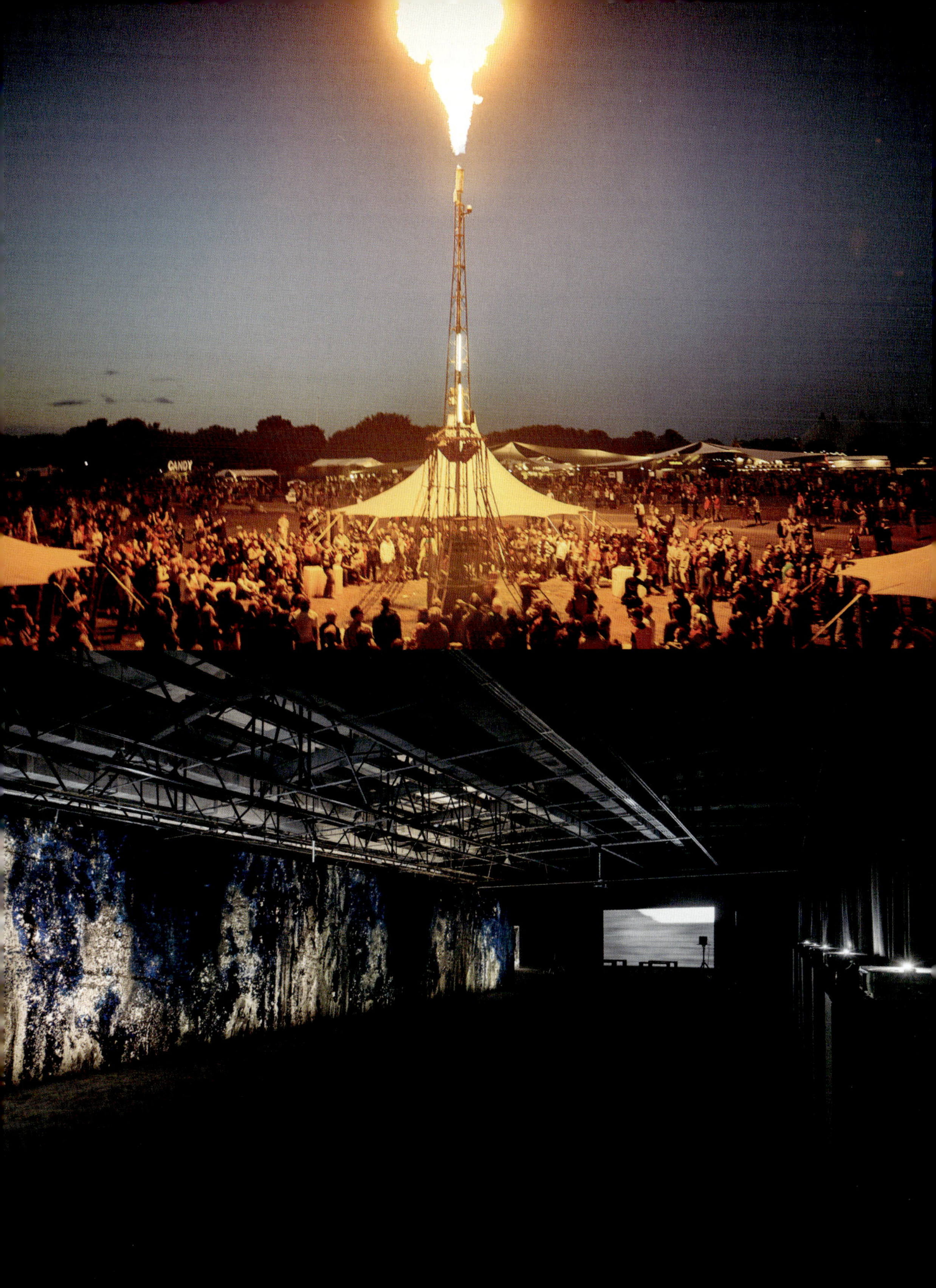

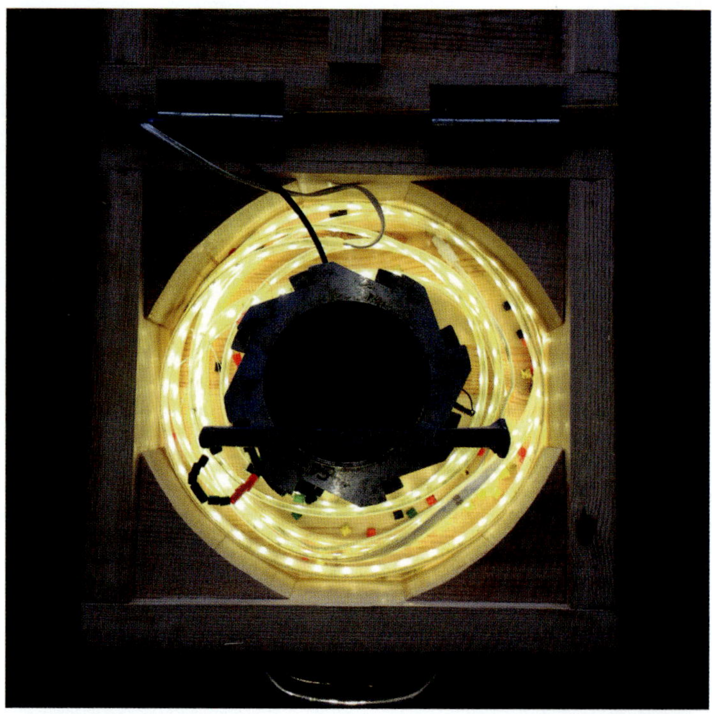

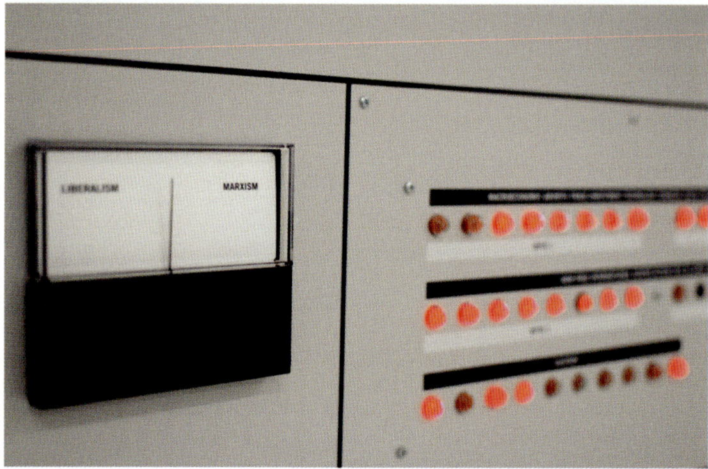

Figure 23. Ewa Jacobsson, *Hearbaricum Fields* (2018), object box one with sound source, 3D Ambisonic work and installation for 24 loudspeakers and four prepared boxes with sound sources, based on field recordings and prepared visual materials. A commission for Notam, Norway. Courtesy of the artist.

Figure 24. Mogens Jacobsen, *The installation S360 (detail)* (2014), interactive installation, 1 m x 1 m x 2 m. Photo by Mogens Jacobsen. Courtesy of the artist.

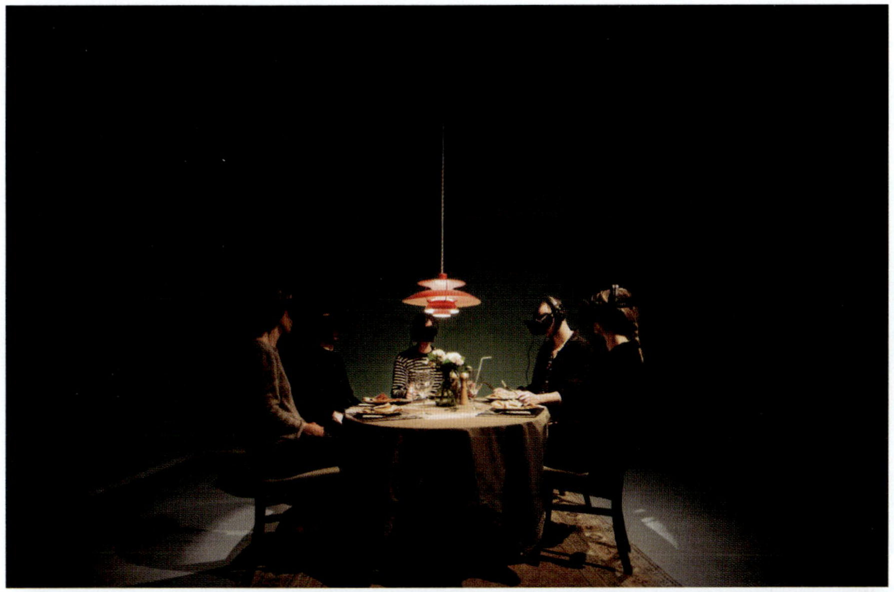

Figure 25. Johan Knattrup Jensen, *The Doghouse, Pos*ter (2014), installation view. Photo by Åsmund Sollihøgda. Courtesy of the artist.

Figure 26. Vibeke Jensen, *Night_Watch* (2008), video projection. Shanghai Museum, Peoples Square, Shanghai, China. Photo by Vibeke Jensen. Courtesy of the artist.

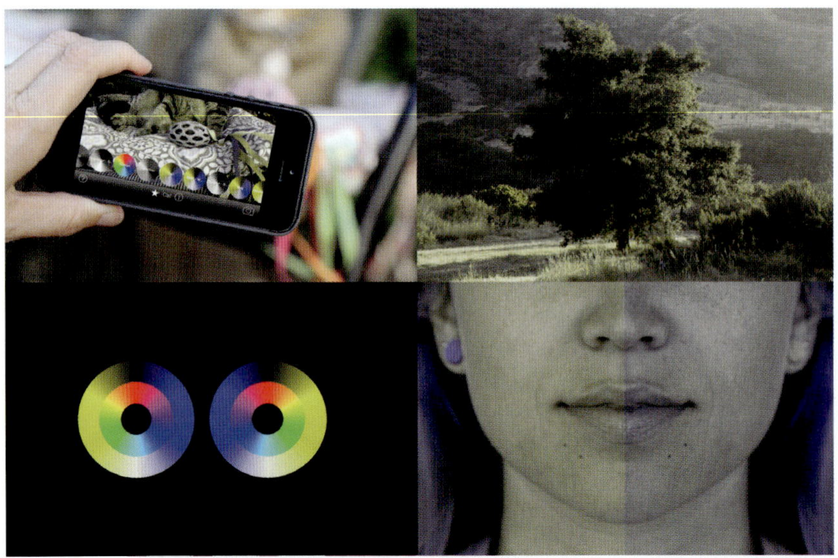

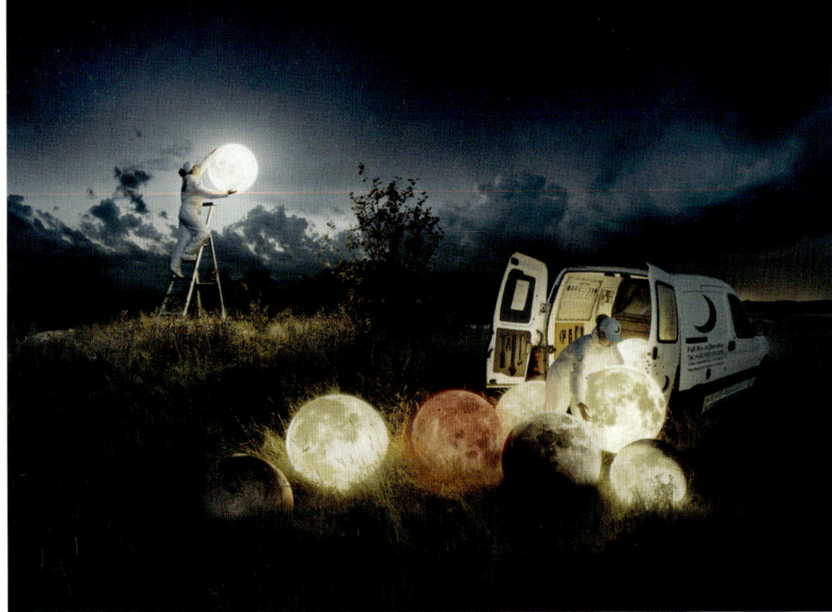

Figure 27. Lisa Jevbratt, *Zoomorph App and Test Images* (2014), iOS App. Courtesy of the artist.

Figure 28. Erik Johansson, *Full Moon Service* (May 2017), digital photo manipulation, 8272 px x 6200 px. Photo by Erik Johansson. Courtesy of the artist.

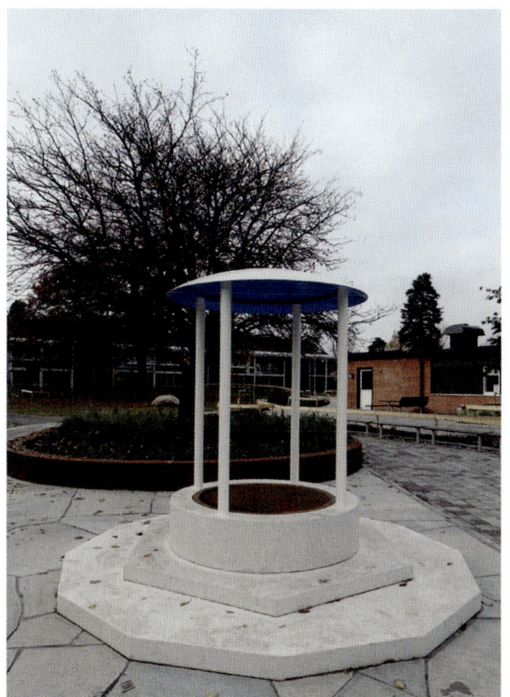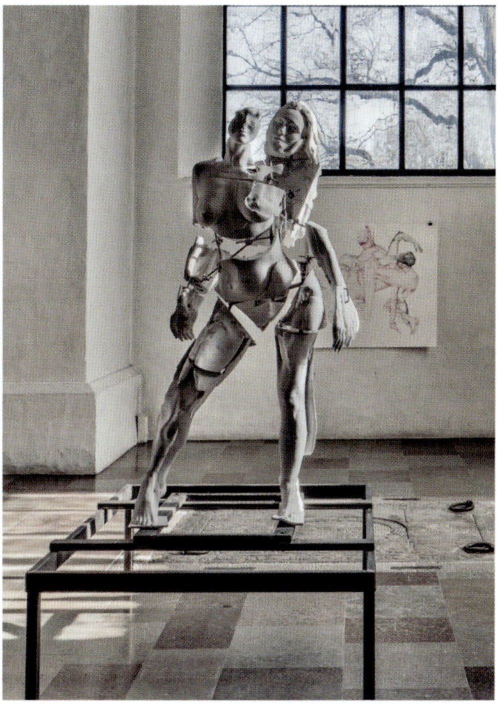

Figure 29. Arijana Kajfes, *Naiad* (2016), terrazzo, painted steel, watercut corten, sound system, interactive software. Public artwork commissioned by KiWi/ÖBO for Vivalla, Örebro. Courtesy of the artist.

Figure 30. Tove Kjellmark, *Inside* (2017), Jesmonite & steel (Hoffman Instrument), 87 in x 60 in x 78 in. Photo by Jann Lipka. Courtesy of the artist.

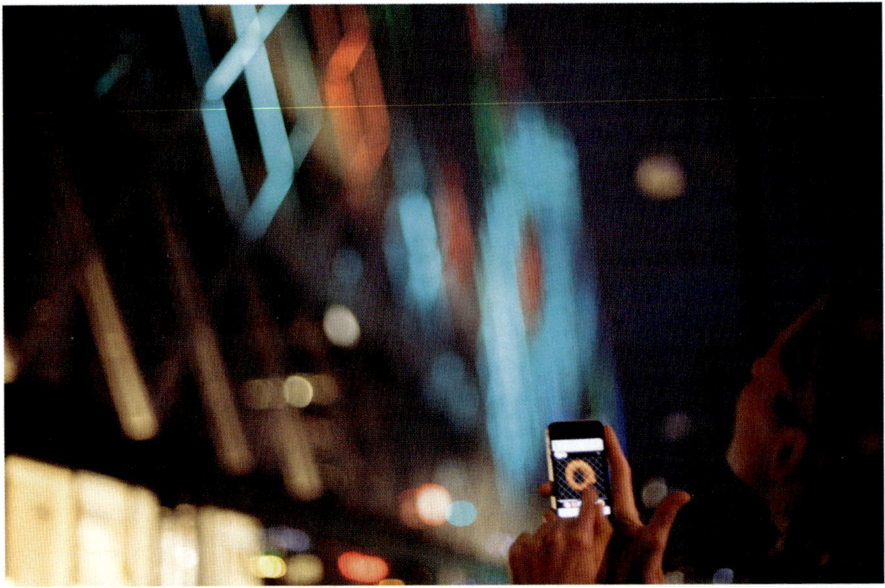

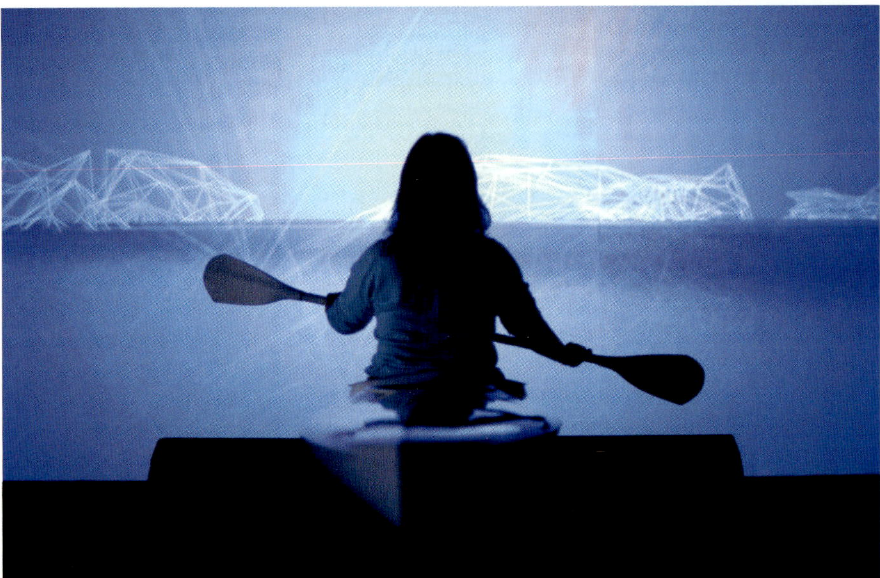

Figure 31. Kollision, *Urban Canvas* (11th October 2013), light installation on the façade of Industriens Hus, Copenhagen, Denmark. Courtesy of the artists.

Figure 32. Jette Gejl Kristensen, *Hyperkinetic Kayak* (2010), installation with interactive Kayak, 3D video and sound, 8 m x 6 m. Photo by Jette Gejl Kristensen. Courtesy of the artist and CAVI, Peter Møller Nielsen.

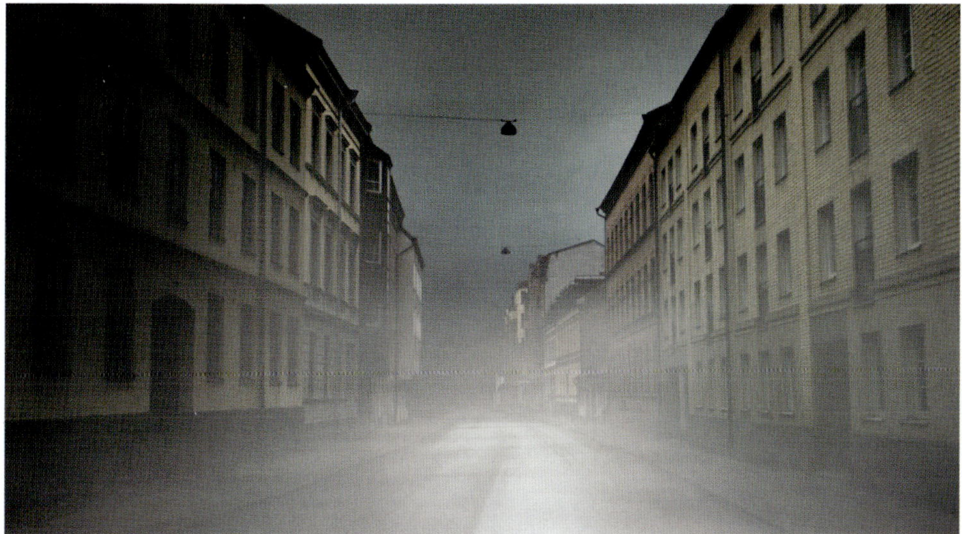

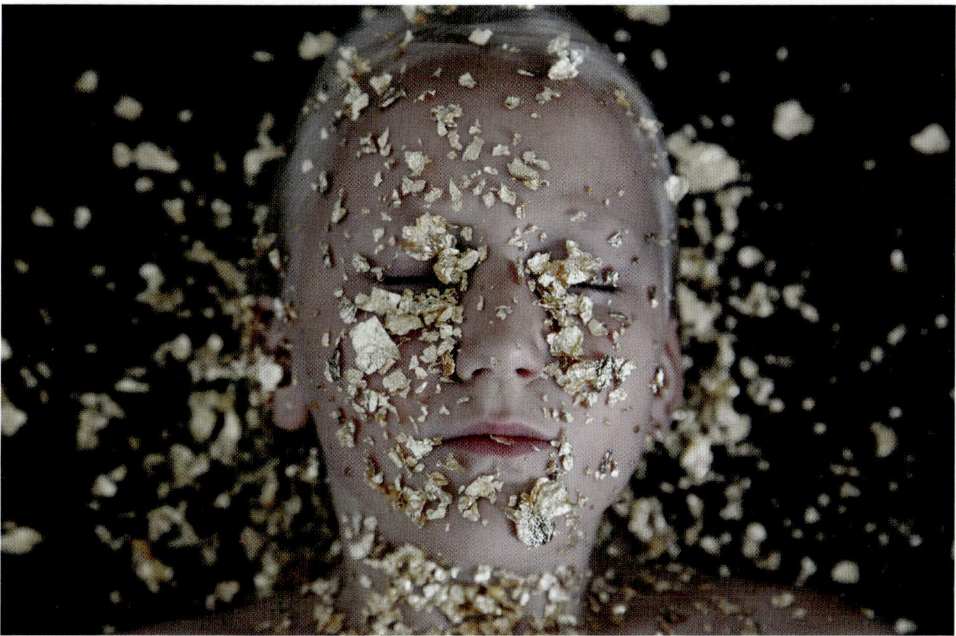

Figure 33. Kristina Kvalvik, *Voices of the Unseen* (28 December 2018), HD photo animation, two-screen channel video installation, 7". Post-production by Simon Möller. Courtesy of the artist.

Figure 34. Marita Liulia, *Vilma* (2016), still photograph from the short film Vilma. Courtesy of the artist.

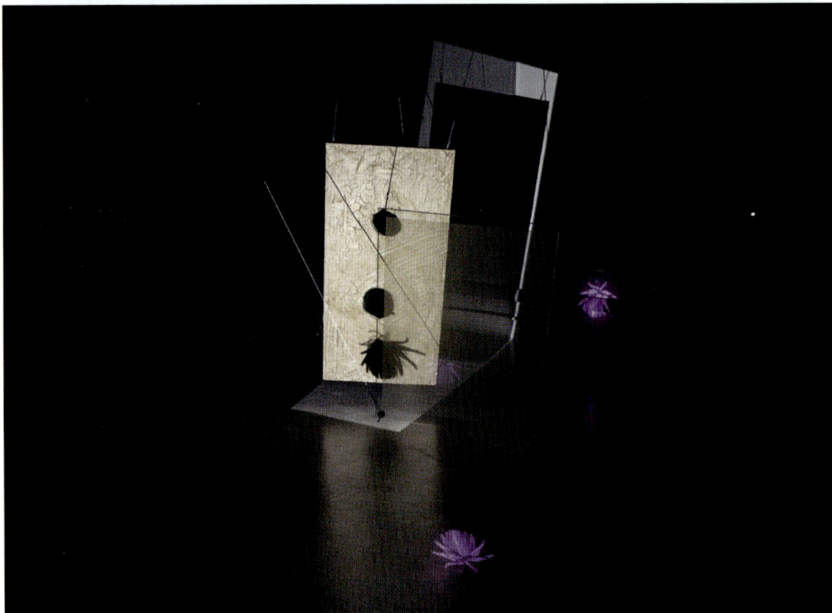

Figure 35. Lundahl & Seitl, *Unknown Cloud on its way to…* (2016). Skinnarviksberget, Stockholm. Photo by Joakim Olsson. Courtesy of the artists.

Figure 36. Anastasios Logothetis, *Sea Deep Web Touble in the Bubble Loop* (2014-2016), multi-channel CGI projection, clay, plywood, steel wire, glass, rear-view projection film, mirror film, dimensions variable. Färgfabriken, Stockholm. Photo by Leif Claesson. Courtesy of the artist.

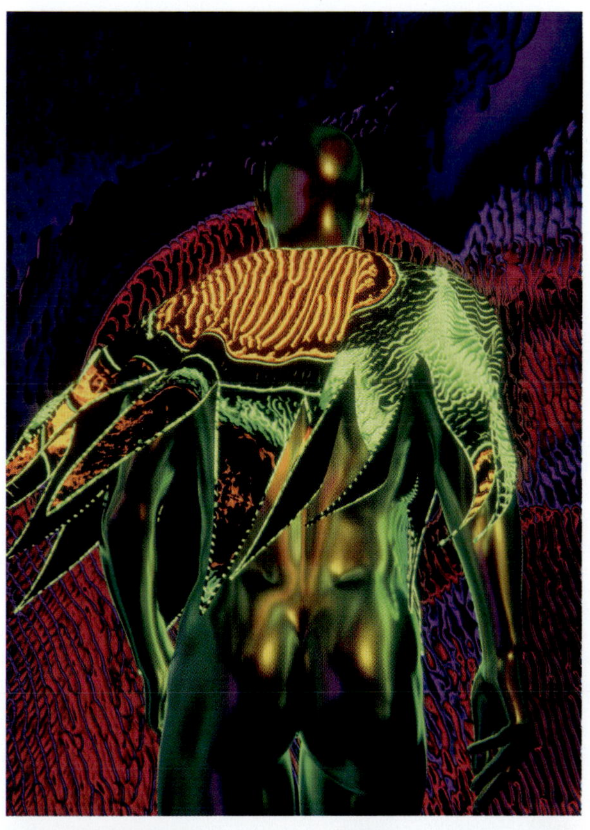

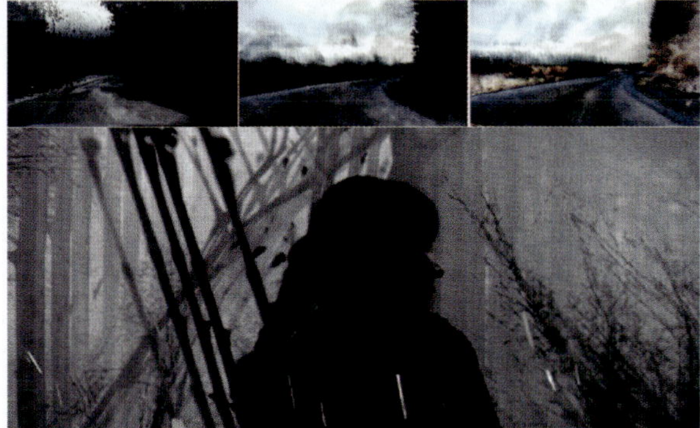

Figure 37. Dark Matters, *DMxDSS* (30th June 2017), animation. Courtesy of the artists.

Figure 38. Mia Mäkelä, *Kaamos Trilogy* (January 2009), digital image (four screen shots from the video Kaamos Trilogu), original video 640 px x 480 px. Courtesy of the artist.

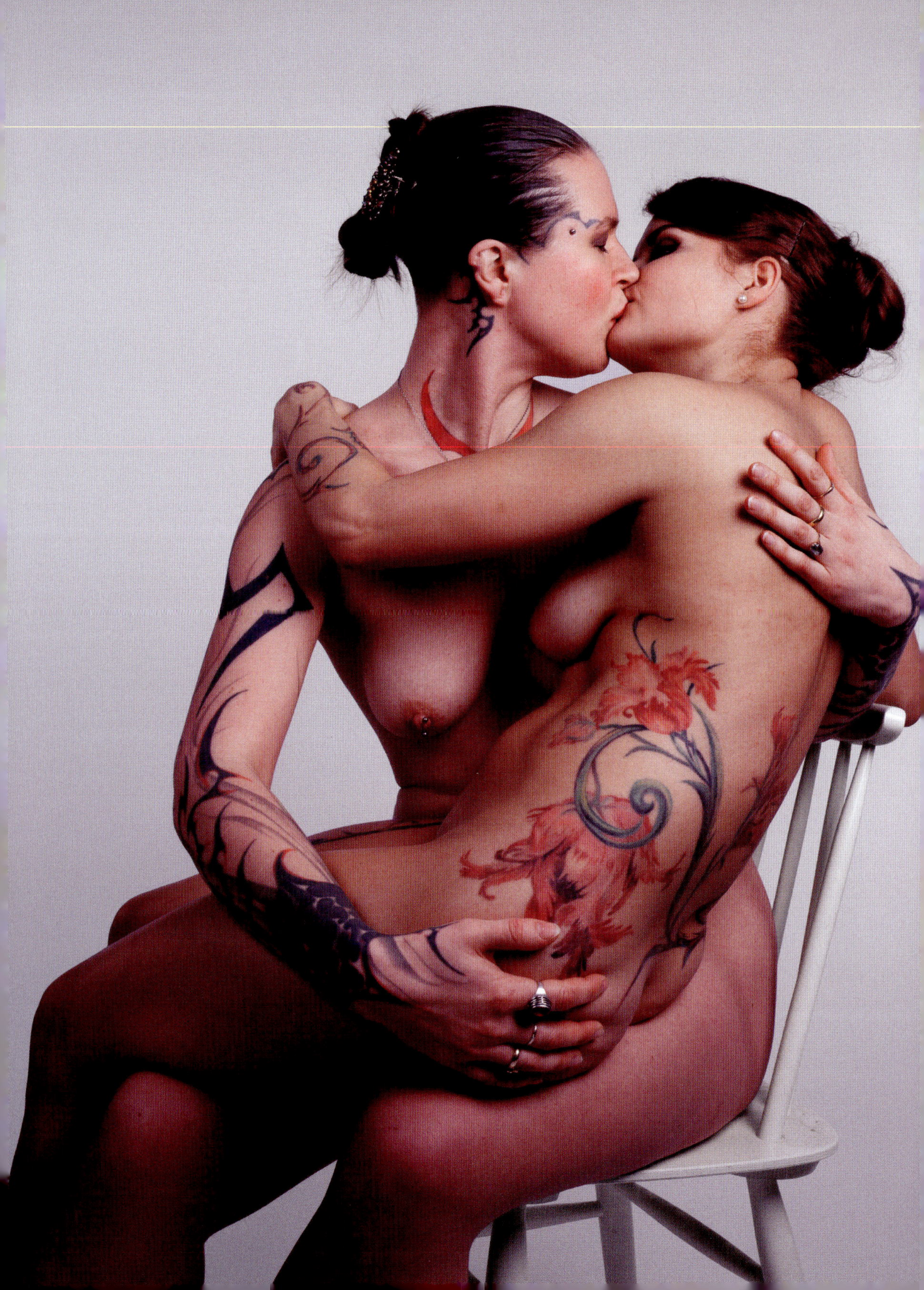

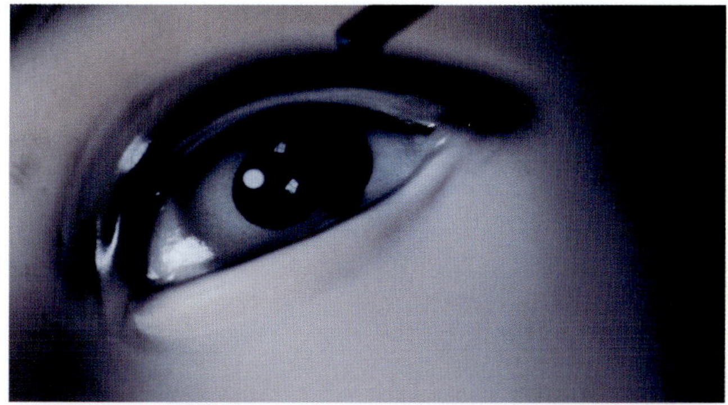

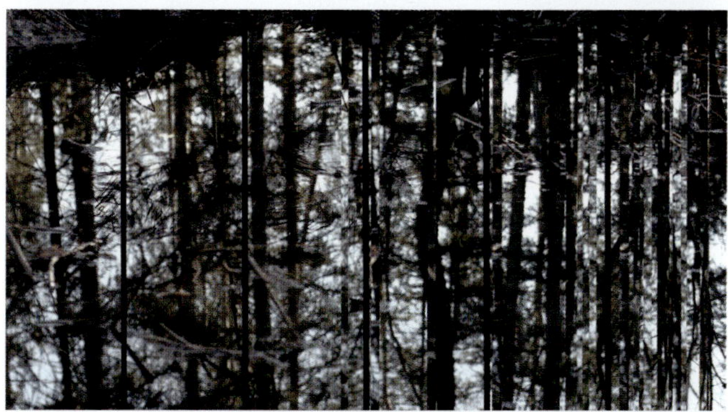

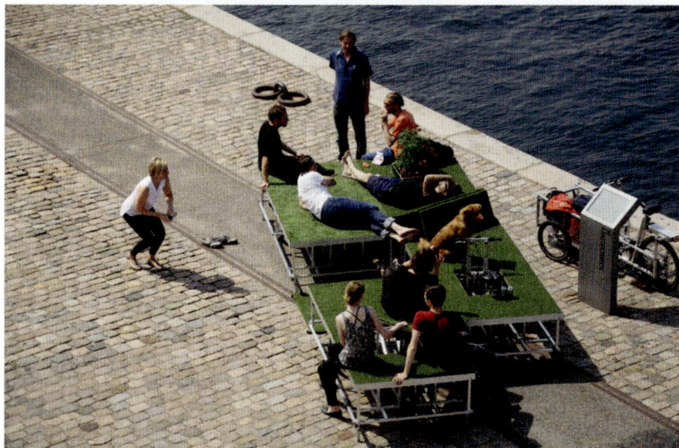

Figure 39. Teemu Mäki, *Kiss* (2015), analogue photograph (extract from a photo tryptichon), 10 cm x 12,5 cm film, scanned and digitized. Assisted by Erica Nyholm. Photo by Teemu Mäki. Courtesy of the artist.

Figure 40. Elisabeth Molin, *Notes on Darkness* (November 2017), photography. Courtesy of the artist.

Figure 41. Tone Myskja, *Still Point of the Turning World* (2015), video installation. Photo by Annar Bjørgli. Courtesy of the artist.

Figure 42. N55, *XYZ Cargo / Parkcycle Swarm* (2013), modular system for building an instant public park. Copenhagen, Denmark. N55 in collaboration with Till Wolder and Rebar. Courtesy of the artists.

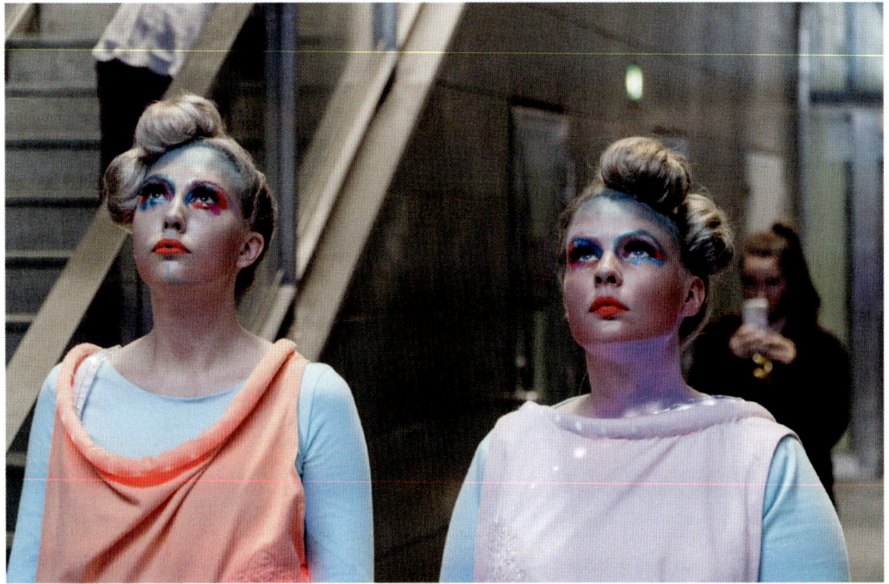

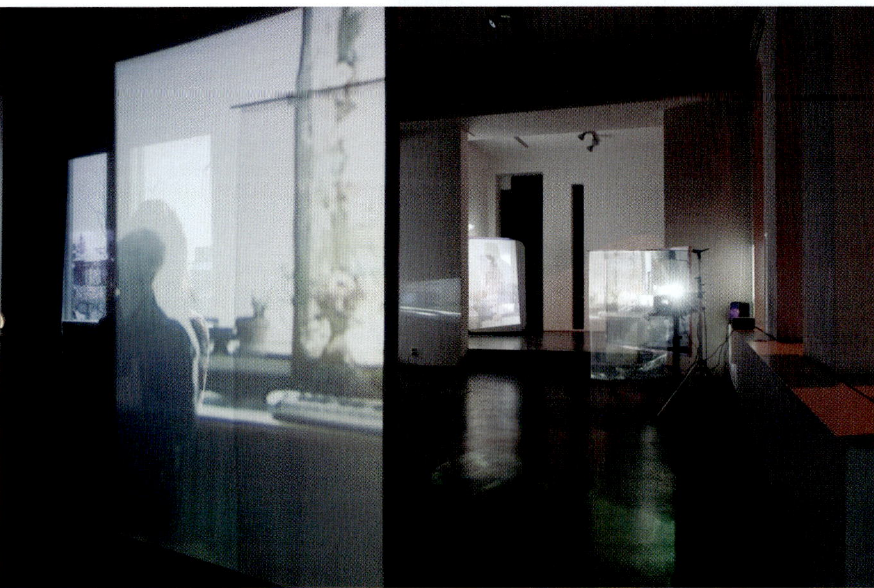

Figure 43. Nuleinn (Rine Rodin & Magga Ploder), *Parasite* (2017), performance in Copenhagen Metro, Denmark. Photo by Oskar Koliander. Courtesy of the artists.

Figure 44. Marjatta Oja, *1, 2 and 3: Detail of 'Transparent' (2009-10)* (2 December 2009 – 3 January 2010), situation sculptures. Galleria Sculptor, Helsinki, Finland. Photo by Petri Artturi Asikainen. Courtesy of the artist.

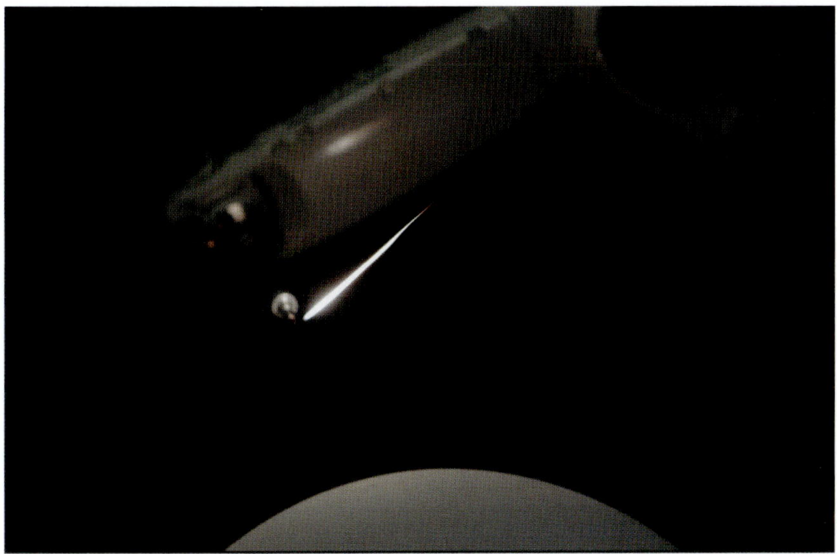

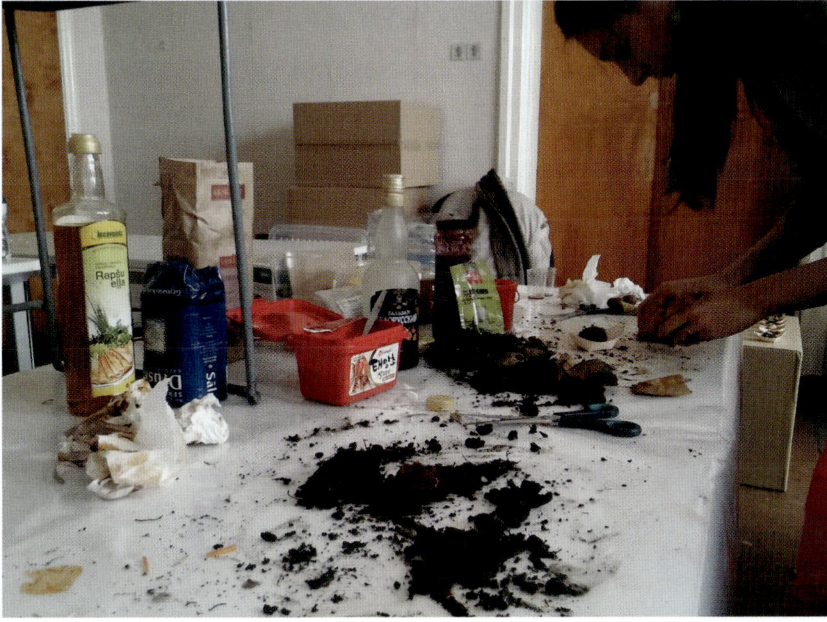

Figure 45. Erik Parr, *Clinamen* (2016), digital photograph. Courtesy of the artist.

Figure 46. Andrew Gryf Paterson, *Gourmet Geophagia.lv* (November 2015), mixed organic and food matter, 2 cm x 6 cm each. Courtesy of the artist.

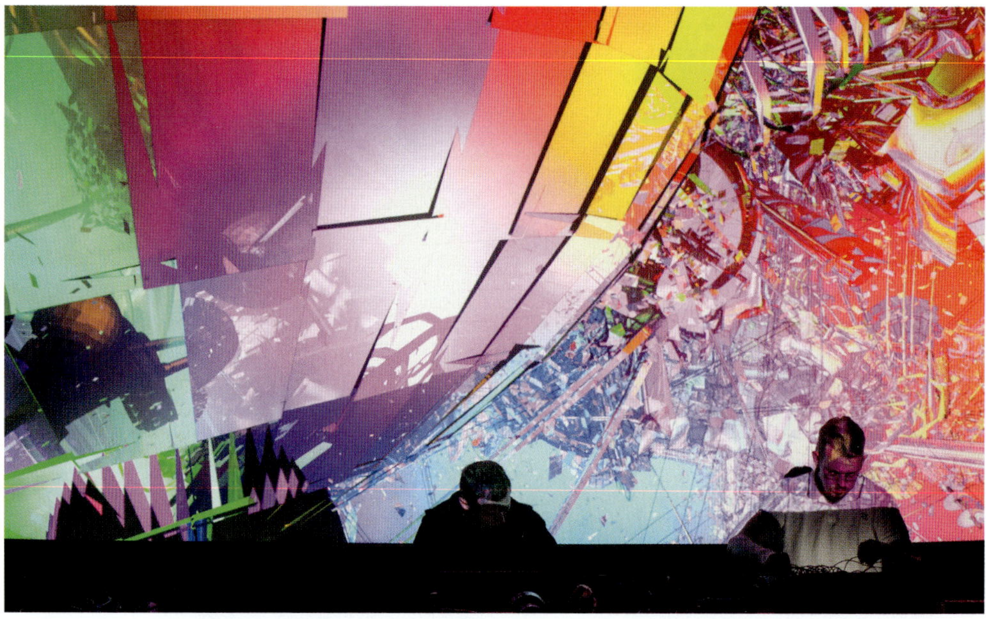

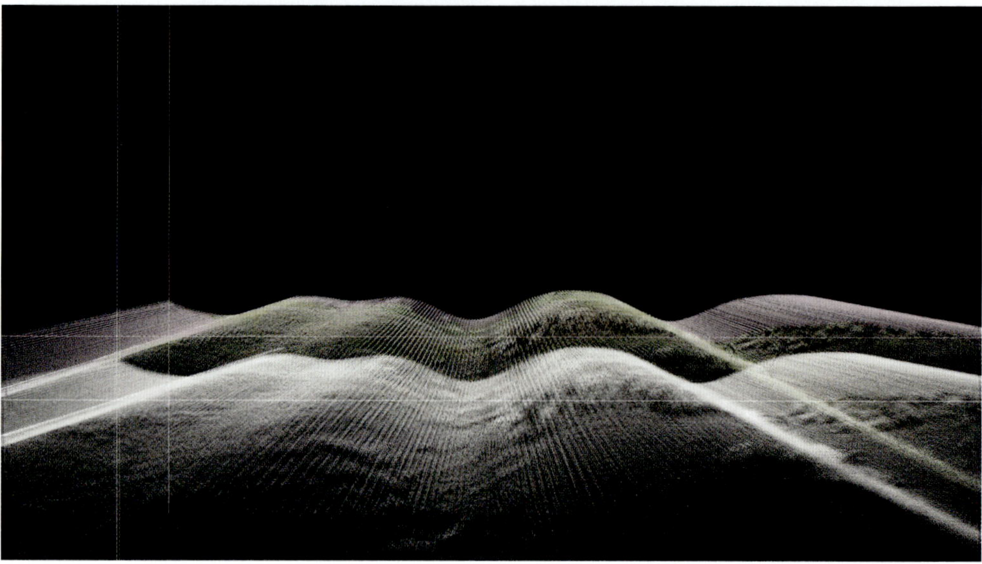

Figure 47. Pink Twins (Vesa Vehviläinen and Juha Vehviläinen), *Pink Twins Live at Swaeg, Niagara, Tampere* (28th June 2015), audio-visual live performance. Photo by Paula Lehtonen. Courtesy of the artists.

Figure 48. Tuomo Rainio, *Untitled (gravitational waves)* (2017), online artwork. Commissioned by Kiasma Museum of Contemporary Art Helsinki. Courtesy of the artist.

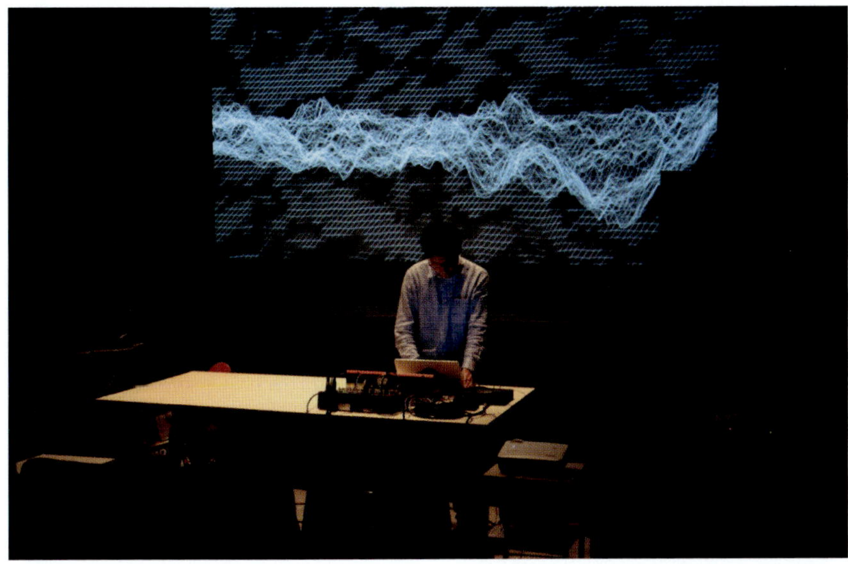

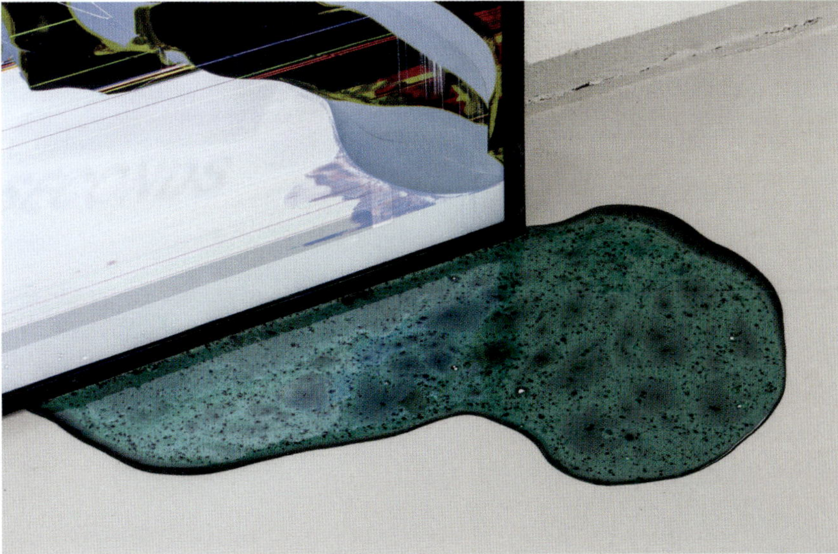

Figure 49. Juan Duarte Regino, *Enactment* (May 2015), audio-visual performance. Institute of Advanced Media Arts and Sciences – Ogaki, Japan. Photo by Yushi Yashima. Courtesy of the artist.

Figure 50. Jacob Remin, *eroding screen landscapes (detail view)* (2017), video on broken LCD screen, honey, coffee, pigment, 0,5 m x 0,5 m x 1,2 m. Photo by David Stjernholm. Courtesy of the artist.

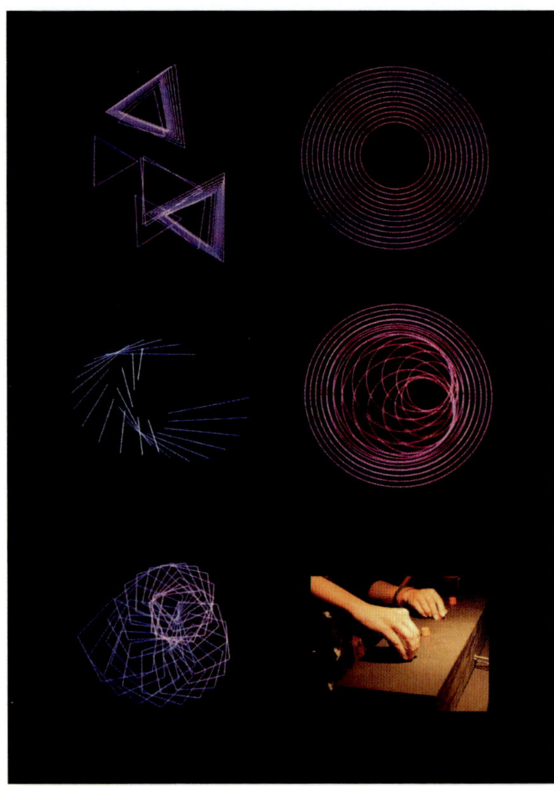

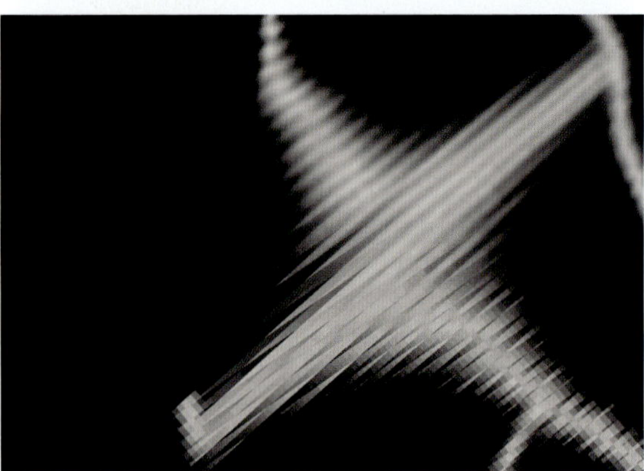

Figure 51. Stian Remvik, *Harmonic Connection documentation* (4th September 2017), interactive installation. Bergen Kunsthal Landmark. Photo by Marieke Verbiesen. Courtesy of Marieke Verbiesen.

Figure 52. Carl-Johan Rosén, *At the Catastrophy-Point* (October 2016), remix of Complementary Cubes by Manfred Mohr. Courtesy of the artist.

Figure 53. Petri Ruikka, untitled new still work (2018), animation, projection, dance. Choreography and Dance by Iiris Talvitie. Photo by Petri Ruikka. Courtesy of the artist.

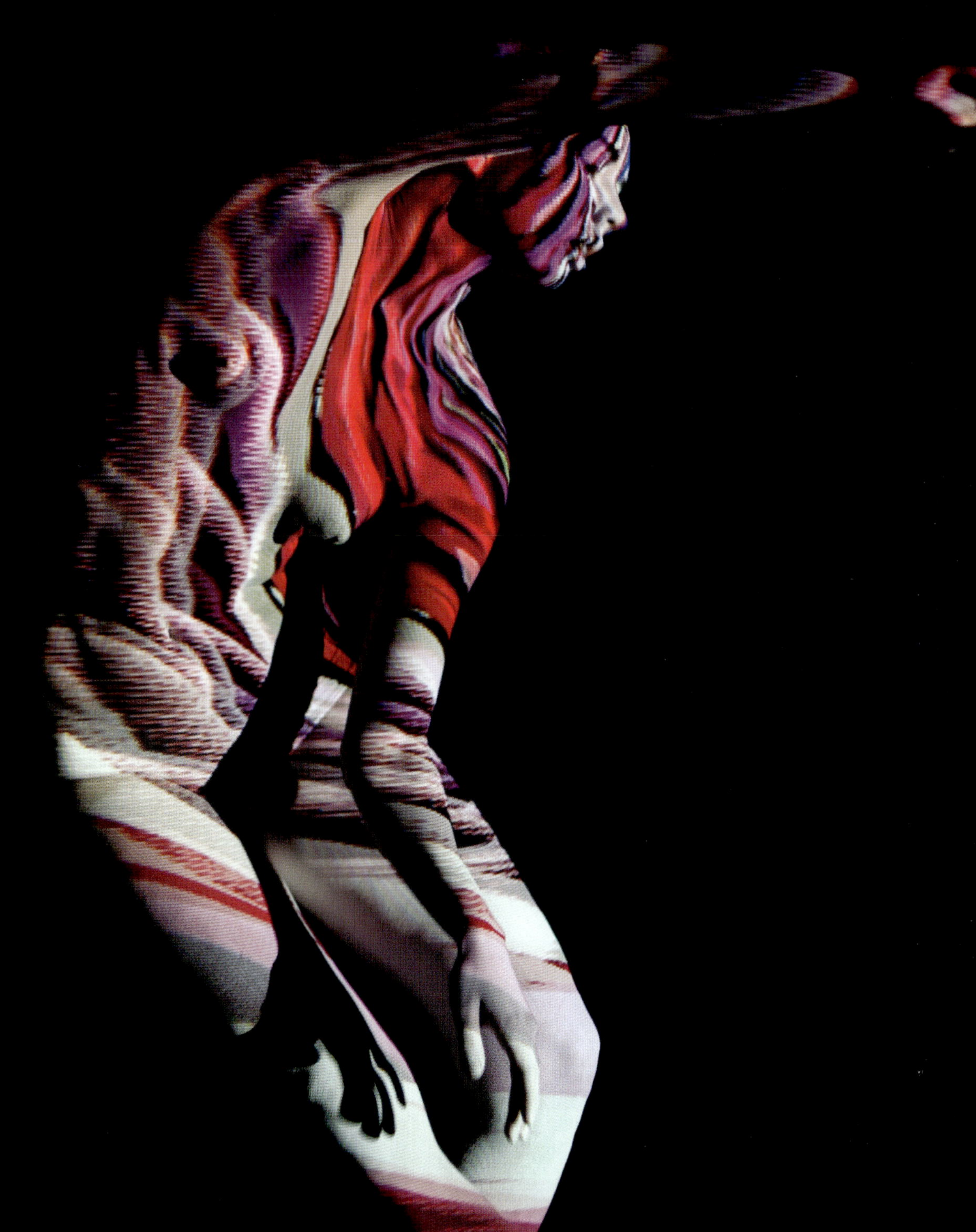

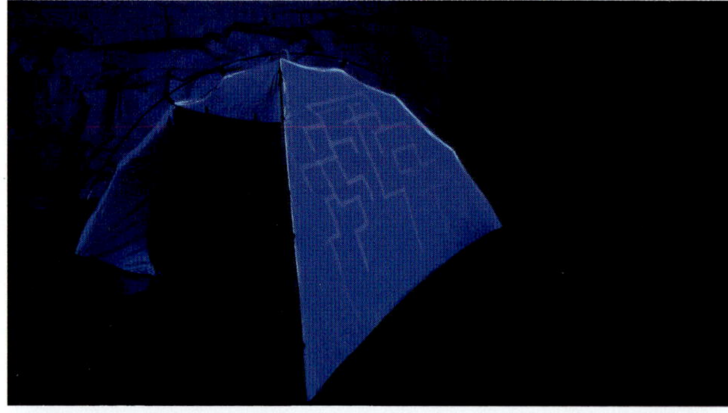

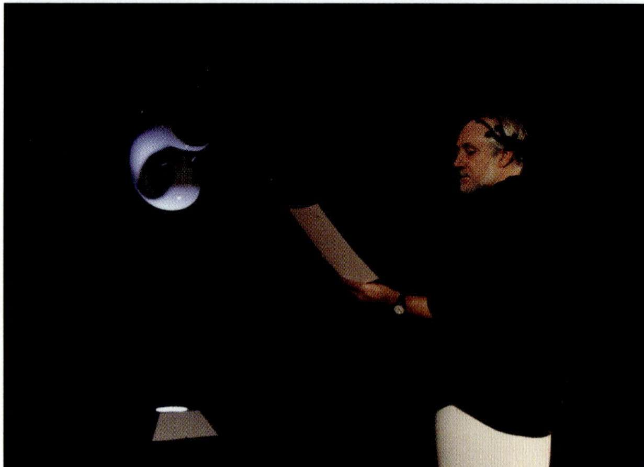

Figure 54. Anne Katrine Senstad, *Color Synesthesia VII* (2015), DV video loop, 16:9, 25' 30". Sound composed by Catherine Christer Hennix. Courtesy of the artist.

Figure 55. Joonas Siren, *Hermanni Keko & Joonas Siren: 4e6f6d6164* (13th December 2017), installation prototype, approx. 5 m x 5 m. Photo by Joonas Siren. Courtesy of the artist.

Figure 56. Mats Jørgen Sivertsen, *Untitled (SubConch at ANX)* (12 February 2014), photography, ANX Gallery, Oslo, Norway. Photo by Mats Jørgen Sivertsen. Courtesy of the artist.

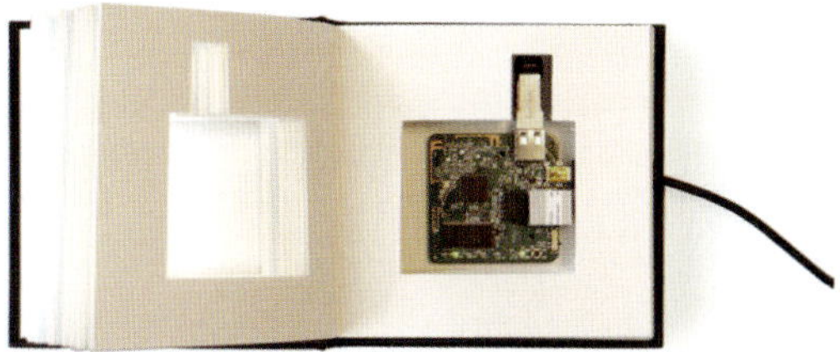

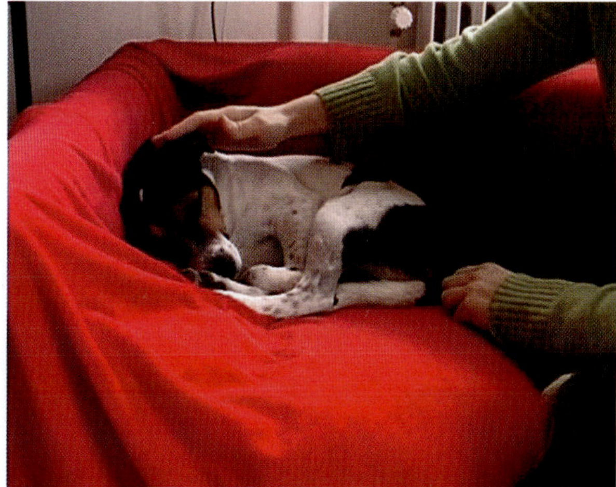

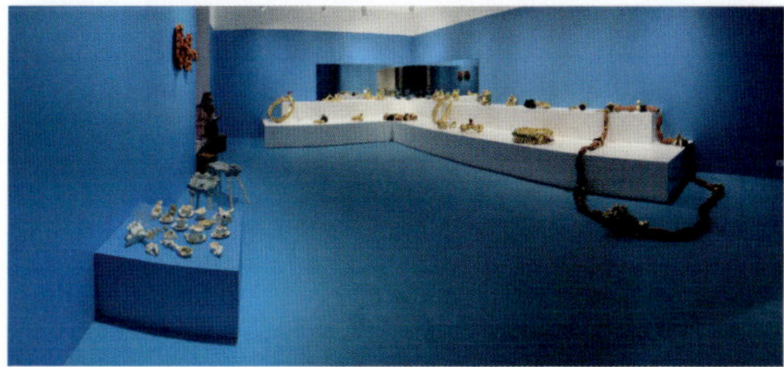

Figure 57. Jacek Smolicki, *On-Going Project. Post-digital archive combining digital and analogue content* (2016), paper, re-purposed router, digital media, 14 cm x 14 cm. Courtesy of the artist.

Figure 58. Lisa Strömbeck, *I Love You – You're Mine* (2001), video, 13 min. Photo by Lisa Strömbeck. Courtesy of the artist.

Figure 59. Egill Sæbjörnsson, from the exhibition Ugh & Boogar – Jewelleries (December 2017), imaginary characters, clay, glass and 22 carat gold. Anhava Gallery, Helsinki, Finland. Courtesy of the artist.

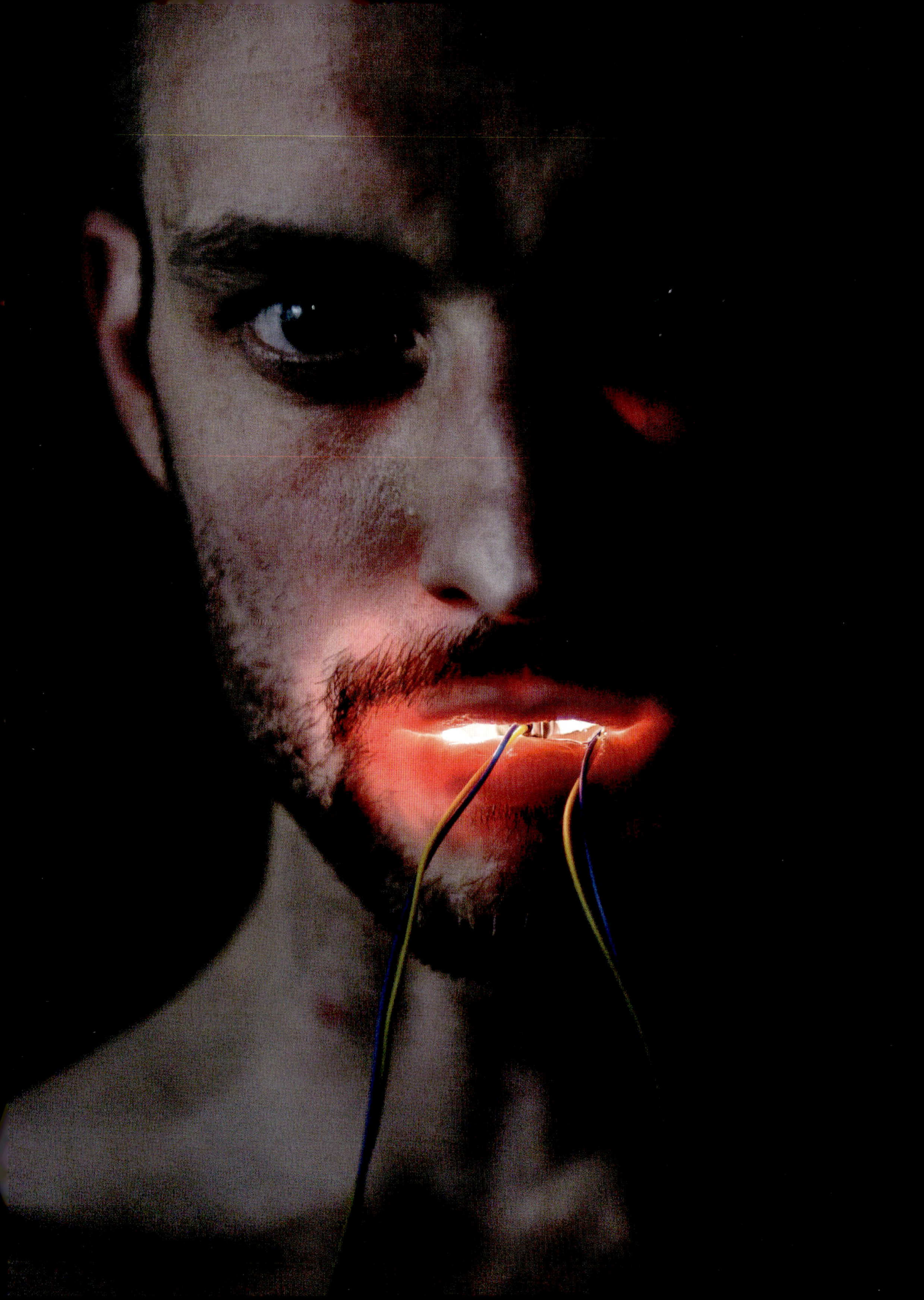

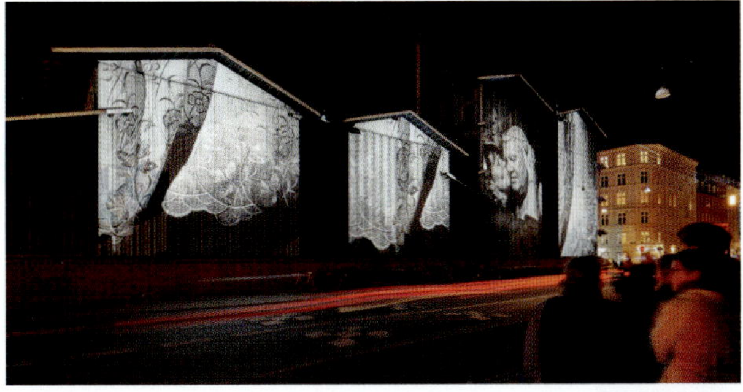

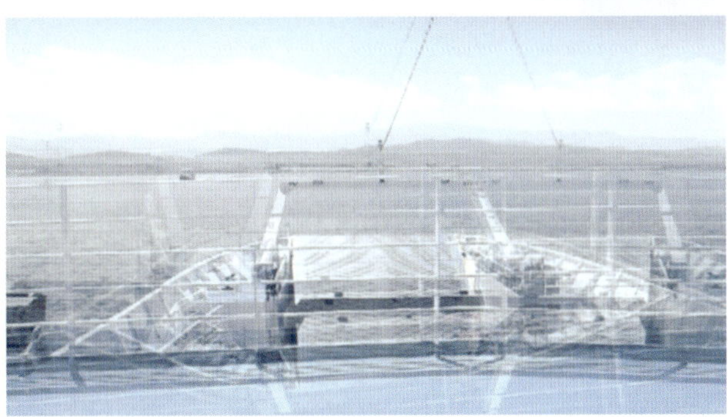

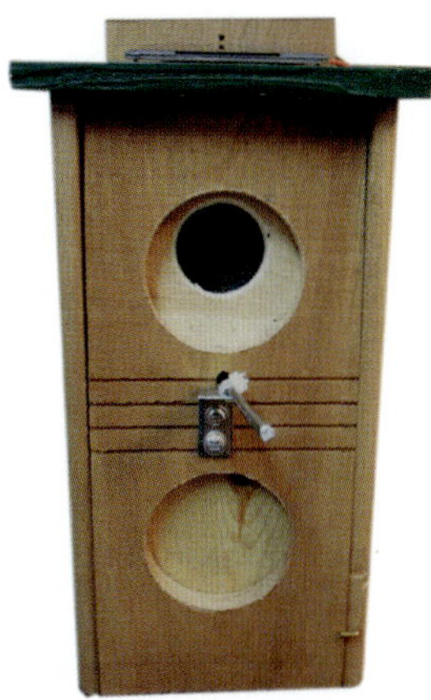

Figure 60. Tina Tarpgaard / recoil performance group, *ON/VOLT* (March 2014), Jonas Örknér, Dance Artist. Photo by Søren Meisner. Courtesy of recoil performance group.

Figure 61. Hanne Lise Thomsen, *Inside Out Istedgade* (September 2015), site-specific video installation. Copenhagen, Denmark. Photo by Torben Esperod. Courtesy of the artist.

Figure 62. Björk Viggósdóttir, *Before Sundown* (June 2008), video still. Photo by Björk Viggosdottir. Courtesy of the artist.

Figure 63. Magnus Wassborg, *Those who discoursed on nature* (2017), bird driven switch for Arduino software starting selected texts, H 430 mm, W 193 mm, D 180 mm. Photo by Magnus Wassborg. Courtesy of the artist.

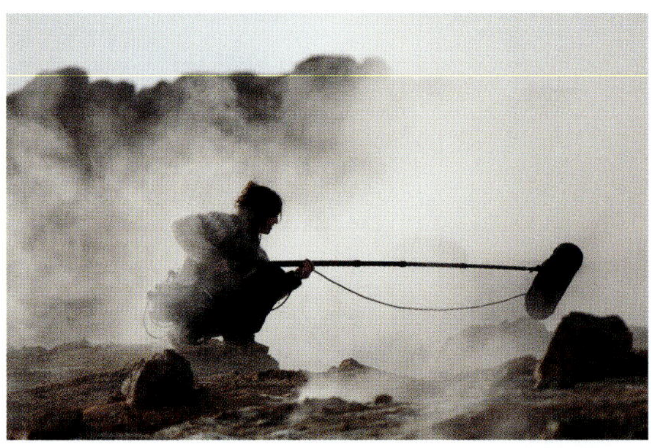

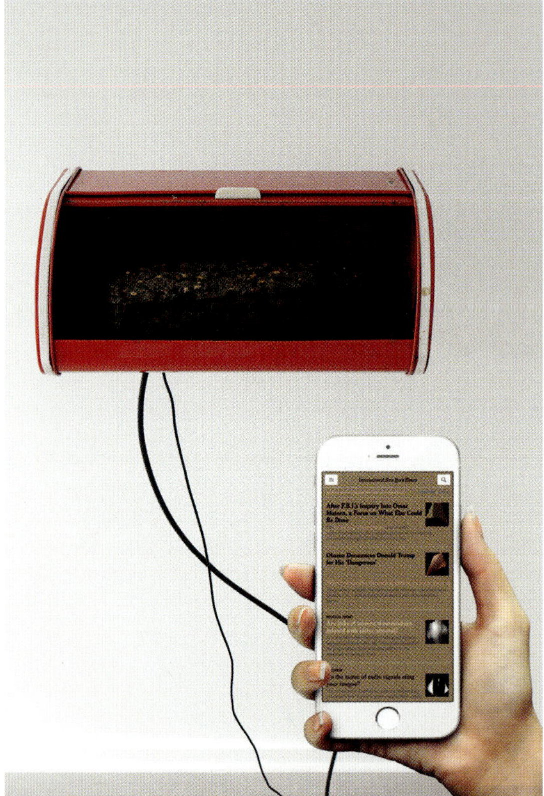

Figure 64. Jana Winderen, *Jana Winderen* (2014). Krísuvik, Iceland. Photo by Finnbogi Pétursson. Courtesy of the artist.

Figure 65. Kristoffer Ørum, *Wireless Tounges* (2016), acrylic composite material, acrylic paint, steel, plastic, wireless router and LAN cable. Photo by Tomas Skovgaard. Courtesy of the artist.

Part 2

Dynamic Seclusion: Nordic Noir and Digital Culture

Jonatan Habib Engqvist

Success is only preparation for the next failure.

August Strindberg

Stepping into the Alvar Aalto-designed pavilion at the Venice Biennale 2015, there is a vague smell of tar, charcoal and jute. In my attempts to navigate in the darkness, I start crushing bits of charcoal underfoot. The national Finnish Pavilion located in Venice Giardinni has commissioned the artist-duo IC-98 and their installation *Hours, Years, Aeons*, with the single-channel digital animation *Abendland* slowly transfiguring on the back wall. It is a dystopic, eerie, associative work about the past, present and future of Finland's forest – an imagining of the future of the country's main natural resource: timber. It is accompanied by the drone-like arrangement for double bass and electronics by Max Savikangas, which reverberates throughout the body (Frame Contemporary Art Finland Official Website 2015). The work is dramatic and dark; the film is incredibly slow and the atmosphere intense. While Isaac Julien is organizing a spectacular marathon reading of Karl Marx's *Kapital* throughout the course of the biennale in the main exhibition venue IC-98's low-key installation manages to capture a prevailing sense of isolation, alienation, seclusion and also, I dare say, something utterly Nordic.

Calling a contemporary art installation 'Nordic' based on aesthetic properties today might well be pissing on the chips. Instead, one should feverishly propagate that the 'Nordic region' is to be understood as a mental, cultural and discursive sphere rather than a geographical area where connecting flights are sparse. This is a feasible and comprehensive position that allows for a more contemporary, inclusive and nuanced understanding of the region, and is definitely more in line with the way we, as cosmopolitan prosumers of contemporary art, prefer to see ourselves. The former position is likely to get you into trouble. Indeed, I would be the first to subscribe to the idea that resistance against stereotyping, becoming stigmatized or turned into commodities of nation branding is a healthy reaction for local artists. Not least if we consider things like diversity and inclusion. However, it could also be argued that the so-called informal milieu of any region is a direct reflection of the funding structures that permeate it. And to make it all a bit more neurotic, many of the Nordic structures are national agencies that are more than happy to fund projects that rejoice in criticizing the idea of 'Nordicness', as this indeed is part of that which constitutes the 'Nordic'. In other words, the chances of receiving funding for a project critical to the Nordic stigma from Nordic funders are pretty high.[1] However, a perceived cognitive dissonance in the general understanding of the Nordic region as a cultural construct and the freedom it entails of not being an art historian encourages me to let go of the safety net and speak speculatively of the Nordic scene in terms of narrative, even affirming the notion of 'Nordique noir' (which potentially could be the horizon of interpretation for any non-Nordic reader anyway), as my hunch is that this notion potentially could be used as a means of unfolding how artists from the region respond to recent technical developments and their sociopolitical effects. Asserting the Nordic cliché in such a manner can, for instance, allow for a questioning of the current status of a crumbling welfare state in the region, and moreover tropes of self-seclusion and suicidal tendencies during the darker six months of the year can address an increasing global political anxiety and depression. Rather than the escapism of *Hikikomori*, the rise of what might be labelled 'Nordic magical realism' (beyond immediate associations to internationally well-established artists like Egill Saebjörnsson, Annika von Hausswolff or Eija-Lisa Ahtila) could potentially be understood as a politically persuasive alternative.

The exhibition *Nuit Blanche – Scenes Nordiques: les années 90* at the Musée d'art Moderne de la Ville de Paris, curated by Laurence Bossé and Hans-Ulrich Obrist in 1998, generated one of the most replicated sentences during the turn of this century:

> Periods when certain places claimed to be the center of the artistic world have come and gone. Such an attitude is old-fashioned in an age in which we see a plethora of dynamic art centers emerging in Europe and elsewhere; centers, which have their own special realities to investigate. In the nineties we saw capital cities like Copenhagen, Helsinki, Oslo, Reykjavik and Stockholm contributing to this trend, along with Bergen, Malmö and Oulu, with an explosion of creativity which seems to signal a genuine 'miracle'. By being places for meetings and for transcending boundaries, these cities constitute a floating network that is at once compact and loose.
>
> (Obrist cited in Collectif 1998)

The phrase 'Nordic miracle' was picked up by a number of people in the art industry and became omnipresent as the Nordics launched a new generation of artists onto the international stage (such as Eija-Liisa Ahtila, Olafur Eliasson, Miika Hannula, Aki Kaurismaki, Henrick Plange Jakobsen, Ann Lislegaard, Bjarne Melgaard and the world's most famous Icelander, Björk). In the Norwegian-Swedish curator Power Ekroth's words:

> This was what it was all about: business. The words 'Nordic miracle' could be turned into green for everyone who had seen the rise of the phenomenon referred to as 'YBA', Young British Art, in the early nineties – a group of artists with Damien Hirst in the foreground and Charles Saatchi as the man behind the scenes promoting the art, the artists, and its grand making in the market.
>
> (Ekroth 2007)

The paradox of a pronounced 'miracle' in the late 1990s and the turn of this century was that it, in fact, augmented many of the myths that it endeavoured to dissolve. In the ambition to prove that the Nordic region was sophisticated and global, the case was made that its expressions could not be boiled down to notions of melancholia, boredom and depression because … 'Hey – we're cosmopolitan'. Ironically, these were the very concepts that became, and to a certain extent have remained, the selling point for Nordic art. All miracles are of course paradoxes, and perhaps one consequence of this miracle paradox is that the notion of Nordicness has become an even more delicate issue to depict in terms of common narrative. Add to this the breakthrough of relational aesthetics in the region during the 1990s and a heavy focus on Institutional Critique in the early 2000s. A curious effect of the situation is that a substantial portion of the research on the Nordic region (as a collected notion) has been conducted by non-Nordic residents on the one hand, and enforced by structures for national branding or other forms of marketing interests on the other hand. Thus, many myths are sanctioned by both the art world and academia once more through interpretations that often have been colonized by a certain stereotypical rhetoric, which many of us 'within the scene' would object to, even though it seems as if this objection might simply be out of habit. Of course, the notion of Nordic noir being toyed with here can be seen as a marketing strategy created long before the millennium trilogy, thanks to Ingmar Bergman and the trope of investigations of suicide. The question whether this affects the arts and digital development is thus ambiguous – but hopefully somewhat entertaining.

My modest proposal is therefore to affirm rather than deny these seemingly inevitable myths of Nordic culture. By 'cannibalizing' and transforming these Nordic sentiments in a manner analogous to attempts by Nordic writers and philosophers of the late 1800s, and the anthropophagite movement of early Brazilian modernism, one might, in the words of the Anthropophagite Manifesto by Brazilian poet Oswaldo de Andrade, '[t]urn taboo into totem' (Andrade 1928). As subjective evidence for this exercise, the visual aesthetics of the Nordic moving image could be connected through precisely the cliché that it has become:[2] The Nordic pathology of constantly trying to save nature from man, to adapt reality to the system instead of the other way around, combined with a cliché culture of melancholia, suicide, silence, intoxication and a breeding season might, in this manner, even have a new meaning in contemporary society.[3] As such, it can even potentially hold global relevance. This is, namely, a culture capable of transfiguring several pathological states of mind that denote and epitomize a neoliberal society currently experiencing something analogous to a dark Nordic December without snow. Indeed, isn't it the shadowy thrillers, laconic works by Halldór Laxness, Aki Kaurismäki or Ingmar Bergman, followed by Norwegian black metal, *The Girl with the Dragon Tattoo* and Danish thrillers that have reached international acclaim in recent years, and truly portray something of relevance for our time?

In Susan Sontag's 1969 text in *Ramparts* she writes that Swedes 'never have a problem with talking: A lean across an abyss [...] Favored topics are: the weather, Swedes never stop suffering from the cold – money and plans of action announcing 'I am going to pee' when leaving the room for a minute to announce vacation' (Sontag 1969: 23–38). Even if Scandinavia has (thankfully) become slightly more multi-ethnic since 1969, it might not come as a surprise that when the satirical online journal *The Onion* in 2013 claimed that Lars Von

Trier was appointed by the tourist board to promote Scandinavia through violence and rape, the Danish newspapers apparently swallowed the bait (Christensen 2010). At the same time the claim might not be as far-fetched as it first seems, given that on a global scale we no longer find ourselves submerged in an existentialist's anxiety in front of our 'being-there' (as it might have been during the period between the 1960s and early 1980s described above). Instead, contemporary Nordic society seems to face a monumental boredom, suffering from the hopelessness of political depression and distress produced by the dematerialization of the welfare state and the impossibilities of contemporary life. Looking at the projects of candidates and graduates of Fine Art from the Royal Institute in Stockholm, one can find several examples of a prevailing sense of narrative combined with influences from surrealism, Dada and existentialism.[4] This might very well be a general sign of the influence of global conflicts on the arts, but transposed to the Nordic context, it seems to take on a form of its own.

The conscious, self-chosen attitude of Nordic melancholia – where we only live two months a year – calmly seems to declare that work, which receives economic compensation but no other vital justification, is sucking up life in western society. It asks: why are we working and for whom are we suffering? From a post-welfare state condition where there is no longer a vision of a better future society, this Dark Nordic voice states that life projects are becoming impossible as employment markets are insecure and not even companies expect sustainable, long-term profits. The significance of a politically depressed Nordic art scene emerges, and it appears to be quoting the writer David Foster Wallace by asking: 'How could we possibly understand our role and place in this society – let alone in the World?' (Foster 1996). If one is not living the dream in contemporary society – it seems to say – you almost need religious faith; a belief in a better life to come, a New Age vision, considering other, occult dimensions of current reality in order for life to have any meaning. Isn't it indeed telling that spiritualist Hilma Af Klimt gets her claim to fame at this point in time as the only Swedish representative at the Venice Biennale 2013 – 60 years after her death?

Another – related – example might be the artist Christine Ödlund who for several years has been investigating communication between plants. By interrelating phenomena such as the chemical communication of plants, synaesthesia and clairvoyant visualization, she pushes toward the boundaries of knowledge itself. She uses various media in her work, including drawings, installations, video, watercolour and sound. Referencing educational botanical illustrations and amateur watercolour studies of nature, she has created an arrangement based on observations of the chemical activity of a population of stinging nettles when butterfly larvae feed on an individual nettle. In her large-scale installation at Momentum Kunsthall in 2015, Ödlund combined explorations of occult chemistry, the theosophist movement and synaesthesia. The work consists of three elements: *Colored light in far-red eyes*, a stained glass window, *Plant perception 1 & 2*, two large paintings and *Tower of Eukaryote*, a sculptural installation where the plants' chemical communication can be sensed through smell. The window uses motifs from chemical signs and symbols of occult chemistry. It is red, green and blue – the three colours that plants can interpret and 'see' in order to orient themselves, but also the colours that comprise a digital screen. The paintings convey some of the possibilities of inter-species communication, and the large Tower of Babel-shaped installation hosts not only hundreds of stinging nettles but also larvae that develop into butterflies during the course of exhibition inside this torture chamber for plants.

The Swedish artist Bella Rune's Augmented Reality apps, Lundahl and Seitl's imaginary universes and Tove Kjellmark's depressed cyberland and dysfunctional renderings might be other examples. Kjellmark's art embodies a continuous and earnest play with the mechanisms behind the way we think:

> In my work, I search for another nature: a nature that refuses to accept a difference between technological and natural forces, between human life and animal life, between mechanics and organics. I explore artistic methods to trigger unsettling encounters between non-living artefacts and living agencies. My art embodies a continuous and earnest play with the mechanisms behind our thinking. Over a longer period of time I have dealt with technoanimalism, giving rise to another type of animality, another type of nature that above all very delicately plays with affecting the involved audience.
>
> (Tove Kjellmark, artist testimonial in this volume: 111)

The Nordic sentiment of geographic and cultural seclusion can likewise be described as a form of tunnel vision.[5] Here, the Nordic sentiment of geographic and cultural seclusion might be particularly relevant as a raster on our contemporary condition. As technological development seems to encourage individualism and simultaneously foster segregated communities into which one can delve and disappear through the personalization of the Internet and an abundant use of cookies and matching metadata algorithms, in the last decade we have seen an emergence of what Eli Pariser calls 'filter-bubbles' and 'you-loops' where data is collected and deployed in a manner that determines not only what we find online, but subsequently also what we seek (Pariser 2012). As our web search queries thus confirm the existing world view of each and every one of us, the Internet no longer becomes a window to the world but turns the screen into a mirror of narcissism. Indeed, it seems as if we're already there: *post-post-Internet, post-critical, post-LOL, post-Berlin, post-ethics –* even if the 9th edition of the Berlin Biennale was deeply criticized for its superficiality, 'LOL attitude' aesthetics, lack of criticality and so on, it definitely serves as a marker for a certain shift in contemporary art. With Swedish Anna Uddenberg as a poster girl, and curated by DIS (their first, and probably last biennale), the exhibition witnessed not so much a lack of contextual and art historical knowledge, but a remarkable lack of interest thereof. I suspect that this was the main provocation. But this overly networked paradigm is also what made it so indicative of our times.[6] The remarkable thing with the Berlin Biennale is that it definitely is not ignorant, or ideologically apathetic, and shows compromised ties to corporate culture and consumerism, or corruption if you want. Maybe DIS is not how to do it. Perhaps we need to be more self-critical and less presumptuous. Allowing ourselves to be offline to understand what it means to be online. The biennale's position is not about showing but inhabiting it without any sense of dissension. In his sharp critique, Jason Farago writes

'I have seen spambots with greater sensitivity' (Farago 2016), and this might well be the point at which that particular Nordic sensibility comes into play.

Long before anyone had heard the term 'selfie', Sweden-based artist Alberto Frigo was hyper-documenting his every move, thought and dream. An early advocate of life logging, he has photographed every object his right hand has used since 24 September 2003, making him perhaps the first person to digitally document his life manually (for over fifteen years and still counting). Frigo's manual process means that he is programming his own behaviour and thus avoids the privacy implications of automated life logging (Frigo 2014). The mundane objects, often related to family life in Scandinavia, paint a portrait of a region both geographically and linguistically secluded, but perhaps a place that also allows for that space of contemplation and naiveté that can remain in the dark but avoid cynicism. The Norwegians' love of their small cabins in the forest or on the mountainside as they talk of their *hytte* the way Swedes cherish their *sommarstugor*, the Icelanders and Danes their *sommerhus* and the Finns their *mökki*. Perhaps the long periods of darkness in the northern parts of Europe, stretching from October to March, make Nordic people seek a much-needed temporary refuge, both physically and mentally. On the flip side, the Swedish word *lappsjuka*, literally meaning 'Sami-disease', embodies the feeling of having been isolated or deprived of contact with others for a long time.[7] It comes close to a state of depression and the experience of panic attacks due to loneliness, desperately craving social interaction. An easy cure for *lappsjuka* is meeting people. Nordic seclusion might thus explain why so many artists from the region travel internationally. Sauna culture necessitates sudden rushes outside.

Seclusion is also a recurrent theme in Nordic literature. Jo Nesbø states that he much prefers to isolate himself, and Halldór Laxness' novels often reflect on rough physical conditions and inner spiritual experiences. Henrik Ibsen's plays overflow with descriptions of darkness and solitude; his writings transmit a sense of isolation and alienation. Many of his plays focus on private interiors, homes into which people withdraw and where psychological drama unfolds behind closed doors. Ibsen himself was known for being sensitive and he shied away from the world: 'But, curiously, isolation was necessary to a spirit such as his; he was endowed with the gift of seeing better from afar […] and by his isolation he was enabled to form a perspective without which he could not have developed' (Moses 2013: 5).

The global political depression of contemporary life is, in other words, a predicament that is reflected in art. Boris Groys has claimed that modernism was a road to the art of a future, just as the goal of society was a better future of equality and justice. But it would seem that contemporary art, which of course is deeply embedded in capitalism, does not always relate to a future. Instead, it relates to what *is* now from the point of view of now. Nonetheless, artistic expression can sometimes take on a social situation by revealing vitalities *not* shaped by the dominant forces. It would seem that we need somewhere to dream. And the visions provided to us by our politicians and the market are not cutting it.[8] And it is precisely from this horizon and such a situation that new meaning and relevance could arise to Nordic cliché culture, as a place that – in terms of narrative – has used its unique funding situation to thrive on depression, solitude and lack of meaning. If we, in Nordic art today, for instance, can trace a desire for the spiritual, one could claim that freestanding from art as an alternative form of life lies an interest for the fairy-tale-like glow that can be found in a darkness that *in itself* affirms the pious, self-righteous clarity and silent feast – the ecstatic states of exception created by apartment-isolated winter-life. This mysterious glow, albeit of hopelessness, shows us that there are still other forces, another vitality in reality than our own, which, perhaps, can save us from zombie-like life or suffocating from despair. In many works from the North, not least in some of those we find in the contexts that attempt to avoid a relation of proximity to the so-called Nordic miracle, there is nevertheless a kind of tainted magical realism, with its own variations of culturally historic-laden terms such as melancholia, the fantastic, realism, loneliness and the pre-individual collectiveness of Dionysus.[9] Through cannibalizing the Nordic myth in its entirety, there lies the potential not only to show hopelessness, but also to reveal its transfiguration in 'magic', absurdity and humour. Thus, a strategy might be developed with the potential to create a cultural machine that turns the hopelessness of contemporary reality into a form of intelligence.

References

Andrade, Oswaldo de (1928), 'Manifesto Antropófago', *Revista de Antropofagia*, 1:1, May.

Batycka, Dorian (2016), 'The 9th Berlin Biennale: A vast obsolescent pageant of irrelevance', Hyperallergic, 24 June, https://hyperallergic.com/306932/the-9th-berlin-biennale-a-vast-obsolescent-pageant-of-irrelevance/. Accessed 26 June 2016.

Christensen, Mikkel Fyhn (2010), 'Falsk Danmarks-reklame af von Trier', 24 February, www.dr.dk/nyheder/kultur/falsk-danmarks-reklame-af-von-trier. Accessed 18 April 2016.

Collectif (1998), *Nuit blanche – Scènes nordiques: les années 90* – Exposition du 7 février au 10 mai 1998 au musée d'art modern de la ville de Paris, Paris: Paris Musees.

Ekroth, Power (2007), 'Pissing on the Nordic Miracle', in *Lights On Norwegian Contemporary Art*, Oslo: Astrup Fearnley Museum.

Farago, Jason (2016), 'Welcome to the LOLhouse: How Berlin's Biennale became a slick, sarcastic joke', *The Guardian*, 13 June, www.theguardian.com/artanddesign/2016/jun/13/berlin-biennale-exhibition-review-new-york-fashion-collective-dis-art. Accessed 26 June 2016.

Frame Contemporary Art Finland Official Website (2015), 'Venice Bienniale 2015', www.frame-finland.fi/en/venice-biennale/venice-2015/. Accessed 18 April 2016.

Frigo, Alberto (2014), lecture during the Information seminar *Tebahism*, Stockholm University of the Arts, 5 November, www.vimeo.com/111724660. Accessed 26 June 2016.

Engqvist, Jonatan Habib, Gudjonsdottir, Birta, Hessler, Stefanie and Lykkeberg, Toke (eds) (2015), *Momentum 8: Tunnel Vision Reader*, Milano: Mouse Publishing.

Momentum Official Website (2015), www.momentum.no. Accessed 29 February 2016.

Moses, Montrose Jonas ([1908] 2013), *Henrik Ibsen: The Man and His Plays*. Rpt. London: Forgotten Books.

Nordic Outbreak Official Website (2013–14), http://nordicoutbreak.streamingmuseum.org/. Accessed 29 February 2016.

Ormeny, Francisc-Norbert (2013), *Darkening Scandinavia: Four Postmodern Pagan Essays*, Cambridge: Cambridge Scholars Publishing.

Pariser, Eli (2012), *The Filter Bubble: How the New Personalized Web is Changing What We Read and How We Think*, London: Penguin Books.

Scacco, Lorella (2009), *Northwave: A Survey of Video Art in Nordic Countries*, Milan: Silvana Editorial.

Sontag, Susan (1969), 'A letter from Sweden', *Ramparts Magazine*, July, pp. 23–38.

Strindberg, August (1901), '*A Dream Play*', World Digital Library, www.wdl.org/en/item/11624. Accessed 24 June 2016.

Wallace, David Foster (1996), *Infinite Jest – A Novel*, Boston: Little Brown and Company.

Notes

1   As an example of this questioning, one might mention Denmark's 2011 pavilion in Venice effectively curated by Katerina Gregos. With the title 'The Freedom of Speech', the concept clearly demonstrated how Denmark's most crucial sales argument at that time was that 'in Denmark we can criticize Denmark' (this was right after the so-called cartoon scandals with Lars Wilks). Make no mistake, there is no judgment being passed. Both the curator and the artists selected for the pavilion – including the Danish collective Superflex, who participated by not participating – managed to produce a remarkable, nuanced, deeply critical and by no means illustrative or politically engineered project that explored the complexities of democratic free speech. The example simply stresses the point that the definition of Nordic as related to funding, including a questioning of the equation between Nordic identity and funding – which, not the least, is applicable in times of economic pressure – is a part of what constitutes the 'scene' and thus 'The Nordic' pathology as such.

2   Examples can, for instance, be taken from the film compilation that accompanies a book on the history of Nordic film and video art *Northwave*, by Italian art historian Lorella Scacco (2009): ...*Memory Backwards* (Rikke Benborg, 2008), *Ground Control* (Eija-Liisa Ahtila, 2001), *The Wind* (J Tobias Andreson, 2007), *Scandinavian Pain* (Ragnar Kjartansson, 2006), *Three Rooms* (Jonas Dahlberg, 2008). To a certain extent, this was also explored recently in the exhibition *Nordic Darkness* curated by Staffan Boije Af Gennäs and Johan Zetterqvist at Kristinehamns konstmuseum in Sweden, 2011. On a theoretical level, other examples can be found in Ormeny 2013.

3   In 2012 some of these ideas were originally conceived for a commissioned proposal for the Nordic Pavilion in Venice by the author together with Lars-Erik Hjertröm Lappalainen and Annika Von Hausswolff and later developed into the cancelled exhibition at Kalmar Artmuseum *Soft Glow of Hopelessness* in 2015.

4   A couple of examples might be: Isak Sundström, *Our Only Hope is to Give up Hope* (Konstfack University College of Arts, Crafts and Design, 2015), Joline Uvman's *The Art of Doing as Little as Possible and Getting Away with It*, where she speaks on Skype with herself and browses her desktop through 'shared screen' (Royal Institute of Art, 2016), or Egill Logi Jónasson's micro-universe of thrift shop material, adapted paintings, a mix

tape cassette and a handmade diary titled *The Tape of H8 – sulking corner that explores the pleasure in not wanting to not want.*

5   The theme of the self-chosen isolation was explored in the 8th Nordic Biennial Momentum, *Tunnel Vision*, curated by Jonatan Habib Engqvist, Stefanie Hessler, Birta Gudjonsdottir and Toke Lykkeberg in 2015 and will serve as one of the examples in the text (Momentum 8 Official Website 2015).

6   One critic writes:

> [W]hat DIS have come up with is an exhibition so vacuous, ideologically apathetic, ahistorical, sarcastic, and dehumanizing, it's a wonder it hasn't been blacklisted solely on account of its conformity to commodity fetishism. Not to mention their ignorance of current events shaping Europe – like the refugee crisis, the rise of the Alternative für Deutschland party, Brexit, neoliberalism, austerity, and the privatization of art, culture, and education. The exhibition is pieced together from the organizers' unfettered acceptance of corporate culture, branding, product placement, and spectacle. Benjamin would likely have described it as an exhibition where a 'circus-like and theatrical element of commerce is quite extraordinarily heightened'.
>
> (Batycka 2016)

7   The indigenous Sámi people inhabit the most isolated northern parts of Norway, Sweden and Finland.

8   See, for instance, the *Dark Ecology* Project – a three-year project collaboration between Sonic Acts and the Norwegian curator Hilde Methi, which was held from 2014 to 2016 in different places in Norway and Russia and included three curated 'Journeys'. *Living Earth* is a recreation of these research trips to the Barents Region, from Kirkenes and Svanvik in Norway to Nikel, Zapolyarny and Murmansk in Russia (Living Earth: Field Notes from the Dark Ecology Project 2014–2016).

9   For instance in the *Nordic Outbreak* exhibition and public program, curated by Nina Colosi and Tanya Toft and organized by the Streaming Museum in New York City and across the Nordic region in 2013–14 (Nordic Outbreak Official Website 2013–14), and the Momentum Biennale of contemporary art in Moss, Norway (Momentum Official Website 2015).

Concretism and Danish Digital Art: New Political Dialogues from an Avant-Garde Perspective

Jens Tang Kristensen

This chapter will demonstrate how the dynamic of technical fetishism in digital contemporary art is rooted in a Danish variant of a broader international post-war avant-garde movement. I will demonstrate that contemporary digital art in Denmark has its heritage in the fascination for technology practiced not only by the historic constructivists, but also later by the post-war concretists. Considering particularly the experimentations of these groups in the areas of light and cinematic arts, today's digital artists may be seen to be continuing the work of the historic avant-garde through sociopolitical engagement. This chapter thus posits that social and political content have not actually been removed from contemporary digital art in Denmark. Rather, new media perpetuate this content through the network-based structure of global communication in attempts to agitate against the notion of authenticity, destabilize the autonomous artist-subject, and sabotage traditional assumptions about the art of the real as a reflection of the state and nation. The goal of what follows is thus twofold: firstly, to analyse the influence of the historical avant-garde on post-war concretists in Denmark, paying particular attention to how this influence led to the early development of new media art; and secondly, to consider the question of how the technical fetishism evinced by both earlier avant-garde movements may be perceived as the historical matrix, of which the dynamics in the contemporary digital art is a partial legacy.

Digital Arts Interventions Considered in Light of the Historical Avant-Gardes

In his classic text *Theory of the Avant-Garde*, Peter Bürger posits that, despite the widely variant circumstances under which they came into being and the broad spectrum of forms they took, the avant-gardes that were born amid the turmoil of the First World War and the Russian Revolution nevertheless shared an alliance of purpose: namely, to protest and mobilize against capitalist, bourgeois, marketplace ideology through political art interventions (Bürger 2004). Bürger sees movements such as Dadaism, futurism, constructivism and surrealism as evidence of the successful emergence of the avant-garde, while the art movements of the post-war period are regarded as indices of its eventual bankruptcy:

> The revival of art as an institution and the revival of the category 'work' suggest that today, the avant-garde is already historical. Even today, of course, attempts are made to continue the tradition of the avant-garde movements (that this concept can be put on paper

without being a conspicuous oxymoron shows again that the avant-garde has become historical). But these attempts, such as the happenings, for example, which could be called neo-avant-garde, can no longer attain the protest value of Dadaist manifestations, even though they may be prepared and executed more perfectly than the former.

(Bürger 2004: 57)

In Bürger's view, the failure of post-war groups to carry on the tradition of the historical avant-garde manifested mostly in their lack of interest in the institutional-critical approach that so deeply preoccupied the earlier movements. It is, of course, difficult to establish that any and all forms of institutional criticism were evacuated from post-war art, particularly in view of examples such as the Situationist International, the Art Workers' Coalition and the Danish Eks School, which all assumed extremely critical social positions and sharply opposed any form of institutionalization or exploitation of art. The present inquiry will attempt to shed some light on the question of whether today's digital art can be seen to occupy a similarly subversive stance in relation to regnant neoliberal social forms and the institution of art in general.

One of the major achievements of the historical avant-garde groups was that they managed, regardless of the different forms and approaches they assumed, to expand and complicate what was considered 'art'. Prior to the First World War, a piece of art was considered a discrete, stable and authentic object, while the artist was defined as a subject of essential genius from which the artwork emanated as a matter of course. After the war, however, the defining parameters of artworks were broadened to include an idea or concept, a design or even a mass-produced product. The artist could, as with Dadaism, work under a pseudonym, creating collective works in collaboration with other artists, or work as an anonymous facilitator of collective enterprises. Within these limits they could even function as a worker or engineer within design-based industries (see, for example, the constructivists). This mutual shift in what was understood by the terms 'art' and 'artist' emerged as a significant feature of the historical avant-garde programme, as evinced not only at the level of the individual work, but also in categories of endeavour such as collective painting, sound poetry, bruit noise music, total theatre and the cinema (as practiced by futurists, constructivists and the various contingents of Dadaism). Indeed, the basic institutional notion of 'artwork' was fundamentally compromised, particularly in political activist forms of art and works that predicted the practice of sampling (e.g. collage, montage, etc.), which were thus resistant to categorization.

It is important to note that the legacy of Dada continued to exert itself in post-war Denmark, as it did internationally, where the advent of Happenings and the resurgence of a post-futurist techno-fetishism corresponded with the development of new technological media. The post-war avant-garde increasingly availed itself of these new outlets, as can be seen in the development of the nascent computer industry. Here, art was increasingly guided by electronic innovations and interventions in the forms of various light- and sound-based installations. This transition in turn became foundational for digital art, which continued to destabilize early modernism's reliance on classical notions of style and art. It was not until the advent of digital art that one could truly regard art as a form of global mass communication, which by definition undermined the place- and site-specificity that had traditionally distinguished a work of art. Interestingly, it is this state that makes it difficult to characterize digital art in regional or national terms (i.e. Danish, Nordic, Scandinavian, etc.) because it is precisely the specificity implied in these labels that its ubiquity precludes.

Notwithstanding such theoretical considerations, however, both Nordic and non-Nordic artists working in the post-war period expressed a new interest in concretism and non-objective art as a potential means of creating an up-to-date art form that was at once social and universal. The intention of the concretists was to create an art of pure form and colour, based on mathematical principles designed to overthrow the prevailing bourgeois values of western European society. In the utopian eyes of the concretists, the sabotage of these values would automatically result in the rebuilding of post-war Europe, assuming a new path towards an international social contract based on socialist, humanist principles. A condition for achieving this was that artists dealt exclusively with purely geometric concretist art; this would not be for private consumption, but, ideally and primarily, for integration into the public sphere and workplace. Concretist art was to be executed in such a way that it became a self-referential form, non-objective and entirely devoid of reference to any reality beyond itself. To achieve a truly socializing art form, it was necessary to dissolve the boundaries and parameters traditionally associated with the individual work of art. Artworks were thus to assume a new form of spatial art, embodied by their composition and the organization of colour, design, architecture, and light and sound art. (It should be noted that, notwithstanding such transformative ideas, many concretist artists persisted in creating works in standard media, such as painting and sculpture, throughout their careers). In these ways, post-war concretist artists manifested a clear legacy of the historical avant-gardes, such as the Russian constructivists and the later Berlin Bauhaus; they also made notable strides toward realizing Thomas Wilfred's idea of an eighth medium for art: pure, immaterial light (Krarup 2000: 21ff).

The concretists of the 1950s and 1960s were fully dedicated to the project of freeing artwork from its historical parameters as a necessary step toward the larger goal of ushering in a new, socially oriented model for society. In pursuit of this, several Danish concretists – including Gunnar Aagaard Andersen, William Soya (1927–94), Knud Hvidberg (1927–86), Albert Mertz and Richard Winther – were pioneer experimenters with electronic art and various forms of light works. Mertz never lost his abiding interest in film, photography and, later, digital photography, and he was in fact eventually appointed as the first professor of video art at the Royal Academy in Copenhagen. Indeed, all of the above-mentioned artists agreed that it was only by integrating innovations within the field of industrial technology into vanguard art practice that artists could realize their societal goals. The Danish artist, critic and media personality Jens Jørgen Thorsen (1932–2000), in a catalogue published for the Herning exhibition *Konstruktion 68* (1968), posited that concretism as a social and political art form could be particularly successful if implemented in the nascent form of computer art:

We are now on our way out of a mechanical epoch of geometric hotch-potch, toward a much more complex field of unimaginable possibilities, guided by computers. Modulated and cyberneticized. And now, as I read the American journals, in their nationalist fervor, searching high and low for leaders of this new wave of Concrete art that has distilled geometry and pure proportions and color down to integral values in and of themselves, I think of Aagaard Andersen and the experimentations he was trying even before 1950; it's clear that he was a pathbreaker of international importance.

(Thorsen 1980: 140)

As early as the 1960s, Aagaard Andersen was being regarded as a pioneer of what may be retrospectively called early international computer-generated art. Andersen had, in fact, urged that the marquee operated by the newspaper *Politiken* in Copenhagen's City Hall Square be reconceived and restaged as an artwork, perhaps recalling his own *Concert for Five Violins and a Slide Projector*, which debuted in 1949 (Kristensen 2014: 210). This composition had called for the slide projection of a five-line musical staff that corresponded to the music that would usually have been accompanied by violins. Experimentations such as this might be said to have beaten posterity to the punch, in terms of the still current interest in light-based art and digital intervention. An interesting aspect of Thorsen's article is its observation of a potential danger inherent in mechanical cybernetics and computer technology: unchecked, they could become a force for the oppression and exploitation of humanity. This was not an apprehension shared by concretist digital and visual artists, who on the contrary regarded these technological advances as conquests in a campaign of artistic emancipation. Nevertheless, there was a currency to Thorsen's argument, especially as he demonstrated that the electronic age required of its artists an enhanced social awareness precisely because their work would be seen and could potentially influence a far larger public audience:

Has art become a value in and of itself, distinct from the utilitarian[,] the practical[,] the functional. These two sides of the coin are at play in the present exhibition [*Konstruktion 68*]. And at stake is essentially each individual artist's entire life's work. The outcome will not here be decided by machine-intelligence sound works of the kind heralded by Hans Jørgen Nielsen and those worldly mongers of the catch-phrases found in career journals such as *TA*. The most significant problem posed by computerized cybernetics lies in the term *feed back*: that is, the ability of these new machines to control, fluctuate, and reverberate a process in reaction to information encountered and collected while the process is still being carried out. Large sums have already been invested in an effort to conquer this problem. The U.S., for example, spends more than $10 million per year on the MacProject, whose goal is to make these machines public property (or will they be rulers of the public, instead?). The result here will not be determined solely by machine feed back. It will be decided above all by *human* feed back. That is the process in which art now intends to involve itself, to alter, modify, destroy, optimize.

(Thorsen 1980: 143, original emphasis)

For the Danish concretists, the point was to create new forms of art for direct installation as components into technological frameworks and the machine industry; only in this way could art be mass-distributed and thus influence societies across geographical and social boundaries. Art historians Marianne Barbusse and Lene Olesen offer the Danish concretist Richard Winther as a prime example of the continuing priority placed on creating a non-objective art susceptible to fusion with the machine in the post-war period. As far as the artists were concerned, it was only in this way that they could succeed in evading the capitalization of art by museums and collectors:

> [To] excise superfluous naturalism, to deal only with pure artistic elements, absolute values. The artwork must operate directly on its own terms, and the obfuscation of foreign elements, naturalistic expressions, inadvertent spontaneity, must be evacuated. The execution must be as technical and mechanical as possible. He [Richard Winther] called this liberating, absolute art synthetic, [and] it was the only truly populist social art.
> (Barbusse and Olesen 1995: 65)

Winther eventually moved into mechanical and computer-generated art, among other media. Indeed, his work in these fields indicates that he shared the concretists' utopian dream of an electronic art that would realize the goal common to all avant-garde movements: a completely autonomous art, released from any and all demands of capitalism and the interests of the mercantile market.

Danish Concretism and Early Digital Art

In the 1960s, long before terms such as 'media art' and 'new media' entered the idiom, Danish post-war concretists such as William Soya and Knud Hvidberg drew inspiration from recent developments in computer technology to develop a series of programmed artworks. Concretist artists worked with art without any literary references and content, which meant that the non-figural content was analogue with its form. For instance, Soya's *Astabile* and *Kommunal Sommernat* (both 1962) incorporated elements such as circuit boards, neon tubes and various other electronic components to create a new type of work that may be described as a 'programmed collage'. As will be discussed, these experimentations anticipated Soya's later work in the fields of electronic and computer-generated art (Soya 1987). In 1970, Soya was granted access to an electronic data-processing unit at the Royal Academy's School of Architecture in Copenhagen. This computer, although primitive by today's standards, allowed Soya to create his first truly computer-generated works, which he then fed through a line printer.

Soya's works from this period were in close dialogue with corresponding tendencies in the international art scene. *Cybernetic Serendipity*, an exhibition at London's Institute of Contemporary Arts in 1968, introduced audiences to new categories of artwork, which, like

Soya's, primarily consisted of graphic works printed on a plotter, various light installations, and aural and robotic art. Soya also executed a number of concretist paintings and works of light sculpture, such as the one that decorates the ceiling of the central library in Kolding, Denmark. Soya often used a computer to complete proposed sketches for painted and sculptural works, which thus first came to life as graphic works when produced by a line printer or plotter. Soya has in fact emphasized that the computer was by definition created on visual and communicative terms, by which he implies a natural and unspoken connection between the visual arts and electronic digital media. The political and social engagement which preoccupied the Russian constructivists in the 1920s, and which later characterized the post-war concretists in Europe, was clearly also present in the work of Soya. For example, Soya worked on the notion of creating a transparent museum, under which rubric the art institution and the art market would be eradicated, as would the assumption of an authentic and autonomous artwork:

> There is also a series of new practical possibilities for museums connected with the databank. It will probably not be long before museums can function as databanks for visual art. Call the museum on a telephone line open all day and night, and have the picture sent directly to your computer; select a picture from a current exhibition, and have some written materials sent along with the picture you ordered. The image can either be created specifically for an electronic database, perhaps even a moving picture, or it can be a picture you can toy with, alter, re-color. Or a reproduction from the museum collection. Or, most intriguing, a series of images, such as for instance a themed exhibition with expository text provided by the museum, created from its own collection or from images gathered from within the country and abroad.
>
> (Soya 1987: 30)

There is an affinity here between Soya's fascination with technological potential and the constructivists' paradigmatic intention that the artistic, the technical and the political – and thus the societal – should be unified as a lynchpin in the international socialist revolution. Soya himself stressed the importance of his art being incorporated into the sociopolitical sphere: 'If my art had no connection to the society I live in, then what I make would not be works of art but rather ritualized, religious narratives on canvas' (Soya 1987: 33).

Soya's ideological objective of creating new forms of social art through computer intervention can also be associated with the work of Kit Galloway (b.1948) and Sherrie Rabinowitz (1950–2013), who work under the organizational moniker Mobile Image. With their *Satellite Arts Project* (1977), Galloway and Rabinowitz created the first example of a satellite sculpture, in which two dance troupes, each in a geographically separate location, performed routines that were integrated with each other via satellite. Danish concretist artists such as Soya, Hvidberg and Mertz in many ways anticipated the anti-authoritarian, experimental approach to art that would later be found in the Internet-based works of such groups as www.0100101110101101.org, the Danish Artsp@ce Copenhagen and Artnode (Brøgger 2008: 398; Schreiber 2008: 31–32).

The constructivist and concretist goal of creating an objective and universal art that ideally would be practiced by all (and would thus result in the dissolution of art as an autonomous category) was in many ways rearticulated and further developed in the transition to the electronic age. Writers such as Lev Manovich, Mark Fisher, David Harvey, Fredric Jameson, Gilles Deleuze, Félix Guattari and Slavoj Žižek have focused on the capitalization of social reality as a particular characteristic of the postmodern aesthetic field. In this connection, Manovich posits that digital artists usually lack critical insight into the media they use – media which are often made available to them by multinationals such as software and computer companies. In this way, Manovich casts digital artists as covert offenders, contributing to the political sterilization of art's critical potentials, which he sees operating on a new and unprecedented scale:

Today, as more artists are turning to new media, few are willing to undertake systematic, laboratory-like research into its elements and basic compositional, expressive, and generative strategies. Yet this is exactly the kind of research undertaken by Russian and German avant-garde artists of the 1920s in places like Vkhutemas and Bauhaus, as they explored the new media of their time: photography, film, new print technologies, telephony.

(Manovich 2001: 15)

Notwithstanding Manovich's critique, the constructivists' wish to engender effective collaboration between engineers, scientists and artists did resonate in the works of early digital artists such as the Swedish artist and engineer Billy Klüver (1927–2004), who founded EAT (Experiments in Art and Technology) in 1966. In total keeping with the historical avant-gardes, Klüver proceeded from the assumption that there was no distinction between the programmer, the engineer and the artist (Paul 2003: 16). The programmed images with which post-war concretists in Denmark worked so closely in a sense also heralded the emergence of a watered-down, digital globalization. From a McLuhanist point of view, this form of commerce exposed the paradigmatic structure of the machine age, in which the notion of artist-as-subject became an armoury for the mass production of 'authentic' and aureate works in the classical mould (McLuhan 1967). Contemporary digital remix culture, in which electronic images create new visual montages, present yet another front in the battle against the artist as a source of production and holder of copyright. In this context, as lawyer and media scholar Lawrence Lessig has suggested, the rules of copyright are regarded as the last desperate attempt of capitalism to sustain by patent the idea of the artist as an autonomous individual with complete legal power over the production of the artwork (Kristensen 2014). As Lessig points out, massive campaigns to eradicate Internet piracy have in fact only resulted in art being crystalized; suspended in a temporary stasis until the moment when it is completely dissolved, with the possible collateral consequence that subversive critics of the capitalist establishment are left with nothing to say (Lessig 2008).

Danish concretist Richard Winther expressed an interest in the constructive possibilities of computer drawings, which also indicated his belief in the necessity for art to continually find new pathways toward total integration into society. In this connection, it is interesting to note Soya's insistence of being the sole programmer behind his artworks. In this way, he remained representative of a generation of artists who were reticent to abjure entirely the importance of the artist for the artwork. Artists like Hvidberg, Mertz, Soya and Winther thus represent a generation in which the artist-subject repudiated their authority only partially in experimentations with new media. As such, they never completely abandoned their faith in what we could call 'authentic art' as a bastion of revolutionary thinking. The use of new media, meanwhile, did result in the creation of a hybrid of new art forms and aesthetics with significant variance from established categories, with the result that art as an experimental form of expression and lifestyle reattained a central position. Writer and critic Hans-Jørgen Nielsen (1941–91) had used one of Denmark's first computers to experiment with concretist poetry and, as with the visual artists, had attempted to disintegrate art through the use of these new media. In a sense, this resulted in the utopian being replaced by the dystopian (Soya 1987: 16; Berardi 2011). It should be mentioned that several of the leftist, socially engaged artists who sought to create new mass-produced imagery in the 1960s and 1970s – for example, Ex-School artist Tom Krøjer (1942–2015), who executed the computer-based image *Datamaskinens børnetegninger* in 1973 – eventually abandoned computer-based creative work because of the tendency for technical innovations to be patented by capitalism. Carsten Schmidt-Olsen (b.1952) revisited a project of serial industrial imagery in the early 1990s, in basic continuance of the constructivists and concretists (Bak 2007: 180ff.). In collaboration with the Center of Art, Science and Technology and the Machine and Production Department of the Danish Engineering Academy in Lyngby, Schmidt-Olsen built a computer-controlled robot that was able to draw on its own. The intention here was not the creation of concretist works in the formal or stylistic sense, although many of the ideological and political positions that motivated the concretists in their battles and interventions against art institutions and tradition did resonate in Schmidt-Olsen's work. The purpose was rather to demonstrate that the knowledge and experience that informed the historical avant-gardes and the neo-avant-gardes must have influenced the digital art of today.

New Nordic Digital Art and its Potential as a Global Political Actor

Of course, we will inevitably find the roots of Nordic digital art in a global and historical field, and that means it does not exist as an exclusive phenomenon. Thomas Wilfred established his Institute of Light in Manhattan in 1930, with the purpose of investigating the use of light as an artistic medium in itself. Five years earlier, he had produced a light concert for 300 participants at the Royal Theater in Copenhagen. In contrast to today's art, which is often protected and/or controlled by patent, Wilfred created his Gesamtkunstwerk ('total work of art') with the absolute conviction that every art form should function within a totality created for the benefit of humanity as a whole. At the opening of the Institute of Light, Wilfred thus proclaimed:

> As my first gift [to the Institute] I grant open rights to all my patents. The collective results of my research. My collection of books, manuscripts, tools and instruments. The rest of my life, dedicated to research, composition, and teaching.
>
> (Wilfred cited in Krarup 2000: 24)

Wilfred's socialized attitude toward his own production was, significantly, not in keeping with the expansion of copyright law that has since dominated the administration of arts and culture, especially within the field of digital arts. In his classic text *Remix*, Lawrence Lessig reminds us that copyright rules were few and rather weak at the beginning of the 1900s (Lessig 2008: 100–01). This continued to be the case through to the emergence of the avant-garde in the post-war period. Lessig demonstrates that it was not until the 1960s that patent law was expanded to include all manner of products, which then engendered a concomitant broadening of copyright regulations. The advent of digital art occasioned another surge of copyright rules, which have since not only functioned as a means of protection, but have also – predictably, perhaps – had a prescriptively regulatory effect on the behaviour of art and cultural producers. Legalisation has thus not only affected the way artists work, but also had an influence on the consumption and use of art and media in the public sphere. In this sense, as Lessig posits, digital art and culture has been neither willing nor able to undermine the global, neoliberal social order or the multinational legislation to which it is itself subject. As he states:

> For the first time, the law regulates ordinary citizens generally. For the first time, it reaches beyond the professional to control the amateur – to subject the amateur to a control by the law that the law historically reserved to professionals [...]. For the first time, the law reaches and regulates this culture. Not because Congress deliberated and decided that this form of creativity needed regulation, but simply because the architecture of copyright law interacted with the architecture of digital technology to produce a massive expansion in the reach of the law.
>
> (Lessig 2008: 103)

The contemporary Danish art group Superflex, which also deals with digital art, has achieved considerable success in bypassing such copyright laws in a substantial series of critical and polemic works. These works (or Tools, as they call them) can be regarded as analogous to what in computer technology is referred to as open-source. Superflex has created a Tool called *Supercopys* (2007), which consists of a large series of works that, despite their widely variant types, can nonetheless be considered in art-historical and institutional terms as a discrete category of artworks. What unifies *Supercopys* is the shared goal of creating works of art that at once amalgamate and negate the market of which they are themselves a part, and that can be both copied and adapted for use by everyone. An example of this approach – not just as an isolated artistic strategy, but as a component of a larger sociopolitical and economic mission – is found in their appropriation and redesign of Poul Henningsen's PH 5 lamp, which Superflex adapted for gas-powered usage by poor residents of third-world countries. Superflex's view of all people as artists, and their resultant wish to serve the global population, is indicated in the digital Tool they call *Superchannel* (1999), which consists of a local television studio from which they produce low-cost programming via the Internet (Bonde and Sandbye 2006: 339f; Gade and Jalving 2006: 148). More than a cultural gesture, *Superchannel* can also become a meaningful sociopolitical organ. For example, the channel can act as an interactive platform that allows people in Karlskrona and Wolfsburg to refashion their respective cities in the form of virtual copies, whereby participants are given agency in a process of political negotiation and collaboration that theoretically could be replicated in real political life. Superflex has thus attempted to create a platform for criticism, in a sense functioning as a micro-political organization. Their soft drink Guarana Power, for instance, debuted in 2003 as a co-development with the people of the Brazilian rainforest as an action against monopolization of guarana nut pricing by multinational conglomerates (Albrechtsen 2013: 292).

Denmark received its first gallery for digital art with the opening of Art Space at Vallensbæk station in 2004. The purpose was to establish a new social space for digital and interactive art, while also broadening the public's understanding of what can qualify as art. Interestingly, the gallery does not distinguish itself significantly from other modes of public art exhibition. So far, exhibitions have been limited to relatively conventional forms of digital work, installed in accordance with state requirements regarding presentation and content. To some degree, this is explained by the fact that the gallery is owned by the municipality of Vallensbæk, which must in turn adhere to the regulations and requirements of the Danish National Railway (DSB), which owns the station. The result is a situation just as restrictive upon the art that is offered as any traditional 'closed' museum space. It should be noted that for Vallensbæk, the utility of broadening horizons through allegedly progressive art is also at stake, which essentially obviates the activist or political potential of the art as a subversive critique of existing social power structures, and precludes polemical inquiries into societal problems and inequities. Generally, it does not seem that the station/gallery distinguishes itself noticeably from the experience economy that motivates so much art and cultural programming today. Furthermore, the site is identified in Simon Anholt's national branding index as one of the most important reinforcements of collective and national identity in Denmark today (Anholt 2007). A recent article in the Danish newspaper *Politiken* notes:

According to the Gallery's producer, Andrea Hasselager, Vallensbæk mayor Henrik Rasmussen (Conservative), along with DSB, had hoped to do something with the Station, which was 'a bit boring' [...]. The initiative also had the goal of putting Vallensbæk on the map as a center for digital art.

(Andersen 2014)

One may also consider the recent sale of the website *If No Yes.com* Developed by the Dutch-Brazilian artist Rafaël Rozendaal, this was the first website ever to be sold at auction, complete with works comprised of pure geometric forms and colours strongly reminiscent of concretist works of the 1950s and 1960s. If this transaction established anything, it is the ease with which digital art is implicated in the neoliberal social discourse, and thereby subsumed by capitalistic market forces. Olia Lialina's *My Boyfriend Came Back from the War* (1996), the first Internet-based work to be sold on the market, similarly demonstrates how this form of digital art enters the mercantile art market in much the same way as other, more classic artworks. Digital art has furthermore come to assume an integral part in those businesses upon which it is also dependent, whereby it is often largely inseparable from software and hardware manufacturers and their related interests. It therefore has difficulty in establishing and/or maintaining autonomy, unless of course this situation can be disrupted from within, as Superflex has consciously attempted to do (Bosma 2008: 223). It thus becomes apparent that digital art allows for its own seamless integration into what I will describe as institutions of traditional arts administration, such as museums, galleries and universities. The political critique levelled by Superflex, through various interventions and Tools that actually involve digital art, thus agitates far more cogently than digital art can. Indeed, it is notable that given its peculiar co-dependence with the tools of its creation, a work of digital art can often only be finished as part of a media platform that is already complete. When Superflex debuted its *Superchannel* in 1999, it was also making use of relatively new media. Only two years previously, the then French president, Jacques Chirac, admitted that he did not know what to call a computer mouse, while the then US president, Bill Clinton, had never even used a computer (Hill 2013: 19). The blossoming of media awareness in the intervening 25 years has actually made it more difficult to mobilize a substantive and politically potent critique of the globally regnant neoliberal structure of society. Symon Hill, in his work on cyber activism, has noted that although digital culture – particularly social media – has become a force for empowerment in various minority groups, it has also been subject to increasing compression of its powers through regulations meant to limit and control what may be disseminated through such media:

This is not to say that social media itself cannot be an important space for resisting injustice. Internet access is sharply increasing but, as we are about to see, governments and corporations are becoming more and more aware of how to use the web to undermine people calling for change. This is the next big challenge for cyber activism.

(Hill 2013: 118–19)

It is my thesis that the historic dynamic of technological fetishism in contemporary digital art may in turn influence its potential as a locus of subversive political resistance against the neoliberal capitalization of everything. Digital art, however, also faces the challenge of finding a way to resist the growing tendency of neoliberalism and capitalism to neutralize ideological distinctions. It is indeed only from this sort of fatalist perspective that there is any value in recognizing certain Nordic digital art as an expression of the increasingly rebellious and yet still not altogether liberated, socially accountable avant-garde. It should be possible to describe the Nordic as a new alternative movement to the global order (it is the case with Superflex, for example) and therefore not as a metaphor for a local nationalistic movement rooted in romanticism. It is only in this sort of social view, present in individual digital works, that the medium can generate adequate means to fight against multinational powerhouses and their channels of distribution. In addition, it is only from this perspective that Nordic digital art can attain a position to evade the nationalist connotations and meanings invariably associated with apparently exclusionary national terminology. If certain parts of 'Nordic digital art' can act as an avant-garde descriptor, it will be through effecting a selective and subversive critique of the neoliberal doctrine that wishes to negate difference in the name of greater freedom and the growth of the anonymous, global, mass-produced marketplace.

If digital artists in the Nordic region wish to intervene in and disrupt the neoliberal capitalization of everything – which David Harvey argues is the overriding characteristic of society today – if these artists wish, in short, to embody the legacy and heritage of the historical avant-gardes, they must continually make use of new media and strategies. The fact that Scandinavian countries have emerged as the vanguard for neoliberal social policy since the 1990s means that the artists from this region must take a stance in relation to this accumulation of power:

> Social democratic states (such as those in Scandinavia or Britain in the immediate post-war period) had long taken key sectors of the economy such as health care, education, and even housing out of the market on the grounds that access to basic human needs should not be mediated through market forces and access limited by ability to pay. While Margaret Thatcher managed to change all that, the Swedes resisted far longer even in the face of strong attempts by capitalist class interests to take the neoliberal road. Developmental states (such as Singapore and several other Asian countries), for quite different reasons, rely on the public sector and state planning in tight association with domestic and corporate (often foreign and multinational) capital to promote capital accumulation and economic growth.
>
> (Harvey 2009: 79–80)

There is no question that several Scandinavian digital artists share a desire to actively distance themselves from those political trends that have emerged from a concatenation of nationalist and neoliberal discourses (Kristensen 2017). It is also clear that these digital artists, much like the historical avant-gardes around the First World War and the post-war concretists, must face the challenge that art often becomes neutralized in the public sphere. This is often because art was transformed to design or decorate in institutions such as schools, factories and public spaces. This is not to say that artworks, such as those created by Superflex, are superfluous as social and cultural weapons; it means rather that approaches other than the digital alone must also be engaged. Superflex's direct engagement with local environments is very important as a subversive strategy. At that level, Superflex also shares many similarities with The Fallen Fruit Project in Los Angeles: 'Part of a larger urban agricultural movement supported by environmental nonprofits and community arts foundations, Fallen Fruit has also turned its attention to different aspects of pomiculture: planting trees and making jam' (Raley 2013: 292).

Since the 1960s, both in Denmark and beyond, artworks have become gradually more mechanized and institutionalized, whereby they have gradually merged with other mass media. I would in fact posit that it has become increasingly difficult for artists to position themselves as revolutionaries, since the era of concretist art gave way to the rise of electronic art as described in this chapter. Even stipulating that digital art is multiplicitous, and therefore exists in a wide variety of forms and contexts, it will nonetheless always be dependent (as were the works of the historical avant-gardes) on its own disintegration, negation and death. Only when art is nullified in the life of society may it extricate itself from the capitalization that art institutions and canonical art history perpetuate, and in which contemporary digital art inscribes itself. Therefore, if digital art is to function as a politically active force, it must avail itself of digital formats as a starting point for heretofore unrealized artistic practices. Consider, for instance, the alternative approaches of West-oriented, libertarian, opposition and activist groups such as Reclaim the Streets, Pussy Riot, Occupy, Pappsatt and Antifa. Among these groups, the impact of physical confrontation, meetings and street action has never been compromised by their parallel artistic or mass communication-based presence, which they continue to develop through electronic media. A comparable viewpoint is proposed by Graham Meikle, a professor of communication, in connection with a commentary on the work of Gabrielle Kuiper:

> Be aware of the Net's limitations, says Gabrielle Kuiper, of Sydney Indymedia and Active Sydney. Don't use it as your primary form of communication. If you are spending your whole day staring at a computer screen and not getting out there and having face-to-face conversations, then it is unlikely you are changing much. It is a valuable communications technology, but it is no substitute for in-the-flesh human communication in all its messy three-dimensional sight, sound, touch, taste and smell interaction.
>
> (Meikle 2002: 179)

Another problem relates to the general rejection, since the fall of communism, of a bipolar world-view structurally based on an ideological opposition between East and West. In this new age, the paradigm has shifted to one in which democracy and the welfare state are to be consolidated and expanded through consumption and free market enterprise. This is despite the fact that the new global order also reinforces the notion of a world driven by migration, which allows that order to be perceived as at once more complex and more compounded than before. These fluctuating and divergent conditions not only make a context for digital art and culture, they also contribute significantly to the difficulty today in establishing a meaningfully subversive and oppositional collective critique of globalized neoliberal ideology. As noted by Luc Boltanski and Eve Chiapello, the victory of capitalism over communist ideology emerged as a natural consequence of communism's political dissolution; these conditions, they posit, have made it problematic to deploy art and electronic media in the fight for social justice:

> In the second half of the 1980s, with the end of the Cold War, capitalism found itself on its own again, without any apparent credible alternative. This belief did not become established only among the managers of a triumphant capitalism. It was widely shared by sympathizers and activists of the old leftwing parties. In order to preserve a legitimacy that was less and less readily accorded them, the great majority of these activists, even when they came from communist parties in rapid decline, were keen to show that they had abandoned revolutionary violence, the project of radical social change, the future projection of a new society and a new humanity, a radiant future – things which full acknowledgement of the horrors that had accompanied the building of Soviet society, obvious to anyone willing to see them for more than fifty years, rendered at once odious, chimerical and ridiculous.
>
> (Boltanski and Chiapello 2007: 324–25)

In order for digital artists in Scandinavia to continue the fight started by the historic avant-gardes and the post-war concretists, it will be necessary to found new artist collectives. These should not simply work with digital art, but also find ways to deploy it in more activist-oriented modes of life-practice, not just for the sake of the state or art, but for all of humanity. Media activism's connection to what I would call 'real-world problems in physical reality' means that any fight for a better future must simultaneously occur in a broader global collective movement. This is because we need both digital and physical activism to fulfil our revolutionary 'utopian dream work' (Berger 2005: 85):

> Another instance of the power of an email campaign was the crash of an Italian Government computer system following a 24-hour global Drop the Debt campaign targeting the Italian Finance Ministry in the run-up to the Okinawa G8 summit in 2000. [...] Although I was traumatized by my experiences in Genoa [site of the G8 Summit in 2001] I have reluctantly concluded that it seems necessary to have both the threat and reality of violence and property destruction and even possible loss of life, in order to force our agenda for a fairer world onto the international stage.
>
> (Berger 2005: 85–87)

Noam Chomsky is also very clear when he says that the political effect of the Occupy movement – with the activist able to mobilize real collective power in social everyday life, in contrast to the liberal individual and free market doctrines – cannot be neglected:

> One of the real achievements of the Occupy movement, I think, has been to develop a real manifestation of rejection of this [the new spirit of the age] in a very striking way. The people involved are not in it for themselves. They're in it for one another, for the broader society and future generations.
>
> (Chomsky 2012: 74)

References

Albrechtsen, Pernille (ed.) (2013), *An Artist with 6 Legs – 253 Works, 20 Years, 8 Curators, 1 Exhibition*, Copenhagen: Kunsthal Charlottenborg.

Andersen, Malene Tabart Lehmann (2014), 'Togstation bliver Danmarks første kunsthal for digital kunst', *Politiken,* 26 March, https://politiken.dk/kultur/kunst/art5508349/Togstation-bliver-Danmarks-f%C3%B8rste-kunsthal-for-digital-kunst. Accessed 4 February 2016.

Anholt, Simon (2007), *Competitive Identity – The New Brand Management for Nation, Cities and Regions*, Hampshire: Palgrave Macmillan.

Bak, Aase (2007), 'Industri- og teknikbegejstring – 1900-tallet', in Hanne Abildgaard and Aase Bak (eds), *Industriens billeder*, Copenhagen: Arbejdermuseet and Nordjyllands Kunstmuseum, pp. 154–84.

Barbusse, Marianne and Olsen, Lene (1995), *De Konkrete – Konstruktive tendenser i dansk kunst – fra kubisme til Ny Abstraktion*, Copenhagen: Gyldendal.

Berardi, Franco Bifo (2011), *After the Future*, Edinburgh: AK Press.

Berger, Sarah (2005), 'From Aldermaston marcher to Internet activist', in Wilma de Jong, Martin Shaw and Neil Stammers (eds), *Global Activism – Global Media*, London: Pluto Press, pp. 84–93.

Boltanski, Luc and Chiapello, Eve (2007), *The New Spirit of Capitalism*, London: Verso.

Bonde, Lisbeth and Sandbye, Mette (2006), *Manual til dansk samtidskunst*, Copenhagen: Gyldendal.

Bosma, Josephine (2008), 'Mellem det modererede og ekstremerne: Spændingerne I forholdet mellem netkunstteorien og den gængse kunstdiskurs', in Jacob Lillemose and Nikolaj Recke (eds), *Vi elsker din computer*, Copenhagen: Det Kongelige Danske Kunstakademi, pp. 211–25.

Brøgger, Andreas (2008), 'Dansk kunst går online – forsøg på overblik over den netbaserede kunst siden 1995', in Jacob Lillemose and Nikolaj Recke (eds), *Vi elsker din computer*, Copenhagen: Det Kongelige Danske Kunstakademi, pp. 393–422.

Bürger, Peter (2004), 'Theory of the avant-garde', in *Theory and History of Literature*, Minneapolis: University of Minnesota Press, p. 4.

Chomsky, Noam (2012), *Occupy*, London: Penguin Books.

Gade, Rune and Jalving, Camilla (2006), *Ny-Brud-Dansk kunst i 1990érne*, Copenhagen: Aschehoug Dansk Forlag.

Harvey, David (2009), *A Brief History of Neoliberalism*, Oxford: Oxford University Press.

Hill, Symon (2013), *Digital Revolutions – Activism in the Internet Age*, Oxford: New Internationalist.

Krarup, Helge (2000), *Lyskunst i Danmark*, Copenhagen: Forlaget Politisk Revy.

Kristensen, Jens Tang (2017), 'En note om artnode', *Idoart*, 14 January, www.idoart.dk/blog/en-note-om-artnode. Accessed 20 February 2017.

Kristensen, Jens Tang (2014), 'Når Linjer trækkes op, skabes der afstand – En ny socialkunsthistorisk analyse af Linien IIs placering og status i den danske kunsthistorie, belyst ud fra en undersøgelse af gruppens forhold til avantgarderne som kunstnerisk strategi og politisk intervention', Ph.D. thesis, Copenhagen: University of Copenhagen.

Lessig, Lawrence (2008), *Remix – Making Art and Commerce Thrive in the Hybrid Economy*, New York: The Penguin Press.

Manovich, Lev (2001), *The Language of New Media*, Cambridge, CA: The MIT Press.

McLuhan, Marshall (1967), *Mennesket og medierne* (trans. Elsa Gress Wright), Copenhagen: Gyldendal.

Meikle, Graham (2002), *Future Active – Media Activism and the Internet*, New York: Routledge.

Paul, Christiane (2003), *Digital Art*, London: Thames and Hudson.

Raley, Rita (2013), 'The ordinary arts of political activism', in Peter Weibel (ed.), *Global Activism: Art and Conflict in the 21st Century*, Cambridge, MA: The MIT Press, pp. 289–98.

Schreiber, Rachel (2008), 'Net kunst: efter det utopiske øjeblik?', in Jacob Lillemose and Nikolai Recke (eds), *Vi elsker din computer*, Copenhagen: Det Kongelige Danske Kunstakademi, pp. 17–38.

Soya, William (1987), *Kunst og EDB*, Copenhagen: Anton M. Jensen.

Thorsen, Jens Jørgen (1980), 'Elektronhjernen og Billederne', in *Friheden er ikke til salg – Synspunkter og essays samlet under et berufsverbot*, Lynge, Denmark: Bogan, pp. 140–46.

The Art of Instituting

Jamie Allen and Bernhard Garnicnig

It was a cold December day, 2011. In a somewhat damp, freshly painted basement space in Sankt Hans Gade, Copenhagen, a small group of artists, researchers, media-makers, programmers, technologists and friends gathered (a co-author of this essay, Jamie Allen, was in attendance). With a downloaded form from a Danish government website, available as a set of role descriptions and mandate templates called *vedtægter* ('listing of statutes'), the attendant group performed a particularly Danish kind of social and organizational alchemy: a few quick signatures founded and instituted a *forening*, a new association or fellowship of artists; a union with a legal, financial and temporal standing in Denmark. Crafted from the standard *foreningsdraft* (literally an 'association draft'), a new collaborative entity called Science Friction came into being. Over the next weeks, a public website was designed and built by its membership (sciencefriction.dk), and rather quickly, Copenhagen, Scandinavia and the world had a new arts organization; in this case, one devoted to technological and media experimentation, and attending to forms of mutual research, support, solidarity and heterogeneity in collaboration.

Section §2 of Science Friction's *vedtægter* outlines its *raisons d'être*: 'to create a foundation for art and culture in the field of art and technology, with particular emphasis on critical attitude towards the same', and to 'operate an office and workshop community for use by active members and other tenants if the space allows' (Science Friction *foreningsdraft*). As Swedish artist Katja Aglert reflects regarding her own interdisciplinary practice in her testimonial in this book, Science Friction attempted experimental institution-making that 'can be imagined and performed without reproducing the static order it attempts to critically reflect' (Science Friction *foreningsdraft*); an attempt to develop collaborative solidarity in study and research, and a means of production that re-envisions the terms of these activities in contemporary art and beyond.

This very Danish, public and relatively common process of self-initiating a *forening* requires no lawyers nor application processes. Unlike other organizations in Denmark and Scandinavia, it invokes no special laws and requires little registration or oversight. Yet it creates a legal entity – one with social and political standing, and a consistency in time and purpose. Importantly, it can be associated with bank accounts and immediately apply for public money in the Nordic region. It is an instaurative act that requires only the time and effort of a set of individuals voluntarily agreeing to its characteristics, and to the fulfilment of some generally accepted criteria for annual meetings and division of roles. To the non-Danish people present at the signing of this particular *forening*, the simplicity and lightness of the entire process was compared to similar activities in other parts of Europe and the

Americas, which would not be as effortless. What culture, what tradition, what bit of Nordic magic allows for such an arrestingly straightforward *instituent* act, the analogue of which might not exist in many other, non-Nordic places in the world?

Illusory Institutions

Institutions – artistic or otherwise – may be real, but they are not entirely *actual*. Rather, they are part of a vast array of imaginary tools and mediums that enable human collectivism. They do not exist as singularly physical, geographical, organizationally constituted entities; they are instead *instituted* – historically, processually, continuously – into our variable present by the stories that we devise for ourselves and relay to one another.

As a noun, the English term 'institution' implies established laws and organizations; in verb form, institute infers practices that are continuously instantiated through belief and action. One example would be the 'institution of marriage', which perhaps captures the dynamic yet perpetual nature of institutional forms more accurately than organizations such as post offices and museums. This example calls to mind those things in the world that are produced by love and commitment, desire and intention; performed acts of restoration, inauguration and speech, projection and imagination; real yet often intangible things that persist, hopefully, almost mystically, through time.

In his leapfrogging deep history and anthropology *Sapiens: A Brief History of Humankind*, Yuval Noah Harari writes: 'There are no gods in the universe, no nations, no money, no human rights, no laws, and no justice outside the common imagination of human beings' (Harari 2015: 178). As with the corporate and governmental entities Harari cites, institutions such as cultural collaboratives and even temporary collective bodies are fundamentally derived from the customary mythologies that exist mostly (if not only) in the imagination of collectives of peoples. These instantiations – evidential forms of collective consciousness – can be large or small in scale. If institutions must be ascribed to a particular domain of existence, they are extant as *fictions*: imagined composites of official policy, built infrastructure, cultural and social tradition, commitment, personal promise, and operational tactics and methods. There is apparent, if not at times inordinate, power and efficacy deployed through these non-real things. Institutional fictions are key to cooperation, incorporation and operativity; when these fictions are enacted, they can result in large numbers of strangers working in concert. As Bruno Latour points out, fictional beings are not only the result of subjective creation – they create us as subjects; as fictions, institutions demand that we 'insignificant amateurs, brilliant interpreters, or passionate critics, become part of [their] journey of instauration' (Latour 2013: 241). Collective myths of common purpose and function are responsible for the vast majority of human endeavour at practically all levels beyond individual, utilitarian action (i.e. we work *for* nation states, neighbourhood watch programmes, corporations, universities and community arts organizations). From the art museum to the activist group, from the Los Angeles Police Department to a tribal village council, orchestration is the result of often invisible conductors at many levels. Harari uses the example of a commercial institution, namely the car company Peugeot, the oldest and largest of Europe's car-makers, to drive this point home:

> In what sense can we say that Peugeot SA exists? There are many Peugeot vehicles, but these are obviously not the company. Even if every Peugeot in the world were simultaneously junked and sold for scrap metal, Peugeot SA would not disappear. It would continue to manufacture new cars and issue its annual report. The company owns factories, machinery and showrooms, and employs mechanics, accountants and secretaries, but all these together do not comprise Peugeot. A disaster might kill every single one of Peugeot's employees and go on to destroy all of its assembly lines and executive offices. Even then, the company could borrow money, hire new employees, build new factories and buy new machinery. Peugeot has managers and shareholders, but neither do they constitute the company. All the managers could be dismissed and all its shares sold, but the company itself would remain intact.
>
> (Harari 2015)

It is hard to deny the effectiveness and real-world impact of this real thing called 'Peugeot', or any other really real creative and imaginary projection just like it. What makes its whole greater than its parts is precisely its enigmatic existence as a kind of multiply transubstantiated aggregate, condensing out of an ether – here and there and now – quintessentially and fundamentally qualifying that which is institutional. These highly conceptual and complex projections – manifested through various media and interfaces, physical actions and material aesthetics, maintaining difficult to define relations to one another – establish themselves in oft-studied consistencies of form, and undergo constant internal and external change. Even the presupposed membrane between the internal and external can be hard to define. It is in the creation of institutional forms, or in the modulation of institutional interfaces, that the projective imaginary of the corporate CEO, the politician, the religious leader or the avant-garde conceptual artist can be said to find common, if somewhat slippery, ground.

In the late nineteenth century, Émile Durkheim famously inaugurated a new science – sociology – as the 'science of institutions, their genesis and their functioning' (Durkheim 1938). Since then, the social-scientific tradition of institutional analysis has given way to political science and theory: economic, legal and humanities-based interpretations (art, history, literature, philosophy, art criticism and art history) of the interactions between institutional bodies, and the various actors and agents 'external' and 'internal' to them. And yet there is at least one question that remains ever-salient: what *is* an institution?

What is the Copenhagen *forening* Science Friction? And what became of its future? Its membership has changed numerous times; its focuses and activities are always shifting; and its means and types of operations (i.e. its physical and decision-making structure) has been in near constant flux throughout its years of existence. Science Friction continues to exist in numerous ways, both online and off. And yet, it is the kind of thing that is difficult to point at, difficult to identify, impossible to simply define.

Critical Impressions and Artistic Critique

For many, the term 'institution' evokes or represents nothing but the worst forces of repression. Diverging responses and associations, anxieties and discomforts abound, and relations of trust and responsibility vary from individual to individual, culture to culture, encounter to encounter. Institutions can both afford and limit individual power and possibility; they are collective social fictions that can produce affects and effects, responses and reactions, ranging from a kind of psychic claustrophobia to sensitively scaffolded creative expression. Perhaps as a result, the indeterminate and indistinct institutions of government, education, art, culture and economics seem perpetually 'in crisis', always anachronistic and failing 'us' in all sorts of ways. Immigration services and government licensing centres are institutional fronts with notoriously recalcitrant, opaque façades that tend to put strategic distance between power and individual people. Within the Danish context, we might ask if it is even possible to develop a critical institutional practice in the context of well-oiled, widely accepted and lauded *forening*-style institutionalism. If the energies required for critical institutional practices come, at least in part, from the inevitable frictions against or within state or societal organizational structures, can these really take root in contexts rife with such smoothly operating institutions, and sophisticated outlets of institutional frustration? What artistic, mediatic or technological frictions can be articulated through such easily and readily instantiated artist-run organizations like Science Friction, in the Danish context?

From Dada and Fluxus to conceptual art and latter-day media and digital art, artists have always had newly invented tools, media strategies and artistic perspectives for creating, questioning, manipulating and representing institutional forms and milieux. The anti-commercial and anti-art sensibility of Marcel Duchamp's *Boîte-en-valise* (1935–41), a self-curated museum in a suitcase, and the artistic form identified as Institutional Critique that began in the 1980s, bookend what art history canonizes as strategies for the production, modulation, *détournement*, critique and deconstruction of cultural institutions. A confluence of cultural, artistic, educational, political or nationalistic mandates has made institutions – and particularly arts and cultural institutions – 'potent material for manipulation' (Bronson and Gale 1983: 7). These strands each evolved to focus on conceptual, critical and research-orientated practices. The post-war period witnessed several waves of critical institutional artistic practices, from those 'challenging the authoritarian voice of museums, corporations, and governments' to those asserting institutional collectivity in opposition to the 'authority of the [artist's] voice itself' (Deutsche 2009: 67 paraphrasing Foster et al., 2004: 624).

Buchloh describes a trajectory of 'moving from the aesthetics of administration of conceptual art to the administration of aesthetics of institutional critique' (Buchloh 1990). In expanding artistic intent away from material art objects and studio production, conceptual art strengthened both the research orientations of critical art theory and the predominance of institutional power, allowing artistic practice to be 'performed by administrative aestheticians, i.e. museum directors, curators etc.', thereby echoing the motivations behind the New Institutionalism in art (Sheikh 2009). In the 1960s, conceptual artists explored the necessity for their work to exist within a 'post-medium-condition' (Krauss 2000), evoked by late-capitalist conditions of art production and the mainstream global art market. By unhinging the dictates of the art market, conceptual artists made 'ideas themselves the machines that make the art' (LeWitt 1967). Aligned with this kind of thinking were early systems and cybernetic arts, which saw the possibility to render immaterial, distributed, transparent and immediate the way both artists and institutions engaged with polity. Conceptual art and emerging computational networks then colluded to provide the conceptual scaffolding for meta-critical perspectives on art, and infused popular, online culture with the brand of ambiguous, neoliberal creative libertarianism that has come to define culture in the West. Genealogically related initiatives and events like Experiments in Art and Technology (E.A.T.) from the 1960s and anti-institutional technocentric developments gave birth to movements such as net art in the 1990s (Allen 2011). In *The Democratic Surround,* cybernetic historian Fred Turner charts the related and parallel proliferation of nonlinear technologies, multimedia environments, and networks that gave rise to the 'alone together' democratic subjectivity of neoliberalism, and the disruptive, almost apocalyptic innovation and digital utopianism that completely transformed cultural, political and scientific institutions (Turner 2013).

One example of this transformation is the aforementioned artistic movement, Institutional Critique – often associated with the works of artists like Marcel Broodthaers, Andrea Fraser, Fred Wilson and Hans Haacke – whose evolution enables a systematic inquiry and exegesis of the inner workings of cultural institutions, archives, museums and academies. Art historian Rosalyn Deutsche has attempted to differentiate between distinct phases of the Institutional Critique movement, showing how the 'first wave' of artists drew 'attention to the presence of economic and political power present in the seemingly pure and neutral spaces of the museum' (Deutsche 2009: 66) by integrating the language, interfaces and constructs of institutionality into their works. Here, art was a vehicle to explicitly expose present relations with the shifting, boundless contexts of cultural institutions. The so-called 'second wave' (Holmes 2009) of Institutional Critique work of the 1990s, furthered by artists like Fraser and Wilson, extended the very scope of art into multidisciplinary research, while inversely questioning the authority and role of individual artists, curators, archivists and educators. These artists opened up particular modes of sociological and ethnographic research into the arts; they probed new institutional-individual relations, and challenged the contradictory autonomy and sovereignty claims of critical artist-labourers working in the authoritarian, corporate and agenda-laden contexts of institutions like national(istic) museums. Raunig terms 'instituent practices' as the very possibility of 'practices that conduct radical social criticism, yet which do not fancy themselves in an imagined distance to institutions' (Raunig

2009: 11); those which subvert or break from rigid institutional relations while drawing on the inventive avant-gardism of the 1960s and 1970s (Holmes 2009).

A great deal of evidence supports this renewed sense of the historic import and current relevance of Institutional Critique, including: *The Museum as Muse: Artists Reflect* (McShine 1999), a large-scale, retrospective group exhibition in the 1990s that included seminal works by Hans Haacke, Michael Asher, Louise Lawler, Andrea Fraser and Marcel Duchamp; a 2016 mid-career solo exhibition of Andrea Fraser's work at MACBA, Barcelona, entitled *L'1%, c'est moi*; as well as recent art theory writings that address and compose the movement's lineage (Martinez 2014). Typifying the Institutional Critique genre, Fraser's solo exhibition used *détournements* of institutional communications media formats (e.g. interviews, museum tours, posters, art magazine essays and organizational diagrams) to present the genealogy of the marketization, globalization and callousness inherent in institutional art environments. In Denmark, a place where cultural welfare and institutions are relatively uncontentious and thought to be well managed, there are those who have claimed that Institutional Critique 'never really found any fertile ground in the specific Danish or Scandinavian context' (Sander 2004).

Artificial Hells (2012a) by Claire Bishop emphasizes how artists' concerns with breaking down cultural-institutional boundaries can wind up exacerbating dominant economic and administrative regimes. For Bishop, the activities of groups like the Artist Placement Group (APG) in the 1960s provide examples of the ambiguous inversions of relationships between artists and institutions. Instead of pulling audiences into the work, organizations like the APG operated on the 'inverse principle of pushing the artist out into society' (Bishop 2012b). By placing artists in institutions of industry and government, the APG proposed a practice of art 'that can cause both business and art to reevaluate their priorities' (Bishop 2012b: 177), thereby pragmatically reinventing creative agency and acting as precursors to these agencies becoming economic commodities. The institutions governing modern human life are always a confluence of educational, governmental and economic interests, and so the APG developed the notion that interrogating or developing new relationships in institutional contexts was 'half the work' (APG's slogan was 'the context is half the work' [Bishop 2012b: 166]). The extension of artistic practices to realms outside of art resonates with Buchloh and Krauss' positioning between those of the Institutional Critique and those of the APG, neither of whose work relied solely on subjective autonomy, tradition or pragmatic adoption of survivalist economic strategies. Instead, they combine intellectual and aesthetic strategies to allow for continual and active questioning of 'what it is we really want from art' and its institutions (Malone 2007). Bishop's research into the APG illustrates how individual agencies can be extended by blurring the always imaginary and projected boundaries between institutional types, yielding metaphors of action and influence in the world that go far beyond 'art'.

The rich set of experimentations, negotiations, investigations and discussions brought to bear by Institutional Critique and groups like the APG have had profound impacts on the bureaucratic and organizational structures of traditional cultural institutions. Ironically, Institutional Critique has become thoroughly institutionalized (Fraser 2005: 278), leading to a transformation of the cultural institution itself. As a result, curatorial and archival practices have shifted to 'follow the artists', as described in the 1990s by the New Institutionalism in art (Kolb and Flückiger 2013). Cultural institutions have assimilated the artistic propensities for fluidity, unpredictability and risk as explored by twentieth-century artistic avant-gardes and Institutional Critique practitioners. New Institutionalism – not to be mistaken nor entirely divorced from related, aforementioned and homonymous developments in social science – underlines how cultural institutions have been reconfigured, reshaped and reactivated as interactive 'agents for change' (Casey 2001) that attempt to build more active, democratic and egalitarian public spheres. Cultural institutions throughout the 1990s and 2000s were inspired by 'participatory' (Simon 2010), 'interactive' and 'interpretational' formats, often enabled through media and the Internet (Allen and Lupo 2012). Later, itinerant and localized gestures of these dynamic, intentionally inclusive and accessible principles included institution-led initiatives like the Centre Pompidou's mobile museum project in 2013, or the artist-led Musée Précaire Albinet, a makeshift museum in a Paris suburb that was initiated by artist Thomas Hirschhorn and run by local residents. The Vietnamese-Danish artist Danh Vō, based in Mexico City, has articulated a number of individual-institutional 'Trojan horses', including exhibiting the collections and work of other artists and non-artists. *I M U U R 2* (2013) at the Guggenheim Museum in New York saw Vo presenting Chinese-American artist Martin Wong's collection of tchotchkes, destabilizing and deferring authorship and accountability of the individual artist to the museum. Continual conceptualization and attempts to revive intra- and trans-institutional developments of this kind are analysed in the literature (Voorhies 2016).

The inspiring and still contemporary rubric of 'extra-disciplinary investigations' (Holmes 2009) is borne from thinking about the tools initiated by Institutional Critique. Moving beyond the 'systematic exploration of museological representation' (Holmes 2009: 57) that examines correlations between arts organizations and economic power as a postcolonial science, extra-disciplinary practices assume interventionist tools and the expansive, boundless scopes inaugurated by artists engaged in Institutional Critique to expand the horizons of research and practice still further:

> The extra-disciplinary ambition is to carry out rigorous investigations on terrains as far away from art as finance, biotech, geography, urbanism, psychiatry, the electromagnetic spectrum, etc., to bring forth on those terrains the 'free play of the faculties' and the intersubjective experimentation that are characteristic of Modern Art, but also to try to identify, inside those same domains, the spectacular or instrumental uses so often made of the subversive liberty of aesthetic play.
>
> (Holmes 2009: 55)

N55 is a Copenhagen-based Scandinavian art collective, emerging in 1994 as a way of developing projects in the public sphere outside of conventional and mainstream galleries and *muséal* arts practices. As an arts practice focused on using open-source tools and methods, N55 makes no intention towards typical art-object sales but instead uses the artwork as a means to develop a set of practices and relations. Furthermore, the group is ambiguously tied to the artistic identity of several individuals, using the institutional and organizational moniker 'N55' to garner international attention for numerous projects in urban planning, architecture and public space reconfiguration. All of N55's ideas and designs are freely accessible and available for no charge to the public, and so their main acumen and aura – if we can call it that – comes from their institutional form: a kind of illusory and effective hybrid entity that makes products, but is not *for* the making of products. N55, as an institutional form, exists, in part, in order to keep existing. In working like this the group articulates the ways that artists can become and remain extra-disciplinary, veering towards any field of knowledge. N55 is an artistic practice-cum-institution, artists-as-organization; administrative and institutional language, tropes, interfaces and communications styles probe the boundaries of their artistic practice via a sort of 'administrative sublime' (Holte 2006).

This kind of *institutional becoming* is part of an extra-disciplinary stylistic and tactical mandate, often integrating unstable, ad hoc architectures (e.g. field tents and mobile museums), as well as social science-inspired research methods (Miessen, Hirsch and Misselwitz 2009). Reminiscent of strands of avant-garde conceptual art in terms of lack of concern for formal or media-specific outcomes, these elements give social-scientific and journalistic inflections to art as practices of research. The artistic interest in aping institutional forms also lies in how media and communications interfaces (i.e. the design of logos, websites, digital publication formats and the equivalency of communications afforded with e-mail) allies this type of activity with what has been termed 'post-digital art practice', or practices that employ digital media not for their own sake, but for their symbolic, organisational and cultural potentials. The artist-becoming institution imitates digital tropes in order to create imaginaries around creative projects through the skilful deployment and modulation of digital, cultural norms (Cramer 2014). They can act and communicate in ways that the general public and established institutions of natural science, social science, politics and art recognize, understand, or purposefully or productively misunderstand, but are nevertheless attuned to and respond to.

In seeking detailed interpretations of the operation of these entities, sociological studies of institutions have cross-pollinated their methodologies with what might be termed 'artistic' (or, alternately, 'representational') methods, media-derived insights, and visual and sensory translations of the lived experience of institutional-individual relations. In the wake of the APG and developments like Institutional Critique, social science has assumed ways of recomposing, reperforming and reconstituting art and media-making as critical knowledge work. In the Nordic context (amongst others), this has given way to highly influential cultures of artistic research, both inside and outside the institution. Annette Arlander cites Esa Kirkkopelto, professor of artistic research at Theatre Academy Helsinki, who links artistic research back to the importance of instituent practices:

Artistic research done by an artist outside institutions is worthy of its name only if it has institutional consequences and if it can articulate itself in relation to institutions [...]. As a consequence, the criteria for evaluation would consist of considering to what extent an artist-researcher is able to present their invention as an institution. If they manage to do that, their research has significance to everyone, it produces knowledge.

(Kirkkopelto cited in Arlander 2013: 157)

Post-Digital Institutions as Artworks

Since the 1980s, close attention has been paid to hegemonic western, nationalist and patriarchal narratives and constructs of the museum. Described as the 'post-reflexive turn' of the 'new museology', this focus has developed into a self-reflexive discourse critiquing the ascendency of artistic and cultural institutional power (Vergo 1991). Throughout the 1990s, museums began to function more as increased public information hubs and digital access points. The administrators and curators of these institutions reacted to this by starting to include multiple voices, non-expert communities and individualist approaches to those collectives formerly known as 'audiences'. Many museums developed into spaces for the enactment of possible futures and became models for extra-artistic social dynamics. Susana Smith Bautista's *Museums in the Digital Age: Changing Meanings of Place, Community, and Culture* (2013) charts the experiments in permeability undertaken by museums to become 'citizens' of the communities they were seeking to engage and communicate with. Bautista cites examples in which the *voice* of the museum is articulated on social media platforms in dialogue with individual community membership. Other examples include projects like the Brooklyn Museum's early 2000s exhibitions, in which publicly sourced online photo feeds were displayed in the museum to provide a kind of collective visual-ethnographic community portrait. A further example from 2013 saw the National Gallery of Denmark issuing advertisements in Danish newspapers to ask the public 'What's SMK to you?' inviting readers to submit answers via Facebook.

The proliferation of communications networks and the Internet in the 1990s exacerbated many aspects of the contradictory conservative inertia and dynamic resilience apparent in institutions. Although institutional change occurs, it is often much slower than other technocultural dynamics. Moreover, the relative stability of institutions appears as an impediment to that which 'makes it possible for human groups to take effective action' in technologically advanced societies (Lustick et al. 2011: 2). Traditional cultural institutions persist, but shifting societal conceptions and expectations constitute and instigate rapid and responsive change, often fomented and exacerbated by changes in media and communications technologies. Artistic and cultural institutions play the role of leading-edge transformational institutions, acting as relatively malleable sites for prototyping institutional styles of engagement. Technological coercion toward the forming of new institutional interfaces is underlined, for example, by the tension between how museums, galleries and other traditional cultural and archival institutions treat the Internet as a secondary space for research, documentation or context. Others simply see it as a distraction, when for many people the normal way to access art and culture is through the Internet. For Zachary Kaplan, an editor and the director of the digital arts organization Rhizome, technological disruption continues to demand a 'rethinking of institutional practices: acts of representation, modes of address, curation, metrics, use of scale and the primacy of the traditional white cube itself' (Kaplan 2016).

Nordic Techno-Institutionality

Examples of the contradictory form that is the anti-institutional institution abound in contemporary artistic practice. Experimental spaces and places for thinking and production that are loosely linked to topics in science, art and technology (i.e. hacker spaces, DIY technology groups, artist-run project studios) are the benefactors of an energizing genealogy of para-academic, anti-institutional and collective forms. The history of these kinds of projects and collectivities roots these often paradoxical *dis*organizations in a tradition spanning twentieth-century avant-gardes, art and technology pursuits, and the digital and post-digital potencies wrought via online, virtual and variegated kinds of belonging and acting together.

Such tendencies are manifested in the Nordic region through the work of groups like the aforementioned N55, whose anti-institutional strategies are focused on building up 'a non- institutional praxis financed by the production and distribution of things, like cargo bicycles' (N55, artist testimonial in this volume: 86). Similarly, as Laura Beloff notes, technologically inclined works are manifested by a 'subcultural art scene – and typically initiated with small-scale associations and organizations' (Laura Beloff, artist testimonial in this volume: 87). These groups have included the stalwart media production crew at Dark Matters and the Copenhagen research, art and pedagogy collective Science Friction, whose foundational story began this chapter. These groups orient their practices towards the disruptive potential of technologies and technological questions, as well as their historical and contextual effects on creative practices. Scandinavia-based artist Alberto Frigo notes how the frames of cultural organization at one point limited his ability to employ or use technological elements in his work:

No longer constrained by the spatial and temporal framework of cultural institutions, I have come to develop a whole encompassing practice, which, through a constant engagement with several aspects of my life, provides me with a new framework of artistic operation. I do not so much play around with algorithms but perform as an algorithm.

(Alberto Frigo, artist testimonial in this volume: 50)

Here, Frigo renders palpable and personal the institutional frame as both inspiring perceptions of limitation and constraint, as well as productive of a reactionary or frictional, avant-garde creative impulse.

Reinstituting Institutions

Although critical, artistic cultures have often treated institutions and their interfaces as impasses to be confronted or surmounted, we also find great promise in the extrapolations and derivations of new orientations, placements and hopeful reconstitutions of institutional forms. Drawing on traditions of assembly, organization and self-led, progressive institutionalization in the Nordic context (particularly in light of technology literacy and sensibilities towards skills in digital design), artists and the arts are poised to enact the transformative power of institutional forms. This lies in a particular flexibility to diversify responsibility across collectives; to proliferate and adopt methods while helping to equalize agencies, energies and temporal resilience. New institutional forms show promise, acting as countermeasures to a contemporary landscape that is marked by the creative destruction wrought through austerity, conservatism, supervision and economization. Cybernetics historian Fred Turner calls for the formation of 'intermediary institutions through which we can act', emphasizing how 'networks are not enough. Individuals are not enough' (Turner 2014). He poses the question: 'Where is the middle range? The credible institution that gives me credible information on which I can take action?' (Turner 2014).

References

Allen, Jamie (2011), 'Could this be what it looks like? Lifelike art and art-and-technology practice', *Artnodes*, 11: November, pp. 74–79.

Allen, Jamie, and Lupo, Eleonora (2012), *Representing Museum Technologies*, Milan: Politecnico Di Milano.

Arlander, Annette (2013), 'Artistic research in a Nordic context', in Robin Nelson (ed.), *Practice as Research in the Arts – Principles, Protocols, Pedagogies, Resistances*, New York: Palgrave Macmillan, pp. 152–62.

Bautista, Susana Smith (2013), *Museums in the Digital Age: Changing Meanings of Place, Community, and Culture*, Lanham, MD: AltaMira Press

Bishop, Claire (2012a), *Artificial Hells*, New York: Verso.

—— (2012b), 'Digital divide: Contemporary art and new media', *Artforum*, September, www.artforum.com/inprint/id=31944. Accessed 13 March 2017.

Bronson, A. A., and Gale, Peggy (eds) (1983), 'Introduction', in *Museums by Artists*, Toronto: Art Metropole.

Buchloh, Benjamin (1990), 'Conceptual art 1962–1969: From the aesthetic of administration to the critique of institutions', *October*, 55, pp. 105–43.

Casey, Dawn (2001), 'Museums as agents for social and political change', *Curator: The Museum Journal*, 44:3, pp. 230–36.

Cramer, Florian (2014), 'What is "post-digital"?', *A Peer-Reviewed Journal About (APRJA)*, http://www.aprja.net/what-is-post-digital/. Accessed 12 June 2016.

Deutsche, Rosalyn (2009), 'Louise Lawler's rude museum', in Gerald Raunig and Gene Ray (eds), *Art and Contemporary Critical Practice: Reinventing Institutional Critique*, London: MayFly Books, pp. 63–77.

Durkheim, Emile (1938), *Rules of Sociological Method*, New York: Free Press.

Foster, Hal, Krauss Rosalind E., Buchloh, Benjamin H. D. and Bois, Yve-Alain (2004) *Art Since 1900: Modernism, Antimodernism, Postmodernism*, New York: Thames & Hudson.

Fraser, Andrea (2005), 'From the critique of institutions to an institution of critique', *Artforum*, 44:1, pp. 278–86.

Harari, Yuval Noah (2015), *Sapiens: A Brief History of Humankind*, New York: Harper.

Holmes, Brian (2009), 'Extradisciplinary investigations: Towards a new critique of institutions', in Gerald Raunig and Gene Ray (eds), *Art and Contemporary Critical Practice: Reinventing Institutional Critique*, London: MayFly Books, pp. 53–61.

Holte, Michael Ned (2006), 'The administrative sublime, or the center for land use interpretation', *Afterall*, 13:Spring/Summer, www.afterall.org/journal/issue.13/administrative.sublime.or.center.land.use. interpre. Accessed 12 March 2017.

Kaplan, Zachary (ed.) (2016), *The Born-Digital Art Institution: The Medium in the Post-Medium Condition*, Santa Monica, CA: Sternberg Press.

Kolb, Lucie, and Flückiger, Gabriel (2013), 'New institutionalism revisited', *On Curating*, 21, pp. 6–17.

Krauss, Rosalind E. (2000), *A Voyage on the North Sea: Art in the Age of the Post-Medium Condition*, New York: Thames & Hudson.

Latour, Bruno (2013), *An Inquiry into Modes of Existence*, Cambridge, MA: Harvard University Press.

LeWitt, Sol (1967), 'Paragraphs on conceptual art', *Artforum*, June, pp. 79–83.

Lustick, Ian S., Nettle, Daniel, Sloan Wilson, David, Kokko, Hanna, and Thayer, Bradley A. (2011), 'Institutional rigidity and evolutionary theory: Trapped on a local maximum', *Cliodynamics: The Journal of Theoretical and Mathematical History*, 2.

Malone, Meredith (2007), *Andrea Fraser, What Do I As an Artist Provide?*, St Louis, MO: Mildred Kemper Art Museum.

Martinez, Chuz (2014), 'The octopus in love', *E-Flux*, 55:May.

McShine, Kynaston (1999), *The Museum as Muse: Artists Reflect*, New York: Museum of Modern Art.

Miessen, Markus, Hirsch, Nikolaus, and Misselwitz, Philipp (2009), *Institution Building: Artists, Curators, Architects in the Struggle for Institutional Space*, Berlin and New York: Sternberg Press.

Raunig, Gerald (2009), 'Instituent practices: Fleeing, instituting, transforming', in Gerald Raunig and Gene Ray (eds), *Art and Contemporary Critical Practice: Reinventing Institutional Critique*, London: MayFly Books, pp. 3–11.

Sander, Katya (2004), 'Criticizing institutions? The logic of institutionalization in the Danish welfare state', *Republic Art*, February, http://www.republicart.net/disc/institution/sander01_en.htm. Accessed 13 June 2017.

Science Friction (2011) *foreningsdraft* [from an email exchange with Jacob Sikker Remin].

Sheikh, Simon (2009), 'Notes on institutional critique', in Gerald Raunig and Gene Ray (eds), *Art and Contemporary Critical Practice: Reinventing Institutional Critique*, London: MayFly Books, pp. 29–32.

Simon, Nina (2010), *The Participatory Museum*, http://www.participatorymuseum.org/read/. Accessed 13 June 2017.

Turner, Fred (2014), 'What Is the Museum of the Future?', Youtube, https://www.youtube.com/watch?v=UOm-dUSAlpI. Accessed 12 December 2018.

Vergo, Peter (ed.) (1997), *New Museology*, London: Reaktion Books.

Voorhies, James (ed.) (2016), *What Ever Happened to New Institutionalism?* Cambridge, MA and Berlin: Carpenter Center for the Visual Arts and Sternberg Press.

Representation, Complexity and Control: Three Aspects of Technology-Based Sonic Art

Jøran Rudi

Today, digital technology permeates nearly all creation of sound for any media. This pervasiveness is the same for other types of content and for society in general. There is hardly any societal problem or challenge where digital technology is not seen as part of the solution – even in cases that on the outset do not seem to be candidates for this type of approach. For example, when refugees from Syria rolled in across the Norwegian borders from Sweden and Russia in 2015, one of the responses was a suggestion for making cell phone apps that would help refugees find the assistance they needed, and to help them find employment and other activities that would further support their integration. On the surface, apps and wireless access seemed an unusual means of helping people who had escaped war and tremendous suffering, but many of those who came were quite vocal about the lack of adequate Wi-Fi access in the temporary shelters where they were housed.

This anecdote has little to do with music but when people – those who have been forced to leave their previous life behind and run – put Wi-Fi access high up on their list of priorities, it says something about how important digital tools have become across the globe. Perhaps the refugees only needed to hear from their loved ones and talk to them, but in light of the importance they put on their portable devices, the idea of the app actually seemed pretty good. It may become a significant form of help, of course in addition to food, shelter, clothing and other bare essentials. The suggestion for an app was, in many ways, a timely response.

Digital media is important in mobilizing community efforts to help in the situation. In Oslo, for example, a Facebook-group started by a couple of artists quickly mobilized a large number of people to contribute their time to distribute emergency aid – in the form of food and clothes – to refugees who were poorly prepared for the winter conditions they met in Oslo in December 2015.

Against this backdrop, it is not difficult to accept the premise set out by the editor of this book that digital technology has profoundly affected tools, creation, distribution, experience and discourse in the arts. Since the art sector comprises a large and constantly developing set of efforts and functions, there are several types of dynamics at play. From the artist testimonials that were gathered in order to form a basis for the essays in this book, a number of topics have emerged as contributions to changing the creation, dissemination, participation and appreciation of artworks. It is also interesting to see a few artists expressing that digital technology has become such an integral part of their life and work that they do not find it necessary to reflect more on its role, and is perceived as 'just another set of tools' with no particular effect on artistic ideas and their execution. Whether this rejection of the imprint of digital technology means that these artists in fact have become cyborgian to the degree that they just can't see the integration with technology in their practices, or that their creative ideas are unaffected, would be an interesting thread to follow, but it falls a little outside of the scope of this chapter, where the theme is the digital dynamics that have influenced representation and identity in the audio arts.

In this chapter, *audio arts* is not considered to be part of either music nor visual and conceptual arts. Audio art is instead thought of as a 'super-category' that encompasses the above. This categorization makes it easier to focus on the continuum of how sound is used in, for example, experimental music and sound installation art, rather than the differences between art genres (Rudi 2008).

The broad topics that have been identified in the artist statements are:

- Fascination and preoccupation with the new tools and affordances of digital technology
- Exploration of particular qualities of digital media and the use of these qualities as artistic material
- Questioning and exploring how the digital paradigm has changed the conditions for everyday existence
- New artistic practices and new types of works (participatory, remote, abstracted)
- The requirement of new competences for visitors and audiences

In addition to these general topics, some of the statements provided by the artists also reflect on globalization, pointing to the future that emerges more rapidly now than before digital technology became omnipresent. While emphasizing their international presence and profile, a few of the artists are also grappling with the notion of 'nordicness', referring vaguely to the importance of context, and the traditional preoccupation with nature. Some also add social perspectives and point to the egalitarian ideas that characterize the Nordic democracies to a higher degree than typically found in more strongly class-divided and hierarchical societies. Thus, two additional topics can be identified in the statements, which will make a meaningful expansion of the bullet list:

- Digitally influenced and digitally determined changes in behaviour
- Consequences of new distribution technology for Nordic identities and globalization in art

The range of possible discussions that follow from this collected bullet list is clearly too wide for one chapter and a choice of a more specific topic must be made. The digital paradigm permeates all sectors of society, and since the seven listed bullet points are interconnected, it is from this web of connections that I draw the topic for this chapter. We will discuss how digital technologies allow any type of digital representation to become material for processing, and how this type of conception and representation influences our sense and understanding of sound identity as well as identity on a wider scale. The focus will be on the audio arts but the perspective will span along a wider sector in order to provide the relevant context. As we all know, sound does not exist in a vacuum, neither as a physical process nor as a social event (really, it doesn't!).[1]

Many of the artist statements mention problematic aspects of the digital presence, and one emerging concern is the flexibility of identity, a flexibility facilitated and encouraged by digital presentation, self-presentation and interaction. Another concern stems from the types of surveillance that result from the constant visibility and the increasing need for confirmation that often follow in the wake of social media. Media use is increasing dramatically; we are, for example, on average, checking our cell phone more than 110 times a day (Woollaston 2013), and in this way we are adding significantly to the growing influence of media content at the same pace with which we reduce our private time for reflection and quietness. Users consciously or unconsciously conform to the norms that fill social media with likes, never dislikes, and smiling displays of success rather than the uncertainty and worry that follows struggle and difficulty. In comparison, the conformism in Woody Allen's film *Zelig* from 1983 seems like an innocent child's play.[2] The Zelig character ingratiates himself in widely different contexts, by radically changing his appearance and behaviour, and seems to completely lack any identity and personality other than those that he adopts. One can arguably say that media influence and praxis with digital media and software tools encourage certain types of self-representation, thus leading to a self-imposed suppression of individual variance in the identities presented in these media. We shape our digital avatars and they shape us.

Distance

Notions of identity and representation are intertwined, and although it might not seem necessary to include much philosophy in this chapter, Martin Heidegger's essay 'The Question Concerning Technology' from 1953 comes to mind. Heidegger was a student of Edmund Husserl and brought with him much of his teacher's thoughts on phenomenology in his understanding of technology's role in how our perception and understanding of the world around us changes, arguing that the character of things emerges when things show themselves in their own way. (This, however, did not bring Heidegger into the essentialist fold. Heidegger believed that identity was processual more than fixed, but a more thorough discussion of this will lead us too far off track in this chapter). What makes Heidegger's essay interesting is that he, on one hand, criticizes technology for creating distance, while on the other hand seems to encourage use of technology in order to not become subservient to it. I have found this dichotomistic relationship to technology in several of the artist statements, which form the basis for this book.

There are many things to criticize in Heidegger's thinking – his politics; his ahistorical view on technology, where older production modes are considered in keeping with natural order (thus not distorting perception) while only new ones pose challenges; his contention of truth, which is rather authoritarian; his reduction of technology to methods and things (ignoring social aspects and competences), and more. Heidegger's views on technology does not necessarily allow for understanding new realizations of this natural order, however, the key point in his text that makes it relevant for our discussion about identity and representation is that something happens to our perception of identity when looking through a technological lens. In digital sound, for example, all sounds become material, rather than having identities of their own. In principle, they are reduced to pure physics – pressure waves that can be measured numerically.

As Mark Blitz summarizes in *The New Atlantis*, 'Heidegger draws attention to technology's place in bringing about our decline by constricting our experience of things as they are' (Blitz 2014). How Heidegger imagines it possible to avoid any cultural filter in order to let things appear unfiltered is not clear, but he fields an important point when arguing that we now view nature, perhaps also including human beings, only technologically – that is, we see nature only as raw material for technical operations. One might, as philosopher Bernard Stiegler, propose that a technological gaze is something inherent for our species, expanding the notion of technology to include a wider set of competences and not only the tools themselves. For example: The idea of a hammer precedes the actual construction, but a hammer is not a technology until someone knows how to use it, and it gains meaning by serving a function. The impetus for development is (probably) unwillingly problematized in the humorous saying that if a hammer is your only tool, all problems will look like nails. Thus, the concept of technology is placed squarely in the social domain – as not only a thing, but also understanding and know-how. Also, to Heidegger the technological lens is restricting, because we will only see the affordances – what is possible with the technology, what the technology 'wants to have happen', in a sense. In our case of sonic art, the technology becomes a means to an end and also directs the human activity, leading the users to perceive only the sonic aspects that technology allows us to grasp, not the sounds as they are. Phrased differently, the nearness of connotations and references that we experience in sounds disappear when the sounds are reduced to spectromorphological changes that tap them of origin, intent and significance. This was the essential intention in *musique concrète* when it was invented in the years following the Second World War. Engineer Pierre Schaeffer and fellow composers at Groupe Recherches Musicales at the French radio were developing a new musical language in reaction to the pompous orchestration in interval-based music such as Richard Wagner's and the serial music of the Second Viennese School. This was the period when purely synthesized electronic music was becoming a distinct genre, with Karlheinz Stockhausen as the most prominent composer. Of course, these musical inventions were analogue, not digital, but the compositional ideas from that time remain in much electroacoustic music of today, with abstracted sounds and musical forms that do not conform to the relatively stable paradigms of music for acoustic instruments.

Interestingly, this removal of references and recognition for artistic purposes is somewhat parallel to the issues that western music has run into when quoting and incorporating music from the developing world. These appropriations most often overlook the cultural framing and aspects of the original music, and the result is often perceived as ignorance, or slighting, of the cultures from where the music has been taken. This type of musical migration is often understood as a form of exploitation, and artists from the developing world who provide this music are not often enough credited or paid for their work – it is only material. A prime example is Brian Eno's and David Byrne's *My Life in the Bush of Ghosts* from 1981, where the work of the North African musicians, radio hosts and others that was integrated at first was not even credited properly, not to mention paid. The artistic licence to quote the work of others is a slippery slope, and in the western music industry often contested as copyright infringement. The most extreme case of this is John Oswald's *Plunderphonics* from 1985 that consists entirely of short music snippets from hundreds of records. The record industry protested Oswald's appropriations, possibly also because Oswald had a political agenda that promoted cultural plunder as a basic artistic right.

For our focus here on the digital footprint in sonic arts, it is interesting to point out that when technological means are used to tease out hidden or less prominent features of sounds in order to exploit them musically, the sound processing itself implies some degree of reductionism. And, referring once more to Heidegger, this type of process is self-sustaining – mastery of the technology reinforces the technological filter. Heidegger's text was published in 1953, and its concerns about the distance that follows from technology use can still be traced in most modern musicology. In discourse of technology-based music, Leigh Landy's article 'The something to hold on to factor in timbral composition' raised related concerns already in 1994 (Landy 1994). In this text, Landy is grappling with the issues of how untrained listeners largely fail to appreciate (complex) electroacoustic music, and how composers might help them develop more fruitful listening strategies. He finds that the use of technical language when describing methods and technologies in the compositions are creating more distance than nearness, thus echoing Heidegger's main argument for the need to experience things as they are, unfiltered.

The difficulties for broad appreciation of technology-based art that Landy points to have roots that reach back to the beginnings of both electric sound and electrically generated images. For example, when A. Michael Noll and Bela Julesz, at the invitation of Howard Wise Gallery in New York, exhibited some of the graphical work they made in American Telephone and Telegraph's Bell Labs in 1965, they did not exactly meet with a warm reception. The harsh criticism that the exhibition received might in part have been motivated by the fact that computer renderings had sprung from military technologies for calculating ballistics (Taylor 2012: 20),[3] however, the main drift of the criticism was that the works 'did not display any fantasy' and that 'they were cold and soulless'. The images had been generated from the calculations embedded in the execution of an algorithm and not drawn by hand. It should also be mentioned that one of the artists, Bela Julesz, was uneasy in calling the works art, while Michael Noll was fine with it. The artists ended up finding common ground when naming their exhibition of generative art Computer-Generated Pictures.

In sound, the situation was similar, although experimentation with unconventional forms and materials were well underway already before the Second World War with the futurists and the Dada movement. In electronic music, Pierre Schaeffer's studies were not well received at first, and the pioneering work of Louis and Bebe Barron in scoring for the film *Forbidden Planet* in 1956 also met with questions of categorization. What was the right name for the soundtrack – music or effects? The original screen credit for the film was supposed to read 'Electronic Music by Louis and Bebe Barron', but this was changed at the last moment at the insistence of the American Federation of Musicians. The new credit read 'Electronic Tonalities by Louis and Bebe Barron'. It was the word 'music' that the musicians needed to see omitted. The economic motive for the union is easy to see – protecting jobs for their members and barring others from infringing on their territory – but the mere switching of the word 'music' with 'tonalities' was sufficient for the musicians to feel that the competition had been eliminated, or at least reduced. The episode shows that the questioning of whether machine-made expressions could in fact be called art held sway also in the auditory arts.

The objections to the early experiments with electronically generated sounds and images seem to have sprung from scepticism towards using machines for generating art. And they seem to be a fairly good match with Heidegger's notion that the use of technology creates distance to the process and identity of the material. But the objections might also indicate that it was the abstracted material itself that made the works difficult to accept. In computer-generated arts, the execution logically springs from human-made rules as an abstract – there are no tangible elements to touch and no method available to experience the thought process as it is deposited into sets of algorithms, rather than into pigments or instrumental performance practices.

These types of critical reactions evidence that strict logic and algorithmic execution does not necessarily result in public acceptance. Interestingly, similar logic and rule-based approaches for estimating artistic quality have been tried. American mathematician George David Birkhoff, for example, published a theory on aesthetic quality in 1933, in a little book where he, in addition to discussing earlier theories on aesthetic quality, also provided a collection of examples where his theory was applied in evaluation of music, poetry, visual and three-dimensional art. His simple formula $M=O/C$, where quality (M) is expressed as the ratio between structure (O) and complexity (C), shows the importance he placed on structure and that the aesthetic quality would increase with the decrease of complexity. Simple and structured was the formula of success. Of course, Birkhoff shows quite a reductionist view on art and he completely ignores receiver competence and context, while concentrating solely on the work itself. It should however be noted that Birkhoff believed that the intuitive perception of art should be considered more important than his formulaic description, so clearly, he had his doubts on the validity of his method, just as Bela Julesz in 1965 questioned whether his computer renderings were artworks. By using mathematics as tool and method, both involuntarily cast light on some of the fundamental problems in using metrics for describing aesthetical experiences.

Nearness

Musical use of technology often entails processing; twisting and turning sounds to tease out content and 'liberate' this content from the context and the more referential qualities of the original sound. This process has been postulated as necessary for experiencing sound as it is, not as what it means in a referential sense. Clearly, this type of abstraction can easily be said to create distance to the sounding object by blurring its identity, however, bringing forth and casting new light on content that has been concealed by established semantics, or generating new sounds from scratch, brings something new and unheard into the world. From this perspective, technology brings closeness and perhaps it is time to remember how Heidegger recalled that the Greek word techne (from which 'technology' is derived) originally meant 'bringing-forth of the true into the beautiful' (Blitz 2014). With this view, it is clear that technology can also bring out essential identity markers, and perhaps Heidegger's main goal with his discussions was to open up the discussion of technology in order to better understand and embrace it, rather than 'hopelessly rebel against it', as Mark Blitz cites Heidegger in his essay in *The New Atlantis* (Blitz 2014). Only by grasping the affordances and making deliberate use of them can we avoid being dominated by them.

This line of argument has a familiar ring in Nordic music contexts, since it was frequently found among Scandinavian pioneers in electroacoustic music from the 1960s to 1980s, such as Knut Wiggen in Sweden and Kåre Kolberg in Norway. Only by using technology in music could composers take part in the development of society and assume their part of the responsibility for its development. Their arguments work well with Heidegger's contention and it is no surprise that this relationship to the current media technologies can also be found in our artist statements, for example, in those of Laura Beloff.

The intention of creating something new is essential in all arts, and several artists in our reference group aim to reveal the affordances and features of technology by using it. Kristina Kvalvik, Niels Bonde and Elisabeth Molin have written about this in their statements. Technological qualities can be revealed by using technologies to 'make' rather than 'consume' something and the responses in, for example, social media-driven interaction will reveal something essential. A perfect example that appeared in the Oslo Press in June 2016 was the art project *iSynx,* where the filmmakers in Volt Film, well known for their documentary film about drone warfare, presented a fictitious contact lens. This lens should significantly enhance the lives of their users and they were looking for beta testers. Their claim was '*iSynx* is a personal AI operating system that will revolutionize your life by enhancing your body and mind'. According to the project's Facebook page they had 700,000 original visitors, of which 1500 had signed up as beta testers (iSynx 2016). The beta testers had signed a contract where they gave away all personal rights, along the lines of normal social media practices, for use of their input to create automatic recommendations for users, based on the typical use of big data. They also gave away personal, medical and financial info, including credit card numbers. The website would record the user's voice and *iSynx* would have the right to sell these recordings to third-party companies, without any restrictions. The invasion of privacy was total – in effect, all sensory impressions captured by the contact lens would become the property of a company to exploit as it saw fit, and despite these harsh terms 1500 people signed up (iSynx 2016).

iSynx was an art project designed to feed into a debate on artificial intelligence, questioning where the delimitations should be for developing such technologies; it was not a real product or business idea. But it is difficult to imagine how an art project of this type could have been launched and be successful without (at least on the surface) being immersed in the technologies it set out to question. The *iSynx* project provides an example of how immersion in a technology is used for making a successful project about the technology itself, thus providing the experience of nearness.

Smartphones are already pointing us in directions where we typically like to go, based on information from us and our friends, and unsurprisingly, the omnipresence of social media is a topic for several artists in our survey, such as Marie Munk and Joonas Siren. But how does this work in the audio field – does digital audio bring the same sense of nearness, immersion or participation? Although the artistic development has resulted in genre-mixing and many grey zones with mixed identities, there are several relatively clear lines of intersection in digital audio art: (acoustic) interval-based vs. technology-based music, electroacoustic music vs. more conceptual sound art, conventional acousmatic music vs. more critical genres such as noise, glitch and other live-based, rebellious and non-institutional forms, etc. These divisions might not all be interesting here, and the types of sounds, the level of processing and the use of conceptual, extra-sonic references vary widely. What is common is that recording technologies are crucial, as in the early electroacoustic music, especially the development of digital equipment. Recorders and microphones of very high quality are available for a low cost compared to the pre-digital situation, and in combination with the dramatically falling prices on computers and software, the economic and institutional barriers for playing around with sound have disappeared. Mats Jørgen Sivertsen from our survey is one of a number of artists who has emphasized the increased opportunities that follow from this, and Mia Mäkelä describes the new technological situation like this: 'My whole art production can be fitted into a two square centimetre physical space (SD card)' (Mia Mäkelä, artist testimonial in this volume: 45).

The availability has opened windows into working with sound, both as abstract material and in a more documentary sense, and the multiplicity of artistic approaches to working with sound is arguably the most important development in the sonic arts; competences have become widespread, and the sensitivities that listening relies on are much better distributed among the population than they were pre-digitally. Digital sound fills media everywhere, and soundtracks in films and games routinely include complex and deliberately constructed psychoacoustically effective soundscapes. This type of first-hand experience brings nearness, and in the instance of the arts (if they are any good) also reflection. The everyday sound environments are effective in their use of technology to make us feel presence, nearness, immersion and overwhelming larger-than-life soundscapes, and with the recent re-emergence of Virtual Reality, we see a huge interest in 3D sound for headphones.

Representation

The principal difference between analogue and digital technology is in the representation. Analogue, physical representation of sound is continuous but digital representation consists of strings of 1s and 0s – and is the same for all types of content. The re-formatting of a continuous signal to discrete numbers is a re-interpretation that makes the content easily available for mathematical operations and is hugely powerful. Since all types of data can be represented digitally, data from, for example, an image can easily be rendered as sound and vice versa. Of course, these types of cross-use of data might not be particularly meaningful, but they are possible.

Arguably more meaningful than this cross-use is the use of sensor data from the environment, findings from the sciences, recorded data from visitor and audience movement and actions, etc. With the right formatting and relevant mapping to sound processes, any data can be used meaningfully, and this type of appropriation is often used for providing artworks with both structure and identity. One of the artists in the survey, Mogens Jacobsen, uses data in this manner and works with computer code in different languages for programming behaviours in different objects. A recent example from his portfolio is the installation work *Probabilistic Audio Dice Roll* from 2015, where a dice is thrown based on data from radioactive decay in uranium glass (Mogens Jacobsen Official Website 2015). The roll is a sonification of radioactive decay, much the same as the Geiger counter that emits a beep for each radioactive emission – a classic example of sonification. Jacobsen brings the process of radioactive discharge from one domain into another, and by making it audible by way of digital techniques he makes it available to our senses.

Sonification is defined as the representation of data by non-musical sonic means, and a humorous example from the Norwegian oil industry is the implementation of a cash-register sound in an analysis software – the sound would be triggered when a possible oil-carrying layer in the geological data from the seabed was found. Possible profits were represented in a tongue-in-cheek manner.

In music, works get a quasi-scientific character when explicit use of numbers from, for example, the natural sciences are used for structure. Clearly, listeners are enabled to experience relationships that would otherwise be unavailable for the senses, but whether this approach results in added artistic value is less certain. Regardless, this type of experiential focus brings new material into the arts, and although it is not always possible to hear what the composers would like to emphasize, the listener nonetheless experiences something that is out of the ordinary. This is an important aspect of digital representations in itself – that they actually make new material available for experience. This type of new content in musical discourse gave an air of 'scientification' to the music, and the language that was introduced for describing these types of works revealed a more research- and technology-oriented approach. It happened in acoustic as well as in technology-based music, and exact analyses of spectra and other measurable impulses were used to give structure and orchestration to music for ensembles of various sizes. The most prominent example of this genre from the international scene is the French spectral school, and the same types of techniques were used by several composers in Scandinavia as well.

Another and simpler example is in the increasingly popular genre of soundscape recordings, where another artist in the collection of testimonials, Ewa Jacobsson, observes the importance of combinations of digital, social and biological processes. Technological advances in portable recording and sound reproduction technology have provided the basis for rapid growing popularity of this art form. Tape reels have been replaced by flash memory, simple microphones have been replaced with microphones sensitive enough to record ants walking, hydrophones are able to capture sound hundreds of meters below the ocean surface, and arrays of microphones and loudspeakers make it possible to render sound in three dimensions for high fidelity. However, by placing microphones or inserting plugins for processing in the studio production, deliberate choices are being made. What is recorded and produced is still a selection, and nature becomes what we make it.[4] Processes and patterns are extracted and put before our senses by way of technology, either through simple editing or by the more technically involved capture of the necessary data that can be used for abstracting principles for further modelling, such as sonification. One early example of this approach is Rob Waring's *Sonomatrix* from 1995, where natural processes are being played out across a grid of 64 speakers (Rob Waring Official Website 2016).

World renowned Norwegian artist Jana Winderen records below the ocean surface, at great depths, and the recordings she brings to the surface reveal a world of sound that few of us would otherwise be able to hear, both because it is difficult to get down into the deep and because the internal noise in our bodies disturbs our ability to listen when we are immersed in water. This type of increased availability is also recognizable in the exoticism of soundscape recordings from endangered ecosystems or in the advanced recordings of microscopic sounds that are well below or above the human hearing threshold, amplitude – wise or spectrally. Digital recording and processing technology brings new content to our attention and this changes our perception of the environments and systems from where the sounds are taken, as well as our notion of what is music. Representation with digital means has made it easy to expand the arts with new material.

Complexity and Control

One of the most important aspects of digital technology is how easy it is to create and control complex dynamics; complexity in how data can be interpreted, information extracted and flexibility in its representation. Analysis of sound, for example, is based on measurements of air pressure – 44,100 measurements/second for CD quality. Each of the measurements gives a number, and by looking at these numbers in different ways, one can find frequencies, rhythms, amplitudes, instrument and sound types, musical qualities and genres, and so on. Mathematical operations are the key in both analysis and processing, and sounds can become twisted and turned in innumerable ways. Sound and acoustics are already complex phenomena and digital tools increase the possibilities for control and development of increased complexity. The sheer number of possibilities seems endless, and the easy use of modern software or apps stimulates meandering exploration without requiring much preparation from the user. The abundance of tools makes it possible to produce musical results without having any idea of which choices have been made in the software, and the result is a steady focus on novelty. Norwegian computer music pioneer Knut Wiggen warned against some consequences of this situation as early as 1970, when he wrote about how the critical potential in the new music could be undermined (author's translation): 'There are several composers today who want new processing equipment – new tools – in order to become the first one with a new type of sound. It makes little difference whether this sound has any basis in their musical imagination. The electronic sound becomes a gimmick. The sounds become a result of how the equipment works and not how we would like it to be' (Wiggen 1970: 61).

In this statement, Wiggen points to the need for understanding the technology in order to realize the artistic ideas. It is not sufficient to just use technology, the artist also needs to understand (at least something of) what is happening in the process. This was a necessary prerequisite in the early computer music but less important in the synthesizer tradition that rapidly gained momentum in the 1970s. These concerns are no less valid today. During the 1980s and into the 2000s, software became increasingly complex and users needed a good understanding in order to make informed choices. A new type of composer or sound artist emerged, an artist that mixed the roles of producer, engineer, technologist, musician and composer. A prime example of this type of composer from the ranks of the early pioneers is Jean-Claude Risset, who was in charge of computer music when the French centre IRCAM opened its doors in 1977. Risset had been active as a researcher, composer and musician since the early 1960s and contributed significantly to the understanding of how musical spectra develop. His work *Sud* (1984–85) fully exploits this acoustic research (Risset 1965).[5]

It was arguably in music that use of data from science and other disciplines first took hold. In Norway, British composer Natasha Barrett made a hallmark for herself already in the 1990s when using data from natural processes to control the generation, processing and playback of sound in installation works such as *Mimetic Dynamics* (1999) and *Displaced: Replaced* (2001). In the years that have followed since, installations and music from her studio show that she has maintained this interest on complex control of sonic events through digital means. And it is not only the works themselves that show this focus on control of complex data; the program notes and other textual descriptions of the works are technically oriented.

Another example of complex sound control has been found in Swedish Åsa Stjerna's installation *Currents* from 2011, where she inputs data from a scientific research project on North-Atlantic ocean currents into a dynamically changing work that was installed at the Norwegian Opera and Ballet in Oslo. In part, the data from the ocean controlled the development of the installation, according to the website of NOTAM (who produced the event), and was piped to Oslo by way of a scientific computing centre in Stockholm.

Key terms in working with complexity and control are co-variation, dependency and coupling of disparate elements. Inserting data and controlling complex systems is essential in many of the digital arts, and there is little doubt that the new tools have changed the artistic approach for many artists. Artists Bjørn Erik Haugen and Tor Jørgen van Eijk discuss in their statements how digital tools have changed both their way of working as well as the content of their work.

Concepts

Perhaps the most interesting artistic results from the adoption of digital technology are within cross-disciplinary and concept-driven arts. Broader perspectives are brought into the arts by defining conceptual links between both disparate elements and constructed connections that can be given physical shape with more ease than with only analogue tools. Visitor movements or deliberate actions can easily be captured and used to control artistic details, and 'live' generative art has become an important genre. One recent example of this approach is Asbjørn Blokkum Fløs commission from Bergen Center for Electronic Art (BEK) in 2015. Here, he grabs sound from a café in real time, analyses and processes it into electric trigger signals that are sent to a number of sculptures shaped as small towers. The triggers activate electromagnets that pull hammers of different materials and sizes, and they beat on steel plates where thicknesses and sizes have been carefully calculated to produce specific sets of frequencies. By combining hammering on the different plates, well-defined spectra are created, and in a way they are direct representations of the captured speech patterns from the café. The title of the work is *Doppelgänger,* the German word for Double, and Fløs gives us another representation of the café conversations, based on conceptual recognition, distortion, materiality and distance. The exactness in this work would have been unattainable without digital technology.[6]

Signal capture, analysis and mapping can be done with ease, and this opens up elements that have previously been unobtainable for reinterpretation and exposure. An unavoidable consequence is that the identity of the material changes and it becomes difficult to see the 'original' – in fact the entire concept of the original is in flux. One example: In the early 2000s, we executed an experiment at NOTAM where we had approximately ten highly qualified listeners (composers of acousmatic music) rate different versions of six to eight genres of music: orchestral, ensemble, folk, ethnic, pop, rock, etc. The versions were simply the originals compressed with different algorithms and to different degrees, and we did this testing in order to help a Norwegian music download service that was being built at the time find the best compromise between download time (compressed file size) and quality. We asked our ten listeners to focus on sound quality – on which version sounded the best – and surprisingly, their ratings were all over the board. There was no consensus. We had been careful not to provide information about which files were the originals and the answers showed that there was no clear identification or agreement of neither original nor quality. With modern production technologies, the entire identity is at play as new aspects are emphasized.

It is perhaps easier to see this flexibility of identity that follows digital technology if we look at the self-publishing that is the backbone of social media, where the selective self-presentation blurs the distinction between reality and fiction, as several artists in our survey have pointed to. Marie Munk is particularly clear in her description of the media-driven presentation as 'the way people behave and communicate with each other'. As technology becomes increasingly immersed with both our bodies and our lives, the way in which we are 'present' changes, both physically and mentally. 'Our bodies are no longer sacred or honest, but highly manipulated – just as any other aspect of our lives. Even nature, which used to be understood as pure, is no longer reliable. Technology is capable of manipulating every aspect of our bodies, lives and nature, which is both intriguing and fear provoking' (Marie Munk, artist testimonial in this volume: 66). Or more briefly, as Joonas Siren puts it: 'I have a real life persona and a digital online persona, and none is more real than the other' (Joonas Siren, artist testimonial in this volume: 34).

Media presentation can be as innocent as the composer's use of sound to guide audiences in installation and performance situations, creating a flow of events that he or she finds attractive, or it can be more politically coloured, as when technologically shaped sound is used to instrumentally change human behaviour. The distribution of technologies and social networks create new behaviours on a broad scale, and this process can be productively described as reprogramming of our sensory apparatus, much like what Marshall McLuhan described in 1967 and has written about several times since (McLuhan 1967). Examples of these types of artistic concerns are found in both Laura Beloff's and Niels Bonde's statements, and they are implicit in Jacek Smolicky's responses to the editor's questions as well. Audio technology is being used to encourage certain behaviours and discourage other types, and the situation is a product of both technical affordances and social framing.

WWW-technologies, that among the pioneers were imagined to be liberating and democratizing, have become an essential part of the society's mainstream and lost the critical potential they were once believed to have. Herbert Marcuse, a popular philosopher in the 1970s, explained that societal acceptance of critical practices actually removes their critical potential (Marcuse 1964), and the self-imposed suppression of individual originality that dominates current social media follows from this type of broad acceptance.[7] Peer pressure seems stronger now than ever before, and the combination with commercial use of big data has a powerful influence.

Closing Remarks

The digital paradigm of binary representation has opened up the arts for new material, and although the technology has lost its allure for some artists such as Vibeke Jensen, who has become 'more drawn to the tactility of physical materials, hands-on situations and processes' (Vibeke Jensen, artist testimonial in this volume: 94), other artists such as Jacob Remin have been using the technology itself as material. In a more comprehensive perspective, Laura Beloff for example is doing the same thing when she exploits our technological competences to deliberately change our behaviours. The technological affordances of media have become tools and topics for artists all around. For audio arts, one can certainly claim, as composer Luciano Berio did in 1953, that artistic use of technology takes place in a continuum and does not appear in a schism,[8] but then one must ignore the particularity of the representation and how it opens new layers of complexity, control and conceptual developments as we have described them above. The distance to the sounding object itself can certainly be said to increase with the digital representation when compared to the analogies that were carrying earlier technologies, but, as a magnifying glass, digital technology brings composers and listeners closer to the sound than before – and it is easier to change focus to new and hitherto unappreciated aspects of the sonic world.

This distance is complicated – on one hand it is a step away from the immediate sensory experience, but it also creates a mental space for more of a conceptual richness and stronger connection to the 'real' world, in fact, strong enough for the distinction between 'real' and 'representation' to become blurred. Heidegger was concerned about distance and argued that it could be overcome by exposing perspectives that emerged with the use of technology itself. In the current digital situation, the distance to the objects that follow from digital representation seems to be a prerequisite for developing the nearness that follows from immersion in the technologies, whether is it the make-believe identities of social media, the micro-approaches in sound processing, or the conceptual manipulation where reality and fiction meet. These abstractions realize the deeply human identity that is embedded in and follows from our technological gaze, and the situation can be likened to Escher's drawing of hands that draw themselves, except that this time it is the human code that modifies its author.

References

Berio, Luciano (2009), 'Musica per Tape Recorder', *il Daspason*, 4:3–4, pp. 10–3. Reprinted in Novati, Maria Maddalena and Dack, J. (eds) (2009), *The Studio di Fonologia*, Rome: Ricordi, p. 4.

Blitz, Mark (2014), 'Understanding Heidegger on technology', *The New Atlantis*, 41, pp. 63–80, https://www.thenewatlantis.com/publications/understanding-heidegger-on-technology. Accessed 21 June 2016.

Flø, Asbjørn B. and Wilmers, Hans (2015a), 'The intrinsic value of timbre in Doppelgänger', *Proceedings of the International Computer Music Conference (ICMC)*, Denton, USA.

—— (2015b), 'Doppelgänger: A solenoid-based large-scale sound installation', *Proceedings of the 2015 International Conference on New Interfaces for Musical Expression*, Baton Rouge.

Higgins, Hannah and Kahn, Douglas (2012), *Mainframe Experimentalism – Early Computing and the Foundations of the Digital Arts*, Berkeley: University of California Press.

iSynx (2016), 'Events', Facebook, www.facebook.com/events/1026794837436396. Accessed 2 July 2016.

Landy, Leigh (1994), 'The something to hold on to factor in timbral composition', *Contemporary Music Review*, 10:2, Reading: Harwood, pp. 49–60.

Marcuse, Herbert (1964), *One-dimensional Man*, New York: Beacon Press.

McLuhan, Marshall (1967), *The Medium is the Massage*, New York: Bantam Books.

Mogens Jacobsen Official Website (2015), 'Probabilistic Audio Dice Roll', https://www.mogensjacobsen.dk/showwork.php?pid=80. Accessed 11 July 2016.

Risset, Jean-Claude (1965), 'Computer study of trumpet tones', *Journal of Acoustical Society of America*, 38:5.

Rob Waring Official Website (2016), 'Sound installation: SONOMATRIX', http://robwaring.info/snmtrx.html. Accessed 8 July 2016.

Rudi, Jøran (2008), 'Sound and Meaning', in J. Rudi (ed.), *Absorption and Resonance – Sound and Meaning*, Oslo: NOTAM.

Taylor, Grant (2012), 'The soulless usurper – Reception and criticism of early computer art', in H. B. Higgins and D. Kahn (eds), *Mainframe Experimentalism – Early Computing and the Foundations of the Digital Arts*, Berkeley: University of California Press.

Wiggen, Knut (1970), 'Den musikaliske bakgrunden för datamusiken', Prisma 4:3, Oslo: Gyldendal.

Woollaston, Victoria (2013), 'How often do you check your phone? The average person does it 110 times a DAY (and up to every 6 seconds in the evening)', Dailymail.com, 8 October 2013, www.dailymail.co.uk/sciencetech/article-2449632/How-check-phone-The-average-person-does-110- times-DAY-6-seconds-evening.html. Accessed 14 February 2016.

Notes

1 As a physical phenomenon, sound is pressure waves and if there is no material in which the waves can be propelled, there can be no such pressure waves.

2 In *Zelig* by Woody Allen (1983), the main character appears in a large number of circumstances and always fits in by changing the way he looks and acts. In the film, this condition is recognized as a disorder.

3 The early computer systems used for this were the ENIAC and EDVAC. Both systems were developed during the Second World War, for military purposes (Taylor 2012: 20).

4 This is an underlying perspective in much of the writings about 'dark ecology', which in essence puts humanity and its activities back into the ecological equation as part of

nature, not separate from it. Important theoreticians are Timothy Morton and Slavoj Zizek.

5 Jean-Claude Risset also published a catalogue of synthesized tones in 1969, where he gave examples on spectral characteristics of intonations on several instruments, written during his time at Bell Labs in New Jersey.

6 A video of the work is available on Vimeo: www.vimeo.com/99662254. For research articles on the engineering aspects of the installation, please see Flø and Wilmers (2015a, 2015b).

7 Herbert Marcuse was a student of Martin Heidegger, and his term 'repressive desublimation' is explained in detail in Marcuse (1964).

8 Luciano Berio wrote: 'the electronic creation or manipulation of sounds should be seen as a phenomenon not of schism but of continuity, springing from the same historical and human motives that guided the development of music from Palestrina to Dallapiccola' (Berio 2009: 4).

Uneasy Listening: Perspectives on (Nordic) Sound Art after the Digital

Budhaditya Chattopadhyay

The coming about of digital technology seems to have disrupted and reconfigured artistic practices. The thematic threads that emerge from a close reading through the artist testimonials in this volume, expressed by artists that are active within the Nordic contemporary art scene, indicate a fertile condition for the reconfiguration of several strongly held concepts, namely: site, object, body and the materiality of things. This disruption is also recognized beyond the geologic Nordic region, if we take a critical look at the international contemporary art scene post globalization. Indeed, contemporary art is struggling with the deconstruction and dismantling of the concept of site-specificity and the artistic object-based materiality after the digital revolution. This is particularly true for sound art, which is perhaps at the centre of the art world's recent fascination. Due to its inherent characteristics, sound art finds legitimacy in the absence of the object, from conception to practice and from the production to the reception of the artwork.

In this chapter, I am interested in developing a discursive context for the purpose of examining the conditions of intensified mobility, deterritorialization[1] and object-disorientation[2] of sound as experienced in contemporary sound art practices after the advent of the digital, both within and outside of the Nordic region. Departing from the vantage point of being a sound and new media artist myself, navigating through 'digital dynamics', I will try to articulate how the digital has triggered particular forms and aesthetics in sound art. Drawing on the conceptualization of sound objects – from the writings of contemporary sound scholars like Brandon LaBelle, Joanna Demers et al. – and on the notions of nomadism and deterritorialization from the seminal works of Gilles Deleuze and Félix Guattari-I intend to develop a primary argument on mobility, deterritorialization and object-disorientation in the so-called post-global and 'post-digital' sound art within and beyond the context of Nordic contemporary art. This argument will respond to the questions of spatiotemporal disembedding of the sonic object and mélange of listening experiences across multiple sites in our contemporaneity milieu. I will show that these kinds of interactions, interpenetration and mélange trigger new forms of subjectivities that incorporate an 'unsitely' and immaterial aesthetics in contemporary sound art; *unsitely* referring to the multiple and diverse ways artists are working in public space within the context of networked digital culture, being in two places at once; or to the super-imposition of real and virtual space that has become our common experience. The digital dynamics in sound art that I examine in this chapter are of particular relevance to investigate these issues in the perspective of the Nordic context, which, as I will later discuss, has been long entrenched in typically familiar and recognizable sound experiences.

Indeed, the emergence of digital technologies kick-started a condition of pervasive connectivity that now instigates perpetual dislocation. In this condition, perceptions constantly shift across unsettled geographies, producing meanings that at times are arguably independent from locative sources or the object of sound.[3] As an increasingly migratory being, a 'listener' wandering around in today's digitally converging cities is sensitive to environmental sounds, navigating through various urban sites and experiencing them as spatio-temporally evolving but gradually disorienting auditory situations, juxtaposed with real-time spatial information and memory of another place in another time. The nomadic subject relates to these auditory situations through contemplation, self-reflective and contingent processes informed by an enhanced sense of mobility. After the digital revolution is over, the contours of this contemporary reality bear the traces of its impacts on collective thinking, artistic practices and larger sociopolitical consciousness. This sense of mobility across the sites and resultant 'object-disorientation'[4] within the sociopolitical mélange and resultant spillovers are addressed in this chapter as driving forces of contemporary sound art practices. These perspectives resonate with the views of the Nordic artists who take sound as point of departure in their works. The chapter contributes to current discourses on the implications of the digital technology in contemporary art, focusing on sound art as a significant mode of artistic production.

The Field of Sound Art

There is some confusion and uncertainty about how to define 'sound art'. The question concerns whether sound art derives from an art music tradition or stems from a derivative of the visual arts. This is the question that problematizes the positioning of sound art in the aesthetic practices at large. Because of this, the somewhat complementary attitudes reflected in many artists', critics' and curators' commentaries explain why the current state of sound art triggers serious thoughts about the taxonomies and structure of the term. From the western art historical tradition, early examples of 'sound art' include Luigi Russolo's noise intoners and subsequent experiments by Dadaists, Surrealists, the Situationist International and in Fluxus happenings and environments designing a trajectory that leads to what Seth Kim-Cohen terms 'the conceptual turn' (Kim-Cohen 2009).[5] Because of the diverging approaches to the term, sound art debates often occur on whether sound art falls within the domain of either the visual art or experimental music, or whether it should be defined in between the categories. Among other artistic lineages from which sound art arguably emerges are conceptual art, minimalism, site-specific art, sound poetry, spoken word, avant-garde and experimental cinema. Sound scholar Christoph Cox suggests: 'At its best, "sound art" opens up or calls attention to an auditory unconscious, a *transcendental* or *virtual* domain of sound that has steadily come to prominence over the course of the twentieth century' (Cox 2009: 19). It is apparent that sound art has taken a definitive surge in aesthetic practice, production and dissemination and gained major attention in recent years, but such developments occur rather 'tentatively and ambivalently' (LaBelle 2006).

Kim-Cohen has described sound art as the unwanted child of music (Kim-Cohen 2009). He has pointed out the boundaries, tendencies and specific shifts in post-war sound art practice after Pierre Schaeffer's experiments with *musique concrète* and John Cage's experiments with silence. Their work, despite a preoccupation with sound's inherent material character, broadly contributed to a sound art history, setting the tone for the conceptual turn. Following traditional scholarship on sound and site, such as Murray Shafer's work at Simon Fraser University (Schafer 1994), terms such as 'soundscape' and 'acoustic ecology' have been used to describe specific sound practices embedded with a strictly environmental aesthetics. I have however argued elsewhere that these practices were inherently constrained with predominantly objective musical structures and locative ecological concerns, such as the perspectives of the acoustic ecology of cities vis-à-vis rural sites (Chattopadhyay 2012, 2013, 2017b). The practices with recorded and composed soundscapes with an environmental and ethical concern for site-specific acoustic ecology do not substantially contribute to the so-called 'conceptual turn' which the emerging sound art would subsequently entail.

Music writer Geeta Dayal argues, while referring to art critic Blake Gopnik, that sound art seems 'less esoteric' in the contemporary 'new media art' environment because of our 'newfound comfort with the immaterial world of pure data and information flowing through the cyberspace' (Gopnik cited in Dayal 2013). The 'new media' allows for the separation of sounds from their locations and facilitate their travel across globally dispersed networks as digital data and information. Sound that is disembodied from its locational specificity falls within multiple layers of mediation across multiple levels of reception and interpretation outside of place, time and context in the new media environment, whether in, for example, an audio-streaming network on the Internet, a multi-channel sonic environment, a telematic performance or an exhibition in augmented space of an interactive installation work. In this space of constant and itinerant flow, the production and reception of sound over greater mobility and interactivity leads to its interpretation as a fertile and more emergent auditory situation, rather than being posed as static material of a sonic artefact. Hence, sound art is more comfortably discussed within the 'object-unspecific',[6] essentially immaterial and multiply interpretative paradigm of new media art. This positioning of sound art in the contemporary art context is necessary in order to comprehend my ensuing conceptualisation, what I term an 'object-disorientation' of sound.

A Closer Reading of the Nordic Context

Traditionally, Nordic sound art is musically structured. Up until the Internet era, the sound of Nordic music was largely geographically isolated from the outside. Music scholar Frederick Key Smith has argued that the Nordic countries' 'lack of a land-based connection with continental Europe and their geographic isolation by the North and Baltic seas, as well as the Atlantic ocean in the case of Iceland, separated them from the bulk of Europe's musical activity until later' (Smith 2002: xv). This geographical positioning impacted 'the sound' of Nordic music and sonic works among others Nordic cultural productions, traditionally instituting a sense of familiarity and comfort. It is no surprise then that a flux of sounds from the outside world in the contemporary milieu would create uncanny and uneasy sensations in the mind of the listening subjects habitually situated within the Nordic region. In my teaching and workshops throughout Denmark and a few other Nordic countries, I have engaged participant-listeners in sound walks who have followed me around the city of Copenhagen while developing their individual experiences of sound walking. I have asked them to write their impressions on a piece of paper. As many of them were local – students based in Copenhagen or other parts of Denmark – sounds of the city of Copenhagen were mostly known or familiar to them. However, in the sporadic occasion of encountering sounds that were not easily located or sourced from their objects or origin, it was apparent that they felt unsettled. I suppose that those moments of uneasiness were caused by the 'unknown' in everyday sonic navigation around a known city.

What is the 'unknown' embedded in a sonic phenomenon? Does it operate outside of the reality of the sonic object-hood and site-specific structures of sonic phenomena? Even object-oriented philosophers like Graham Harman have argued that the reality of anything outside of a correlation between thought and being remains unknowable (Harman interview in Kimbell 2013). This unknowable sound or 'noise' enters the Nordic sonic palette and disrupts the familiarity. Likewise, researcher Thomas Bøgevald Bjørnsten argues:

> During the past decade an increased attention has been paid to, for instance, a category such as 'sound art' together with an equally strengthened interest in phenomena and concepts that fall outside the accepted aesthetic procedures and constructions of what we traditionally would term as musical sound – a recurring example being 'noise'.
>
> (Bjørnsten 2012)

Sound art after the digital in the Nordic context brings this 'unknown' into the foreground and forces the listener to ask: 'Is there any difference between music and sound art, when music is something that constantly opens up to the world of sounds around music?' (Vandsø 2015). Here music acts as a traditional setting and sound art disorders the sense of ease to trigger a renegotiation of the listening experience.

The Impacts of the Digital Technology

Digital technology introduced a range of tools, techniques and practices pushing for innovations not only in artistic production, but also the way we interact with site and object as artistic experience. Scott Contreras-Koterbay and Łukasz Mirocha argue:

'The expanding use of digital technology has been increasingly recognized as worthy of interest in aesthetics and in the art world; from projected cybernetic utopias and virtual realities to global awareness of artistic trends and unique art worlds, from the direct use of digital techniques as both the means of production and as art itself to its use as a means of facilitating new insights into art history, digital technology's impact has become pervasive and even, perhaps, common'

(Contreras-Koterbay and Mirocha 2016: 11).

This pervasive and common impact of digital technology over artistic production is exemplified by the way Nordic artists express their concerns about the intrinsic and momentous shifts they experience. These shifts are primarily felt in terms of the redefinition of the artistic object and the renegotiation of the art's site-specificity. Often disruptive, the digital seems to alter the artist's conceptualization and handling of these fundamental aspects of the approaches and methods of aesthetic practices. From the artist testimonials collected for this publication, artist Anne Senstad states: 'The digital allows me to intersect and interfere with space, large spaces, site-specificity, transformation of spaces, the psychological space, mobility, and physical displacement' (Anne Senstad, artist testimonial in this volume: 41) Artist Arijana Kajfes experiences a 'shift of materiality, time and space' working in the digital technological realm (Arijana Kajfes, artist testimonial in this volume: 42).

These practice-based perspectives on imbibing digital technology into the artistic production underscore a sense of uncanny, discomfort and uneasiness. This prevalent sense of 'the uncanny' comes from the observation that artists find themselves at the crossroad of changing the way artistic objects have been perceived and produced so far. The uneasiness also pertains to the possibility of leaving a secured comfort zone of established approaches and methods of working, as well as to experiencing artworks.

At the same time there is a sense of euphoria about unwrapping the possibilities that the digital offers. The artist duo Bombina Bombast (Emma Bexell and Stefan Stanisic) states: 'the digital has made us look out from our black box and search for other spaces than the given. The digital has meant for us a higher level of interaction and mobility'(Emma Bexell and Stefan Stanisic, artist testimonial in this volume: 43). The artist group IC-98 (Patrik Söderlund and Visa Suonpää) notes that: 'another important level of the digital is its infinite reproducibility' (IC-98, artist testimonial in this volume: 43). Artist Hrund Atladóttir states: 'The freedom and range of possibilities always pull me back into the digital' (artist testimonial in this volume: 36). While artist Jesper Carlsen claims that art 'has become more democratized' in the digital realm (Jesper Carlsen, artist testimonial in this volume: 44). New media theorists have also identified these aspects of digital media technology – namely interaction, mobility and reproducibility – for example Lev Manovich in his seminal works (Manovich 2001, 2013).

In the field of sound (art) production, with the advent of digital technology, widely available and easy-to-handle recording devices, applications and facilities have made various options and formats available to sound practitioners. Scholars of sound production

Tomlinson Holman and Mark Kerins inform us that digital sound systems (DSS) have introduced a number of creative possibilities, including significantly larger dynamic ranges in sound recording, a larger headroom (the amplitude above a designated reference level that a sound signal can handle before it distorts or clips), multi-channel formats, wider panning for sound spatialization and full-frequency channels (20 Hz–20 kHz) with a flatter response (Holman [1997] 2002; Kerins 2011). These capacities have made possible new production practices – a wider range of dynamics in sound as well as increased complexity in mixing and spatial fidelity (Kerins 2011) – while recording and processing the available depth, perspective and width of sound. Film scholar Vivian Sobchack takes account of 'shifts of emphasis and attention in both sound technology and our sensorium', predicting the future of sound production in terms of (digital) technological innovations to produce works rich in spatial dimensions stimulating a sonic sensorium (Sobchack 2005: 2). Creative practices with sound in the digital realm lead to new experiences in which audiences engage with sites and objects often through immersive listening, involving novel spatial engagements with sound.

As it is clear from these practical and conceptual considerations, in the digital realm, sound phenomena and the so-called sonic object or site often disentangle from each other, making sound's materiality a case for artistic intervention and transformation towards a virtual mode of spatial experience where the sensorium of the listener is triggered. Indeed, sound is more easily 'torn' from their objects, sites and sources in the digital realm and this condition contributes to the often uncanny and uneasy 'object-disorientation' of sound beyond geographical and sociocultural sites to be reconfigured into a new unsitely 'spatiality' in the hand of the artists (Schafer 1994).

Moreover, digital communication devices and technologies facilitate the condition of extensive nomadism of agents attuned to the psychogeographic evocation of physical locations and corporeal places in the post-globalized universe of intense mobility. In this universe, we encounter an immediate place and situate ourselves within it in ways that are intertwined; they are not only discreet physical experiences but sometimes appear as hybrid and syncretic environments. For example, my smartphone records sound from a place and sends it elsewhere to someone else via applications like WhatsApp; one place becomes merged with another as I overhear it in a Skype chat from someone far away, thus I move, migrate and navigate from one place to another *mentally* more than physically. The sonic interactions with these multiple sites through which I move and the expanded objects that I encounter, tend to be unfixed and evolving rather than having a concrete structure (Chattopadhyay 2013).

Status of the Site and Object in Sound Art After the Digital

In the field of contemporary (sound) art, the topics of site – as well as materiality and object-hood – have been challenged. In recent years, it is observed that sound-based art has seemed to move away from the digital and post-production sound in a turn back to emphasize the materiality of sound. Sound in these practices is not a transparent medium played through hidden speakers but is instead employed to investigate materials – and is itself produced through materials, such as field recordings that have various histories, including social, cultural, political, art historical, geological and ecological histories. However, one may ask if 'sound' can be 'exhibited' as an artistic object. It seems to be a basic fallacy considering the nature and characteristics of sound predominantly emerging as an ephemeral and immaterial phenomenon. The dichotomy between materiality of sound recording and immateriality embedded in personal listening experience problematizes the positioning of sound art in the contemporary field of artistic and curatorial practices demanding renewed inquiry into the complex relationship between sound and artistic objects within a context of digital technology's impacts on contemporary art. After the advent of digital technology this debate about sound's site-specificity and object-hood is intensified largely because sound is often easily dislocated beyond its sited source or object in a digital milieu, as I have argued earlier in this chapter.

In classical Sound Studies, scholars have already underpinned the issue of sound's problematic relation to its object or source and emphasized its interpretative nature following its production: 'Sound is not actualized until it reaches the ear of the hearer, which translates molecular movement into the sensation of sound' (Altman 1992: 19). Altman speaks here of a sound event as defining the trajectory of the essential production and subsequent reception of sound content. Its narrative, as Altman terms it, is hypothetically bound to the source that produces it. These spatial sources of sound, or the sounding object when producing sound, are spatially defined or connected to a place, but are not rendered until and unless they are carried by a medium (such as a tape recording) to reach the point of reception and subsequent interpretation. By the same token, a sound is remediated whenever it is digitally converted from its analogue recording source into the digital format. Digitization further dislocates sounds from their sources, turning them into discreet data in the nebulous post-digital environment as discussed before. Sound content enters the domain of digitalization – a condition of constant travel, flexibility and flow at different stages of digital mediation. This condition reaches saturation – a state that can be termed 'post-digital' – to denote a hybrid economy/ecology. In this process, sounds are freed from the object or source. As such, sounds, in the post-digital condition, imply mobility and subsequent object disorientation. However, the process of interpretation is more complex than it appears at its perceptual level. Contributing to this discourse on the sound object, new media scholar and theorist Frances Dyson suggests to 'first, find a way of discussing and representing sound unhinged from the visual object; second, find a device (the tape recorder) that will somehow enable such a representation; and finally, mask the mediation of that device by arguing for an ontological equivalence between the reproduced sound and the original sonic source' (2009: 54). This suggested ontological equivalence might be difficult for a listener to establish in a nomadic condition in which a specific sound presents a multitude of amorphous listening states inside the listener's mind, leading to a sonic explosion of site-unspecific and object-disoriented sensations and mood-based streams of contemplations outside the traditional settings of place and object, but inside a nomadic listener's consciousness.

The Emergence of Field Recording and Other (New) Spatial Practices

A 'field recording' employs the methodology of recording site-specific ambient sounds outside of the studio. The practice is also known as 'phonography' – a term used to signify its similarity to photography. Field recording was originally developed as part of a documentary approach in anthropological field research; it also stands analogous to location recording in filmmaking, albeit being largely controlled by the predominant narrative strategies of cinema. With the introduction of high-quality portable recording technologies after the digital revolution in the 1990s, it has subsequently become an independent and evocative art form in itself within the realm of sound art and new music. The current form of field recording practice often involves capturing of environmental sounds that vary between animal sounds from the remote corners of the wilderness to the everyday urban sounds subliminal in volume and low frequency in content; therefore, they tend to be complex in texture, tone and characteristics (Lane and Carlyle 2013). In response, artists have often pushed the technical limits of sound recording, demanding low noise and extended frequency response in portable, easy to use recording formats, ranging from high-resolution multi-track recording gadgets to self-made technologies of DIY contact microphones.[7] The emergence of digital technology actually made it possible to approach such recording techniques and methods. The digital era turned out to be an ideal situation for the emergence of field recording-based sound art, enabling diverse approaches to capturing sound from a site. After the advent of digital technology in the late 1990s, widely available and easy-to-handle digital sound recording devices, applications and facilities made various options and formats available to contemporary sound practitioners. As a sprawling practice in the contemporary realm, field recording-based sound art facilitates recording of sound on location with intricate details: deeper depth of field and wider dynamic range of frequency, including more precise, controlled and accurate documentary evidence of the site. These recording capacities allow for reaching out to the uncharted territories of the universe – including locations under water, below the ground, in the Amazonian forests, arctic landscapes and even in outer space.[8] Contemporary practices with sound are acclimatized by the saturation of digital technology in recording, production and reproduction. This condition gives birth to a new context that can be termed 'post-digital', characterized by intensifying technological convergence, aesthetic inclusivity and artistic freedom (Chattopadhyay 2014a; Cramer et al. 2014). In this post-digital territory, field recording is being amply advanced by recent developments in gadgets with multi-track recording options having greater flexibility, access to the farthest corners of the location and by applications with precise control over each recorded audio clip. Options for keeping numerous tracks open up possibilities for recording a larger number of sound elements and working with multiple layers of sound captured from a location. In the studio scenario, there are plenty of choices for processing sounds (digitally or with retro-aesthetic means, e.g. analogue) towards spatialization and multi-channel composition.

Sound art practices, such as noise-work and field recording, are facilitated by these post-digital processes resulting in sound's dislocation and object-disorientation (Chattopadhyay 2014a, 2017a). The representation of a site in the form of field recording tends to develop more into idiosyncratic, playful, and often subjective constructs of site and object-hood. These constructs are typically a result of intricate interplays between recognition of the site and its abstraction in the compositional stages, utilizing the digitally recorded sounds from the field as compositional ingredients or raw materials. Field recording-based sound artworks often transcend the Schaferean notion of typically site-specific (urban and rural) soundscapes and acoustic ecology.[9] These works neither give substantial importance to underscoring what Schafer refers to as stereotypical 'soundmarks' of the site, nor do they intend to enhance the 'ecological' discourse of differentiating between 'lo-fi' and 'hi-fi' environments of a site (Schafer 1994). These works, in my assumption, encourage a rather subjective interaction with the site. As Brandon LaBelle articulates: 'artistic production is but a mirror of the artist's own image: mimesis depicting interior states, psychological anxieties, euphoric hopes and ecstatic dreams. Art represents life at its most poignant, its most dramatic and its most memorable' (Labelle 2006: 212). The artist's own impression of a site as derived from the interaction with the site while doing field recording frames the selfhood to be inscribed in these sound artworks. The artist's subjectivity also reflects in the way these works are transformed and composed. What is unique is a distancing from an ontologically driven approach to a site; rather weaving it into an ambivalent reproduction that is open to multiple contingent interpretations. It is no surprise that sound scholar Joanna Demers finds sound in a contemporary artistic context 'a tantalizing phenomenon that simultaneously discloses and hides a great deal about its origin'. Her statement sheds light on the issues of estrangement and dissociation of the site-specificity and object-hood from digitally recorded sound in field recording practices and its composition in a sound artwork (Demers 2010: 115). These works demand the listener to participate and imaginatively construe new sites and objects upon listening, often experienced otherworldly and outside of the present.

Sound art indeed becomes overly perceptual and participatory in the (post-) digital milieu. A given auditory situation of a traditional exhibition or public showcasing of sound art appears to a drifting listener as liquid and amorphous. This ambivalence triggers and drives the aural imagination of the listener wherein the intended artefact posed in the foreground of the exhibition dissolves. In this context, the participation of the listener becomes a crucial factor for the artistic experience to be conveyed. Therefore, it becomes more important to create fertile auditory situations where sound can affect and activate a multiplicity of interpretations, experiences and moods in the listener's end than trying to pose a material object or artefact in its so-called 'exhibition' in situ.

If we take the ontologically questionable space of the exhibition as a critical juncture, a number of contemporary Nordic sound artists (e.g. Lars Lundehave Hansen, Jacob Kirkegaard and Christian Skjødt) process or intend to reorganize the conventional form of the exhibition as a space for participation and engagement. Lars Lundehave Hansen's recent works, such as *The Space Between the Silence* (2017), exemplify an effort to create an unsitely and object-disoriented parallel universe. The Danish artist converts the site of Møstings House, a small country house now used as an exhibition space in the Frederiksberg district of Copenhagen, to a world where time, causality, objective and spatial logic is suspended. Sound is manifested to create a new reality with dramatic effects that challenge the familiar senses of sited-ness and object-specificity.

In my own work as a sound artist, operating internationally with a primary base in Denmark, I intend to reconfigure the association of sound with the site and object, wherein I take a departure from the Schaferean soundscape.[10] I make an artistic intervention in the site and render a transformation of the sound object in the practice of field recording to produce an 'expanded object' in its composition as an artwork. Sound scholar Joanna Demers notes how in the field recording 'audio footage ties a soundscape composition to the ecological, social, historical or cultural dynamics of a specific location, which both personalizes and politicizes the act of listening' (2010: 120). What she means is that the material layers of ambient sound collected through field recording from a particular site always carry some documentary evidence. However, the composition of the field recording also allows the listener to personally engage with the construction of the site as an imaginary formation. To give the listener a fertile space or open-ended situation to listen in an engaged, re-embodied and subjective way, the artist's intervention in the site and its transformation into a new spatiality presents field recording as sound art beyond its immediate site-specific evidence.

My work *A Table is a Table* (2014) – exhibited in an underground basement as part of a show with the nomadic gallery Nålen in Copenhagen – takes our contemporary context as a point of departure to negotiate the above-mentioned divergence between the phenomenological and experiential aspects of listening and the material object-hood often demanded from the works of sound art. The work produces a site-specific installation of sound and found objects, employing digitally enhanced 'sonification',[11] to create fertile auditory situations that trigger the listener to interact more actively and associate with sounds beyond the immediate site and object into virtual territories. In this work, sonification transforms everyday objects into the realm of sound art by making them vibrate, augmenting and expanding their materiality in nuanced ways. In this project I intend to develop a series of installations that involves creation of a fluid auditory situation in a sonic sculptural form, involving playful sonification of found objects in situ to pose the problem of recognition. The works intend to underline the role of what Jean-Luc Nancy has called the 'listening subject' (Nancy 2007) by 'holding open the threshold between sense and signification' (Kane 2012). This process operates between dissemination of sonic artefacts and exploration of the perceptual and cognitive realm of listening, asking for participation and intervention of the listener.

My more recent work *Exile and Other Syndromes* (2016–17) responds to the current indisposition of migration, mobility, placeless-ness and nomadism, which are considered as impulses of a contemporary condition that eventually blurs the boundaries between the digital and the corporeal, between local and the global, or between private and enhanced access and freedom of the public domain, helping a nomadic subject to emerge as an elevated and emancipated self.[12] The project intends to examine these contemporary realities as manifesting in an augmented environment that incorporates multi-channel sound diffusion and visualization of field recordings in generated and live-modulated text. This generative and interactive methodology intends to develop fluid sculptural forms of sound intersected with sound-generated texts. The work transmutes the contemporary city's volatile, oppressing and tensed environments to reorient the navigational mode of listening by involving an elevated sense of poetic contemplation and transcendental thought-streams of the listener navigating the intercepting urban spaces. The work considers aspects of a 'deterritorialized' and nomadic mode of listening and explores its introspective capacities. Here I use the concept of 'deterritorialization' to denote the transcending of the local to be part of a trans-local context to develop new spatial narratives, drawing on the ideas of Deleuze and Guattari (1986, [1972] 2004). Transcending the barrier of immediate meaning of sound in terms of its site or object touches upon the poetic attributes of listening. The work was conceived in Copenhagen during 2012, and the fieldwork (site-specific sound recording) was conducted mostly in Denmark and other parts of Europe and Asia covering a period of over four years. The work was produced during my residency at Kunstuniversität Graz between September 2015 and January 2016; the pilot version was premiered at CUBE, Kunstuniversität Graz. The work relies on intuitive capacities of listening rather than the ontological and epistemological reasoning involved in deciphering the immediate meaning of sound. In seeking to make inward contemplation and subjectivity available to the wandering urban listeners, the work explores the poetic-contemplative possibilities embedded in everyday listening in the city to counter the neurosis of contemporary urban living. The particular emphasis on the poetic attributes of an expanded mode of listening provides a context for exploring the unexpected splendour of everyday urban sounds and their transcendental potential. Emergence of contingent moments in the urban listening experience expands the Cagian idea of chance composition towards a context of fluid and nomadic interaction with everyday sounds in contemporary cities.

Sounding the Outside: Analysis and Concluding Remarks

All of the above-mentioned works (by Lars Lundehave Hansen, Jacob Kirkegaard, Christian Skjødt and myself) have a common thread: They suggest a condition of deterritorialization manifested in a sense of site-unspecific otherworldliness as I have explained. As noted, Gilles Deleuze and Félix Guattari used the term 'deterritorialization' to describe the condition of the disembedding and re-embedding of social relations from various objects and sites (Deleuze and Guattari [1972] 2004). The term describes any process that decontextualizes a set of relations, rendering them remote and virtual and preparing them for more actualizations outside a fixed local territory. Many anthropologists use the term 'deterritorialized' to refer to a 'weakening of ties' between culture and place; meaning the removal of cultural subjects and objects from a certain location in space and time.

Deterritorialization implies that certain medial and cultural aspects tend to transcend specific territorial boundaries in a present world that consists of things, objects and places that are fundamentally in constant mobility, flux and transformation under the spectre of the contemporary condition. The intensified process of mediatization in present times works as a preferential source of deterritorialization, while it becomes a catalyst for other sources of deterritorialization (e.g. migration and mobility). As I have shown above, digital technology operates in the works of Nordic artists as a catalyst to push the established 'difference' between sites and objects towards facilitating a sense of fluidity dissolving the site-specificity and object-hood of sound. Often this condition provides a new spatial context for the audience/listener to come at the centre of experiencing an artwork by intervention and active participation. In other words, these works – made with the help of digital technologies – with 'post-digital' hybrid aesthetics are marked by multiple interpretations and multiple levels of meaning making at the listener's end.

As increasingly migratory beings, listeners wandering around in today's post-global cities, with post-digital mobile devices in their hands, are sensitive to contemporary urban sound navigating through various alienating and dehumanizing hybrid post-industrial urban spaces. They may consider these sounds as spatiotemporally evolving but gradually disorienting auditory situations, informed by real-time spatial information and juxtaposed with memory of another city in another time. The nomadic listener relates to these situations through contingent processes of contemplation and self-reflection prompted by the enhanced sense of mobility across various sites.

These constantly changing sites and landscapes tend to transcend the boundaries between global, local and discreet digital environments. Due to the extensive mobility, for a contemporary urban listener, the perception and cognition of sounds cannot be posited within a specific place-based source or object, nor can a locative identity be extracted from the sound because of its transient nature. As the nomadic movements intensify, it becomes difficult to relate oneself to one place at one time – the sense of 'rootedness' dissolves into a perpetual nomadism by itinerant sonic interaction with semi-known and/or unknown places and pseudo-locales perceived in the mind. In this nebulous cosmos of rapid flow, the interpretation of sound contents contributes to the formation of speculative notions like 'post-global', 'post-local' or 'post-digital' via the extensions of social networks, greater interactivity and multiple interpenetration and psychic personalization of (sound) media. These features result in an increase in flexibility and disembedding of sound contents from their sources as social acts beyond mere geographical limits and identities. Within the merging local-global boundaries, one culture develops constant awareness of the existence of another. Cultural components like sound recordings travel through this dispersed space in mutual interaction, influencing and infusing each other. These 'deterritorialized' wanderings substantially contribute to an emergent condition of primarily mobile and itinerant beings engaged in the liberated ebb and flow of events, phenomena and ephemera, which operate 'beyond digital essentialism' (Negroponte 1998; Cascone 2002).

For the uninitiated (Nordic) artists, thinkers, scholars and art goers who are resistant to change, contemporary (sound) art may 'sound' uncanny and may develop uneasy sensations in the context of the contemporary conditions marked by a globally dispersed flow of placeless and faceless data across open-ended national borders. However, an inclusive approach would render these artworks less uneasy – an expanded mode of listening would accommodate the unknown transcending the immediate site towards the virtual spaces and transform set objects into fluid situations. This is the context within which contemporary sound art breaks new grounds.

References

Altman, Rick (1992), *Sound Theory/Sound Practice*, New York: Routledge.

—— (2012), 'Four and a half film fallacies', in Jonathan Sterne (ed.), *The Sound Studies Reader*, London: Routledge, pp. 225–33.

Bjørnsten, Thomas Bøgevald (2012), 'Sound [signal] noise: Significative effects in contemporary sonic art practices', *Journal of Aesthetics & Culture*, 4:1, pp. 1–8.

Braidotti, Rosi (2012), *Nomadic Theory: The Portable Rosi Braidotti*, New York: Columbia University Press.

Cascone, Kim (2002), 'The aesthetics of failure: "Post-digital" tendencies in contemporary computer music', *Computer Music Journal*, 24:4, pp. 12–18.

Chattopadhyay, Budhaditya (2012), 'Sonic menageries: Composing the sound of place', *Organised Sound*, 17:3, pp. 223–29.

—— (2013), 'Auditory situations: Notes from nowhere', special issue, *Journal of Sonic Studies*, 4.

—— (2014a), 'Object-disoriented sound: Listening in the post-digital condition', *A Peer Reviewed Journal About Post-Digital Research*, 3:1, http://www.aprja.net/object-disoriented-sound-listening-in-the-post-digital-condition/. Accessed 6 June 2018.

—— (2014b), 'Sonic drifting: Sound, city and psychogeography', *SoundEffects*, 3:3, pp. 138–52.

—— (2017a), 'Beyond matter: Object-disoriented sound art', *Seismograf/DMT*, special issue: Sound Art Matters, November.

—— (2017b), 'Audible absence: Searching for the site in sound production', Ph.D. thesis, Leiden: Leiden University.

Contreras-Koterbay, Scott and Mirocha, Łukasz (2016), *The New Aesthetic and Art: Constellations of the Postdigital*, Amsterdam: Institute of Network Cultures.

Cox, Christoph (2009), 'Sound art and the sonic unconscious', *Organised Sound*, 14:1, pp. 19–26.

Cramer, Florian (2014), 'What is "post-digital"?', *A Peer-reviewed Journal About Post-Digital Research*, 3:1. http://www.aprja.net/what-is-post-digital/. Accessed 6 June 2018.

Dayal, Geeta (2013), 'Sound art', 6 August, http://www.theoriginalsoundtrack.com/2013/08/06/sound-art/. Accessed 10 March 2017.

Deleuze, Gilles and Guattari, Félix (1986), *Nomadology: The War Machine* (trans. B. Massumi), Cambridge: The MIT Press.

Deleuze, Gilles and Guattari, Félix ([1972] 2004), *Anti-Œdipus* (trans. R. Hurley, M. Seem and H. R. Lane), London and New York: Continuum.

Demers, Joanna (2009), 'Field recording, sound art and objecthood', *Organised Sound,* 14:1, pp. 39–45.

Demers, Joanna. (2010), *Listening through the Noise: The Aesthetics of Experimental Electronic Music,* New York: Oxford University Press.

Dyson, Frances (2009), *Sounding New Media: Immersion and Embodiment in the Arts and Culture,* California: University of California Press.

Helles, Rasmus and Jensen, Klaus Bruhn (2013), 'Introduction to the special issue – Making data: Big data and beyond', *First Monday,* 18:10, http://firstmonday.org/article/view/4860/3748. Accessed 5 September 2018.

Holman, Tomlinson ([1997] 2002), *Sound for Film and Television,* Boston: Focal Press.

Kallinikos, Jannis, Aaltonen, Aleksi and Marton, Attila (2010), 'A theory of digital objects', *First Monday,* 15:6, http://firstmonday.org/ojs/index.php/fm/article/view/3033/2564. Accessed 5 September 2018.

Kane, Brian (2012), 'Jean-Luc Nancy and the listening subject', *Contemporary Music Review,* 31:5–6, pp. 439–47.

Kim-Cohen, Seth (2009), *In the Blink of an Ear: Towards a Non-Cochlear Sonic Art,* New York and London: Bloomsbury.

Kimbell, Lucy (2013), 'The object fights back: An interview with Graham Harman', *Design and Culture,* 5:1, pp. 103–17.

Kelman, Ari Y (2010), 'Rethinking the soundscape: A critical genealogy of a key term in sound studies', *Senses and Society,* 5:2, pp. 212–34.

Kerins, Mark (2011), *Beyond Dolby (Stereo): Cinema in the Digital Sound Age,* Bloomington: Indiana University Press.

LaBelle, Brandon (2006), *Background Noise: Perspectives on Sound Art,* New York: Bloomsbury Academic.

LaBelle, Brandon and Martinho, Claudia (eds) (2011), *Site of Sound: Of Architecture and the Ear,* vol. 2, Berlin: Errant Bodies Press.

Lane, Cathy and Carlyle, Angus (eds) (2013), *In the Field: The Art of Field Recording,* London: Uniformbooks.

Manovich, Lev (2001), *The Language of New Media,* Cambridge: The MIT Press.

—— (2013), *Software Takes Command,* New York: Bloomsbury Academic.

Metz, Christian (1980), 'Aural objects' (trans. G. Gurrieri), in Altman, Rick (ed.), *Yale French Studies 60: Cinema/Sound,* New Haven: Yale University Press, pp. 24–32.

Nancy, Jean-Luc (2007), *Listening* (trans. C. Mandell), New York: Fordham University Press.

Negroponte, Nicholas (1998), 'Beyond digital', *Wired,* 6:12, https://www.wired.com/1998/12/negroponte-55/. Accessed 6 June 2018.

Schafer, R. Murray (1994), *The Soundscape: Our Sonic Environment and the Tuning of the World,* Rochester: Destiny Books.

Smith, Frederick Key (2002), *Nordic Art Music: From the Middle Ages to the Third Millennium,* Westport: Greenwood Publishing Group.

Sobchack, Vivian (2005), 'When the ear dreams: Dolby digital and the imagination of sound', *Film Quarterly*, 58:4, pp. 2–15.

Vandsø, Anette (2011), 'Listening to the world: Sound, media and intermediality in contemporary sound art', *SoundEffects*, 1:1, pp. 68–81.

―――― (2015), 'Music, sound art and context in a post-Cagean era', *Seismograf/DMT*, www.seismograf.org/node/6605. Accessed 10 March 2017.

Notes

1 Gilles Deleuze and Félix Guattari coined the term 'deterritorialization' in *Anti-Oedipus* (1972) to refer broadly to the fluid, dissipated and schizophrenic nature of human subjectivity in contemporary capitalist societies. In a broad sense, deterritorialization has connections with the idea of the 'disembedding' of social relations if globalization is understood in cultural-spatial terms.

2 Some everyday sounds may suggest transcendental experiences beyond their intended immediate meaning or sonic object-hood. I have argued elsewhere (Chattopadhyay, 2014a, 2017a) that such experiences are intensified when the listener is in a mobile and deterritorialized mode of listening to opening up the experience for multiple interpretations beyond a specific place, such as in the digital or virtual domain. The listener is almost certain to simultaneously create imagined gestures or link a sound to its illusory myriad of sources, evoking some kind of contemplative and thoughtful imagery in this process of mental resonance and personalization of sounds into poetic-contemplative listening states. I coin this condition as 'object-disorientation' to underscore a sound's multiple meanings and manifold usage accross places, situations and listening contexts.

3 I have discussed this issue of the disruption of the sound and object relationship after the coming of the digital in artistic production, in a number of my writings (Chattopadhyay 2013, 2014a, 2015).

4 As I have shown in my article 'Object-disoriented sound: Listening in the post-digital condition' (Chattopadhyay 2014a), contemporary urban sounds often present a multitude of amorphous listening states inside an itinerant listener's mind, leading to a sonic explosion of object-disoriented but mood-based streams of thoughts within the nomadic listener's consciousness.

5 Seth Kim-Cohen diagnoses this conceptual turn in sound art after the groundbreaking intervention of Marcel Duchamp. He states, '(S)ince the 1960s, art has foregrounded the conceptual, concerning itself with questions that the eye alone cannot answer, questions regarding the conditions of art's own possibility. The conceptual turn is not intrinsically an inward turn from gaze to navel gaze. Instead, conceptualism allows art to volunteer its own corpus, its own ontology, as a test case for the definition of categories. […] A conceptual sonic art would necessarily engage both the non-cochlear and the cochlear, and the constituting trace of each in the other'. (2009: xxi)

6 In their work 'A Theory of Digital Objects', Jannis Kallinikos, Aleksi Aaltonen, and Attila Marton claim that 'digital objects are marked by a limited set of variable yet generic

attributes such as editability, interactivity, openness and distributedness that confer them a distinct functional profile'. This leads to a profound sense of 'instability' as evasive and fleeting artifacts that contrast with the solid and self-evident nature of already-old sound media, such as sound recordings on tape, CD, file systems, or other types of storage. The fluid and mutating nature of that universe of digital objects and their diffusion across the social fabric makes them difficult to authenticate, preserve, or archive in the social memory and knowledge base. The elusive flow of digital objects, carrying a multitude of sound contents, problematize their (sound's) object-hood, rendering them more as ephemera than even discreet artifacts (Chattopadhyay 2014a: 4).

7   As an example, Danish sound artist Jacob Kirkegaard uses various kinds of contact mics.

8   Examples are the field recording works of Andrea Polli and the NASA sound archive.

9   I have shown in my recent writings (2017) that the Schaferean notion of the soundscape has had a particular aim 'to draw attention to imbalances which may have unhealthy or inimical effects' (Schafer 1994: 271). This 'moralizing' tendency can be problematic while discussing sound art.

10   Ari Kelman (2010) in particular has been a strong critic of the idea of soundscape as conceptualised by Schafer.

11   *Sonification* refers to the emerging areas of sound practice such as VR, sonic interaction design, HCI, and Augmented Reality, where the term has been used in reference to novel approaches to auditory practice that convey information, meaning, and spatial qualities in the interactive context of media art environments

12.   The full version of the work was exhibited (for multichannel sound and 3-channel live visuals) at the Rogaland Kunstsenter as part of the Screen City Biennial, Stavanger, Norway, 12–31 October 2017.

Reformulations of the 'Natural' World: Jana Winderen's Sound Installation *The Wanderer*

Ulla Angkjær Jørgensen

In his lecture 'Waiting for Gaia', French philosopher and anthropologist Bruno Latour evokes the question of the sublime. Today there are no places left on Earth untouched by human hand and therefore no possibility for experiencing the sublime wonders of nature, he says. This is due to the fact that:

> Nature is no longer what is embraced from a faraway point of view where the observer could ideally jump to see things 'as a whole', but the assemblage of contradictory entities that have to be composed together. [...] We can still feel the sublime, but only for what is left of nature *beyond* the Moon and only when we occupy a View from Nowhere. Down below, no longer any sublime.
>
> (Latour 2012)

The idea of a sublime nature, which we have inherited from Romanticism as something wilder and greater than our comprehension, something beyond the reach of human hand and mind, in which we can seek comfort away from the burdens of civilization, no longer fits in with reality. Today, 'nature' is scientific data and we are left feeling disconnected from our own nature and *umwelt* on the edge of ecological catastrophe. One of Latour's cures for this imbalance is aesthetics; according to him we need to connect to the world and this can only happen through a heightened attention to sensory perception (Latour 2012).

In the present chapter, I want to ask in which ways technological works of art can help humans connect to the *umwelt*. Contemporary art is becoming increasingly engaged in problems of climate change, but how can works produced for the art sphere ever hope to help solve global ecological problems?[1] The Norwegian artist Jana Winderen (b.1965) – with a background in the biological sciences – also worries about the ecological imbalance on earth. Her participation in the *Dark Ecology* project in Northern Norway 2014–16 is a testimony of her concern (Dark Ecology Official Website 2016). She designs local spaces of aesthetic experience from sounds recorded in nature, but unperceivable to the naked human ear. Her audio-visual works are assemblages of information data made available to local listening in art installations and online. Her work includes soundscapes in different formats, only I will take a look at the sound installation *The Wanderer*, created by invitation for the Norwegian Lorck Schive Art Prize in 2015.[2]

To understand this genre of art, another of Latour's concepts will prove useful. To think of the artwork as a quasi-object, an object bridging different fields of information and competence and addressing audiences in and outside the art institution seems more in line with this genre than clinging to art as mere concept. Jana Winderen's works are produced with and performed by technological means and they spring from her knowledge as a student of biology. Furthermore, the art gallery (or museum) is only one platform among others where she lets her soundscapes be performed.

In which ways do technological renditions of sounds take part in aesthetic reformulations of human-nature relations? Or, to formulate it in a more adequate way for the present purpose, how can they be seen to be locally produced and experienced connections with the *umwelt*? If we are indeed living in the Anthropocene, we need, as many are quite aware of, to think beyond the nature-culture divide and technology-human binary to envision a future for humans and fellow beings.

Science, Technology and Art

Winderen's soundscapes are technological works that problematize the modern concept of nature as a pure phenomenon and something radically different from culture, science and technology. They are good examples of Latour's hybrids and quasi-objects that make the division between man-made objects and given phenomena obsolete. But they also challenge the modern concept of art as a linguistic utterance produced only for the discursive field of an isolated art scene in order to *speak* critically about what goes on 'out there' in the world. Winderen's works are, of course, part of the discursive field of contemporary art but they are also *real* objects having *real* effects on *real* bodies. They push the boundary of art in the direction of a technological aesthetics that seems preoccupied with addressing environmental issues through the sensuousness of the body in an environment and they challenge the frame of the gallery.

Winderen's works belong to different spheres that cannot solely be spoken off in discursive and representative terms. They are not conceptual in character but more like aesthetic environments in themselves. But how are we to think of these hybrids? Latour is critical of the hegemonic status of semiotics in the humanities and social sciences because the linguistic sign cannot count for the complexity of quasi-objects. He writes:

> The various forms of semiotics offer an excellent tool chest for following the mediations of language. But by avoiding the double problem of connections to the referent and connections to the context, they prevent us from following the quasi-object to the end. These latter, as I have said, are simultaneously real, discursive, and social. They belong to nature, to the collective, and to discourse.
>
> (Latour 1993: 64)

The material world cannot be divided according to binary oppositions. Accordingly, if we try to envision the world corresponding to French philosophers Gilles Deleuze and Félix Guattari we get a sort of multi-dimensional grid where everything can intersect with everything; and with Latour in mind you could say that these intersections are where quasi-objects appear. In this perspective, there are no universal hierarchy of orders; language never has universality in itself or form a metalanguage (Deleuze and Guattari [1987] 2002: 111ff.). It belongs to the material world like any other regime of signs. Nor do Deleuze and Guattari base their system on a divide between nature and culture where nature is something pre-existing culture, in fact, they do not talk much of nature and culture.

When Winderen sets out to record sounds in a given environment with all her equipment, she works as a scientist on fieldwork. She collects her material in places (micro-cosmoses) where humans never go, but which are all touched by human interference one way or another. She moves her microphones and hydrophones across micro-territories, recording sounds of materials, animals and microorganisms from the most unlikely places on earth, inside ice glaciers and crevasses, and underneath the deep-sea. But as she says, no sound milieu is pure natural and cleansed from the sounds produced by human intervention. Afterwards she samples and manipulates her soundscapes on a computer. Unlike the British Library Sounds project, which separates natural from cultural categories, Winderen's project is about the compound quality of the sound environment. The British Library points out that it was composer R. Murray Shafer that coined the term *soundscape* and quotes G. Wagstaff for defining a soundscape as sounds that 'describe a place, a sonic identity, a sonic memory, but always a sound that is pertinent to a place' (British Library Sounds Official Website 2016). The British Library's project is a preservation project and it seems that a soundscape to them is something essential formed by the connection of certain sounds to a particular place. To Winderen, a soundscape is different.[3]

In digital postproductions, she composes compelling sound assemblages that form soundscapes in their own right. Each soundscape is a compilation of material from diverse biotopes and does not refer to one specific place. They form intersections of different matter; they are hybrids. For instance, *The Wanderer* is a sound installation of sixteen channels in which the viewer-listener finds herself immersed in a roar and rumble from Zooplankton and Phytoplankton recorded in the Atlantic Ocean between the North Pole and the Equator. It is an everywhere and a nowhere, a place and an event that only materialize for the human ear in this particular work. The 'places' of *The Wanderer* are the different social situations it produces at different times and in different locations with and for different listeners. For example, I have experienced it twice under different circumstances at Trondheim Art Museum, one time alone and one time with a group of students. But I have also bought a digital copy online that I listen to on my computer. This work comes both as an audio-visual installation and as an audible file. It can be listened to in diverse settings like any other piece of music, or you listen to it like you read a book.

The Wanderer, Soundscape and Interface

At Trondheim Art Museum, you found yourself experiencing the piece in a dark room, where a dim light shone from the glass coffered ceiling. This was a specific visual and sensuous setting that promoted the idea of being under water. You could barely see the two benches at the centre of the room covered with blankets and inviting you to sit down. The space was darkly lit in order for the viewer to concentrate on listening. You found yourself immersed in a deep and strange soundscape provided by sixteen loudspeakers around the wall base. The utilization of the glass ceiling was a given yet intelligent feature to convey an underwater experience, the glass ceiling serving as the surface of the sea and supported by the dark painted walls of the room. You would hear different strange sounds, some deep and resonant, some crackling waterish, some reminded of whales singing, some were silent and sizzling, some would come out distant like a wind going down. In between, breaks of silence would appear but also deep, loud and resonating sounds from a hollow space. Creepy-crawly sounds made you think of insects, blowing sounds of a faraway wind, but there were also metallic sounds, honking sounds or the resonating sound of rolling bodies of water, and howling and whistling, and even sounds of almost melodic quality. Though I am trying here to establish the sounds as distinct entities, they would intermingle and form an assemblage. Altogether, this was not a sound environment known to you beforehand, it was not a representation of something in the least familiar.

The sound installation created spaces through the fading of foreground and background, like a modernist painting experimenting with space on the picture plane. The space would stretch and contract. The deep roaring sounds increasing in intensity would hit your stomach while the high sizzling sounds spoke to the upper regions of your body. The soundscape stimulated an evocative and physical experience, yet the ephemerality of sound was insistent in the flows of different sounds coming and going. It was an entirely unexpected experience, but most strikingly what hit you was how the sounds stood out almost material in character and how you found yourself embraced by the utterly plasticity of the whole thing. It was almost a literal illustration of Deleuze and Guattari's idea of the work of art as 'a bloc of sensations, a compound of percepts and affects' (Deleuze and Guattari [1991] 1994: 64). This was because the sounds had a thingish quality about them, they stood out as 'thing-sounds'. To Deleuze and Guattari the artwork is sensory becoming, an event that happens in the here and now. It does not refer to anything prior to its own existence; it does not represent. Yet it is composed by someone – a human being – who knows perceptions and affections for he 'himself is a compound of percepts and affects' (Deleuze and Guattari [1991] 1994). In Deleuze and Guattari's theory, percepts and affects are condensations of perceptions and affections, and they are realized and come together through materials in the work of art.

There may be a conceptual side to art too, but this is not what constitutes art, the conceptual side is secondary according to Deleuze and Guattari. Even so-called concept art is determined by its sensorial constitution; this is what makes it art and not just idea. Jana Winderen had framed her work in conceptual terms at the entrance, because she wanted to remind the visitor about the environmental state of the oceans. And in so doing she addressed the discursive field of contemporary environmental debate. She had written two statements:

1. The world's marine population have halved since 1970
2. Phytoplankton produce half of all oxygen on Earth

But these statements did not explain the soundscape, nor were they a prerequisite for the work. They were occasional statements and taken together with the experience of the work they would guide the visitor into thinking about it along certain lines. My argument for the work's environmental modus operandi lies not in this linguistic message, but in its aesthetic and sensory ways of taking place. The reformulation of the 'natural' world lies neither in the representational nor in the conceptual register, but in its digital aesthetics. Deleuze and Guattari's thinking about art is fruitful because it allows for the work of art to be a result of sensations unfolding over time through material and as part of that same process, to be material passing through sensation to become art (Deleuze and Guattari [1991] 1994: 173). The digital process facilitates the captured sensations to become art through their digital materialization and the material to become yet more sensations. *The Wanderer* is a bloc of affects and percepts that constantly multiply. The installation forms an interface for exchange between two levels of sensorial activity, events that already have taken place and some that are about to take place. The 'captured' percepts and affects are technological, processed into new percepts and affects. This interfacial level is where the viewer/listener is activated. I will come back to this, but first I will characterize the special milieu created by the installation.

Sound and Space: An Atmosphere

I will use German philosopher Gernot Böhme's term 'atmosphere' to describe what the acoustic artwork produces and why it is appropriate to call it a soundscape. Winderen's own reflections on sound and human perceptions of sound are accurate: 'The sensory impression of sound is very physical. Depending on the materials around you, you can feel it in your bones, or as a sensation in your nostrils, or vibrating under your feet' (Winderen cited in London 2013). She is describing synesthetic experience, the interaction between the hearing capabilities and feelings in the body's muscular and bone structure. Her physical understanding of synaesthesia is a precise description of Böhme's idea of synaesthesia as concrete perceptions and the precondition for the production of atmosphere. In his understanding, synaesthesia is not metaphoric and has nothing to do with language – though the traditional understanding of synaesthesia in western thought is linguistic (Böhme 2001: 87ff). Rather, synaesthesia is the precondition for what he understands as atmospheres (Böhme 2001: 96).

Atmosphere is the primary object of perception, but it is more on the side of the thing than the 'I', meaning that it is more of an objective phenomenon than it is of subjective origin. You sense an atmosphere affectively when it hits you, Böhme declares (Böhme 2001: 45–46). However, there is also some ambiguity attached to the concept, for another place he states that: 'Atmosphere is something between the subject and the object; therefore, aesthetics of atmosphere must also mediate between the aesthetics of reception and of production' (Böhme 2014: 43). So, if one is to conclude on the somewhat sliding usage of terms, I would say that atmosphere is the production of space by means of synaesthesia. Atmospheric space is produced with or without human interference, this is its objective origin, but synaesthesia is also experienced in/with the human body and this is its subjective origin, which makes it 'something between the subject and the object', in Böhme's wording. It might even be a quasi-object in my opinion. I would prefer to say that it is not a matter of 'in between' but rather a case of two sense regimes that meet and form a specific hybrid event. *The Wanderer* is a soundscape because it produces an aesthetic sense of space through sounds, something that can also be called an atmosphere.

Winderen's soundscape reformulates the idea of a biotope because it brings different 'natural' biotopes together in new constellations to form other 'natures', or it multiplies a normative and universal sense of nature. Nature appears to be sensorial exchange but it also seems to be the physical experiences of the audience. Nature's place is no longer 'out there' far away from culture and the museum. Nature is right here. Or, one could also take a critical position and claim that nature is no longer an appropriate term as it requires its cultural other.

The Viewer's Part

So far, *The Wanderer* has shown that the idea of a 'pure' and 'pristine' nature far away and outside human cultural environments is problematic. But there is also the perspective of the viewer, whose experience I was beginning to develop earlier. For when talking about art it is hard to disregard the fact that humans are involved, both as producers and recipients. There is always an experiential side to an artwork and at times this quality is considered an asset by the artist. With *The Wanderer*, Winderen has gone to some length to make the viewer aware of his or her presence in the particular environment a sound installation is. In painting the room dark and placing the benches at the centre, she had staged a specific relation between artwork and viewer to focus attention on the listening body in an atmosphere. She had paved the way for a certain phenomenological experience of the installation. The phenomenological perspective shows itself to be relevant in this particular situation because it acknowledges that humans are part of nature as well as culture; the phenomenological perspective situates the human body at the crossroads between 'nature' and 'culture' and focuses on the human body's perception of its nearest surroundings.

According to American philosopher Ted Toadvine, phenomenology invites a 'Janus-faced aspect of perceptual experience' that accounts for the fact that 'nature is in us as well as outside us' (Toadvine 2010: 353–55). Following Merleau-Ponty's phenomenology of perception, Toadvine outlines how the human body and the perceived thing enter in a kind of 'coition', in which the same properties are revealed in both thing and body, the perceived thing acts as a 'correlative' to my body Toadvine (2010: 354). This, our perceptual reciprocity with the thing, shows the nature in the human condition as well as the nature outside the human. It complicates the problematic binary opposition of nature versus culture, for the human experience of the natural world is also always marked by cultural influence. When

I experience a tree with my whole sensory apparatus, I recognize its perceptual qualities because they correspond with my bodily apparatus, i.e. its 'nature'. But at the same time, I meet the tree through images of trees from paintings I know, postcards, etc. and perhaps it reminds me of a table I once owned or a memory from somewhere else. I meet the tree with cultural inscriptions that are specific to my personal history and to the culture I live in (education, gender, class, television, arts and so forth). There is no unfiltered perception, but cultural inscriptions and perceptions together form my specific experience of a particular situation. As my sensation of the tree gets filtered through images of trees from visual culture, my image of the tree gets filtered through my perceptions in a situation, in the atmosphere that surrounds the tree.

It is this ability to 'hold together the two horns of our seemingly paradoxical experience of nature' that, according to Toadvine, makes phenomenology such an apt tool for environmental thought (2010: 348). On the one hand, nature is that, which reveals itself to us through our own experience of it; on the other hand, nature presents itself to us as autonomous and independent other, something prior to our understanding of it. Moreover, we are situated within it as well as emerging from it; it is our existential, but paradoxical backdrop.

A Sonic Aesthetics

In my experience of *The Wanderer* I was placed in a situation where my immediate cultural references were of little help. My previous attempts to give language to the sound assemblage shows how unfamiliar its aesthetics appeared to me, however, my poor attempts also prove just how persistent the human mind works to come to terms with the unknown and express it in familiar language; my cultural inscriptions did not fail me. It seems fair to assume that Winderen wished to convey the strangeness and beauty of the unseen in her work, after all this is one of art's classical objectives and I am convinced that those who sat down trying to take in this unfamiliar soundscape would most likely have found both its beauty and its strangeness. This would also be possible to explain within a phenomenological approach, for as Toadvine stresses, one of nature's qualities is 'its alien and reticent withdrawal before our perceptual grasp' (2010: 349). There is always some extent to which the stone will 'hold back' its 'stoneness' from my experience, even in our shared 'co-natural' existence, meaning that there is more to nature than is perceivable to the human sensory apparatus. 'Wildness is the backside of every perception and experience', says Toadvine (2010: 349). This could to some extent serve as a plausible explanation for beauty, but to my temper it leans too heavily on ideas of idealism and essentialism.

I would rather turn to Deleuze and Guattari's dynamic sign pragmatics to see what goes on in/with this particular artwork and how aesthetics emerge. With Deleuze and Guattari one could claim that *The Wanderer* is an 'abstract machine' and displays an 'assemblage'. The abstract machine is a sort of generator in the semiotic process; it is a moment where matter gets activated, it is a level of potentiality. '[The abstract machine] or diagrammatic machine has a piloting role [...] it does not function to represent, but constructs a real that is yet to come, a new type of reality' (Deleuze and Guattari [1987] 2002: 142). At an abstract level, it is a device that transforms matter. This is what *The Wanderer* does to the digital material it is fed with, but it also performs to us, the audience, an assemblage of a-signifying signs, signs that do not belong to a conventional signifying regime. *The Wanderer* plays its small part in the endless transformations of semiotic systems and shows the material basis of some signs. It displays the process where material gets transformed into aesthetics and cultural form. For instance, technology becomes part of the aesthetic expression by expanding the natural world perceived by the human body. Technology is not just a vehicle for recording and playing sound, it is integrated in the digital aesthetics and the soundscape's creation of a new register of sonic signs. The dynamic sign pragmatic approach is illuminating because it explains how art takes part in the continuing creation and transformation of semiotic systems, in this case a sonic aesthetics.

Conclusions

Latour's outrage against the concept of nature comes as a last-minute cry for help on behalf of the planet. With his laconic, provocative and double bind critique of nature, he calls for a realist concept that focuses on the planet's ecological balance and is able to gather common ground among different sciences and policies. The problem with the present understanding of nature is that it is too big, too 'pure' and too historically tainted, and therefore not very helpful in developing long-term solutions for the global ecological crisis. One problem is that our present understanding of nature excludes technology leaving it on culture's side. This is a problem as technology is part of the solution. We need to acknowledge that technology is not in opposition to 'nature'.

Like Latour, Böhme is critical of the modern nature-culture divide, only he calls for a return to aesthetics of nature (*Naturästhetik*) that got lost in the modern separation of spheres. When Latour welcomes hybrids, or quasi-objects, Böhme returns to nature. In his environmental aesthetics, nature is nature as it appears *to us humans*, as we sense and perceive it; it is not nature as an object of science as in the natural sciences (Böhme 2001: 23). Böhme's philosophy is like Latour's: a reaction to the huge environmental problems all earthlings face now and in the future, and like Latour he takes aesthetics to be part of the cure. Only, in his thinking, aesthetics is to begin with part of nature. Even though he turns to aesthetics of nature, he is also critical of the traditional divide between nature and culture, 'We are already living in a cultural and civilized nature' he says, and he emphasises the point with his notion of atmosphere that he calls 'environmental aesthetics' (Wang 2014).

In Winderen's demonstration of how technology, on the one hand, enhances the human sensory register and, on the other, opens up to new aesthetics, her work takes part in the reformulation of the 'natural' world as well as points to the fact that humans are undisputedly dependent on and immersed in the surrounding world. Her works make it clear that technology is no antithesis to 'nature', rather its natural extension, and that scientific data easily transform to aesthetics. Art has moved beyond the classical limits defined by form, image and meaning, as well as the enunciation paradigm or institutional theory that dominated twentieth-century theory on art. Today artists participate in the creation of events that open up to techno-aesthetic diversity in and outside the walls of the museum.

References

Böhme, Gernot (2001), *Aithetik. Vorlesungen über Ästhetik als allgemeine Wahrnehmungslehre*, Paderborn: Wilhelm Fink Verlag.

—— (2014), 'Urban atmospheres: Charting new directions for architecture and urban planning', in C. Borch (ed.), *Architectural Atmospheres: On the Experience and Politics of Architecture*, Basel: Birkhäuser, pp. 42–59.

British Library Sounds Official Website (2016), 'Soundscapes', https://sounds.bl.uk/Sound-Maps/Soundscapes. Accessed 3 January 2018.

Dark Ecology Official Website (2016), www.darkecology.net. Accessed 3 January 2018.

Deleuze, Gilles and Guattari, Félix ([1987] 2002), *A Thousand Plateaus: Capitalism and Schizophrenia* (trans. B. Massumi), London: Continuum.

—— ([1991] 1994), *What Is Philosophy?* (trans. G. Burchell and H. Tomlinson), London and New York: Verso.

Latour, Bruno ([1991] 1993), *We Have Never Been Modern* (trans. C. Porter), New York: Harvester Wheatsheaf.

—— (2012), 'What does it mean to bring the fate of the Earth into daily politics?', International Center for Climate Governance, Venice, 14 September 2012, https://www.youtube.com/watch?v=oSLBVabDgF4. Accessed 3 January 2018.

—— (2015), 'Waiting for Gaia: Composing the common world through arts and politics', in A. Yaneva and A. Zaera-Polo (eds), *What Is Cosmopolitical Design?* Farnham: Ashgate, pp. 21–33, www.bruno-latour.fr/node/446. Accessed 3 January 2018.

Lazzarato, Maurizio (2014), *Signs and Machines: Capitalism and the Production of Subjectivity*, Cambridge: The MIT Press.

London, Barbara (ed.) (2013), *Soundings: A Contemporary Score*, New York: MoMA.

Toadvine, Ted (2010), 'Ecophenomenology and the resistance of nature', in T. Nenon and P. Blosser (eds), *Advancing Phenomenology: Essays in Honor of Lester Embree*, Dordrecht and New York: Springer, pp. 343–55.

Wang, Zhoufei (2014), 'An interview with Gernot Böhme', *Contemporary Aesthetics*, 12, www.contempaesthetics.org/newvolume/pages/article.php?articleID=713. Accessed 3 January 2018.

Notes

1 Among recent exhibitions on the topic of climate change, see *Rethink Relations* (National Gallery of Denmark, 2009) and *Hybrid Matters* (Nikolaj Kunsthal, Copenhagen, 2016), and art projects *Biospheres* by artist Tómas Saraceno.

2 Jana Winderen's *The Wanderer* (2015) is available at: www.janawinderen.bandcamp.com/album/the-wanderer

3 There is an art historical point in using the term 'soundscape' as opposed to sound installation, which I use for the specific installation in the museum. The term soundscape automatically associates with the traditional art historical genre of landscape painting and the work therefore also contributes to the reformulation of a well-known genre.

The Intertwining of the Digital and the Biological in Artistic Practice

Laura Beloff

In the last two decades, we have witnessed a gradual shift observable in the approaches of artists working with technology. This shift can be characterized as moving from the digital and virtual realm towards the physical world. More recently, this can be seen in terms of an inclusion of the biological realm into experiments and artworks that address a wide range of technological developments and their impact on society. Many of the artists working in this field – broadly termed 'art and science' – have a background in digital arts. This chapter traces specifically the emerging inclusion of the biological realm into the technology-based arts as a trajectory towards which the field of digital art appears to be developing.

Given that readers of this chapter probably have general knowledge about digital and technology-based art as an existing field, it focuses primarily on artistic interests that involve biological organisms and living matter in combination with technology. The trajectory is introduced through the actors and milestones in the development of Nordic new media art. It continues with examples of Nordic works, artists and active organizers who are working with a combination of digital and biological matter. The chapter divides the artistic examples into works that focus on the environment and those that focus on humans as biological organisms. Underlying the chapter is my first-hand experience in the Nordic development of new media art and my recent interest in, specifically, biological matter with digital technology. This development has two historical predecessors: one is based on the traditions of art and technology; the other is based on the traditions of landscape art and earth works. The chapter addresses our evolving understanding of concepts such as real, natural and artificial, as well as biological and technological.

The Existing Relationship Between the Technological and the Biological in Art

The employment of biological and living matter in artworks has a long history in art, as does art that incorporates technology, yet these two categories are typically considered separate genres. Technology-based art, or new media art, produces works that are based in digital media, including interactive installations, network art, physical computing works, wearable technology design, and many others. Art history presents examples of artworks and genres that employ biological matter, such as environmental art, eco art, land art and other single experiments. Recently, we have seen novel developments that combine biological and living matter with technological approaches and structures. These novel artistic interests are strongly influenced by developments in technology and the sciences in general. For example, in recent years, we have witnessed a rapid advancement in synthetic biology and biotechnology at large. Moreover, there are also revived interests in technological development that has its roots in the biological world, including areas such as evolutionary computation, machine learning and bio-inspired robotics. All these practices – from synthetic biology to bio-inspired computation – have characteristics that are creationist and grounded within approaches in engineering. Comparable approaches are also present in art and design. Ingeborg Reichle has argued that with the recently developed field of bioart, biotechnology has now become part of the art world; this has consequently raised many questions about biology being treated as technology, and about ethics of manipulating living organisms (Reichle 2014). Both art and science that concern living biological organisms are in some way dealing with manipulation of life – or creation of life from scratch, as the popular synthetic biology slogan claims. One of the differences in their approaches is that the artistic side typically focuses on ethical, critical and philosophical questions concerning this line of work, whereas the scientific approach is typically focused on concrete problem-solving tasks.

Finnish art and science pioneers Antero Kare and Erkki Kurenniemi are two good examples of the earlier generation of practices. Antero Kare is an artist and pioneer in the field of bioart. He started working with micro-organisms in the mid-1980s, and conducted investigations on them in various science labs, which he visited as an artist. He has used bacteria with specific colours as living paint in his artworks. Kare's primary interests have focused on 'deep time', a concept of geological time, which is visible in his artistic practice and interests. More recently, he has also included video, light and media technology as part of his installations that use bacterial growth. Nevertheless, the core of his work concerns biological and geological investigations (Kare 2013).

Erkki Kurenniemi was a Finnish artist, inventor, scientist and techno-visionary whose works and experiments assessed the impact of new technologies on the evolution of human beings (Huhtamo 2003). His body of work from the 1960s and 1970s includes experimental short films, computer graphics, electronic music recordings and theories about the mathematical foundations of harmonies. He also designed and constructed several digital musical instruments in a series called *DIMI*. These experimental works address ideas such as real-time transmission of data and the use of technology as a basis for art practice, and have a clear relation to cybernetics; they also anticipated interactive installation and performance art by several years (Huhtamo 2003). Some of Kurenniemi's experimental works cross over to the biological side through focusing on humans and including them as a core element. For instance, his interactive musical instruments were controlled through biofeedback: *Dimi-S* (1972) was based on the electrical conductivity of skin, while *Dimi-T* (1973) measured the electrical activity of the brain (Wikipedia 2016).

Also visible in the examples of artists given above is a division of artistic interests that concern biological matter, which are categorized into two fields: works that focus on humans and works that are focused on the environment (Beloff, Berger and Haapoja 2013). This division is still visible in many of the works produced today, albeit to a lesser degree. For example, there are works that address climatic and environmental changes caused by human actions, and works that address human existence, adaptation and survival in the changing environment. These kinds of works address the contemporary worldly conditions of humans, their habitat and their actions, and are often coloured with technological practices.

I call works and practices which combine technological and biological actors 'techno-organic'. I have previously defined the term in relation to art as the merging of technology and organic matter, which may include humans, non-humans and the environment (Beloff 2012). Techno-organic practices can refer to developments that increasingly reshape the boundaries between the technological and the biological. This new term allows one to think about single entities that are a conglomerate of biological and technological aspects and actors. For example, Roy Ascott has been a long-term proponent of what he calls the 'syncretic condition' in art. Ascott believes this condition 'will arise when the two apparently opposed technologies are used in tandem; not simply cross referenced in an academic or analytical way, but brought together in a concerted conjunction of actions' (Ascott 2005).

Similar problematizing between the technological and biological and their shifting borders is present in a graphical illustration developed by Pier Luigi Capucci, which divides art that addresses the idea of 'life' into two main fields: the non-carbon realm and the carbon-based realm (Capucci 2008). The non-carbon realm includes mainly technological or new media artworks that address 'life' (for example, genetic art that is made on a computer). On the other hand, the carbon-based realm contains various genres of art that include biological matter and wet laboratory techniques. The concept was further developed by myself, together with Capucci, to include a few recently emerging and re-emerging areas, including artificial life, robotics and synthetic biology (Beloff, Berger and Haapoja 2013).

One of the insights this chart produces is clarity on the fact that an artwork that incorporates biological matter or addresses 'biological life' will always be based on manipulation of living organisms. This is true even in the cases where the work is critical towards manipulation and the use of living organisms. It is obvious that there is no 'natural' situation in art that deals with life, but rather this kind of life is always under the impact and manipulation of the artist's intentions.

Art that is based on computing and technology is not necessarily directly involved in the manipulation of living organisms. For example, the artificial life (A-Life) movement generated a lot of interest among artists in the late 1980s and throughout the 1990s, when the field was evolving within the sciences and technology. The initial quest was not for 'life as we know it' but 'life as it could be' (Langton 1996). Interest in A-life gradually faded, but has recently emerged again due to developments in machine learning and artificial intelligence (AI) that employ deep neural networks. One of the continuously present questions within the field has been what constitutes life and artificial life; what characteristics or properties does an artificial entity need to have for one to call it 'alive'? This argument has divided scientists into two camps: proponents of the so-called 'strong A-Life' believe that virtual creatures truly exist in computer memory and (as is often represented on the screen) can be genuinely alive. On the other hand, practitioners of the 'weak A-Life' use computer models to express and test theories about living things, but do not claim that the models are really alive (Boden 1999).

It is clear that novel forms and concepts will emerge with currently developing techno-organic practices in the arts and sciences. For example, the concepts of 'natural' and 'artificial' require rethinking. Until now, it has been quite easy to recognize a difference between things that are constructed (by humans) and things that are grown (biologically in nature). However, with developments in synthetic biology, unconventional computing and material sciences, for example, this is no longer an obvious issue. As such, the perceptual recognition of the difference between 'artificial' and 'natural' is disappearing.

This section has presented a short overview of developments that are ongoing in the arts, and which have their point of origin between two art genres: one that employs technology and one that deals with biological matter. The next part focuses specifically on the Nordic scene, and introduces actors, artists and activities that are part of these developments.

Digital Art in the 1990s Nordic scene

One can ask: what typical artistic practices are evident in the Nordic scene that span digital and biological art? The digital art field – sometimes referred to as 'new media art' – has never been a strongly visible trend in the art scene in the Nordic countries, especially not in comparison to the Central European scene of the 1990s, which already had several festivals and events presenting artworks that used digital media, as well as established courses in some of their major art universities.[1]

In the Nordic region, there have been several attempts and events that could be described as milestones in efforts to introduce and establish new media art, and which ought to be mentioned in order to give credence to these. Examples include the *ISEA* exhibition in 2004 in Helsinki (m-cult Official Website); the *Outoäly* exhibition in Kiasma, Finland, in 1999, curated by Erkki Huhtamo (Valvomo Official Website 1990); the establishment of the Interactive Institute in Sweden that strongly supported experimental digital art and design during its early years (RISE Interactive Official Website 2016); Gallery Otso in Espoo, Finland, which occasionally exhibited new media art under the leadership of Päivi Talasmaa; the Finnish festival Avanto that exhibited sound-related digital art installations at several small galleries, including MUU Gallery, Galleria Huuto and Mediatheque (Avanto Festival Official Website 2000–09); and some one-off exhibitions, such as *Digitally Yours* in Ars Nova museum in Turku in 2007 (Ars Nova Official Website 2006). One important factor was also the establishment of the Pixelache festival and association that is still active today (Pixelache Official Website 2016). Another surprisingly early actor on the scene was Rauma Art Museum, with their annual Electronic Art Week event[2] that has been left almost unnoticed by the main art scene. Looking through the list of participants in Rauma, it reveals many well-known figures who today are active and influential international artists.

The above list of activities is by no means complete, and the given examples are mainly from Finland, but one can assume that there are comparative lists of similar events within other Nordic countries.

From a practitioner's perspective, the overall situation of new media and digital art in the Nordic region during the 1990s was quite scattered, and not much continuity was established that could have supported artists' initiatives or their education in the field. This resulted in many young artists going abroad for their education or pursuing their digital art interests in countries that had more enthusiasm for the field. This obviously did not help the situation in the region in establishing a good basis for the field.

One specific feature in the development of the Nordic field of new media and digital art is worthy of pointing out. While in Central Europe the field has traditionally been dominated by men, in the Nordic countries – specifically in Finland and Norway – there have been many females involved in the developing and experimental visual art field.[3] However, from a critical viewpoint, even though this was the case in the 1990s and early 2000s, women in the arts working with technology have often been marginalized in the main art scene in the Nordic countries and considered exceptions in the technological art field. This does not mean that they would not have been successful internationally, but rather that they have lacked recognition in their own country. In Finland, it has generally taken quite a long time before digital artists gained mainstream recognition. For example, it took until 2010 for the first digital arts practitioner to be nominated for the Ars Fennica prize in Finland. Since then, the candidates for the prize from the field of digital arts have included Charles Sandison, Mika Taanila, the Pink Twins (Juha and Vesa Vehviläinen) and Terike Haapoja (Ars Fennica Official Website 2016).

Activities and Actors Crossing the Digital and the Biological

My focus in this section is not digital art and its trajectory in the Nordic countries during the last few decades per se, but to give an overview of the current situation. I will focus on actors that have shifted or extended their focus from digital media and technology to include biological matter.[4]

In the Nordic region, the growing interest in the inclusion of biological matter alongside the technological is visible in the activities of small grass-roots organizations that arrange workshops and various events for artists and biohackers. The most active ones today include the Finnish Bioart Society; i/o/lab in Stavanger, Norway; Biologigaragen in Copenhagen; and BioNyfiken in Stockholm. In addition to these small organizations, there has been a growing interest among university arts and humanities departments in developing educational activities that address these novel trajectories. Also, the emergence of artistic works that use digital technology in combination with organic matter is gradually growing. Furthermore, my own long-term practice – which spans from a focus on humans and technology to an emphasis on nature/environment and technology – is an example of artistic work in the

Nordic field (a couple of these works are described later in the chapter). To make obvious the connections between digital art and the current tendencies in art and science and bioart in the Nordic scene, one should mention that many of the artists and organizers who are active in these novel developments have a previous practice or interest in digital art.

When considered from a wide perspective, early incarnations of new media and digital arts were quite different to current developments in the field of art and science. Specifically in Finland and Norway, the digital art field throughout the late 1990s and 2000s was gradually attracting enough interest to create more formalized structures that enabled active individuals to pursue their initiatives.[5] Today, these same infrastructures and previously learned experiences function as models for the developments that engage with crossovers of technological and biological realms.[6] It is evident that the development of new emerging art fields in the Nordic countries is dependent on groups of active individuals who initiate new topics and activities, and who also further develop them as formalized structures, such as small art organizations (which are eligible for state art funding).

This shows that the model previously developed for supporting digital and media art initiatives has proved to be functional, and thus has been adapted for new initiatives. However, this does not mean that it is easy to receive funding and establish support for these kinds of experimental activities, which are often left outside of mainstream art. Without enthusiastic and active individuals who have the energy, year after year, to submit funding applications and pursue organizational activities, the scene would not exist.

One of the most well-established and visible actors in this field is the Finnish Bioart Society, which has focused on the realm of art and science since its founding. The Society was established in 2008, with the aim of developing bioart in Finland. Its primary means of doing so was through organizing an artist residency program at Kilpisjärvi Biological Station at the University of Helsinki (Berger and Beloff 2014). In recent years, the Finnish Bioart Society has grown to become a well-functioning and influential Nordic actor in the international art and science scene. It does this through leadership in many different activities, from international collaborations funded by the European Commission and Nordic Culture Fund to organizing art and science workshops for professional artists and students (such as those run in collaboration with Aalto University); it also curates exhibitions, organizes artists-in-residences in Kilpisjärvi, and presents the Society and its interests in invited lectures.[7] Incredibly, in spite of its clear impact on the development and visibility of the field within the wider Nordic and international art scenes, the Society still functions today with a small yearly budget.

One of the core focuses of the Society has been an interest in the biological (or 'natural') environment: namely, how the environment and our perception of it are impacted by today's scientific and technological development, and by a human desire to manipulate other organisms. The Society's focus on environments has been affirmed by its tight connection to Kilpisjärvi Biological Station (Beloff, Berger and Haapoja 2013). This environmental interest does not refer to traditional 'land art' or 'environmental art' practices, but is focused on technology-driven investigations of environments and their organisms. These include activities in a laboratory setting with technological tools, working with biotechnology methods, as well as using digital media to investigate environments onsite, such as video, sound, General Positioning System (GPS) tracking, drones and environmental sensors.

A key actor in the field is the Danish open space Biologigaragen, which was established in 2010. Biologigaragen has a different focus to that of the Finnish Bioart Society in that it is an example of DIY citizen science activism and bioactivism, albeit with strong connections to the cultural scene (Biologigaragen Official Website 2016). Biologigaragen and its activities provide a good example of crossover activities between hackers, biologists, artists, cultural workers and citizen-science activists in the Nordic region. It is worth noting that this Copenhagen-based initiative shares its physical space with the hacker lab Labitat, which supports hackers and thinkers in their initiatives in relation to DIY technological developments and digital fabrication (Labitat Official Website 2016). Labitat is a part of a well-known international phenomenon of establishing hacker labs. Similarly, Biologigaragen belongs to a network of DIY biodevelopers and activists, which typically focuses on open-source development between biology and electronics.

Other Nordic organizational actors or initiatives that deal with biological and/or technological arts include Norway's Kunsthall Porsgrunn, who run an art and technology exhibition series; the Biofilia laboratory at Aalto University in Helsinki, which offers educational activities within the field of biological arts; the Oulu region of Finland, who currently have a regional artist dedicated to bioart; Pixelache, an organization in Helsinki that has been arranging an annual international festival with a focus on electronic art and subcultures since 2002; and Click Festival in Denmark, which has had a subtheme on art and technology, and in the last two years has shown a growing interest in biological arts with their bioart panels and exhibits.

Unfortunately, it is not easy to pinpoint the significantly Nordic aspects of art practices that have been developing between technology and biology on the global scene. However, it may be easier to see the connections to biological matter through Nordic cultures' close relationship with nature, which is present in various Nordic mythologies, especially given that environmental arts have had such a strong presence in the Nordic region (Fortune 2014; Hakuri 2014). In a sense, one can argue that dealing with the environment and biological matter is almost a natural direction for Nordic art, even when it appears as a component of art dealing with technological matter.

One interesting sociopolitical question concerning this developing field in the near future would be: when increasing numbers of artists are educated in the art and science field, but the majority of museums and galleries ignore exhibiting this kind of experimental art, where will these artists exhibit, and how will they be able to continue their practice? However, this question will not be addressed here. Instead, the following two sections will introduce a selection of artists and works where the relationship between the biological and the digital realms becomes explicit.

Environment – Digital

The previously stated claim that art involving the environment, biological matter and nature is almost a presumable direction in the Nordic art scene can be followed with a question: what does 'nature' mean for us today? One plausible initiator for the increased interest in scientific research by artists could be the involvement of science and technology in forming the role of nature in our contemporary society. Science has become a primary tool to perceive, domesticate and reconstruct nature, often from a perspective that turns nature into a rational study or resource for economic gain. In recent years, the sciences have developed engineering methods that propose possibilities to construct a completely new kind of nature (for example, through developments in biotechnology and, specifically, through synthetic biology). The novel possibilities for human-designed nature are based on comparable thinking processes that are present in other technology-based design disciplines, such as engineering. In fact, today's technology-driven thinking model is penetrating the biological realm concerning living organisms.

What kind of nature is present in the work of Nordic artists working with digital and biological media? The following section presents works by Finnish artists whose works address the environment and/or include biological matter alongside digital components.

The project *Tracing* (2015) by artist and naturalist Antti Tenetz investigates the presence and impact of animals in their environment through their tracks, movements and actions (Antti Tenetz Official Website 2015). The artist has primarily focused on migrating trout species and male wolves, both of which are tracked via technological means, such as underwater and aerial cameras, GPS and drones. Tenetz describes this work as a search for new aesthetics that could expand our perception of nature and time. An interesting element of this project is the emergence of a novel hybrid animal: a combination of a wild, biologically evolved organism that lives free in nature, and GPS technology, which connects the animal to a global-scale technological infrastructure (i.e. through satellites). This set-up produces a very different image of a wild animal than what we are used to. In addition to the idea of nature, what this work produces is definitely not the traditional and familiar Nordic idea of nature that stands for purity, wildlife and, in a sense, also for innocence.

Artist Johanna Rotko's project *Yeastograms – Vanishing Images* (2015) is based on biological matter but creates a reference point to traditional photographic techniques (Johanna Rotko Official Website 2016). The Yeastogram technique is a process developed within DIY bioactivities whereby light-sensitive living organisms are substituted for traditional photographic chemicals (Pavillon 35 Official Website 2013). The produced images, which are based on yeast cells that are provided the necessary light and nutrition conditions, are visible only temporarily before life and growth takes over. Although Rotko's work does not precisely utilize digital technology, it references both the history of technology and the forces of life in the biological realm (Rotko 2015).

Artist Terike Haapoja's work *Dialogue* (2008) creates a connection between humans and trees through whistling and breathing (Terike Sade Haapoja Official Website 2008). The exhibition set-up includes live trees, sensors, sound and light. The work enables an audible dialogue between breathing and the plants' photosynthesis process. When visitors breathe out, they release carbon dioxide into the atmosphere, which photosynthetic organisms can absorb and then release, with oxygen as a by-product. When the visitor whistles to the trees, they respond by whistling back. The interaction between species becomes physical, as they are considered in the work to belong to the same metabolic system. In another project titled *Carbon Tree* (2016), Haapoja collaborated with researchers from the Department of Forest Sciences at the University of Helsinki (Carbon Tree Official Website 2016). This online project presents a real-time carbon flow of a tree located at Hyytiälä Forestry Field Station as an animation. We see the real-time representation of this tree's actions online, diffused into a stream of data.

My own work *The Condition* (2016), a collaboration with Jonas Jørgensen, also deals with trees, but ones that are already modified. Cloned Christmas trees, which are currently being researched and developed in Denmark, are manipulated further by being placed into continuously rotating boxes that form a micro-gravity environment (Beloff and Jørgensen 2016; Hybrid Matters Official Website 2016). In essence, the trees live in gravitational conditions, which clearly differ from our normal terrestrial gravity. The varying direction and speed of the twelve rotating boxes are based on downloaded data from a satellite that observes space weather conditions. This data is downloaded every few minutes and, through the use of intelligent self-organizing methods, the data for the set of boxes are organized so that they can be observed by visitors at different speeds. In this way, the set of trees is treated as one entity, a kind of a forest, instead of individual trees in individual rotating boxes. The work creates a living condition for the biological organisms in which the environment is based on digital control and technological manipulation. In the work, the Christmas tree is presented as a post-natural organism that is both biological and cultural, selected based on aesthetic criteria and manipulated for economic gain. The work points to how biotechnology is deeply tied to our capitalist consumer culture.

In another work I play with the replacement of technology with biological organisms. In a manner comparable to Johanna Rotko's use of biological organisms as the photographic medium, the *Fly Printer* project (2014–16) treats fruit flies as a printing apparatus. They are fed with specially prepared food that is mixed with ink; the flies are then able to print on a piece of paper that is placed underneath their spherical transparent habitat. In the latest version of the work, *Fly Printer – Extended* (2016), a collaboration with Malena Klaus, the set-up is extended with an AI component that observes the images printed by the flies, and interprets for us what it recognizes through the use of convolutional neural network learning. Both of these described works address and investigate the connections between humans, non-humans and AI from an artistic perspective.

An example with a slightly different approach to the environment that neither uses nor addresses living biological matter in the work, but which deals with our planet's environment as a large-scale phenomenon, is Finland-based artist Erich Berger's *Polsprung* (2012) (Randomseed Official Website 2012). The focus of this technological installation is the reversal of the earth's magnetic poles, which has been proven by scientists to have happened in our geological past, and which can be expected to happen again, leading to increased gamma radiation (among other issues). This might potentially destroy our technological infrastructures as well as increase biological mutations. As a visitor of the *Polsprung* installation, one can hear and feel the actual fluctuations of the earth's magnetic fields in real time – an experience Berger describes as 'radical witnessing' (Berger 2016).

Human – Digital

One can argue that the central perspective in works that address the environment is in fact a human one – they are created from the human perspective and typically for human audiences. Similarly, it is even more obviously the focus of works that concretely address humans and the human body. The intertwining of biological and technological matter includes not only environmental aspects and non-human organisms, but also a human–technology merging.

This is an area in which we have seen a growing interest by artists, especially in the fields of human manipulation and human enhancement. This enthusiasm may be partly due to advancements in medical and life sciences, but it has also been impacted by the continuously decreasing size of technological devices and components.

In this section, human enhancement primarily refers to enhancements that are not physical and permanent, and which are achieved via use of digital technology. Experimental practices addressing human enhancement in the arts often propose concepts that go beyond 'the repair of the body' phase common to medical science to focus on repairing the body to its so-called normal state.

One of the best known international artists working in this area is Australia's Stelarc, who has a long-term practice in human enhancement through technology. Stelarc has focused on extending the capacities and overcoming the physiological limitations of a body, which is visible in many of his projects (Stelarc Official Website 2009). Stelarc's performative practice merges with cybernetic machines that transform his body's functions and abilities (Clark 2003). When looking at his projects, one can understand the claim made by cybernetics that the boundaries of a human are constructed rather than biologically determined.

In comparison to artists working with the environment, there are few Nordic artists that work on human enhancement through technological means or who generally address the topic of human manipulation. The following introduces a few works by Nordic artists who have addressed the biological human body using the digital or biotechnology.

My personal artistic practice has evolved from a long-term interest in human enhancement and human interweaving with technological infrastructures (such as networks) towards investigations concerning the environment and its technological enhancement. These investigations are centred on relationships between humans and nature, which is strongly rooted in Nordic cultures and typically considered as natural, primary, almost sacred. In Finland, for example, nature is seen as a protector, and an unwritten belief exists among Finns that they have a stronger relationship to nature in comparison with people from Central Europe or elsewhere. However, the increase in modification of biological organisms by humans, and the simultaneous modification or 'enhancement' (Juengst and Moseley 2016) of ourselves with technology, is now impacting and even reconstructing our relationship with nature. Based on these developments, my artistic research asks: when both the human and her/his environment are technologically manipulated and enhanced, how does that affect the pre-existing understanding of the human–nature relationship? This hypothesis has driven most of my artistic research and works in recent years, typically incorporating technological components with biological ones as an inherent part of my art.[8] In some of these works, a human presence is built into the piece as a required component in the form of a carrier of networked wearable artefacts; other works speculate on concrete and novel technology-based possibilities as a means to connect with our environment. Many of my works address our desire to control nature and question the way technology enforces this desire.

For example, *Appendix* (2011) is a networked tail designed for a human being. This technological device was constructed to challenge the traditional perception of the human body, its borders and its desire for control. The *Appendix* tail is connected through a network to predefined environmental events. These connections are chosen with the intention of having no self-evident or easily interpretable meaning for the user. The tail becomes a part of the user's physical body, yet the user has no control over the movements of the tail. The tail moves based on data streams received via networks from environmental events: the horizontal movement is determined by the real-time movement of the number 3 Helsinki city tram, while the vertical movements are triggered by the real-time wave height of the Baltic Sea. In *Appendix,* real-time technology provides a foundation for the novel human body part and its faculty. With this work, I wanted to experiment with techno-organic connections, which merge the user's biological body and the physical environment via the use of technology into a single entity (Reality Dysfunction Official Website 2011).

Norwegian artist and organizer Hege Tapio has created a work titled *Human Fuel* (2016), which repurposes the human body's excess fat as a material resource for the production of biofuel (Hege Tapio Official Website 2016). For this, the artist went through an invasive liposuction procedure to remove her body fat; this was then manipulated to produce a usable biofuel, which potentially could be used as fuel for a car. The work points to the way we manipulate our biological bodies using technological means, and questions the underlying motives for this kind of manipulation, as well as our morals and ethics for manipulating other non-human species. Even if this work does not directly address digital technology, it addresses the blurring borders between the biological and the technological, which also concerns acceptable procedures for our own bodies. The development of biotechnology is bridging the gap between biology and digital technology at an increased speed.

Stahl Stenslie, another Norwegian artist and researcher, has created a series of works that focus on enhancing the experiences of the human body (Stahl Stenslie Official Website

2016). His early projects *cyberSM* and *Inter_Skin* (1993–94) experimented with virtual environments and computer-controlled interfaces to enable someone to 'touch' another human being across large distances. These projects included connected wearable bodysuits that made one's physical body a living interface for input and output. In a way, a biological human being in these works is seen as a cybernetic organism that is controlled by digital technology (Inkinen 1999).

The Finnish collective Brains On Art crosses several fields in the arts and sciences in their work, which focuses on utilizing human brain functions as the base for their artistic experiments (Brains On Art Official Blog 2016).[9] For example, in the *Poet's Helm* (2014), a helmet measures the user's brainwaves to generate a poem in real time, which is printed on a small piece of paper. In a performance-based work titled *The Suit* (2014), the performer is equipped with galvanic vestibular stimulation electrodes, which are triggered based on stock market data. The performer, who is standing on a bench in a public space, will lose his balance based on the fluctuations of the Helsinki stock market index. Both of these works point to issues of control concerning biological organisms (humans) and technology. In the *Poet's Helm*, the helmet, as a biological human faculty or 'brain', is connected to a technological machine that produces the end product, whereas in *The Suit*, technology takes over the control of the biological body through manipulation of the performer's sense of balance.

The artworks described in the previous two sections refer to a new kind of hybrid ecology that includes technological and biological actors, which have merged to form a new entity. Within these works, a new perception is emerging concerning both technology and biology. From them, it becomes utterly clear that the idea of nature is not what it used to be. It is also important to ask, when we refer to the concept of nature, if we are conscious of what kind of nature we are talking about. With what kind of mindset do we manipulate biological matter? And what role does technological development have in this?

Conclusion: Affiliation with the *Real*

Through the introduction of several Nordic artists and actors in the field, this chapter has built a trajectory from the development of the Nordic digital art scene to the growing interests in the intertwining of digital technology and biological matter. These experimental and novel practices that deal with technology and the sciences have received an increasing amount of attention from the wider contemporary arts field. But can we pinpoint characteristics or inherent properties that are commonly shared among these kinds of works that potentially differ from other, more traditional, approaches to art?

One interesting characteristic of these kinds of works is their affiliation with the *real* – with living organisms and planetary phenomena. For example, Johanna Rotko's *Yeastograms* uses living bacteria and its inherent biological functions by exposing the bacteria to specific light conditions, enabling it to either flourish or die. This is also true in uncontrolled situations or in 'wild' nature. My work *The Condition* connects to the real at two levels: through a network connection to data received from a space weather satellite, and through use of living plants in the installation. Erich Berger's work *Polsprung* makes palpable the real, ongoing, planetary-scale reversal of the earth's magnetic poles. Furthermore, a speculative work such as Hege Tapio's *Human Fuel*, which is based on biotechnological processes, has its base in the real world – liposuction being a commonly used procedure in the cosmetic industry, with the waste product used in the work – body fat – retrieved from living organisms.

These exemplary artworks no longer simulate nor create representations of the world – they deal with the actual *real*. They use existing living organisms and earthly conditions as the basis for the work, which are then presented, investigated and manipulated in order to point to defined issues and create experiences for the audience that have their grounding in our biological and physical world. In comparison to the wider contemporary art field, this kind of art intervenes with real life in the world and with living conditions in a much stronger sense than other, more traditional, art forms.

It is interesting that this aspect of the real is obviously prominent in these kinds of works at this moment in time – i.e. when we are experiencing an increase in the blurring of borders of reality, for example through technology-based extensions such as Augmented Reality that combines digital technology with our physical world.[10] This blurring of the concept of reality and our perception of what is real is possibly underlying the emergence of works that aim to intertwine with our comprehensible physical world. In a situation in which our reality seems to drift ever further away from our reach, we are looking for traces and areas where things are connected to 'the most real'. One of these areas seems to be the biological world and its connection with other living organisms.

The possibilities for the manipulation of biological matter via technological methods, and vice versa, will increase in the near future. But what kinds of divisions between biological and technological, between real, non-real and artificial, and between human intelligence and other intelligences, will form in the future? The artists discussed here have already addressed this question and opened up the field for experimentation. What is more, they are pointing to many ethical and moral questions that these practices raise.

Notes

1   For example, the Academy of Media Arts in Köln established a degree program in 1990. See Kunsthochschule für Medien Köln Official Website (2018).

2   In the 1980s, the Rauma Art Museum started presenting media art by organizing an annual week of video screenings called Electronic Art Week (Sähköisen Taiteen Viikko). This event was extended in 1992 with the inclusion of other thematic exhibitions presenting computer-based and electronic artworks. The last exhibitions in this series were organized in 1997 and 1999 (Rauman Taidemuseo Official Website 2011).

3   In Finland, the previous decades of media art have given rise to artists such as Marikki Hakola, Marita Liulia, Eija-Liisa Ahtila, Pia Tikka, Laura Beloff (the author of this chapter),

Minna Tarkka, Hanna Haaslahti, Minna Långström, Mari Keski-Korsu, Merja Puustinen, Mia Mäkelä, among many, many others. In Norway, the list includes Kristin Bergaust, Marianne Selsjord, Vibeke Jensen, Amanda Steggell, Maia Urstad, Jana Winderen, Hege Tapio, Ellen Roed, Maja Ratkje in music, among many others. And, of course, one should not forget Iceland's electronic art pioneer Steina Vasulka.

4   This also elaborates on my own interests that have developed in this direction over the last decade.

5   These actors include Pixelache and m-cult in Finland; in Norway, the structural organization of the field in the country was supported by the Trondheim Electronic Art Center (TEKS), Ateljé Nord, i/o/lab, the Bergen Center for Electronic Art (BEK) and especially Production Network for Electronic Art (PNEK). Recently, new initiatives in the field of digital arts have been established (for example, Kruks in Finland).

6   Examples of the widened interest in bioart and art and science by former digital art associations include i/o/lab's Article festival, Piksel festival in Bergen, the Metamorphosis Biennale (organized by TEKS) in Trondheim, as well as Pixelache in Finland, which includes several collaborations with the Finnish Bioart Society.

7   Further examples of projects by the Society include: collaboration with the Environmental Research Unit at the University of Helsinki (resulting in the *Prima Materia* exhibition in 2013); establishment of the Field_Notes laboratory in Kilpisjärvi in 2011, 2013 and 2015; running the Making_Life educational workshop series on synthetic biology in 2014–15 and the *Hybrid Matters* collaboration project in 2015–16; and an exhibition at Oulu Art Museum in 2017 (The Finnish Bioart Society Official Website 2016).

8   I have defined this kind of human existence as the 'hybronaut' (Beloff 2012). A selection of works is available at www.realitydisfunction.org.

9   Art expert Kasperi Mäki-Reinikka is a member of this group (Brains On Art Official Blog 2016).

10   For example, in July 2016, a new Augmented Reality game, *Pokémon Go*, was published. In the game, players run around in the physical world to catch Pokémons, which appear on their mobile phone screens. This game was the first commercially successful game of this type, but it was not the first to combine physical location with mobile technology. FLIRT, a project by Dunne & Raby (1998–2000), developed games for mobile phones along the same lines: '*The Lost Cat* is a virtual creature that lives and roams within Helsinki's cellular network occasionally jumping onto people's mobile screens. It appears at certain places in the city at certain times and if you regularly pass those places it even starts to follow you. But like a real cat, it's very independent and easily distracted, moving on and finding new people to love' (Dunne and Raby Official Website 1998–2000).

References

Antti Tenetz Official Website (2015), 'Home page', http://www.tenetz.com/. Accessed 15 July 2016.

Ars Fennica Official Website (2016), 'Home page', www.arsfennica.fi. Accessed 15 July 2016.

Ars Nova Official Website (2006), '*Digitally Yours*', www.aboavetusarsnova.fi/fi/nayttelyt/digitally-yours. Accessed 15 July 2016.

Ascott, Roy (2005), 'SYNCRETIC REALITY: Art, process, and potentiality', http://www4.pucsp.br/pos/tidd/teccogs/artigos/2009/edicao_2/1-syncretic_reality-art_process_potentiality-roy_ascott.pdf. Accessed 1 March 2018.

Avanto Festival Official Website (2000–09), 'Home page', www.avantofestival.com/?ln=en. Accessed 15 July 2016.

Beloff, Laura (2012), 'The hybronaut and the umwelt: Wearable technology as artistic strategy', Plymouth University, https://pearl.plymouth.ac.uk/handle/10026.1/1247. Accessed 15 July 2016.

Beloff, Laura, Berger, Erich and Haapoja, Terike (2013), 'Between landscape and laboratory: An introduction', in Laura Beloff, Erich Berger and Terike Haapoja (eds) *Field_Notes: From Landscape to Laboratory – Maisemasta Laboratorioon*, Helsinki: Finnish Society of Bioart, pp. 8–12.

Beloff, Laura and Jørgensen, Jonas (2016), 'The condition. towards hybrid agency', in *ISEA – Proceedings of the 22nd Interational Symposium on Electronic Art – CULTURAL R>EVOLUTION*, Hong Kong, 16–22 May, Hong Kong: School of Creative Media, City University of Hong Kong, pp. 14–19.

Berger, Erich (2016), personal communication, April.

Berger, Erich and Beloff, Laura (2014), 'Ars bioarctica – Viisi vuotta taiteen ja tieteen yhteistyötä', in Järvinen Antero, Tuomas Heikkilä and Lahti Seppo (eds), *Tieteen Ja Taiteen Tunturit*, Helsinki: Gaudemus Helsinki University Press, pp. 263–72.

Biologigaragen Official Website (2016), 'About Biologigaragen', www.biologigaragen.org/about. Accessed 15 July 2016.

BioNyfiken (2018), https://www.facebook.com/BioNyfiken/. Accessed 1 March 2018.

Boden, Margaret (1999), 'Is metabolism necessary?', British Journal for the Philosophy of Science, 50:2, pp. 231–48.

Brains On Art Official Blog (2016), 'Home page', www.brainsonart.wordpress.com. Accessed 20 July 2016.

Capucci, Pier Luigi (2008), 'The double division of the living', www.noemalab.eu/ideas/essay/the-double-division-of-the-living. Accessed 15 July 2016.

Carbon Tree Official Website (2016), 'Home page', www.carbontree.fi. Accessed 15 July 2016.

Clark, Andy (2003), *Natural-Born Cyborgs: Minds, Technologies, and the Future of Human Intelligence*, New York: Oxford University Press.

Dunne & Raby Official Website (1998–2000), 'PROJECT #26765: FLIRT, 1998–00', www.dunneandraby.co.uk/content/projects/72/0. Accessed 15 July 2016.

The Finnish Bioart Society Official Website (2016), 'Home page', www.bioartsociety.fi/. Accessed 15 July 2016.

Fortune, Bonnie (ed.) (2014), *An Edge Effect: Art & Ecology in the Nordic Landscape*, Chicago: Half Letter Press.

Hackteria Official Website (2018), 'Home page', www.hackteria.org/wiki/Main_Page. Accessed 15 July 2016.

Hakuri, Markku (ed.) (2014), *Place or Space*, Helsinki: Aalto University Press.

Hege Tapio Official Website (2016), 'Human Fuel™', www.tapio.no/wp/humanfuel. Accessed 15 July 2016.

Huhtamo, Erkki (2003), 'Kurenniemi, or the life and times of a techno-visionary', *dOCUMENTA (13)*, http://d13.documenta.de/research/assets/Uploads/KurenniemiHuhtamo1.pdf. Accessed 15 July 2016.

Hybrid Matters Official Website (2016), '*The Condition* – Cloned Christmas trees', https://investigations.hybridmatters.net/posts/the-condition-cloned-christmas-trees. Accessed 15 July 2016.

Inkinen, Sam (ed.) (1999), *Mediapolis Aspects of Texts, Hypertexts and Multimedial Communication*, Berlin: Walter de Gruyter.

i/o/lab Official Website (2016), 'Home page', http://iolab.no/nb. Accessed 15 July 2016.

Johanna Rotko Official Website (2016), 'Home page', www.johannarotko.com/. Accessed 15 July 2016.

Juengst, Eric and Moseley, Daniel (2016), 'Human enhancement', Edward N. Zalta (ed.), *The Stanford Encyclopedia of Philosophy*, https://plato.stanford.edu/archives/spr2016/entries/enhancement/. Accessed 15 July 2016.

Kare, Antero (2013), 'Microbes and a symbolic journey', in Laura Beloff, Erich Berger and Terike Haapoja (eds), *Field_Notes: From Landscape to Laboratory – Maisemasta Laboratorioon*, Helsinki: The Finnish Society of Bioart, pp. 94–115.

Kunsthochschule für Medien Köln Official Website (2018), 'Media and fine art degree', https://en.khm.de/mediale_kuenste/. Accessed 15 July 2016.

Labitat Official Website (2016), 'Home page', www.labitat.dk/. Accessed 15 July 2016.

Langton, Christopher (1996), 'Artificial life', in Margaret A. Boden (ed.), *The Philosophy of Artificial Life*, Oxford: Oxford University Press, pp. 39–94.

m-cult Official Website (2004), 'ISEA 2004,' https://www.m-cult.org/projects/isea-2004. Accessed 20 July 2016.

Pavillon 35 Official Website (2013), 'Recipe #1 – *Yeastograms*', www.pavillon35.polycinease.com/category/recipes/. Accessed 15 July 2016.

Pixelache Official Website (2016), 'Home page', www.pixelache.ac. Accessed 15 July 2016.

Randomseed Official Website (2012), 'Polsprung', www.randomseed.org/web/polsprung.html. Accessed 15 July 2016.

Rauman Taidemuseo Official Website (2011), 'Sähköisen taiteen näyttelyt' ('Electronic Art Exhibitions'), www.raumantaidemuseo.fi/suomi/nayttelyt_sahko.html. Accessed 15 July 2016.

Reality Dysfunction Official Website (2011), '*Appendix*, 2011, by Beloff', www.realitydisfunction.org/appendix/txtFrame.html. Accessed 21 May 2016.

Reichle, Ingeborg (2014), 'Speculative biology in the practices of bio art', *Artlink*, 34:3 (September), pp. 32–35.

RISE Interactive Official Website (2016), 'Home page', www.tii.se. Accessed 15 July 2016.

Rotko, Johanna (2015), 'Katoavat kuvat hiivagrammeja ja muita viljelyalustoja – kokeellisen taiteellisen tutkimuksen raportti' ('Vanishing images, *Yeastograms* and other agar plates – Experimental artistic research report'), Aalto University, www.urn.fi/URN:NBN:fi:aalto-201603291490. Accessed 15 July 2016.

Stahl Stenslie Official Website (2016), 'Works', http://www.stenslie.net/. Accessed 21 May 2016.

Stelarc Official Website (2009), 'Stretched skin', www.stelarc.org. Accessed 21 May 2016.

Terike Sade Haapoja Official Website (2008), *Dialogue*, www.terikehaapoja.net/dialogue/. Accessed 15 July 2016.

Valvomo Official Website (1990), 'Kiasma, Outo äly / Alien Intelligence', www.valvomo. fi/?portfolio=kiasma-outo-aly. Accessed 22 June 2016.

Waag Official Website (2018), 'Home page', www.waag.org/en. Accessed 15 July 2016.

Wikipedia (2016), 'Erkki Kurenniemi', https://en.wikipedia.org/wiki/Erkki_Kurenniemi. Accessed 22 June 2016.

In Between Worlds

Björn Norberg

My youngest daughter has spent quite some time in front of different computer games. It started to escalate with Sims but about two or three years ago she discovered the MMORPG (Massively Multiplayer Online Role-Playing Game) Starstable. For intense periods of time she has been glued to the computer. She is not the only one. At the moment the game gathers over ten million players worldwide, mainly girls but not exclusively. I have studied her playing and the strategies she has developed together with her friends, friends in physical reality and online.

The online version of Starstable was launched in 2011 and the story that the game is built around is quite sophisticated. Your character arrives at a summer camp stable. The goal is to qualify to the Jorvik Hippological Institute on the Jorvik Island. You will ride and train horses, take part in competitions and you will get daily missions. But mystic things start to occur, and you are then asked to help in fighting the Dark Core, a mystic evil multi-national company run by the Dark Riders and Mr. Sands. This is when the real adventure starts, and you will explore it together with other online players. There are chat-rooms and you can start clubs and communities to discuss and meet within the game. But of course, with three million players, there is a whole cult growing around the game with fan-fiction, blogs, walk-through films, forums and the special Jorvikipedia were you will find out everything that is going on in the Starstable world.

Watching my daughter play, I have noticed some interesting tactics and behaviours that she and her friends have developed. Sometimes riding around with the horses seemed to be enough, just playing, chatting and discussing the horses. They were playing with the game just as they played with dolls or dollhouses. But even more interesting was watching them while doing 'events'. Creating an event will give you benefits. A call to the 'event' is sent out, inviting others to join at a certain time and place. Several online players then turn up and do things together. This is in the virtual game, of course. Some of the players my daughter has met online, on different occasions, and she would recognize them. They can communicate via the chat bar. Some of her real friends from physical life join in with their characters as well. My daughter and her friends would then set up another communication link. Next to their computer screens they put up an iPad or cell phone and interconnect via Skype, which allows them to – in real time – comment on the other characters and their behaviour. I guess similar alternative communication lines are put up in between most players, it seems like a normal thing. The physical rooms are then connected via the Skype community, to comment on what is going on in the virtual Starstable world. At the same time, the Starstable game probably very much projects games and plays that the kids also play in the physical world, in the school yard or at home.

It all seemed so natural and self-organized, but I could not help wondering how the kids manage to overlap the different worlds and how they understand and interpret different platforms and media. Another thing that interests me even more is if and how their use of technology and visuals will change their way of understanding media and images, how their perception and understanding of realities will change and how the access to the communication technologies will change their expectations to film, entertainment, images and communication in the future. For these kids it seems normal to exist in many worlds at the same time, as they easily go from one to another.

I started to work as a curator in the mid-1990s, a time when the first MMORPG appeared, video art had just started to be a more accepted art form and when digital editing equipment started to be accessible and affordable. Maybe not for everyone, but artists forming collectives could now fundraise for equipment such as video editor stations and DVD-burners. There are several examples of such collectives in Sweden. Creative Room for Art and Computing (CRAC) was formed in Stockholm in 1997. Some people saw it as a lab for art and technology but the majority of the members of CRAC (in their prime CRAC gathered over 300 members, artists from all over Sweden) saw them as a workshop where you could put your hands on expensive equipment. CRAC were among the first places in Sweden to buy a DVD-burner, which attracted a lot of artists. Also, they had Photoshop stations and a large digital printer and this equipment gave many photographers new opportunities.

I missed the first steps of the activities that emerged around CRAC and I hardly noticed the new generation of video artists and people interested in the digital communities that CRAC organized. During a larger part of the 1990s I worked in a very traditional museum where we rarely had the possibility to show anything but drawings, sculpture and paintings in traditional ways. Besides my job at the museum, I was very interested in the arty and abstract techno scene and acts such as The Future Sound of London, Autechre, The Black Dog and LFO. They were hacking the rhythms and seemed to end the connection to the analogue beat. It sounded as if their music was not generated organically or deriving from an instrument but instead it was the sounds of bits and zeros and ones, and they seemed to know something about a wired, interconnected and digital future. The music provided visions that I could not find in the art at the time.

Enter Internet. Boom! I think it was in 1995 I tried to 'surf' the net for the first time. The graphics were hopeless, the speed and the cost of the communication bizarre but the opportunities and the information availability seemed endless. At the museum I had fallen in love with the archives and the Internet seemed to be the best archive in the world. I saw a future of total access to all music, literature, film and archives ever made. But it took until the end of the 1990s before I finally understood the opportunity of using the Internet and computers to make art. I had totally missed the net art hype a couple of years earlier.

In the year 1999 or 2000 I met with a group of artists who called themselves Beeoff.[1] They had an idea of using the Internet to stream moving images from one place to another, with

TV-quality. At the time net art was strictly bound to the browser and the low bandwidth aesthetics. The net artists would try to break the boundaries of the browser's window frame, make it flicker, change colours and make it behave like the computer was threatened by viruses. The only moving images were in ASCII or GIF, and the images were very much low-res. Few people had broadband, and downloading high-res images and films would take a long time and block the telephone line for hours. Even starting a discussion on how to stream moving images in TV-quality (HD was not in our vocabulary yet) sounded like a very futuristic idea.

Beeoff had a studio in a suburb south of Stockholm. I was supposed to go there for a meeting on how to stream a piece of art from their studio to the museum where I worked. They had done some tests, but they did not seem to have the capacity of describing their project or the connections among institutions to make the project grow. What they had was the studio, some equipment and collaboration with the Swedish telecom company Telia. The potential of their project seemed to be huge. You got a feeling of stepping into a very special atmosphere. I stayed a few hours more after the meeting and after that I voluntarily started to help out to create the curatorial format of a TV-channel that was labelled nonTVTVstation. We then started to stream steadily in 2001, to museums, art centres and in lower resolution even to the web.

The name nonTVTVstation was very accurate. By the standards of the time it was not a TV-channel. It did not have a proper schedule and proper shows, but there were broadcasts – or streamings. The format was simple but in many ways demanding: all artists on nonTVTVstation were asked to create a piece of art that would be produced or generated in real time, 24/7 and for at least 30 days. The output should be an audio/video signal. The piece was then streamed directly to a network of museums in Sweden and later also abroad. The streams measured 2 MB/s. This is not much with today's standards, but at the time it meant that the infrastructure in Sweden had to be changed and this was one of the reasons why Telia got interested in the project. They wanted to know what the future would demand.

NonTVTVstation was not about the browser. It was more about a cinematic experience; an experience of time and duration. Beeoff themselves were rooted in the period of the beginning of video art. They were discovering the camera and the streaming technology just as Nam June Paik, the Vasulkas, Joan Jonas and others had done in the 1960s and 1970s. They were exploring the equipment in the studio, the video cameras, the computers, the streaming devices, as well as a small but growing library of philosophy and science fiction literature in the studio. There were many late nights of discussions about room, image, perception, film, the physical and virtual room and time and the now. The first piece they ever made was called *Head*, this was in 1996, long before they started up the streaming business. It was a traditional video-feedback. They had put a sticker on a TV-set spelling the word, 'HEAD'. A video camera was pointed to the screen and fed back to the monitor. The feed was used as an input to create noisy sounds that followed the visuals perfectly. Later they would create a number of similar installations, adding layers of physical objects. Sometimes their work reminded me of what Joan Jonas had made years earlier. The interest in video distortions and feedback combined with more spatial experiments would lead them into a couple of projects where they collaborated with architects and where they used computers to process the distortions. This would give them more control over the image than the analogue equipment. As a result, *SAPS – Streaming Architecture Projective Spaces,* was shown in a gallery in Stockholm in 2004. The gallery walls were covered with screens, all with complicated geometric forms and non-flat surfaces. The images were projected via mirrors, so they appeared from the backside of the screen. The streaming was distorted in real time in a way that compensated the complex geometric forms. The result was that when you were in the room, you understood that the surface was not flat, even though the images appeared to be flat. This was most disturbing, and the image transformed the physical properties of the room. Today we are more used to façade projections that transform and reshape a building, but this was working in an opposite way, as the screens would transform a distorted image back to normal.

Other projects that Beeoff was working with were trying to connect two physical spaces using streaming and sometimes physical objects. *Tentacle* was a sculpture that existed in an edition of three objects that could be interconnected. They placed one in New York at Eyebeam, one at Kiasma at the ISEA 2004 and the third one was placed at the La Numerique exhibition at La Villette in France. The slots at each venue did not really match, and the New York installation happened after the ISEA and Numerique and was instead matched with an exhibition at the Museum for Samtidskunst in Roskilde, Denmark.[2] The main idea circled around the real time and the idea that the Internet would connect people all over the world and that this would give us an opportunity to share time and space. Each sculpture was a part of an organism, a tentacle. The tentacle picked up sounds and images from one space and broadcast it to the studio in Stockholm. There, sound and images were mixed with the video and sound feed from other tentacles. Then the mix was processed and finally it was streamed back to the inner body of the sculpture where it was projected on the inside of the semi-transparent sculpture body. As an object it was visually appealing, but as an interconnecting organism it was more a prototype or a theoretical explanation of a future that we saw was coming, where visual technology and visual culture would break the physical borders between rooms and worlds and where physical objects and virtual images would merge together to create something totally new.

The activities of nonTVTVstation were very much coloured by the frames that we set up: a one-month video feed created in real time. Also, they were heavily influenced by continuous discussions about space, time and physical contra virtual realities. Artists solved the problem of duration in very different ways. In 2001 Ilona Huss Walin created a piece called *What if I was a rat?* For the piece she constructed a model of an apartment, with furniture, a fully functional TV-set, kitchen with running water and so on, in perfect scale for a family of five rats. The apartment was monitored by eight video cameras 24/7. The piece was streamed to the web and to several museums, including Moderna Museet in Stockholm. People followed the activities of the rats on the web and it created a buzz around the project. Suddenly, a journalist from El País in Spain wanted to do an interview. For the first time nonTVTVstation was functioning as a television channel – but mainly with the web as a platform (Caldana 2004).

Elin Wikström, another Swedish artist, had a totally different approach when she made a one-month long performance where she was counting money, 100 kronor bills. You would see her hands and would hear her voice counting: '100 kronor, 200 kronor, 300 kronor' and so on. It was an impressive work. Italian artist Alberto Frigo also made a one-month long performance. This was in 2005. He had just started his now quite famous project in which he takes a photo of every item that he touches with his right hand. At the time I think he had over 30,000 images that we printed out as thumbnails. They were then sorted using a certain algorithm. This was pre-Facebook, but it is still a perfect visualization of how we control and mediate every second of the ordinary everyday life and how algorithms are controlling our lives and our consumption by offering us products that we did not know we needed. In the end of the performance, when each image was carefully laid out in a pattern on the floor, Frigo brought out an industrial vacuum cleaner and cleaned the floor.

Finnish artists Pink Twins and Juha Huuskonen both worked with software that would download images from the Internet and distort them in diverse ways. Pink Twins were using their software Framestein and the piece was called *Let It Beep* (2002). They have been working very consequently in a similar way since. They create a digital mayhem and a world where the pixels seem to float out of position, making everything around us collapse. Psychedelia and digital visualization meet. Also from Finland, Juha Huuskonen created a piece called *The Moment of Long Now* (2002). It was inspired by the philosophy of the Long Now Foundation and the idea of slowing things down. Each day, Huuskonen's piece would download a short sequence from the BBC News and stretch it to 24 hours. What usually looks as flickering news images from crises and catastrophes all over the world would then appear almost meditative with an added soundtrack of ambient electronic music.

Cable TV was something that many artists used as a source. Sometimes they would randomly use a TV-show or channel; sometimes they would carefully choose one as a kind of readymade content. Very often TV images were just a neutral source and they were edited and distorted so they would not be recognized. In September 2001 Beeoff member Martin Thulin was working in the studio. He had built up a wall of TV sets and was working with several cameras and inputs creating various kinds of feedbacks and distortions that were planned to be used in a piece that he was developing. The wall of television sets, constituting some ten or fifteen sets, was showing the CNN live broadcast. This was a very normal set-up, so he did not pay too much attention to what was happening on the screens. One time he glanced at them and saw an airplane flying into the Twin Towers of the World Trade Center in New York. He stopped working and sat down watching.

I believe that my way of understanding Internet and images changed a lot after 9/11. I finally realized that what was going on at a certain place could be streamed to any other place live, without any editing. We could exist in many rooms at the same time. At the time we were just spectators, but it was clear that more sophisticated technologies could be developed and that they would bridge different spaces and mix different worlds in a way that would sound and look like science fiction for most people.

Most of the nonTVTVstation productions were made in the studio in Stockholm. It was a technological and administrative challenge to make the productions and the streaming from other venues. The artistic concept had to be strong if we were to put the effort into moving the streaming equipment to other places. Icelandic artist Egill Saebjörnsson came up with an idea that challenged us to move the streaming equipment to Reykjavik Art Museum. This became a very popular piece. In *The Sofa* (2004), Saebjörnsson placed a sofa in front of a green screen. A camera was set up and the audience were invited to sit down and interact with the piece. Sitting in the sofa you would see yourself on the monitor. As a surprise, different animations would appear on the monitor and it looked like they popped up behind the sofa. Some visitors would turn their head to see if there was anything there, just to find the empty green screen behind them. Saebjörnsson managed to mix animation and physical reality and he invited the audience to climb into a virtual space. This virtual space, the image, was then live-streamed to the web and to other museums that were connected to nonTVTVstation. This mix of physical objects, animations, film and performance can be found in many of Saebjörnsson's works.

In the spring of 2016, Occulus Rift launched a public version of their VR glasses. The company is owned by Facebook and the company's founder Mark Zuckerberg declared that this technology is the future for social media (Olson 2016). It is clear that Facebook – as well as many other companies – believes that the communication on social media is developing towards VR. We will not only share our activities, post still images of dinners and selfies to a web platform; we will soon share physical rooms. We will transfer a physical site to a virtual world in real time, and in this room we can meet friends from all over the world. Occulus Rift is a VR technology. Microsoft has their glasses, the Hololens. The Hololens project is based on Augmented Reality. With this technology you come even closer to the future that Zuckerberg described. The glasses combine the physical room around you with a virtual animation in real time. Since it is an animation it can be streamed to any other platform, to other Hololens glasses or to a monitor. On top of this, the room, with layers, can be shared with others. Hololens is just one of several similar technologies. Sony has even revealed plans of a contact lens equipped with similar possibilities (Lavars 2016).

These innovative technologies will offer sensations that are similar to the experience that Martin Thulin had of 9/11 or to what Egill Saebjörnsson created with *The Sofa*, but it will bring these experiences to completely new levels. Also, it is not far away from the set-up that I described above, the set-up my daughter and her friends build up around Starstable. For them, an implementation using Hololens or any other similar technology will be familiar. The comparison to the kids' way of gaming is relevant in many ways. The Internet had a big breakthrough in the mid-1990s. There is now a whole generation of young adults that have been brought up with the Internet. They have been wired since they took their first steps. For them, the web is the natural source of information. Not the libraries, not books, not the newspapers nor paper magazines. And they do not watch TV either. They are used to finding what they want when they want it and they are used to getting it for free. This generation has probably developed a critical view that differs a bit from older generations. But young or old, we all seem to have problems judging how reliable online sources are. 'Alternative' news platforms have established and provide a most subjective point of view. Often, they focus on certain topics and are centred around conspiracy theories telling that the traditional media and public service media try to hide facts and that they are controlled by certain agendas.

With all the voices on the Internet and in social media it is hard to distinguish between truth and hoax, real or unreal, facts and misinformation. This creates a situation that subversive extremist groups as well as presidents and candidates take advantage of. The truth or facts are not worth very much anymore. What counts are the clicks and shares you get and by telling something in a very concrete and aggressive way you will get your message out. Rapper BoB started a Twitter campaign stating that the Earth is flat. It was most likely a way of drawing attention to his music, but he probably also gained followers that do believe the Earth is flat (Brait 2016). BoB's tactic is however not unique and is used in political campaigns as well as in a growing cyber war. Donald Trump's campaign in 2016 is an obvious example. This blurs the reality and the real, and creates suspiciousness and vagueness. Maybe a developed and stable democracy, together with a strong digital infrastructure combined with an open cultural scene, will be more resilient to that kind of development.

Swedish artist Peter Hagdahl has for a very long time been exploring the connections between actions in media, economy and other virtual spaces and actions in real life. In the 1990s he started to work with video installations where the spectator triggered changes in the image. His interest lies in complex systems, how small incidents can lead to dramatic causes and how we always interact with a virtual world, where in our daily life we make marks that linger as a 'virtual subconsciousness'. 'It's very Freudian in a way', Hagdahl once told me.[3] In parallel to computer-based video installations he has been working with more physical installations. Often, they seem to be constructed as rebuses where objects, drawings and even paintings together with computer animations and videos have created a model over cosmos and life itself. There is a balance and clear relations in between the various parts.

Peter Hagdahl's ideas have been influential since he was professor at the Royal Institute of Art between 1999 and 2009 and was the founding director of Mejan Labs. One of his former students is Jens Evaldsson. He developed a piece for Mejan Labs and the exhibition *From Reality and Back* that Hagdahl and I curated in 2008. For the exhibition we had rented a full body scanner. It was quite advanced even if the resolution was not as good as more contemporary scanners. It would still scan a full body in only four seconds. You stepped into the scanner and a few seconds later appeared a 3D animation portrait on a computer screen. Evaldsson created an empty landscape where you could choose to put your 3D figure. It was soon filled, and people started to make certain poses to fit in better in the digital world as they were scanned. Evaldsson would also take some of the 3D images and pimp them a bit using Maya, a 3D computer animation software, and they could then be printed using a 3D printer.

I chose the title for this exhibition, *From Reality and Back*, because the scanning let us travel from reality into a virtual world and then to a plastic physical form. The dimensions were blurred, and it engaged me as well as the students. I believe the exhibition became important for many artists. One that would spend some time at Mejan Labs was Tove Kjellmark, at the time a student of Peter Hagdahl. She has since developed a large part of her practice around scanners and 3D printers. Central to most of her work is the human body, which she explores between practices of drawing, painting, sculpture and video. She has used the scanner to scan both her own and other people's bodies and has developed an aesthetic method by investigating what motion means to the scanned image. The glitches that appear when the scanner does not reach hidden parts of an object, or that are created when the object moves, have particularly interested Kjellmark. Her scans look like objects that are falling apart into fragments, not far from the aesthetics of the Finnish artist duo Pink Twins. She has experimented with different printing methods and uses different plastics, plaster and metal. Once the object is scanned and printed, she used the printed object and scans it again, and this sometimes enlarges the glitches or reshapes them. Both Evaldsson and Kjellmark seem to travel in between virtual and phylical realities with comfort, elegance and ease. Again, I cannot help but associating it to my daughter's Starstable set-up.

The future probably belongs to a generation who can bridge between the worlds. Or why not totally mix them? Swedish/Greek artist Anastasios Logothetis has, in a series of works called *See Deep Web Trouble in the Bubble Loop* (2017), combined digital animations, sculpture and projection tricks. These clay sculptures look very primitive when you see them alone. They are made of non-fired ceramic placed on sheets of glass and resemble the result of a clay workshop in a kindergarten. But when Logothetis adds a projection to the sculpture, a suggestive layer is added. The sculpture is suddenly doubled as the glass sheet starts to work as a semi-mirror and reflects onto other glass sheets belonging to the installation. Suddenly a door to another dimension is opened. Another universe is revealed, and in that universe Logothetis has placed 3D animated treasures and fantastic creatures. The result is quite mind-blowing. What seemed to be dull and primitive is now cooking with alien life. This is augmented reality in a most suggestive and surreal form.

A trip to another universe is also offered by the Swedish artists Lundahl & Seitl. In 2015 they participated in the Momentum 8 Biennial in Moss in Norway with their piece *Symphony of a Missing Room*. I had the chance to get a private performance of the piece after the biennial, in the stairwell outside the artists' apartment in Stockholm. I was blindfolded and got a pair of headphones. The piece can be described as an interactive radio theatre taking place in a physical room, as well as in your mind. Without any visual impression, the focus on sound, touch and orientation is increased. A voice will guide you where to go but also describes what type of room you are entering. You move your body. You feel a wind. You feel a touch from another human being. Those impressions are real. But the rooms that the voice describes are totally virtual. I experienced this in a very limited environment, but still I was completely lost in another universe. At the biennial, the choreography and the experiences of orientation were far more elaborated, ending up in a situation where you, still blindfolded, climb into a car that starts to drive away. In the spring of 2017 Lundahl & Seitl opened their largest exhibition so far at Kunstmuseum Bonn in Germany (Kunst Museum Bonn Official Website 2017). Here the audience was invited to experience a selection of the museum's collection guided by an audio guide on a cell phone that the artists provided. After a while the voice in the guide asked you to put the phone into a pair of VR goggles and a story would begin, where you – by visual fragments and sound – mentally travelled into the artworks. Finally, you took the goggles off and entered a room with copies of the pieces you had just seen. The first impression was that you were back where you started, but you would soon find differences and discover that details of your memory of the room did not match with this second space.

Technology has always revealed new dimensions and universes. The telescope, the microscope, photography, film, television and digital animations have helped us to visualize what is too small or too far away to see, what is in the past and even in the future. These optical inventions have been crucial for our understanding of reality as well as the development of society, as noted by Paul Virilio (Virilio 1994). Augmented Reality, and the work of the artists mentioned here, seems to however suggest something else. They do not zoom in on the universe but rather create hallucinations. Their works reflect a reality where the unreal and the real have merged together and it becomes hard to distinguish between the worlds. At the same time, a large part of our lives has moved to a totally virtual platform. Information about our behaviour, habits and lives are collected in the clouds and is being used to suggest to us solutions and products that we want but did not know that we needed. Around the corner are the smart environments and the Internet of Things where the clouds will connect directly to the world and the objects around us.

So, what happens when we can no longer distinguish between virtual and real? Paul Virilio discusses this development in *The Vision Machine* and as always he cries out a warning:

> To my mind, this is one of the most crucial aspects of the development of the new technologies of digital imagery and of the synthetic vision offered by electron optics: the relative fusion/confusion of the factual (or operational, if you prefer) and the virtual; ascendancy of the 'reality effect' over a reality principle largely contested elsewhere, particularly in physics'.
>
> (Virilio 1994: 60)

Virilio published this in 1988, at a time when he could only guess of what was coming. Still, I think we have already been there for a while, where the boundaries between physical and virtual, and between truth and lie, are definitively gone. Trolls and hoaxes are common parts of the Internet. Studying them individually, they normally behave in an absurd way spreading absolutely garbage, but they will always trigger discussions and they create an uncertainty. They plant a disbelief of the entire system. And what is absurd is also thrilling, engaging and fun, and it gains attention, likes, clicks and shares. Likes are more important than telling the truth. It is interesting that Microsoft in the spring of 2016 had to stop their tweet bot Tay shortly after it was released. Tay had a twitter account and started to interact with other twitter users and mimicking their language. It did not take long until the bot turned racist and celebrated Nazism, and it was then shut down (Victor 2016). Racism, fascism, Nazism, terrorism and all kinds of extremism are frequent on social media. The trolls who want to spread the propaganda have very loud voices, and the robot Tay acted as many others: it started to mirror the thoughts of the trolls.

By repeating obvious lies, the propaganda of the trolls creates uncertainty. This tactic works well even for presidential candidates and as a weapon in digital warfare. In Sweden, many people think that we are a leading country when it comes to the development of digital technology. We were early adopters of the Internet; the Internet infrastructure was built early and people like to point out pioneering Swedish companies such as Spotify and Skype. But we are only beginners when it comes to Smart Cities and Internet of Things, compared to many countries in Asia.

The 'smart' technology will definitely help us to use resources in a more sustainable way and create a greener future. It is at the same time however exploiting our privacy, and I think this slows down the enthusiasm for the technology in Sweden. There is a genuine scepticism against technology when it threatens our privacy and integrity. This is probably a healthy attitude. Stockholm city has set up goals for Stockholm, called *Vision 2040*. Here the city states four various aspects of sustainability: ecological, social, economic and democratic sustainability. The document also states that Stockholm is the most Internet-connected city in the world and that Stockholm has a leading role in the ICT-development and, maybe most interestingly, it states that Stockholm aims to be the 'smartest city in the world'. It is understood that this will not wait until 2040 and that this shift is to happen now (Stockholm's Stad 2017). If this high-tech-driven aim is combined with the above-mentioned scepticism it could lead to a future society that is not just smart but also resilient to non-democratic attacks. Keeping in mind the foreign cyber-attacks shutting down important parts of society recently, we need to remember the vulnerability of the digital systems.

I started out by describing my daughter and her friends' way of playing the MMORPG game Starstable and their ease of travelling in between the digital environment in the game, the tele-presence through Skype and the physical room. To me, the development is very much about the dualities: the virtual world/the physical world, truth/lie, and real/unreal. The development runs towards a point where the distinctions are finally and totally blurred. It is becoming lesser and lesser important to separate the dualities.

The Swedish artist Christian Andersson has circled around reality and illusion in his practice. In his piece *Soft Drink Stand* (2001), an old projector beams a slide onto a wall. The slide shows a quote from Philip K. Dick's novel *Time Out of Joint* from 1959:

It's happening to me again. The soft-drink stand fell into bits. Molecules. He saw the molecules, colorless, without qualities, that made it up. Then he saw through, into the space beyond it, he saw the hill behind, the trees and sky. He saw the soft-drink stand go out of existence, along with the counter man, the cash register, the big dispenser of orange drink, the taps for Coke and root beer, the ice-chests of bottles, the hot dog broiler, the jars of mustard, the shelves of cones, the row of heavy round metal lids under which were the different ice creams. In its place was a slip of paper. He reached out his hand and took hold of the slip of paper. On it was printing block letters. SOFT-DRINK STAND.

(Dick 2012: 45)

The piece, as well as the novel, makes a perfect illustration of a world that is built up of illusions and hallucinations. In the novel, everything is blurred. Evil and Good. The virtual and the real. The main character of the novel, Ragle Gumm, lives in a constructed reality that starts to fall apart right in front of his eyes. It is an interesting novel that points out several existential and philosophical questions, but mainly it is sending out an early warning about the vulnerability of the technological development. Translated to our time, it seems to pose the question: is the smart technology smart enough to be sustainable, or is it creating a virtual reality that functions as a surface that obscures a society that is falling apart?

Just as I am summing up this essay, my attention turns to an article in *The New Yorker*. On the 9th of June 2016, Joshua Rothman wrote an article with the headline 'What are the odds we are living in a computer simulation?' (Rothman 2016). The article takes off from a recent quote from entrepreneur Elon Musk and then describes 'the simulation argument'. The argument is not brand new and was given a definite form in a paper written by the Swedish philosopher Nick Bostrom. As Virilio did earlier, Bostrom warns us about the development and initially states,

> that *at least one* of the following propositions is true: (1) the human species is very likely to go extinct before reaching a 'posthuman' stage; (2) any posthuman civilization is extremely unlikely to run a significant number of simulations of their evolutionary history (or variations thereof) and (3) we are almost certainly living in a computer simulation. It follows that the belief that there is a significant chance that we will one day become posthumans who run ancestor-simulations is false, unless we are currently living in a simulation.
>
> (Bostrom 2003)

If we find a life in a simulation depressing, a recent Elon Musk quote will help us: 'Maybe we should be hopeful that this is a simulation [...] either we're going to create simulations that are indistinguishable from reality or civilization will cease to exist. Those are the two options' (Rothman 2016).

References

Bostrom, Nick (2003), 'Are you living in a computer simulation?', *Philosophical Quarterly*, 53: 211, pp. 243–55.

Brait, Ellen (2016), '"I didn't wanna believe it either": Rapper BoB insists the Earth is flat', *The Guardian*, 26 January, https://www.theguardian.com/music/2016/jan/25/bob-rapper-flat-earth-twitter. Accessed 19 June 2016.

Caldana, Stefano (2004), 'NonTVTVstation, una televisión artística por Internet en tiempo real', *El País*, 29 January.

Dick, Philip K (2012), *Time out of Joint*, New York: First Mariner Books.

Kunst Museum Bonn Official Website (2017), 'Lundahl & Seitl, new originals', www.kunstmuseum-bonn.de/nocache/en/exhibitions/preview/info/ex/lundahl-seitl-new-originals-3147/. Accessed 20 April 2017.

Lavars, Nick (2016), 'Sony files patent for contact lens that records what you see', *Gizmag*, 5 May, www.gizmag.com/sony-contact-lens/43157/. Accessed 19 June 2016.

Olson, Parmy (2016), 'Mark Zuckerberg and virtual reality outshine Samsung's Galaxy S7', *Forbes*, 22 February, www.forbes.com/sites/parmyolson/2016/02/22/mark-zuckerberg-virtual-reality-samsung-galaxy-s7/#64ed74654a64. Accessed 19 June 2016.

Rothman, Joshua (2016), 'What are the odds we are living in a computer simulation', *New Yorker*, 9 June, http://www.newyorker.com/books/joshua-rothman/what-are-the-odds-we-are-living-in-a-computer-simulation. Accessed 19 June 2016.

Stockholm's Stad (2017), 'Vision 2040 – Ett Stockholm för alla', www.stockholm.se/OmStockholm/Vision/. Accessed 19 June 2017.

Victor, Daniel (2016), 'Microsoft created a Twitter bot to learn from users. It became a racist jerk', *NY Times*, 23 March. www.nytimes.com/2016/03/25/technology/microsoft-created-a-twitter-bot-to-learn-from-users-it-quickly-became-a-racist-jerk.html?_r=0. Accessed 19 June 2017.

Virilio, Paul (1994), *The Machine Vision* (trans. Julie Rose), Bloomington: Indiana University Press.

Notes

1 At the time (around 1999–2000) Beeoff consisted of Olle Huge, Tomas Linell, Mikael Scherdin and Martin Thulin. Thulin would soon quit the group and moved to south of Sweden. Beeoff worked together until 2005.
2 'Get Real!' Exhibition curated by Björn Norberg and co-curated by Morten Söndergaard and Perttu Rastas.
3 Peter Hagdahl and Björn Norberg, conversation in October 2012.

Virtual Worldmaking: Cultivating Digital Art Practice

Elizabeth Jochum and Mads Deibjerg Lind

When working with emerging technologies, artists find themselves at the nexus of many systems and practices that traverse the public and private sectors. Virtual Reality is both an artistic medium and a technological complex that involves layers of digital infrastructure, information and communications technologies (ICT) comprising software and hardware systems. Like radio, television and the Internet, VR is not a singular technology but a complex, layered system designed primarily for transmission and reception, 'with little or no definition of preceding content' (Williams 2003: 25). From the content perspective, the openness of the medium provides fertile ground for developing new aesthetic experiences alongside more practical products and applications. VR has proved valuable in manufacturing, military and health applications, including immersive surgical training platforms and tactical military training (Carson 2016). VR has also made important inroads in creative industries such as gaming, film-making and new media art (Zabel 2014). As with all new technologies, there must be sufficient infrastructure in place before content creators (be they artists or entrepreneurs) can fully harness the power of VR. Government incentives that support digital growth combined with private sector efforts to promote digital tools and services help pave the way for greater experimentation and development of VR as an artistic medium. The concept of digital aesthetics in VR is best understood within the matrix of activities that traverse the borders of art, entertainment and industry.

This chapter explores the VR technological complex in the Scandinavian context by focusing on the activities of Danish artists working with VR. Rather than focus on individual artworks, we read artistic practice in light of public policy initiatives aimed at promoting digital growth and digital industries at the national level, teasing out the relationships between public and private funding for artistic practices that utilize digital technologies. The goal is to locate artistic practice in this matrix and thereby demonstrate the interdependencies of VR as both an artistic medium and a technological complex. We begin with a brief overview of the origins of VR, tracing the development in research labs through the present. The proliferation of prosumer tools (360-degree action cameras, editing software, smart mobile phone technologies, computer graphics hardware and VR headsets) afford artists increased access to hardware and software tools. Accessibility to VR tools is buoyed by policy initiatives aimed at digitalization to promote digital growth. We present two case studies: the Danish media-based company Makropol and the non-profit BIBIANA Danmark, whose respective artworks and outreach activities promote VR tools and practices across disciplines.

From Pygmalion's Goggles to the Rift

The foundations of VR, which is not a singular technology but a complex of technological tools and systems that span hardware, software and ICT, have been long in development. As with many other technological innovations, artists and science fiction authors imagined the possibility for virtual worlds long before the existence of technologies to construct them. Stanley G. Weinbaum's short story 'Pygmalion's Spectacles' (1935) described a pair of goggles that immersed a person into a three-dimensional, sensory world composed entirely of moving images, sounds and graspable objects, complete with smells and tastes. Antonin Artaud used the term 'virtual reality' in his 1938 essay collection *Le Théâtre et son double* (*The Theater and its Double*) to describe the 'alchemical mirage' found in live performance (Artaud 1958: 49). Artaud believed that theatre could generate virtual realities by physically placing audiences in the centre of the performance space, creating a revolving spectacle 'in order to attack the spectator's sensibility on all sides' (Artaud 1958: 86). Artaud's vision of an immersive spectacle is often cited as a foundational vision of the type of immersive experiences now associated with VR.

It was not theatre but film where VR made its first developmental leap. During the 1950s and 1960s, researchers experimented with pioneering tools that shaped the development of today's VR tools. Following his 1955 essay 'The Cinema of the Future', Morton Heilig developed and patented one of the first multimodal experiential technologies to create a cinematic viewing experience to stimulate all five senses. The Sensorama featured 3D motion pictures, vibrating seats, stereo surround sound and powered wind and scents to create the illusion of an alternate reality. Another notable contribution is Heilig's Telesphere Mask (1960), a stereoscopic-television apparatus designed for individual use, which is recognized as the first proposed head-mounted display (Flores-Arredondo and Assad-Kottner 2015: 424). A motion tracking feature was accomplished the following year when Philco Corporation engineers developed Headsight, the first telepresence system that used two video screens and a tracking system connected to a closed circuit camera, allowing the user to view the surrounding environment by turning their head (Jerald 2015). Computer scientists were quick to realize the potential of computers to generate virtual worlds: in the 1960s Ivan Sutherland developed the *Sword of Damocles* (1968), a preliminary instantiation of the groundbreaking concepts described in *The Ultimate Display* (1965). The *Sword of Damocles* was the first head-mounted display controlled by a computer rather than a camera, creating new sensory experiences of objects and spaces in a virtual environment. The system was so heavy that it had to be suspended from the ceiling, and the crude graphics only depicted simple objects and rooms, but it was enough to generate proof of concept. Shortly after, Myron Krueger's series of interactive art installations *Glowflow* (1969), *Metaplay* (1970) and *Psychic Space* (1971) experimented with computers to generate what he called an 'artificial reality'. Krueger saw responsive environments as spaces for interaction between computers and humans: his *Videoplace* (1974) enabled people to communicate and manipulate objects in virtual environments while being physically separated from one another (Krueger 2003).

Sutherland and Krueger's contributions illustrate two fundamental aspects of virtuality: immersion and interactivity.

The next wave of enthusiasm for VR came in 1987, when Visual Programming Languages (VPL Research) founder Jaron Lanier coined the term Virtual Reality to describe computer-generated immersive environments (Zabel 2014). VPL Research was central to moving VR technologies out of research laboratories and into the hands of consumers: they were the first company to sell VR equipment, including goggles and gloves, and developed products such as the EyePhone head-mounted display, the Audio Sphere and the Dataglove (Parkin 2016). Other companies quickly followed, including Virtuality Group's Arcade Machines, Nintendo's Virtual Boy, Sega's Sega VR, Virtual IO's iGlasses and Forte Technologies' Forte VFX1. The commercial VR products from the late 1980s and 1990s were small and lightweight and were significant improvements over earlier designs. But the expensive price tags and relatively low-quality graphics failed to live up to the expectations hyped by the companies. The most significant progress in computer graphics would come not from gaming but from the simulator industry. Learning to operate complex machinery (such as flying an airplane) is a both dangerous and costly task. During the 1990s, simulators were seen as an effective solution to replace training situations for some military and flying operations (Steed 2014). Until the 2010s, development of VR was mainly left to researchers and industry-specific applications and faded away from the public consciousness, eclipsed by the growing interest in Internet technology.

Public enthusiasm and speculation in VR exploded in 2014 when the social media company Facebook announced plans to acquire Oculus, a tech start-up founded by Palmer Luckey in 2012 and funded primarily through a Kickstarter campaign. In a Facebook post, founder and CEO Mark Zuckerberg announced the acquisition and heralded VR as a revolutionary new communication platform (Zuckerberg 2014). Other companies quickly got into the mix: Sony, Samsung, HTC and Valve, Google and Microsoft all announced plans for future products, which included mobile phones designed for use together with portable head-mounted displays. Powerful mobile technologies, such as smartphones that feature 3D visual capabilities and high-quality displays, have significantly contributed to the popularization of VR, while low-cost products such as Google Cardboard viewer turn every smartphone into a portable VR theatre. Previously, VR equipment was prohibitively expensive for artists, requiring investments up to hundreds of thousands of dollars and corporate or government sponsorship (Zabel 2014). The affordability of VR tools and the push for more advanced graphic processing units (GPUs) on consumer-priced mobile devices have contributed to the re-emergence of VR. Increased computational power has raised the standards for computer graphics and improved display technologies, and artists now have access to a vast range of software systems to experiment with, including advanced tracking systems and real-time networking. Improved VR tools open up new aesthetic possibilities for Augmented Reality and virtual environments. While VR tools still prioritize vision and physical orientation – and do not approach the fully sensorial experiences that Weinbaum and Artaud envisioned – the public now has unprecedented access to both high-end and low-end tools for experiencing and producing creative content. Artists are among the core group of developers experimenting with VR to create new aesthetic experiences.

The applications for VR are vast, and developers are keen to investigate the medium's full potential. Following the example of Google Glass, where prototypes were made available to selected 'Glass Explorers', Oculus (the Rift) and HTC (Vive) distributed their platforms to selected first-users in order to generate enthusiasm and creative applications across diverse industries. Thus far, the experiment has proved more tractable than Google Glass: by the time the products became commercially available in 2016, there was already widespread familiarity with the hardware and software tools for generating original content. Online communities of users have developed around these programs for knowledge sharing and design solutions, easing the barrier for entry and creating more possibilities for access and experimentation by artists.

Digitalization and VR in Scandinavia

VR is a system of technological tools that rely on digital infrastructures, and these tools have converged independently of content and application. In Scandinavia, governments have taken a strong interest in promoting digital products and services because of their strong link with innovation and productivity. Government initiatives that promote infrastructure contribute directly to accessibility and advancements of digital technologies and services, and these initiatives help cultivate VR as an artistic medium by supporting the institutions and individual artists working with new media. Since 2011, the ministries responsible for business and growth in Denmark, Sweden and Finland each have developed strategic agendas for digitalization. Government policy statements make concrete recommendations for how to best develop and implement strategic actions for supporting digital infrastructure, accessibility and incentives in the public and private sectors (Danish Ministry of Business and Growth 2013; Government Offices of Sweden 2011; Ministry of Transport and Communications 2015). These initiatives have far-reaching consequences for business and cultural actors, from the development of fast broadband speeds to digital archival resources for cultural content and production, to the digitization of cinemas and museums.

In Denmark, policy initiatives such as the Innovation Strategy and the Growth Team for Creative Industries and Design make explicit the importance of digital development for the creative industries and across other sectors of the economy. Their report makes recommendations about how to best support and develop emerging digital products and services in both the public and private sectors (Danish Ministry of Business and Growth 2013). Such recommendations are tied to the support of infrastructure that support digital technologies – a process known as digitalization – but also contribute to commercial and artistic projects that advance digital aesthetics. Implicit in these policies is an acknowledgement that governments must work closely with public actors and private companies to ensure robust communication and Internet services. As VR is a communication platform embedded within the larger area of digital media, innovation in digital aesthetics happens across – and often in between – the fields of governance, culture and industry. Like other media, VR reveals a complex entanglement between emerging technologies, aesthetics and society. This entanglement takes on significance in the Scandinavian context, where funding for arts and ICT often explicitly call for innovation and outreach or cross-disciplinary activities.

Two companies that illustrate the matrix of digital aesthetics and infrastructure in Denmark are Makropol and BIBIANA Danmark. Makropol is a media company founded by artists and entrepreneurs dedicated to exploring new modes of storytelling with new media. BIBIANA Danmark is a non-profit cultural organization that designs illustration art exhibitions and events for children in Denmark and Slovakia. Both are relatively young organizations (Makropol was founded in 2012 and BIBIANA Danmark in 2011) that received VR hardware in advance of commercial release. While the artistic missions of the companies are vastly different, their use of VR and active engagement with artistic communities reveal the relationship between emerging technologies, artists and society. Makropol and BIBIANA Danmark both create original artworks, but they also coordinate events to educate and develop their audiences and engage other artists curious about the potential of VR. As case studies, these companies demonstrate how VR is poised to transform traditional media and artistic genres: Makropol uses VR to remediate film and develop new platforms for the production and reception of visual storytelling, while BIBIANA Danmark uses VR to remediate illustrative drawing and to explore new approaches to architectural design. Both companies are funded by government-sponsored organizations as well as private cultural and financial institutions. Grant monies do not merely fund individual artistic projects, but also finance open studios/laboratories for workshops and training of artists in collaboration with cultural and educational institutions. A consideration of Makropol and BIBIANA Danmark's activities in light of the Scandinavian responses to digitalization reveals the contributions of individual artists and companies to digital aesthetics.

Makropol

Makropol is a creative media agency based in Copenhagen, and their work spans interactive art, film, live performance and the development of digital software and applications. Makropol obtained VR platforms from Oculus in 2013 and developed their first VR first-person cinema experience, *Skammekrogen* (2014), an interactive film/art installation. Since then, founders Mads Damsbo and Johan Knattrup Jensen, both graduates of the independent film school Super16, have actively promoted VR film-making across Scandinavia. In 2015, they co-produced a weeklong VR film-making workshop together with the Copenhagen documentary film festival, CPH:DOX. The company has continued to develop immersive VR performances, including a full-length VR feature film. A short VR film introducing *EWA* premiered at the Cannes International Film festival in 2016, among several other experimental, animation and action VR films. The ambitious breadth and scope of Makropol's activities demonstrate a commitment to exploring the potential of VR films while also educating audiences, funding agencies and other artists interested in VR.

Skammekrogen is a short film that is shot and experienced from five different points of view: five characters are seated around a family dinner table and audience members choose a seat that corresponds to one of the five characters. The twenty-minute long film pioneers new methods in first-person cinema, using expanded 360-degree cameras and head mounts for the actors to record their positions and interactions. The technique allows viewers to embody individual characters and experience the film from a subjective, privileged point of view (POV). The film is immersive insofar as the audience is physically situated in the installation and encouraged to identify with the character they inhabit. Audiences can touch the real objects in front of them that correspond in space and dimension to the virtual objects depicted in the film. Audiences have some freedom to look around and explore the virtual environment while the film plays, even if they cannot directly alter the character's actions or the events. Rather than modelling the real world using real-time engines or animation, the film is shot using customized digital cameras, which creates a kitchen sink realism aesthetic.

Skammekrogen's use of VR and multiple POVs is more than a technological embellishment: it is fundamental to the narrative structure that allows for five distinct, simultaneous experiences. *Skammekrogen* challenges the categorical distinction between mimetic and diegetic drama. In mimetic narratives, the audience experiences the events as they unfold: events move towards a conclusion that is completely unforeseen by the characters in the drama or the audience. In diegetic narratives, the story is told through the perspective of the character, and the audience's experience of the narrative and the events are always associated with the narrator's perspective. Diegetic narratives provide a kind of doubling effect: what Paul Ricouer calls a 'continuous visibility' or double vision that enables the audience to see the events and at the same time observe the effect of those events through the lens or perspective of the narrator. For diegetic narratives, the question of POV is usually straightforward: the drama unfolds in relation to the narrative consciousness that recounts it. But when five simultaneous POVs operate independently in the same narrative landscape, the audience experiences simultaneously the imitation of an action and the subjective experience of the event. Spectators are visually and audibly immersed into a narrative universe, aware of the experience of the other viewers/characters and that they are prevented from grasping the experience in its entirety. The audience's physical experience of the narrative aligns so closely with the physical bodies of the characters, creating an embodied experience of narrative consciousness that film, theatre and live performances can only indicate. In this work, VR facilitates corporal empathy between the audience and the character they inhabit, which in turn shapes how audiences experience and remember the event. This mode of storytelling calls attention to how we experience daily life, and the impossibility of perceiving life events in totality. Inside the body of the characters, viewers experience an uncanny otherness in their own skin and take voyeuristic delight in the little fictions that mask the realities of daily living. The film invites viewers to reflect on the peculiar way memories are constructed, formed and recalled. The subjective, individual experience prevents the possibility of convergence, troubling the shared experience that film and live performance typically afford: audiences experience the film alone, together.

Early access to VR equipment was vital to *Skammekrogen*, and the budget for the production, which totalled 700,000 Danish crowns (95,000 euros), was funded principally by grants from the Danish Arts Foundation and the Danish Film Institute. These agencies are interested in exploring the potential of VR film, but because the genre is so relatively new there are obstacles to production and release that need to be addressed before VR can take hold. There are no established distribution models for VR films and no dedicated, networked spaces for viewing. As a genre, VR film has yet to demonstrate the ability to match the economies of scale that traditional film affords; therefore, a large investment in an artistic project that has a limited release for relatively few audiences presents a challenge to funding organizations used to conventional models of production and presentation. *Skammekrogen* did not premiere in a cinema but at an art gallery, and the first extended installation of the film took place in Nikolaj Kunsthal during the 2014 video arts festival Focus (Tabart 2014). Since then, the piece has been screened at art and film festivals, in museums, and at special events hosted by universities and cultural organizations.

Given the digital content and the ubiquity of VR viewing devices paired with smartphones, a VR experience like *Skammekrogen* readily lends itself to a mobile platform. The variable modes of presentation point up the difficulties involved with the emergence of a new medium that has yet to settle into established modes of production and reception. Some film-makers have experienced difficulty receiving funding for VR projects, partly because the medium is seen as simply too experimental. A significant aspect of fundraising for VR films involves educating the cultural community about the potential of the medium and persuading investors that such projects are financially viable. To this end, Makropol collaborated with the established film festival CPH:DOX to produce a VR workshop for Scandinavian artists.

CPH:DOX/VR:Lab

Skammekrogen demonstrated the potential of VR to influence new approaches to storytelling and film-making. Motivated by an interest in developing a network of artists new to VR, Makropol produced a ten-day VR laboratory for twenty Scandinavian artists and producers in collaboration with the Copenhagen Documentary Film Festival (CPH:DOX) in 2015.

Participants came from Denmark, Sweden, Iceland and Norway and were selected by Damsbo and Jensen based on their previous works.[1] The participants were paired in teams of two – an artist and a producer – and the workshop resulted in ten, original point-of-view (POV) VR films that were exhibited at the festival. The films were later made available online through a custom application for mobile phones. The purpose of the workshops is to create a network of artists and researchers working in Scandinavia and connect to international artists.

It is worthwhile examining the considerable role that digitalization and digital growth initiatives play in supporting and developing VR film. VR:Lab aimed to develop an audience and artistic network, educating audiences about the medium's potential and providing artists the tools to explore the aesthetic possibilities and potential applications. It remains to be seen whether the film industry or the art-film scene are ready for VR, however many international film festivals have launched VR workshops and events. Sundance Institute's New Frontier initiative has been running since 2007, featuring labs and residency programs that promote independent artists and creative technologists working with VR, and Venice Film Festival and Cannes Marché du Film have both featured VR films. Workshops at major film festivals are essential grassroots efforts to change the culture of film-making and, to a certain degree, legitimize VR film as an artistic and financially viable medium. The politics of funding and policy initiatives that support such activities are deeply embedded in how the artworks get made, and ultimately determine what kind of works are produced outside the commercial sphere. VR:Lab was supported by the Nordic Culture Fund, Bikuben Foundation, as well as donations of VR gear by Google, Oculus and Samsung.

BIBIANA Danmark

The project M/S BIBIANA is an art and education initiative aimed at school-aged children throughout Denmark.[2] The three-year project ran from 2015 to 2017 and was funded by the private foundation Nordea Fonden (9 million Danish crowns). The platform was a repurposed ship that travelled along the coast of Denmark, visiting between ten and twelve harbours each year to conduct residencies and workshops designed to help children to think creatively about issues surrounding design and use of public space. The project was a platform for education and learning through art and focused on re-thinking the cultural and aesthetic functions of Danish harbours in the changing industrial landscape. In 2016 M/S BIBIANA sailed the coast of northern Denmark under the title *Børn bygger havn – den eventyrlige havn (Children Building Harbour – The Magical Harbour)*. The ship was the site for art and design activities developed in collaboration with professional architects and artists. Artists and educators led children in a variety of activities that included building physical models and designing imaginative spaces in VR studios on board the ship.

M/S BIBIANA is part of BIBIANA Danmark, a non-profit organization dedicated to teaching and inspiring art and culture for young people. BIBIANA has a close collaboration with the world's leading children's book illustrators and continually create participatory experiences that incorporate novel educational and exhibition methods. BIBIANA Danmark believes illustrative drawing, and specifically children's literature, can foster innovative understanding and contribute to aesthetic design in the real world. The interest in innovation and acknowledgment of the power of fantasy as a means for imagining new realities motivated the company's interest in VR: while the company has primarily focused on illustrative drawing and painting (they frequently collaborate with the children's book illustrators at the Biennale in Bratislava), VR tools presented a new method for conducting their education and artistic practice.

The M/S BIBIANA project has three goals: the first is to advocate for children's artistic voices by creating situations where children can experience, share and create. Secondly, M/S BIBIANA is dedicated to working across all of Denmark, not restricting its activities to high-density cities but reaching suburban and rural communities. Finally, the company is a major proponent of visual storytelling and narratives through illustrative drawing. During the expedition, M/S BIBIANA set up two Virtual Reality studios on the ship using HTC Vive VR equipment and Google's Tilt Brush software. This set-up allowed visitors to step into an environment where they could create real-time animations and virtual worlds using a set of handheld controllers with a host of features and illustration tools. No prior knowledge of animation, programming languages or video gaming was required for users to enter the virtual environment and quickly start designing their own virtual worlds. The ease of the intuitive user interface was integral to the workshop's success: learning to use the technology is rather straightforward and therefore it is a prime site for teaching innovative approaches to design. More than a mere attraction, the introduction of VR tools in this context accomplished new artistic and educational goals that are connected to the process of digitalization and development of ICT tools. Architect Janne Bech, the director and curator of BIBIANA Danmark, describes the advantages of VR as a platform for children to explore art, culture and architectural drawing. Whereas a professional architect's tools and methods are based on precise measurement units, proportions and rules, VR enables the child to readily step into the role of the professional creator/designer, where knowledge of proportion, perspective and physics are already accounted for – or do not necessarily apply. With the software Google Tilt Brush, the animation and illustrative drawing process goes directly from (child) artist to audience. It also puts children into direct contact with digital tools and provides a platform for artistic communication.

An old fishing boat might seem an unlikely venue for an art workshop – much less a VR studio – and this unexpected venue confronts audiences in a different way than if the activities were conducted in a museum or gallery. Furthermore, the project highlights Denmark's maritime history by focusing on the country's numerous harbours and waterways. Before designing a world in VR, children are immersed in the world of the harbour and the smells, sights and sounds of the surrounding sea, experiencing the gentle movements of the boat before they begin designing new architectural spaces for harbour fronts. The entire sensory system is activated differently when working on a boat: even if the connection is not explicitly stated, the site-specificity and sensory experience influence the artistic outcomes. As the child enters the VR environment, they bring these subjective, sensorial experiences into their virtual world-making.

The use of VR as an artistic and educational tool is a gateway for digital media and IT education, and is one outcome of this project. The applications for VR in educational settings are vast, and VR is posed to impact education not only as a knowledge tool but also as an artistic medium for young artists. BIBIANA Danmark found VR a useful platform for stimulating creativity and imagination, allowing users to create and animate three-dimensional worlds using their whole body. From an architectural point of view, VR allows users to embody architectural designs in new ways, providing a corporeal experience of walking through spaces and buildings in a way that traditional sketching or CAD programs do not allow. It can be difficult for children (and others) to conceptualize the concepts of room and space without mentioning four walls. Using VR, one gains a different relationship to physical phenomena when actually designing life-scale spaces from their imaginations. VR can promote understanding of spatial properties, scale and perspective, while enabling users to communicate ideas directly through digital aesthetics rather than language or physical media. Finally, VR readily lends itself to a collaborative workspace and virtual social networks. On M/S BIBIANA, children are asked to generate ideas in groups and to collaborate on a shared 3D model in the virtual environment. While most VR experiences are individual, there is a strong interest in developing social VR platforms to offer multi-person experiences. While the technology to achieve this is still in development, the possibility of collaborative art making in virtual environments seems within reach.

Emergence

In many ways, we are only beginning to understand how VR aesthetics will shape and be shaped by the new digital landscape. Immersion and interactivity remain central to VR aesthetics and because of public and private initiatives aimed at digital growth and the creative industries, artists experiment with VR tools to create new aesthetic and educational experiences. The works by Makropol and M/S BIBIANA are just a few of many ongoing VR experiments across Scandinavia. KHORA is a private media company that develops content together with *Cityscape Repairmen*, the first Danish video game to be acquired and made available in the Oculus Gear VR store. KHORA maintains a lab in a pop-up space in Copenhagen, which has become a hub for VR enthusiasts. The shop opened in 2015 and has been a workshop location for school children, ICT companies, private industry and the general public to test VR tools and explore potential applications. The laboratory also functions as a meeting place for local artists and content creators interested in developing new projects and forming collaborations. KHORA founder Peter Fisher, an American entrepreneur, developed the idea of a collaborative workshop model to create a hub for artists, developers and designers in Denmark. The space has a unique atmosphere – a mix of art gallery, training seminar and technical workshop. The physical environment reflects the technological complex of VR and instantiates the types of networked activity that we have suggested are essential for the development of VR aesthetics. In our interviews with KHORA, BIBIANA Danmark and Makropol, we learned that the artists all knew one another and have collaborated, either by sharing equipment, training or design solutions. What unites these companies is not only the tools or status as first-movers of VR in Denmark, but the network of activities aimed at developing new audiences and new applications. These activities demonstrate how digital media and artistic practice are embedded in social and economic practices.

Analysing specific case studies of artists and companies experimenting with VR in light of policy and economic imperatives – especially those that strengthen ICT and digitalization practice – we see how artists not only condition the future art scene but also shape industry and culture. The combination of affordable VR tools and infrastructure that ensures wide coverage for broadband and mobile technologies create a population of users able to generate, share and distribute content with relatively few barriers. As cultural institutions begin to incorporate Augmented Reality and VR tools into their services and experiences, traditional art practices such as painting, sculpture and the performing arts are mediated and transformed by digital tools. Increasingly, artists who do not necessarily work with technology find new avenues for experimentation with digital tools. Recognizing that these artistic experiments and interventions operate within a complex network, VR emerges not only as an aesthetic medium for artists but as a vital, accessible playground for many. The accessibility and exposure afforded by projects like Makropol and BIBIANA Danmark contribute to an ecology of practice that is vital to the development of VR.

As an immersive sensorial experience, VR experiences still leave much to be desired. While users might experience corporeal empathy with the characters in *Skammekrogen* and may even experience strong physical reactions to events in a virtual world from a first-person perspective, the experience is still limited to passive viewing where the body is embedded in a virtual world but not part of it. A young artist may be able to design a dynamic, recreational space along a harbour front, but until they can jump off the edge and feel themselves immersed in the water, the experience remains only partial. And as long as VR experiences remain individual, there is a limit to how immersed audiences will feel. For VR to be truly immersive, it will need to develop the facets of corporeal empathy with the avatar and other bodies that inhabit the virtual world. For now, this remains a compelling but impossible ideal.

References

Allen, Rama (2016), 'Exploring the VR "Innerverse" at Cannes Lions', Lbbonline.Com, www.lbbonline.com/news/exploring-the-vr-innerverse-at-cannes-lions/. Accessed 5 October 2016.

Artaud, Antonin (1958), *The Theater and Its Double*, New York: Grove Press.

Carson, Erin (2016), '9 Industries using virtual reality', *Tech Republic*, 10 March.

Danish Ministry of Business and Growth (2013), 'Denmark's digital growth 2013 – Policy statement to the Danish Parliament', Copenhagen: evm, https://eng.em.dk/media/10599/29-05-13denmarks-digital-growth-2013.pdf. Accessed 11 October 2016.

Flores-Arredondo, Jose H and Assad-Kottner, Christian (2015), 'Virtual Reality: A look into the past to fuel the future', *The Bulletin of the Royal College of Surgeons of England*, 97:10, pp. 424–26.

Government Offices of Sweden (2011), 'ICT for everyone – A digital agenda for Sweden', http://www.cgil.it/admin_nv47t8g34/wp-content/uploads/2017/03/SVEZIA-ICT-for-everyone-a-digital-agenda-for-sweden.pdf. Accessed 28 August 2016.

Jerald, Jason (2015), *The VR Book: Human-Centered Design for Virtual Reality (ACM Books)*, Williston: Morgan & Claypool Publishers.

Khora Official Website (2017), 'Khora virtual reality', www.khora-vr.com. Accessed 28 August 2016.

Krueger, Myron (2003), 'Responsive environments', in N. Wardrip-Fruin and N. Montfort (eds), *The New Media Reader*, London and Cambridge: The MIT Press, pp. 379–89.

Ministry of Transport and Communications (2015), 'Finland to become operational environment for digital business', https://www.lvm.fi/en/-/finland-to-become-operational-environment-for-digital-business-796825. Accessed 28 August 2016.

Parkin, Simon (2016), 'Enthusiasts go back to the future in a Virtual Reality boom', *MIT Technology Review*, www.technologyreview.com/s/525301/virtual-reality-startups-look-back-to-the-future/. Accessed 21 August 2016.

Rhodes, Phil (2016), 'VR in the Cannes spotlight', *KFTV*, 12 May.

Salter, Chris (2010), *Entangled: Technology and the Transformation of Performance*, London: MIT Press.

Steed, Anthony (2014), 'Recreating visual reality in virtuality', in M. Grimshaw (ed.), *The Oxford Handbook of Virtuality*, New York: Oxford University Press, pp. 420–43.

Tabart, Malene (2014), 'Nikolaj Kunsthal byder på virtual realitymiddag i skammekrogen', *Politiken*, 7 February, www.politiken.dk/kultur/kunst/art5501363/Nikolaj-Kunsthal-byder-p%C3%A5-virtual-realitymiddag-i-skammekrogen. Accessed 28 August 2016.

Williams, Raymond (2003), 'The technology and the society', in *Television: Technology and Cultural Form*, London: Routledge, pp. 1–25.

Zabel, Gary (2014) 'Through the looking glass: Philosophical reflections on the art of virtual worlds', in M. Grimshaw (ed.), *The Oxford Handbook of Virtuality*, New York: Oxford University Press, pp. 407–19.

Zuckerberg, Mark (2014), 'I'm excited to announce…', Facebook, 25 March, www.facebook.com/zuck/posts/10101319050523971. Accessed 29 August 2016.

Notes

1 A full list of workshop participants, and the films, can be found at www.cphdox.dk/en/more-than-films/vrlab/participants/.
2 One author of this chapter, Mads Lind, was employed by the M/S Bibiana project and toured with the organization in fall 2016. Part of his responsibilities included providing an impact assessment of the project.

Computational Diffusion and Art's Radical Rematerialization

Tanya Toft Ag

Today we ought to examine anew art's potential role as architecture and foundation on which our future societies might be built. Art has always been integrated into cities with aims of both optically augmenting and materially constructing our surroundings. We can trace the conceptual and physical integration of art in society's architectural structures back to ancient civilizations, from rock art to frescos, reliefs and mosaics, stained glass and architectural sculptures. Today, however, the digital has realized a potential in art to diffuse new 'material' manners into our actual world. As art becomes digital fabric, made up of pixels, 0s and 1s, artists explore new ways of writing the art directly into the systems and sensibilities that increasingly make up our environments, architectures and sensible infrastructures, while continuously seeking new manners for art's interference and engagement with societal change. The digital enables new ways for art to further integrate into society and everyday life and engage with how the world is organized materially. It enlivens renewed attention to art's life and impact outside of the white cube and encourages a potential in art for acting as a political-aesthetic impulse implicated with processes of change.

In this chapter, I wish to leave behind a conceptualist notion of digital or media-based art as 'immaterial' or 'dematerialized' and instead point at a processual quality in the art's behavioural nature. I will propose that contemporary art potentially participates in 'rematerializing' our world, a quality I refer to with the conception of 'radical rematerialization'. With this concept, I suggest that art's digital material not only blends with the materialities (surfaces, architectures and digital code) that increasingly build, 'upgrade' and reorganize our environments, infrastructures and everyday experience but also actively and transformatively operates on these materialities. The quality of 'radical rematerialization' is reflective of a broader digital cultural dynamic of diffusion of digital aesthetic and computational material with urban surfaces, materials and architectures of our world.

'Immaterial' Art and Urban Surfaces

Since around the 1980s, we have witnessed the coming about of a digital dynamic of diffusion of computation emerging with the implementation of computers in our work spaces, homes, architectures and pockets, which has changed our lives and reorganized society: from the micro level of how things work and how we connect with each other to the macro level of our world's informational ecosystems. Computation shapes our surfaces today, not only advancing fixed electronic screens to become responsive, intelligent and analytic, but also increasingly and seamlessly integrating into communicative environments that connect and facilitate our social structures and attention. Incomprehensible pools of data and machinic sensibilities in 'the cloud' are channelled through hybrid interfaces to efficiently make our lives more convenient and guide our navigation, orientation and behaviour. Computational surfaces – two-dimensional, three-dimensional, and augmenting, virtualizing and mixing with our 'natural' environment – increasingly make up 'materiality' in our life world. The diffusion of computational function and intelligence in urban surfaces will soon shape every perceptual dimension of our lived environments.

This condition of computational diffusion has encouraged critical responses in artistic and curatorial practice. Following an imperative formulated in especially the western art context in legacy of installation art, conceptualism and Institutional Critique of the 1960s (as well as attention to site-specificity and relational-aesthetic orientations in contemporary art), and following practices with expanded cinema evolving up through the late 1960s and 1970s, art and curatorial practice have explored various idioms of artistically engaging and questioning urban computational surfaces. This concern has evolved alongside developments in 'media architecture' as both an umbrella term for term for hybrid media structures and interfaces, the integration the integration of digital and intelligent lighting schemes and modular displays into architectural structures, and as a metaphor used to describe grand, architectural-size art installations. Artistic engagement with urban computational surfaces also evolves from explorations of art as a tool for urban renewal or regeneration in urban development processes and morally motivated civil art projects (in particular since the 1980s), which we find in pragmatic ideas of 'useful art'. In the Nordic context we find as an example the urban regeneration project LYSLYD (2008–10), which in collaborations with artists, architects, urban planners and politicians used especially light and sound to revitalize and engage urban spaces in the Copenhagen area.

Today, artists increasingly find or 'make space' (and audiences) for their art in different contexts – from festivals, laboratories, online exhibitions, independent installations and public space to the privatized spaces of shopping malls, airports and transport hubs. As the art progresses with technological culture and becomes increasingly ubiquitous, artists experiment with installing their art beyond computational surfaces of urban screens and architectural 'media' surfaces, and hence move beyond the concept of screen or delimited visual display area as an urban alternative venue or open museum or gallery space for time-based media art. Digital and media-based art in the urban domain today takes up all thinkable material and immaterial forms and durations – from physical to augmented or purely virtual environments.

In the Nordic context, experimentation with digital and media art on urban electronic and/or computational surfaces might have been less progressive than in other art contexts of for example more established cultures for audio-visual experimentation or of stronger traditions of resistance and using technology for amplifying counter-political messages, like we find in São Paulo, Brazil; or in contexts of strong traditions of DIY (do-it-yourself) and maker cultures that use and develop new tools from digital technology, like we find in Berlin, Germany, among many other places.

In the Nordic context, we can rather trace a strong cinematic heritage that has informed exhibition discourse for video art, and which has migrated to urban and non-gallery 'exhibition contexts' for digital art. We recognize the cinematic heritage in initiatives such as the Screen City Biennial in Stavanger (existing since 2017, previously Screen City Festival 2013–15), which is 'dedicated to presenting the moving image in public space', and in the EU-funded initiative Smart Kreativ Stad (2015–20) in Stockholm, which examines 'new perspectives on moving images in the public space' through film, TV and digital media (Screen City Biennial Official Website 2017; Smart Kreativ Stad Official Website 2017). Operating in the realm of artistic and curatorial practice with video, media and digital art in urban spaces beyond the white cube, these initiatives also reflect a system of generous funding structures of both pan-Nordic and national funding bodies, which have enabled relatively large-scale productions in public space and supported costly initiatives of both institutions and independent artists, curators and cultural producers.

From Dematerialization to Rematerialization

The impact of digital technology on contemporary art involves the emergence of art forms and artistic practices that are sometimes characterized by their 'immaterial' qualities, for example, in artistic employment of neon lights, projection technology, laser lights, searchlights, monitors, lighting technology and Virtual, Augmented or Mixed Reality, as well as light transmission via fibre optics in mobile devices, sound systems, gaming devices, cameras, drones, and various other computational elements and functionalities. The attention to art's immaterial qualities found grounds long before (new) media art was articulated as an artistic domain in the 1990s, notably in Lucy Lippard and John Chandler's formulation of the 'dematerialized art object' from 1968. This concept involves the idea that the thinking processes relating to art are considered more significant than the actual material object or outcome (Lippard and Chandler 1968: 31–36). In lieu of the conceptualist reaction towards the objectification – and valorization – of the modernist art 'object' and announcement of the conceptual vision of the art object's disappearance, the idea of dematerialization in art has been explored in various conceptual and performative manifestations, which have contributed to expanding the field of contemporary art.

However, while digital or media-based contemporary art might be temporal and ephemeral in nature, current digital expansions of art in adaptable, processual and immersive-behavioural forms increasingly manifest themselves in interferences with surfaces, systems and architectures, in manners I suggest actually actually 'materialize', or 'rematerialize', our environments and life worlds anew. The migration of digitalized art to urban surfaces and spaces therefore concerns not merely art as 'dematerialized' matter but rather its diffusion into the sensible fabric of society by which the art becomes implicated with rematerializing our environments.

The idea of 'rematerialization of the art object' has been suggested by professor of digital media art Dew Harrison in relation to a post-conceptual shift in artists' returning to solid form. This she locates in a tendency in contemporary artistic practices with digital technology of solidifying virtual objects into physical form – through for example 'accumulated painting' with digital tools and code, in 3D surface computing, printing and prototyping, in virtual art installations and manifestations of Mixed Reality techniques and interfaces, among others (Harrison 2013). In Harrison's conception of rematerialization, she emphasizes artists' implementation of the digital, cyberspace and the Internet of Things into the 'real', whereby artists explore various materials, processes and means of production to formulate new approaches to making and to acquiring new skills and craftsmanship (2013).

My conception of rematerialization in relation to art concerns not merely the solidification of the digital into solid art form, but rather the diffusion of art's matter – with the digital – into digital or hybrid materialities and architectures of our everyday lives. With 'rematerialization', rather than 'dissolved matter' in and of itself I consider contemporary art's digital material as matter that can affect and be implemented into physical, digital and virtual 'materialities' in the real world, whereby the art as a digital substance engages with processes of 'rematerializing' (changing and remaking) our environments. This evokes a dynamic of computational diffusion, which announces how spatiotemporal 'materialities' of virtual forms, images, objects, systems and environments fuse into both the physical forms and digital infrastructures that make up our environments today.

Change Through 'Radical' Rematerialization

When the dynamic of computational diffusion comes into effect through art, the opportunities inscribed with digital elements entwine with a growing inquiry in artistic thinking today of engaging new modes of political aesthetics in the art in response to the conditions of everyday life. These are forms of political-aesthetic manifestations beyond a post avant-garde discourse of merely presenting counter forms to the visual messages of capitalism informed by objectives of reclaiming increasingly commercialized public space, and beyond guerrilla manifestations of resistance and protest with aims to subvert or interrupt habitual perceptions, experiences and uses of public space.

From the testimonials in this book, we get a sense of what motivates artists to work beyond the confines of the exhibition space – exhibiting their art in the urban public domain, in site-specific manifestations, in urban electronic infrastructures of screens, or projection surfaces, in (media) architectures or urban design, or via mobile devices, apps, on YouTube, or via other wide-ranging networked platforms or interfaces.

Laura Beloff notes 'My aim is that my [wearable] works should be used by the public and integrated into their lives, rather than hanging in a museum' (Laura Beloff, artist testimonial in this volume: 98). Anne Senstad describes how the digital allows her to 'intersect and interfere with space, large spaces, site-specificity, transformation of spaces, the psychological space, mobility, and physical displacement' (Anne Senstad, artist testimonial in this volume: 41).

HC Gilje describes how he is 'interested in the manifestation of digital systems in physical reality, moving from the general digital to the specific physical':

> For many years I have been working with an over-arching concept I call 'Conversations with Spaces' where I look at different ways of transforming and activating spaces using light, projection, sound and motion; ephemeral media that create temporary transformations of physical spaces, which again influence how we experience these spaces.
>
> (HC Gilje, artist testimonial in this volume: 94)

Nuleinn (Rine Rodin and Magga Ploder) explain:

> Working with the digital, the artist is able to remove herself and the art from the boundaries of the typical art institution, and out into public space. We have used this as an agenda in our work, creating installations for public transit spaces. With the performance *Parasite* from 2017, for example, we used the Copenhagen Metro as a host for an interactive performance. By using these different contexts, the art is exposed to different audiences and reactions, as well as the digital, activating the audience in a completely new way.
>
> (Nuleinn, artist testimonial in this volume: 96)

Kristoffer Ørum states:

> The reason why the digital interests me is because the use of mobile phones or screens in public spaces affects and interferes with daily life. It is not so much the technology in itself that interests me, but the exploration of the role that digital technologies play in our understanding of the world around us, in our self-images, and in turn our behaviour and imagination.
>
> (Kristoffer Ørum, artist testimonial in this volume: 37)

The Danish design group Kollision expresses:

> Using the digital to augment physical spaces and infiltrate artistic domains is to us an almost evolutionary step to take. Digital stuff is all around us, it is only natural that it also pervades artistic practices – and that those practices in turn trickle into society, as art has always had a way of doing. Digital tools allow for constant reconfiguration and interactivity, which is much more in tune with the pace of our society than having urban spaces, buildings or artworks remain unchanged and almost sacrosanct for millennia.
>
> (Kollision, artist testimonial in this volume: 95)

From these statements we can see that the exhibition and engagement of art in the urban domain is particularly tied into incitements of audience activation, transformation and change. These ideas evoke how, throughout recent (western) art history, art has engaged with various trajectories of 'change' in inquiries seeking to change society in one way or another. In the 1910s, in reaction to the innovative rhythms and images of the industrial marketplace, mass media and urban popular culture, the vanguard artists demanded that true art should go beyond the intellectual to transform daily life. Later, the Dadaist artists advocated for nonsensical behaviour in response to the horrors of the First World War, and the Fluxus movement sought to promote a revolutionary quest in 'living art' and 'anti-art'. In the late 1960s, the Situationists enacted tactics of *dérives* and *détournements* in attempts to create spaces for alternative appropriation with aims of transforming urban spaces and their behavioural-infusing meanings, while various forms of protest art have advocated for direct action through artistic resistance to politically unjust and other urgent issues. These are just a few examples of art movements whose inquiries have concerned transforming contemporary society and everyday life within it. Especially since the 1960s, the belief in art's ability to engage with politics and potentially to change the world has expanded, with various artistic orientations grounded in goals relating to visions of change rather than handcraft skills or conceptual experimentation. In the legacy of these movements, we can consider how artistic discourse today has formed with a sense of hyper-political self-consciousness.

With the idea of *rematerialization*, I wish to engage a notion of change in the sense of a 'radical' dimension in contemporary art. I am interested in a form of radicality that is located in the digital reinforcement of art's subversive nature, by which the artwork – by evoking a new form of political aesthetics – operates radically through being directly embedded in society's 'material' structures. This form of radicality differs from discursively common trajectories of change in contemporary art, as have been located by art historian Mikkel Bolt along three overall tendencies of either interventionist, solution-oriented or relational art practices. While interventionist art practices can be found in so-called semiotic terrorism, guerrilla communication or tactical media, rooted in an avant-garde discourse of transgression, breakthroughs and making visible institutional power structures, solution-oriented art practices seek to bring solutions to specific societal problems, and in relational art practices of typically socially engaged art (also referred to as dialogical, community-based, participatory or collaborative art) artists are deeply committed to making work that addresses pressing social issues and that change the way we perceive the world (Bolt 2011: 175–81).

Widely evolving from ideas of critical theory, in the Nordic artistic context we find a strong influence of the relational artistic discourse. Perhaps echoing a certain pursuit of collectivity in the Nordic region, reflecting the social democratic project of the welfare state, artistic attention has especially been paid to a sense of 'social aesthetics' and the creation of socially engaged and participatory art (Larsen 2006). We recognize this orientation in for example the practices of Hanne Lise Thomsen, Johan Knattrup Jensen and Mads Damsbo, Dark Matters, Andrew Gryf Paterson and N55, as described by the artists themselves in this book. This may also reflect the strong social realist cinematic tradition in the region, which is manifest in a discourse of attention to societal, communal and real-life scenarios, everyday life-worlds, and existential concerns and social consciences of ordinary people.

My attention to art in relation to change here however differs from the relational discourse. Rather than 'relationality' as an ontological premise and attention to direct relations (between humans, and humans and the world), I am concerned with how particular conditions stimulate our relations; how we are embedded in the world's immediacy, which I will return to shortly.

The notion of *radicality* I wish to evoke also differs from how the term 'radical' is oftentimes used to denote art of an activist revolutionary (or 'artivist') nature, as characterizes a strong trajectory in contemporary art today (Weibel 2015). I am not talking about a radical-left sense of resistance in the art (for example, towards capitalism and the culture industry). I also wish to avoid the term's superficial connotations and to aestheticize a sense of 'radicality' in association (but not seriously engaging) with activism. I am thus avoiding the depiction and celebration of 'radicality in art' as an aesthetic trope while washing away a pure radical intent and action as is a core quality in activist practices. As such, without seeking to lay claims to radical politics per se I am instead exploring a conception of 'radical rematerialization' in terms of a sense of direct and operative mode of political aesthetics that the digital affords contemporary art.

Radical rematerialization concerns mechanisms by which art actively participates in processes of change in real-world materialities. For example, when art participates in (re)designing technological interfaces and architectures, disrupting our media landscape and use of social networks, or intervening in infrastructures for networked processes of democratic participation. In evoking a sense of realism, radical rematerialization concerns an interest in the actual and real rather than the abstract and speculative, thereby setting the conception aside from an idealist or utopian focus on abstract visions of a world imagined or yet to come.

Radical rematerialization denotes a quality, which I argue is particularly potent in digital art, of intervening directly in real-world conditions, in real-time. Real-time in this perspective involves that the art's temporal aesthetic material 'acts' upon our reality in the present moment; perhaps by presenting real-time data, by facilitating a telepresent meeting or interactive experience with the art, or by enabling interference or interaction with matter directly in mediated experiences that differ from experiences offered in regular (non-art) conditions of mediation but which might take place in the same sites. In the urban domain, I thus consider 'real time' not strictly in terms of an instant computational response or as necessarily reflective of a real-time networked dimension of the artwork. Instead, I consider the real-time aspect with regards to the art's direct interference with our urban reality, its processes and development; how the artwork's aesthetic material engages with things, surfaces and interfaces in a manner of being embedded in their visual or invisible appearances, materialities and behaviours.

We can further anchor this notion of 'radicality' by engaging what Richard Grusin has proposed with the concept of 'radical mediation' to denote an understanding of mediation in terms of something we are 'in the middle of'. This can be a process, action or event that generates or provides the conditions for the emergence of subjects and objects, as opposed to something that 'relates' objects or subjectivities otherwise considered to be distant from each other (Grusin 2015). In this conception, rather than relating to things and people, 'mediation' is a condition of being within the world, evoking a particular sense of presence in which our conceptual and affective states might actively transform – as theorized by Gilbert Simondon with the concept of *individuation* and Joseph Stiegler in the conception of *technogenesis* (Simondon 2009, Stiegler 1998). The notion of mediation in terms of 'immediacy' is thus opposed to an understanding of mediation in terms of something that happens in-between pre-existing objects, subjects, phenomena, categories or events (in-between us and things in the world); something that by way of a relational quality is connecting or negotiating between these entities that are considered to be already there. The account of mediation in terms of 'immediacy' – which falls in continuation of twenty-first centuries theories in the legacy of Edmund Husserl, Henri Bergson and Martin Heidegger, among others – challenges an ontological distinction between representations and what they may represent, as filtering, limiting, constraining or distorting an immediate perception or knowledge of the world. The 'immediacy' of a mediated experience, for example with art, is not what is displayed or represented (i.e. an artistic vision somehow mediated to an audience), but rather a matter of affective embodiment.

In this understanding, art is not a delimited field of experience (like a painting in a frame or the film reel in the cinema that we 'look at'), nor does it operate in a manner of relationality or distance from the world and its phenomena. Art is rather perceived as embedded in its contexts and contingent with the forms, ideas, actions and materials that make up these contexts. And digital art is particularly contingent with (and taking advantage of) contemporary technological contexts and the communicative infrastructures both employed and questioned by artists, oftentimes at the minute of or even before their release; sometimes invented by artists ahead of their availability to mainstream culture, and sometimes developed in counterposition to mainstream technologies.

In current artistic discourse dedicated to excavating 'the contemporary' we must acknowledge a value in contemporary art practices that engage the present-day matter of how digital materials are organizing contemporary life. These artistic inquiries are brought into social and political conditions when acting as processual impulses in these materials. Perhaps rather than occurring as critical antitheses to society, these practices invoke change at much more senseable scales through affecting our human-bodily perceptual experience. From this perspective, we can consider questions pertaining to aesthetics in media-based art to coincide with our ontological experience with media aesthetics in our contemporaneity at large.

New Political Aesthetics with Radical Rematerialization?

In the merging of Grusin's notion of radical mediation with my account of rematerialization into the conception of 'radical rematerialization', I have considered how art, when embedded in both our physical and digital materiality, can affect the fabric of this reality in such a way that new modes of artistic intervention may emerge that blur anew the aesthetical and the political.

The digital influence and hybridization of contemporary art has reconfigured art's relation to society and its implementation within it. With the shift from object to process in the 'dematerialization of the artwork' within conceptual art of the late 1960s and early 1970s, text, language and dialogue became tools and forms of artistic practice. Today, much of our text, language and dialogue exist in computationally maintained social networks – made of or facilitated by code. Contemporary art is made of the same 'material' as our environments; it is generated from pixels and series of data facilitating computer processing in a numerical format of binary numbers. These are the same materials as those structuring our increasingly immersive lives today that continuously evolve with ever-more complex, interconnected ecologies, exchanges and formations of relationships.

Some artists express in their testimonials a strong sense of reflexivity and awareness about how their art practices employ the same technologies as those that are developing society today. For example, Tuomo Rainio describes:

> all digital information is related through a common structure. For an artist working in the post-conceptual era of image making it is fascinating to find an underlying digital structure where ideas and concepts can be turned into codes, and further, into images. Not only images relate to each other, but the whole realm of digital information.
>
> (Tuomo Rainio, artist testimonial in this volume: 56)

He continues:

> I am interested in the points of access where the borderline between the autonomous field of art and the societal context breaks and creates a new energy flow that benefits both the art world and the world outside it. Digitalization brings forth one of these access points, since images that did not earlier (before digitalization) have any connections with each other are now relatives and originate from the same mathematical foundation.
>
> (Tuomo Rainio, artist testimonial in this volume: 88)

What makes media art distinct from other kinds of media aesthetics is therefore the mode by which it intervenes in 'images' of everything else and interferes with our perceptual (sense-)experience.

Artists have always been curious to explore the contextual limits and applicability of art; however, the digital has enabled a new level of fusing art's inquiries with processes of change in everyday life. Digital art potentially intervenes directly in the appearance of our surroundings: how we use our mobile computing devices, the optics and lenses through which we experience the world and affect our literacy and consciousness as political subjects. For example, when net art interferes with websites and online experiences; when sound art augments urban or natural environments; when media art engages architecture and affects the changing expression of a building's skin; when mobile art interferes with our psychogeographies and urban paths; when the art of coding or an algorithmic procedure integrates in social media networks or digital communication cultures and the functionality of urban systems; and when art creates the infrastructures of websites, templates and constructions of meaning in society in relation to our communicative existence. When digital art does these things, it directly integrates, modifies and mixes up with our reality, affecting our immediate experience (by way of reconfiguring what conditions our experience) rather than mediating representations of the world to us.

Digital material has enabled art's images to become active in a different way. Digital and media art makes use of the same material that makes society today. We can locate a particular contemporary dimension in this by means of the art's contingency with the materials, technologies and 'things' of everyday life (as well as with other disciplines and aesthetic orientations). The digital thus conditions how the artwork operates as a contemporary art form while offering opportunities for the art to interfere with the materialities that condition our experience and imagination – something I have examined in previous writing (Toft 2017). From this we can consider that the digital has enabled what might be seen as a new form of political aesthetics in artistic materials and behaviours – as a potentially instant, processual and living impulse.

Art has always been political in terms of interrupting the 'distribution of the sensible' in our everyday life (Rancière 2015). French philosopher Jacques Rancière sees the aesthetic effect in art not necessarily in the sense of producing a kind of 'energy for action' or 'form of deliberation' about the situation, but rather in how the art creates new forms of perception and interpretation by interrupting and supplementing our everyday sense-experience with a sense-experience with the artwork that has no part in the perceptual coordinates of the community, and which thus modifies the 'aesthetic-political field of possibility' (Rancière 2015: xiv and 80). Here, I put aside a notion of art as directly resistant antithesis to cause-and-repair logic. Instead, art may have more long-term effects on the everyday workings of society that subtly impact our ways of doing, seeing and making (Rancière 2015: 41–42). The kind of political aesthetics that I suggest the digital has enabled in contemporary art is not necessarily one of instant revolution but rather one that operates through a sense of *longue durée*. From this we ought to not expect an immediate impact of the art but rather fertilize a sense of 'immediacy' in the artwork and acknowledge its immediate and gradual participation in transforming how things appear, how they work, or expectations or perceptions that surround them.

In this line of thinking, digital art holds a potential for interfering with our distribution of the sensible, which today is made up of the same material, signifying and a-signifying signs, that develops and increasingly constitutes our material and sensible worlds. It can thus be argued that digital art is inevitably political since it affects our sensible distribution in society – namely, by affecting our sense-experience. Media-aesthetics in art engage our sensible system just like any other media-aesthetic experience, combining with image impressions of everything else during our experience with it. When intervening in discourses and situations dependent on the same digital material, art holds the potential to deconstruct, re-abstract and reorganize the situations of mediation that structure everyday life – like a kind of Trojan horse with implicit differential modes of resistance.

What I am proposing here is a critical potential in art that becomes apparent when not setting oneself aside from the system and critiquing it from a distanced or relational position. Instead, art's critical potential is found when it works with and within the system in terms of rematerializing its appearances, behaviours or protocols. This proposal leans on a conception of what Irit Rogoff has named embedded criticality rather than distanced criticism and critique (Rogoff 2003).

However, when embedded in society, environments or other locations of operation, art must simultaneously deviate from the protocols, ideologies, logics, knowledge structures and habits that the system maintains. When art becomes almost indistinguishable from technocultural forms, it could be argued that the dissolution of the material art object coincides with a disappearance of art's aesthetic autonomy, thereby raising the risk of it becoming enmeshed or of complying with the institutions, political power structures or corporations the artwork would otherwise seek to dismantle. Thus, the question remains: when inside the system, how can art still resist this system?

In response to this question, I suggest that art can be critical by way of thinking through the conditions of production that prevail in a particular historical context. Art needs to preserve a gap between the atemporal conditions of its production and the linear temporality of the political process it evokes – free from the instrumentalities of 'immediacy' and 'effectivity' otherwise enforced by the logic of neoliberal capitalism. In order to achieve this, artists and curators need to continuously rethink the parameters of the political aesthetics they enact. We might therefore need to reformulate our imaginations of art's autonomous position, when emerging from digital material and networks; when art operates while embedded in the real, digital and virtual architectures and social systems of everyday life as it is today.

Conclusion

Compared to other countries, the Nordic context does not have a rich historical past of resistance and activism. Rather, the Nordic culture has a tradition of 'sensitive resistance', formed of free expression, discussion and consensus, where public dissatisfaction can openly fuse into the political system. This culture might inspire the conception of 'radicality' that I engage with the notion of *radical rematerialization* in this chapter in the sense of change through sensible redistribution.

I propose the conception of radical rematerialization in an attempt to embrace art's real-time implementation in and modification of the digital, virtual and physical structures of our reality. This suggestion however invites for continuous effort to understand the complex ecologies of which art form a part (in terms of application, fusion and potential actual rematerialization of the 'materialities' of our reality), by which the art simultaneously tweaks the interfaces that condition our ways of seeing, doing and making in society. This conception of art's 'work' concerns how digital and media-based art increasingly permeates our infrastructures and participates in materially and virtually shaping the sensible standards and norms by which we will mould our future. In this, I propose, lies a political-aesthetic potential. In perspective of a long-pursued democratic aim of making art and art's spaces accessible and relevant to everybody, which reflects how art is historically anchored in 'radical' orientations of merging art and everyday life, digital and media-based art has the potential to become part of our everyday spaces and 'material' environments. Art can be an impulse of difference that operates – perhaps 'permanently' – in the systems and surfaces of everyday life.

In the quality of radical rematerialization I see a particular potential in digital art as operative and transformative material, for example in showing ethical and reflective manners that may inform the design principles for the next visual media façade or the architecture of a future Augmented Reality game, or that critically 'educates' people's literacy towards (or sensible reception of) future innovations with media aesthetics. Or, art may provide our computationally diffused surfaces and systems with an altered algorithm that modifies the apparent possibilities and delimitations of engaging with services or experiences in our world. It matters greatly how we formulate the imperatives behind aesthetic innovation, not least considering how media aesthetics and the computational diffusion they mobilize increasingly create the architectures, infrastructures and ambiances of our everyday life.

We need to further examine the trajectories by which contemporary art can engage with processes of change in the world – beyond our societal imaginations – and discuss how we can understand the 'value' of these new modes of change. We also need to discuss how art's autonomy and independence from a (western) delimiting and rational-thinking societal imaginary can be maintained. Further inquiries into these questions will benefit current and future scenarios for art to participate in discussions of how social, political, ecological, urban and technological dimensions of our world will develop. If we are to leave art out of these discussions, by keeping art within the confines of the white cube and the discourses on the exhibition and 'presentation' of art that this institutional concept embodies – perhaps in fear of losing out on some of art's autonomy, aura or value when integrating with our actual world – we risk delimiting art's role as a technique of embellishment or entertainment. And then, we might fail to include the essence of 'art' – the free spirit of the human, poetic, sensible, social and sustainable being – while racing towards 'smart' but also alarmingly technocratic futures.

References

Bolt, Mikkel (2011), *En Anden Verden*, Copenhagen: Forlaget Nebula.

Bourriaud, Nicholas (1998), 'Relational aesthetics', in Claire Bishop (ed.), *Participation*, London: Whitechapel, pp. 160–71.

Grusin, Richard (2015), 'Radical mediation', *Critical Inquiry*, 42:1, pp. 124–48.

Harrison, Dew (ed.) (2013), 'The re-materialisation of the art object', in *Digital Media and Technologies for Virtual Artistic Spaces*, Hershey, PA: Information Science Reference (an imprint of IGI Global).

Larsen, Lars Bang (2006), 'Social aesthetics', in Claire Bishop (ed.), *Participation*, Cambridge, MA: MIT Press, pp. 172–83.

Lippard, Lucy and Chandler, John (1968), 'The dematerialization of art', *Art International*, 12, pp. 31–36.

Rancière, Jacques (2015), *The Politics of Aesthetics* (trans. and ed. Gabriel Rockhill), London and New York: Bloomsbury Academic.

Rogoff, Irit (2003), 'From criticism to critique to criticality', *European Institute for Progressive Cultural Policies*, www.eipcp.net/transversal/0806/rogoff1/en. Accessed 15 January 2018.

Screen City Biennial Official Website (2017), 'Home page', www.screencitybiennial.org. Accessed 5 January 2017.

Simondon, Gilbert (2009), 'The position of the problem of ontogenesis', *Parrhesia*, 7, pp. 4–16.

Smart Kreativ Stad Official Website (2017), 'Home page', https://smartkreativstad.com/en/. Accessed 5 January 2017.

Stiegler, Bernard (1998), *Technics and Time, 1: The Fault of Epimetheus* (trans. Richard Beardsworth and George Collins), Meridian: Crossing Aesthetics series, no. 1, Redwood, CA: Stanford University Press.

Toft, Tanya (2017), 'Images of urgency: A curatorial inquiry with contemporary urban media art', Ph.D. thesis, Copenhagen: University of Copenhagen.

Weibel, Peter (2015), *Global Activism, Art and Conflict in the 21st Century*, Karlsruhe and Cambridge, MA: ZKM Center for Art and Media and The MIT Press.

Critical Thoroughness: The Dynamics of the Artist as User and Producer of Digital Elements

Mette-Marie Zacher Sørensen

*I don't think of materials as media or mediators for me or my artistic intention, but rather as
a kind of 'collaborators,' for lack of a better word. The mediation that takes place is mutual:
the material mediates me and I mediate the material.*
(Marie Kølbæk Iversen, artist testimonial in this volume: 56)

When, in her artistic statement, artist Marie Kølbæk Iversen describes the relationship between herself as an artist and the material with which she works in terms of *collaboration*, she emphasizes an interesting dynamic between the two entities: 'artist' and 'material'. The artist's material may be paint on canvas, marble, software or social processes. Marie Kølbæk Iversen's use of the word 'collaboration' demonstrates an almost animistic perception of the material with which she as an artist works. The material has a form of agency; it provides for cooperation and a dynamic, complex relationship. In this chapter, I am interested in this *collaboration* between artist and digital material, which reflects a dynamic of digital material crafting. I am interested in how Nordic artists implicitly or explicitly communicate a kind of attitude in their works towards the material with which they are 'collaborating'. Is the premise for the collaboration humble, curious, wondering, or impressed, critical or teasing? Is the attitude towards the material a proud display of what this material can do or does it represent a contemptuous attitude to 'see what the problem with this material is'?

I will focus on a project by the Danish artist Kristoffer Ørum and, in part, the artistic practice of Swedish artist Goto80. Both artists use strategies in which collaboration with digital material can be characterized by what I call *critical thoroughness*. I use this term while specifically referring to how, instead of accepting and using available digital elements and tools, the two artists insist on different ways of producing their digital elements from scratch. The artists thus investigate digital media by being the producers of digital tools. In Kristoffer Ørum's performative lecture *The Futuer* (2014), the performer (Ørum) browses the Internet, displaying Google results, websites and videos found on YouTube and Wikipedia pages. The sensational thing (which is never directly revealed to the audience) is that Ørum has produced it all himself (Ørum 2014). This means that, instead of accepting the system developed by Google, for example, with its inherent logics, Ørum is the developer of his own parallel system. Instead of accepting that we are 'communicated to' and even communicate via a 'language' on which we do not have any influence, the artist has learned the language of coding and regains some sort of technological power as an artist, insisting on *techne* (by being the producer of digital tool with 'his own hands'). Kristoffer Ørum's critical thoroughness is comparable to that of the Swedish artist and composer Goto80, who – also associated with the glitch movement – uses the sounds of low-tech computers to perform, record and release music:

> For my art-oriented performances, I try to be less of an artist and more of a worker. Instead of using pre-made music and algorithms, I use software that forces me to do most things by hand. I program sounds and compose music from scratch […] I often play with the idea of ownership and copyright, especially in relation to the political economy of music.
> (Goto80, artist testimonial in this volume: 50)

With the use of Vilém Flusser's concepts, it can be argued that many media artists today meet his definition of being *tool-makers* as well as artists (Hayles 2014: 165). As the process becomes more sophisticated, it moves from object to tool. With the right technologies, artists may trigger preconditions for the processes, which their works constitute. Kristoffer Ørum, in his own words, 'hope[s] to challenge existing systems of knowledge and technology' (Kristoffer Ørum, artist testimonial in this volume: 59). It is not my ambition to prove that a critical thoroughness – in dealing with the digital material – is a specific Nordic trend, but rather to explain an interesting attitude I observe among some Nordic artists towards digital material. Perhaps a curiosity and sincere thoroughness occurs because this generation of artists has been a part of a Nordic educational infrastructure where new media art and digital media has not been on the school curriculum. In their respective geographical areas, some Nordic artists have been lonely 'first movers' in the interrogation of new media for the production of art and music.

I will approach the artistic strategy of critical thoroughness from a familiar distinction in art history between 'art' and 'craft' and through a critical sociological analysis of the relationship between users and producers of contemporary digital media. When, as users of digital media, we create a website, do a status update or share a YouTube video, we are producers; we communicate. But we are also limited in our communication due to the logics and constraints in the digital tools we are using. As Bernard Stiegler has put it, today's technologies have the ability to communicate to us while we communicate through them (Stiegler 2009: 37). In this sense, technologies may be considered to have agency and make a powerful influence on visual and medial discourses in general. José van Dijck argues that, in a contemporary social media context, 'creativity should be accredited to a complex amalgam of actors' (van Dijck 2013a: 45). In the following, I shall investigate issues concerning dynamics of agency in the relationship between digital technologies and their users and demonstrate how my selected examples of Nordic digital art challenge this dynamic through critical thoroughness as an artistic strategy. I will define and discuss the concept of critical thoroughness and argue how it simultaneously relates to and differs from the internationally recognized concept of glitch (understood as an artistic use of flaws and errors). I will do this by first outlining two examples of self-portraits by Nordic artists, one of which can be characterized as a critical thoroughness strategy, while the other is a glitch strategy.

Bodybuilding, Marble Sculptures and the Failure of 3D Prints: On the Difference between Critical Thoroughness and Glitch

The Danish artist Lea Guldditte Hestelund's work from 2015 titled *Self-portrait as Discobulus* is a photograph of the artist posing as Myron's ancient marble sculpture, the *Discobulus*. Initially practicing as a sculpturer and working with marble, prior to producing this work, the artist exercised bodybuilding and had a special diet. A process requiring tremendous discipline, placing herself in a fitness environment that was otherwise foreign to her, the artist worked with a personal trainer while striving to emulate the ancient sculpture. She says in an interview that it was important for her to go 'all-in' with the bodybuilding world in order to thematize and criticize questions about body ideals.

> At that time, I was outside the fitness environment and had never really been in a gym. In fact, I was probably a little distant to it all, but I decided that if I have to work with this, then I needed to know what it is. One cannot criticize something you're totally unsympathetic to. [...] It has always been important for me to have a foot in both camps. I try to relate critically to a lot of things around the body cult, but at the same time it has become a part of my life – a part I have been very happy about. I had never imagined beforehand that I would like to lift weights, but I have discovered that there is a huge sense of freedom in being able to lift your own weight.
>
> (Cited in Steiwer 2015)

For me, the self-portrait made by Lea Guldditte Hestelund and the process it represents is an example of critical thoroughness precisely because of the attitude towards the 'material' (her own, analogue female body as well as bodybuilding as a strategy and technology), which possesses a duality as expressed in the quote by Guldditte Hestelund. She is critical but has a sincere interest in the 'material' and is involved in this. Thus, there is no critical distance as such, but a genuine involvement.

I shall argue that, unlike Lea Guldditte Hestelund's sincerity in her dealings with her artistic material, Martin Erik Andersen's self-portrait (which, curiously, also relates to an ideal sculpture from Greek mythology) has a different attitude towards the material being processed. Martin Erik Andersen has worked with a self-portrait that utilizes 3D technology. His sculpture *Kontrapost: In Order to do Good* from 2010 is a 3D printed figure based on photographs of Martin Erik Andersen himself, who stands in the same posture as the classic depictions of the Doryphoros (one of Greek antiquity's famous statues illustrating Polykleitos' theory of perfect proportions).[1] Rather than pursuing a perfect scan, he has retained the errors and the lack of information that occurs in the scan. This results in partially distorted 3D prints in which certain parts of the sculpture consist of faults and smoothed-over ambiguities (Jacobsen 2015: 7). The attitude towards the material seems critical, humorous and indulgent to me, like saying 'look what my material and technology can achieve, but see, too, what they cannot'. Unlike Lea Guldditte's sincerity and thoroughness,

I would rather put Martin Erik Andersen in the tradition of glitch. I shall explain the concept of glitch and my concept of critical thoroughness in the following.

GLITCH – 'to interrogate conventions through crashes, bugs, errors and viruses'.
(Menkman 2011: 14)

The 3D sculptures made by Martin Erik Andersen could be considered an example of glitch. In her book on glitch, *The Glitch Moment(um)*, Rosa Menkman defines glitch as an '(actual and/or) simulated break from an expected or conventional flow of information or meaning within (digital) information systems that results in a perceived accident or error' (Menkman 2011: 9).

Menkman defines glitch as a mode of noise in a theoretical context of early information theory, as formulated by Claude Elwood Shannon and Warren Weaver (Shannon and Weaver 1963). In Shannon's communication model introduced in 1948, noise is not something that disturbs information. Rather, glitch and noise break the ideal of 'perfect transmission' (Shannon 1948). As the media theorist N. Katherine Hayles has pointed out, there is no such thing as 'perfect transmission': noise is a precondition for information because, to be able to pass on information, there must be a risk of something going wrong. One can also say that information consists of a strange paradox between predictability and unpredictability. In order to hand over information, there must be something that is predictable in advance, i.e. something that exists as possibility. But if everything is predictable, information no longer exists (Hayles 1999: 30–32).

Rosa Menkman describes how the dominant modernist (and twentieth-century) ideal for technology has been the notion of *the transparent channel*: 'Within media design and development cultures, the pursuit of ultimate noise-free and hi-fi channels and supposed highest levels of "reality" has tended to be the holy grail' (Menkman 2011 14). Glitch, as an aesthetic strategy, disturbs this ideal, and the concept has, in my view, some similarities with Bertolt Brecht's famous *Verfremdung* concept – the effect of making the familiar strange. Roughly speaking, one can say that developers of commercial enterprises strive for the noise-free, the highest levels of 'reality', while glitch as an artistic strategy reminds us of the noise, the 'materiality of the medium'. Glitch provides a glimpse into normally obfuscated machine language. Rather than creating the illusion of a transparent, well-working interface with information, the glitch captures the machine revealing itself. Menkman mentions the development of the computer's graphical user interfaces as an example of a tendency to strive for transparency. User interfaces were developed to let users interact with multiple electronic devices using graphics rather than complicated text commands. The development of user interfaces made technologies more accessible and widespread, yet more obfuscated in their functionalities.

Consistent with this description of the historical development of media forms, Bernard Stiegler has analysed the differences in (1) language, (2) mass media, such as television and radio, and (3) contemporary interactive media (that present the graphical user interfaces

Menkman is talking about). Stiegler explains how 'interlocution' is the life of language, referring to how the person addressed must also be able to answer (Stiegler 2009: 37). His point is that audiovisual mass media, such as TV and radio, spoil this interlocution because they produce a dissociation process in which I am spoken to (addressed) without being able to speak myself. Stiegler argues that we have undergone a (positive) development from the reduction of the recipient by radio and TV to a mere recipient of communication to the Internet's designation of us as both senders and receivers – for instance, in social media. However, he also notes that language (communication) is substantially dialogical, and that a problem arises when the person you are communicating with is an algorithm whose language you do not speak and whose development you cannot influence. This involves technologies that communicate to us and help us communicate even though we do not understand how they are created. Hence we participate in symbolic milieus that develop us as individuals even though we ourselves cannot contribute to developing them. Therefore, I do not take part in the collective individuation (Stiegler 2009: 38), i.e. in the ongoing transformation of both the milieu and myself. This, according to Stiegler, is detrimental to democracy/political life.

Glitch, in Menkman's words, catches the machine revealing itself and thereby reminds us of the technologies behind the transparent interfaces. How does critical thoroughness relate to this strategy, and how does it differ? I have already mentioned a difference in attitude towards the material. Whereas glitch points towards the materiality of the medium and the presuppositions for information, through its highlighting of noise and mistakes, my concept of critical thoroughness denotes a rather humble, curious and sincere attitude towards the materiality of the medium. Both glitch and critical thoroughness demand a certain degree of craft from artists. Critical thoroughness tries to a certain degree not only to capture the machine, the technology or the medium revealing itself, but also to develop the machine, technology and the medium before even using it for production. Thereby the strategy of critical thoroughness is somehow responding to Stiegler's criticism of a short-circuiting in which we communicate via a medium or programming language that we do not actually understand, by being the producer and not only the user of digital tools. In the following section I will explain how this production – and critical thoroughness – is carried out in Kristoffer Ørum's performative lecture *The Futuer*.

Kristoffer Ørum – The Futuer

In 2014, Kristoffer Ørum was invited as keynote speaker at a conference arranged by the Danish Association of Science and Technology Studies, with the theme *Enacting Futures* (Ørum 2014). At the conference, he delivered a performative lecture in which he explores various websites relating to the topic of time and the future. Ørum speaks and displays Google results from his computer on the big screen, demonstrating what happens when you misspell something in a Google search – 'future' becomes 'futuer', and 'time' becomes 'thyme', which ends in a humorous and poetic examination of the double meaning of the two words. In the performative lecture, Ørum displays a website that, by using access to his own personal data, visualizes his financial future and also visualizes estimations of his level of happiness in the past and in the future. He also visits a webpage with TED talk videos and displays a music video with a singer who sings pop music in a spherical universe, as she reads Immanuel Kant.

At one point during the performative lecture, the computer stops and displays the graphic circle on the interface that signals that processing is underway. While waiting, Ørum keeps talking and he reflects on how his early computer days were spent waiting – like listening to an old clock at his grandmother's. Suddenly, the minimalist graphic circle changes character, and the audience laughs and watches in wonder until the rotating circle is replaced with a photograph of a rotating piece of thyme. This reveals a rupture or difference in the visual interface signal. Ørum is not simply browsing Wikipedia and homepages on his computer, connected to the Internet. The truth is that the artist has made everything himself: Visual representations of Google searches, websites, Wikipedia entries, the music video. Everything! Ørum is not a 'browser', like a collector of other people's material on the Internet. He has also not added data into an existing home page with graphic calculations on predictions of the future. He has made the whole page, produced and directed the video, the graphic design, the programming and so on. Ørum has thus produced his own (in some cases, visual representations of) interfaces, websites and programs, rather than utilizing existing digital tools or elements.

Kristoffer Ørum's critical thoroughness is comparable to Swedish artist and composer Goto80 when he uses the sounds of low-tech computers to perform, record and release music: 'I try to be less of an artist and more of a worker. Instead of using pre-made music and algorithms, I use software that forces me to do most things by hand' (Goto80, artist testimonial in this volume: 25). He prefers to make everything from scratch. The artistic strategies of these artists raise issues concerning the relationship between user and producer in our contemporary digital environments, which I will examine in the following section. They also raise issues concerning the role of the artist as a producer of tools, as well as concepts such as *techne* and craft from a historical perspective.

In his book *The Invention of Art*, Larry Shiner argues that, before the eighteenth century, there was no distinction between art and craft. This was first introduced with the modern concept of art:

Before the eighteenth century, the terms 'artist' and 'artisan' were used interchangeably and the word 'artist' could be applied not only to painters and composers but also to shoemakers and wheelwrights, to alchemists and liberal arts students. They were neither artists nor artisans, in the modern meaning of those terms, but only the artisan/artists who constructed their poems and paintings, watches and boots according to a *techne* or *ars*, an art/craft. But by the end of the eighteenth century, 'artist' and 'artisan' had become opposites; 'artist' now meant the creator of works of fine art whereas 'artisan' or 'craftsman' meant the mere maker of something useful or entertaining.

(Shiner 2005: 1)

I argue that media art today – exemplified, for example, by Kristoffer Ørum's performance *The Futuer* – is disrupting the distinction between artist and craftsman that developed with the modern concept of art. The concepts are not as such being mixed together. Ørum's status is far from being the same as a developer at Google, who has produced something 'useful', but it is a necessity for Ørum's project that he is able to produce a visual reproduction of a Google search that is just as convincing as a real search. And herein consists his thorough involvement with the digital elements. Of course, this is not to say that artists in the modern concept of art are not thorough or able to handle their specific medium in a thorough way. The difference lies in the development of new tools rather than using what is available, and this is the critical aspect in the digital practices of Ørum and Goto80. José van Dijck describes how 'Michel de Certeau, in *The Practice of Everyday Life* (1984), proposes that people use *tactics to negotiate* the strategies that are arranged for them by organizations or institutions' (van Dijck 2013b: 6). Using de Certeau's distinction between tactics and strategy, we might say that strategy is the framework while tactics are behaviour within these strategies.[2] With critical thoroughness, I would argue that one is inside and altering strategies, not just creating new tactics. The artists are not only users of existing tools and digital elements but also toolmakers. When I highlight craft and artists who make things from scratch as a critical position, however, it can also be seen from another perspective. As the digital poet and net artist Mary Anne Breeze points out in her article 'Inappropriate format][ing][: Craft-orientation vs. networked content[s]':

[I]t seems evident that various web/net/code artists are more likely to be accepted into an academic reification circuit/traditional art market if they produce works that reflect a traditional craft-worker positioning. This 'craft' orientation [producing skilled/practically inclined output, rather than placing adequate emphasis on the conceptual or ephemeral aspects of a networked or code/software-based, medium] is embraced and replicated by artists who create finished, marketable, tangible objects; read: work that slots nicely into a capitalistic framework where products/objects are commodified and hence equated with substantiated worth.

(Breeze 2003)

You could say that Kristoffer Ørum avoids a production of 'crafted' objects by creating a work that is not turned into an object, because the performance has an ephemeral character. Within a capitalist logic, one can argue that it is a waste of time because it does not leave a salable, bounded object, although it has taken lots of 'craft' to produce.

The Relation between Users and Producers in a Media Sociological Context

The artistic strategy of critical thoroughness, in which artists are the producers of the digital material, can be written into a larger cultural and critical media sociological context with an interest in the relationship between the producers and users of digital content. Christian Fuchs has been dealing with web 2.0 optimism and current critiques of it – especially when it comes to the dream of social media and users as producers. He has been analysing YouTube and the utopia of the free, democratic public sphere in which everyone can produce and contribute, but the fact is that on the top ten list of the most viewed YouTube videos by 2011 we only find one video 'produced' by amateurs (the legendary 'Charlie bit my finger'), while the rest are primarily music videos produced by commercial industries (Fuchs 2013). Since around 2013, amateur YouTubers such as Pew-die-Pie started to emerge. A Swedish teenager sitting in his room commenting on computer games suddenly had 60 million followers. Nevertheless, the media theorist Olga Gurinova characterizes the general media user of our contemporary culture as a lurker (Gurinova 2017). This concerns the relationship between sender and receiver in a variety of media types, which I have dealt with in perspective of Bernard Stiegler's theory of the relationship between user and recipient and their interaction in historically-developed forms of media, such as language, radio and television, and new digital and social media. José van Dijck makes the important objection that the relationship between active and passive must be qualified. In particular, our utopia of what she calls the UCG [user generated content] sites must be revised: 'The implied opposition between passive recipients defined by old media (e.g. television) and active participants inhabiting digital environments, particularly UGC sites, is a historical fallacy' (van Dijck 2009: 43).

As Bernard Stiegler has put it, today's technologies have the ability to communicate to us while we communicate through them. In this sense, technologies have agency and a powerful influence on visual and medial discourses in general. As mentioned in the introduction to this chapter, José van Dijck argues that, in a contemporary social media context, creativity should be accredited to a complex amalgam of actors, but the fact is, according to her, that web 2.0 users are often more passive users than active creators (van Dijck 2009: 43).

Conclusion

That users of television and radio were passive while web 2.0 set the stage for interaction and user-generated content is a historical myth. This is an image that needs nuancing, according to van Dijck; and, according to Stiegler, it is problematic that, when we communicate on the Internet, we are doing it via frameworks and tools about the production of which we know nothing and to the development of which we contribute nothing. Stiegler is interested in the development of new technologies. How do they determine our opportunity to communicate something and what do they communicate to us? Do we know how technologies function and are we able to be involved in developing and changing them? This raises very real political implications in our contemporary media landscape – must we accept a communicative economy in which our behaviour, communication and interaction are disciplined, determined and interpellated by tools we do not understand, influence or develop? A problem arises when the entity with which you are communicating is an algorithm whose language you do not speak and whose development you cannot influence. This concerns technologies that communicate to us and help us communicate even though we do not understand how they are created and why we participate in this way in communicative milieus that develop us as individuals, but to which we ourselves cannot contribute. Should we teach our children programming in school and change legislation so that we do not become subject to the existing tools and their (secret) logics and restrictions? It is in this light that Ørum's practice exhibits critical thoroughness in that he does not make use of existing material but is himself the producer of both content (music video) and tools (the system for data visualization).

I have tried to explain in this chapter what is meant by critical thoroughness in contemporary Nordic art. I have placed the concept of critical thoroughness in relation to – but also as distinct from – the concept of glitch, in which the difference, among other things, consists of the attitude towards the material used. The glitch movement seems to have a desire to recall noise and error as the prerequisites for information, whereas critical thoroughness demonstrates a more sincere attitude towards the material used.

In perspective of Nordic art, and of the art in dialogue with society, critical thoroughness embodies a call to politicians in the Nordic countries to take digital education seriously. If you teach school children to program and gain an understanding of the production of digital tools, they become engaged in the communication that takes place via digital media and not just passive users of digital tools. As Bernard Stiegler argues, the act of being the producer and not only a user is a precondition for democracy.

The artists I have associated with critical thoroughness often prefer to produce their own tools and digital elements, becoming producers and not only users (albeit in a discreet and humble way), and thereby touching on issues and institutional strategies with regard to our contemporary media culture. Critical thoroughness refers to making things from scratch and, although still within the complex framework of contemporary art, to be both an artist and a worker.

References

Breeze, Mary Anne (2003), 'Inappropriate format][ing][: Craft-orientation vs. networked content[s]', *Journal of Digital Information*, 3:3, (n.pag.).

Bürger, Peter (1974), *Theorie der Avantgarde*, Berlin: Suhrkamp Verlag.

Dijck, José van (2009), 'Users like you? Theorizing agency in user-generated content', *Media, Culture & Society*, 31:1, pp. 41–58.

—— (2013a) 'Social media platforms as producers', in T. Olsson (ed.), *Producing the Internet – Critical Perspectives of Social Media*, Gothenburg: Nordicom, pp. 45–62.

—— (2013b), *The Culture of Connectivity – A Critical History of Social Media*, New York: Oxford University Press.

Fuchs, Christian (2013), 'Social media and capitalism', in T. Olsson (ed.), *Producing the Internet – Critical Perspectives of Social Media*, Gothenburg: Nordicom, pp. 25–44.

Gurinova, Olga (2017), 'The lurker and the politics of knowledge in data culture', *International Journal of Communication*, 11, pp. 3917–33.

Hayles, Katherine N. (1999), *How We Became Posthuman: Virtual Bodies in Cybernetics, Literature and Informatics*, Chicago: University of Chicago Press.

—— (2014), 'Speculative aesthetics and object oriented inquiry (OOI)', in R. Askin et al. (eds), *Speculations V: Aesthetics in the 21st Century*, Brooklyn: Punctum Books, pp. 158–79.

Jacobsen, Lise Skytte (2015), 'Print dit skrig – 3d printningens kunstneriske potentiale', *Billedpædagogisk tidskrift*, 3, pp. 4–9.

Menkman, Rosa (2011), *The Glitch Moment(um)*, Amsterdam: Network Notebooks 04, Institute of Network Cultures.

Shannon, Claude E. (1948), 'A mathematical theory of communication', *Bell System Technical Journal*, 27:3, pp. 379–423.

Shannon, Claude E. and Warren Weaver (1963), *The Mathematical Theory of Communication*, Champaign: University of Illinois Press.

Shiner, Larry (2001), *The Invention of Art*, Chicago and London: University of Chicago Press

Steiwer, Louise (2015), 'Som var hun hugget i marmor', *Kopenhagen*, http://kopenhagen.dk/magasin/magazine-single/article/som-var-hun-hugget-i-marmor-lea-guldditte-hestelund/. Accessed 3 February 2017.

Stiegler, Bernard (2009), 'Teleologics of the snail: The errant self-wired to a WiMax network', *Theory Culture Society*, 26:33, pp. 33–45.

Ørum, Kristoffer (2014), 'The futuer', YouTube, https://www.youtube.com/watch?v=UmgSc TtokSk. Accessed 20 June 2016.

Notes

1 The sculpture is also used by Martin Erik Andersen in his hybrid installation *In Order to Do Good (Acoustic)* from 2010.

2 It would be interesting to discuss these issues with the distinction between system-immanent criticism and self-criticism, which Peter Bürger in his *Theorie der Avantgarde* (1974) borrows from Marx.

Interactivity Dynamics

Lorella Scacco

In the 1990s, globalization, access, flexibility and openness created the conditions for the expansion of personal experience, with the spread of digitization processes enabling the automatic processing of information. Cyberspace, our computerized environment that embraces many computer users and computer data, has facilitated connections, coordination and synergies between individual intelligences. This fluidity of thought has increasingly marked our society, thanks to the spread of social networks. Evolution today seems to concern more co-evolution: we learn and grow through a variety of encounters and relationships, whether real and/or virtual. Things are no longer governed by one sovereign principle but rather by a phenomenon of 'reciprocity'. It is the part of the whole that the self expands. Now, keywords are 'sharing' and 'interacting'.

This is significantly the case for contemporary art where cohabiting styles, languages and techniques are very different from each other in the single artwork. The digital revolution has made the image infinitely more malleable, with great cost and time advantages. The term 'interactive' can be used to mark this age. The dynamic of interactivity that guides my essay is investigated not only as a tool but also as an ongoing interchange of digital information, culture and lifestyles. To interact means 'to act reciprocally', to cause and undergo at the same time. The desire to actively involve the viewer into the inception, creation and completion of the same work of art is a phenomenon that has its roots in the historical avant-garde. Just think of Marcel Duchamp's *Bicycle Wheel* (1913), where a wheel rotates on a painted stool inviting the viewer to turn it, to 'interact' with the ready-made. The birth of binary language has allowed artists to have increasingly powerful and engaging interactive devices. In the case of Nordic artists, for instance, the digital dynamics have introduced a new hybrid relationship with nature and with that altered the ancient Nordic canon of nature.

Interactive Devices

In computer culture, interaction is the active participation of a user through a data, information or image transaction. The physical devices that perform this connection function are called 'interfaces': they transform and reconvert movements, audible signs and visual signs at will. The information is not limited to an exchange of electrical impulses but goes through the gestures and sounds of the people who produce the interaction. Through interactivity, the work of art is 'in our hands', that is, you can participate in its construction or re-invention. It is not just a mode of participation in the construction of its meaning (as with 'traditional' art), but a co-production of the work since the viewer is often called upon to directly intervene and create a sequence of signs or events. It is a collective creation, often a work-event, meaning the final result of interactive or participatory work is determined by the actions of the public. Interactive artists like Jeffrey Shaw, Lynn Hershman and Perry Hoberman, encouraged the audience to create their own narratives and associations with their actions. We can recall the interactive environment *Lorna* (1979) by Californian artist Lynn Hershman, which critics widely consider to be the first 'interactive media art' piece (Rush 1999: 203). The video presents the story of a woman, Lorna, who lives in her apartment without any contact with the outside world. Through the video, the viewer can communicate with the woman's world and save her from her loneliness. The changing on-screen sequences determine the development of the story, creating a personal version.

The latest technologies – and in particular interactivity – are oriented towards the stimulation of our multi-sensory experience, which simultaneously target many of the recipient's senses. Interactivity in art not only involves the eye but increasingly engages touch, kinaesthesia and proprioception. The 'point of view' is flanked by proprioception, that is, from the information gathered by our muscles and tendons, which allow us to identify, for example, our position in space. The design of these 'virtual' spaces also exploits temporal processes of our senses. Changes in our awareness of time are adjusted by our emotions (you only need to think about how different time is experienced when you are waiting or if you are angry). In these virtual and interactive environments, our involvement depends upon the relationship that is going to be established between the environments and our temporality. Digital technologies are developing new perceptual alphabets that we are learning to understand and use. They create new sensibilities, which interlace, analogize, overlap and blend between the digital and analogue, between the organic and the inorganic. Today, we live – increasingly – in the oscillation between physical/material perception and virtual/intangible perception. We can live without continuity between these two dimensions.

Digital and Biological

Scientists are transforming computers into organic machines. Whilst the scientist Gerald M. Edelman claimed that the computer cannot hear, Marchesini has announced that:

> new 'bioputer' is born, a biological computer system. In America, DNA molecules are already being used to perform complicated calculations. Other experiments use leech neurons connected to chips, which are a hybrid of silicon and carbon, of technology and essence of life, producing autonomous biological realities.
>
> (Marchesini 2009)

The new intelligent machines will be a mix of consciousness, emotionality and social skills. They are currently somewhere between interactivity based on silicon and that which comes from organic life. In that case we have to deal with a new kind of sensory communication between us and the machines.

Laura Beloff is working in this direction and may be considered one of the pioneering artists in this area of research in the Nordic countries. The Finnish artist has always been interested in the crossover of science, technology and art to make the public aware of important issues and get their opinions on them, as shown by her first interactive installations that created new inclusive realities rather than simply reproduce reality in a virtual way. In these experiments, based on the physical and emotional effects of an interactive system in real time, Beloff very soon noticed that the strong expectation from viewers of what would happen after their interactions became a limit for the development of her work. So her attention shifted from the reactions of people to the reactions of 'systems', since they allowed her to work on a technological element that fed on her own life and was modified according to her environment with less dependence on public actions. In her 'wearable works' such as *Head* (2004–7) and *Heart Donor* (2007) the role of the target audience is fundamental. These works are designed to increase new potential users over a long period of time rather than to get quick responses to their actions. In this sense, Beloff hopes that this technological clothing will be used in peoples' everyday lives instead of only being shown in museums.

After this phase of research, Beloff has explored the divide between the digital and physical universe, for example in *Seven Mile Boots* (2003–4). Here the person who wears the boots designed by Beloff, along with Berger and Pichlmair, can simultaneously 'walk' in the physical world and the Internet world whilst listening to various chats. The work is 'open' (Eco [1962] 1989), expanding upon the semiotic concept of such words in a technological way, which brings together real people in real time, or rather, in 'real life', as the artist herself states. It creates

a possibility of space which pushes the users forward in a search for more. This deficit creates the desire for substance, a desire to consume and to experience. The piece seduces in one hand with knowing and on the other hand with not yet knowing; What will happen now? What will be the next response?

(Randomseed Official Website 2003–04)

It is a work in progress that evolves in close contact with the users and the real and digital space that surrounds them.

The perfusion of bio-technology connection and the connectivity of technological support made the miniaturization of computer systems possible, allowing the creation of hybrid products in continuous transformation and redefinition. Recently, Laura Beloff has created new bio-technological connections in perceptual or experiential fields by working towards a university research project titled *Hybrid Matters*. One of her experiments predicts the inclusion of non-human biological organisms inside technological networks, as in the recent project titled *Fly Printer*. One of the three finalized versions, *Fly Printer – Extended* (2016), is a work that raises philosophical and existential questions about standardized methods of printing, and therefore on the current predominance of a uniform and standard visual communication. The artist has created three versions of the installation, which consists of a printing device where a glass sphere is home to a group of midges. These small organisms feed on inks mixed with food and, after digestion, form small coloured dots in no particular order on paper placed under the transparent globe. Biological organisms must therefore replace a technological function of our common printer. *Fly Printer* indicates a gap between the engineering and the organic and at the same time holds back human control on information and biological species. The results of the printer designed by Beloff are indeed uncontrollable because the printouts are random traces of biological processes. As the artist, along with co-creator of the installation Klaus, states:

> The biological and the cultural are reunited in this apparatus as a possibility to break through a common way of depicting the world, trying to find different surfaces and using a strange apparatus to insist in the interstice of visibility. Through the *Fly Printer* happens the becoming of a colourful dot, what is there to be seen? To be interpreted? This is a disruption of the chances of sense.
>
> (Laura Beloff Official Website 2017)

In another version of the printing device, the artist presents advancement in research by inserting the Artificial Intelligence reasoning to interpret the coloured dots left by midges. In *Fly Printer – Extended*, biological organisms are in fact considered elements of signs that produce technology, but the printer also includes an intelligent system with a camera and convolutional neural network (CNN) to recognize and interpret the images. So the installation creates a system that first produces images with flies; secondly, an artificial vision system observes these images as models and finally, artificial intelligence (CNN) will interpret these abstract images to a human observer. The observer will see on the one hand the real dots produced by flies (under the sphere), and on the other hand the interpretation of the dots made by artificial intelligence (in projection) being able to make comparisons in its subsequent decoding. Here the interactive artwork is no longer 'in our hands' because the viewer is not directly involved in its construction or re-invention but is allowed to interrogate it to form their own opinion about the meaning of a hybrid nature work. This establishes a comparison between biological and artificial interaction with an evolutionary and synergetic potential to be discovered. With the *Fly Printer* project, Laura Beloff and her co-author raise questions about digital aesthetics and its future developments.

Life Space

The atypical nature of some projected, particularly moving, images in some places and the ability to interact with them raises new poetic imagery and extraordinary physical entanglements. Take for example Mona Hatoum's installation *Corps étranger* (1994) in which the artist made the public experience a 'simulated walk' inside of her vital organs by projecting them on the floor. The author had inserted a small camera inside her body, which recorded the functioning of her internal organs. Ever since this innovative installation, contemporary art has continued to impress us with exciting new forms and expressions.

From the point of view of perception, objects – regardless of whether they are real or virtual – never refer to a homogeneous reality; objects are never 'all in one piece', passive and unchanging in front of us. Already in the 1930s, Kurt Lewin, the father of topological psychology, suggested the perception of objects to be studied in the context of what he called the *life space* (Lewin [1936] 1961). This is a heterogeneous, complex and articulate space, which of course includes objects and the relationship between things and people, not just between people and places. Norwegian artist HC Gilje works in this direction with his installations, seeking to stimulate a resonance between the physical space and the mental space of audiences. The artist conceives his work as a moment of pulsating life in inanimate environments with the goal of transforming the place. Although starting from the concept of a dialogue between himself and the site preselected for the installation, his spatial projections and moving light installations trigger new perceptions in the audience. This happens for example in the installation *Projected Light Objects: Circles* (2011), which revolves around the boundary between projected light and real space through a series of circular projections, which constantly change the perception of the physical circle, and in *Revolver* (2013), where the shadow of the viewer interacts with the light and shadow installation.

The Norwegian artist uses technology to control our perception of motion. The slightest change, or lack thereof, also has an impact on our experience of time. As Gilje himself states: 'If there is little or no change in an environment, this affects our experience of time. If there is motion happening at various speeds (like the pulses of light in *Trace*), both the experience of space and time seem to expand and contract' (Gilje 2016). The installation *Lightspan Forest Flares* (2014) triggers our perception in a similar manner. Originally situated in a forest outside of Oslo, pulsating lights moving on a string between trees allow us to briefly discover a clearing in the forest before it closes again in the dark. In the installation *Flimmer* (2015), black strips are hanging from a gallery ceiling, and light breaking through the strips and their shadows animate the space, as wind passes through it. Gilje's light installations distort the concept of static space and container objects. In another of his installation works, *In Transit* (2012), hanging white frames are lit gradually by a passage of light, one by one marking the space and moving the homogeneous environment. The site-specific installation *Snitt* (2010) is a straight line that slowly moves through the three rooms of the gallery space, 'cutting' the environment into different sections. The movement of the line, viewing the space from various angles, focuses the viewer's attention on the physical quality of the gallery, like the walls, ceiling, floor, door openings, pipes, lighting, etc. The moving line of light, however, modulates and interrupts its straight linearity with a series of continuously evolving segments according to the observer's position and the angle of the line, with respect to the architecture. The theme of movement is still under investigation in *Puls*, which is a light installation from 2010 commissioned for the Bybanen-Bergen city tunnel. This is formed by two waveforms lights with a total length of about 400 metres, in one side of the tunnel blue and white and in the other side red and white. The movement of a train through the tunnel makes the waves appear as if animated, creating an emotional state in the traveller.

The concept of *life space* returns in Mogens Jacobsen's installation entitled *Hörbar/Audiobar* (2006) at the Museum of Contemporary Art in Roskilde, Denmark. This installation allows you to explore a large collection of sounds through social interaction with physical objects – bottles, which can be placed on a table in the middle. The visitor can interact with the sounds in the 'audio-bar' by way of moving the bottles. As the Danish artist explains: 'The bottle- and bar-metaphor was chosen to facilitate social interaction between the visitors at the *Hörbar/Audiobar*' (Mogens Jacobsen Official Website 2006). Each bottle has a label indicating its contents, which may have different percentages of rhythms and vocals. All sounds gathered come from the Art Museum of Roskilde's collection of international audio-art from 1890 to present day.

Renowned as a Danish pioneer in 'net art', in 2001 Jacobsen nonetheless left behind the monitor and the computer as a means of expression, which he felt to be too limiting, and dedicated his practice to creating objects and installations with electronic and algorithmic elements (Jacobsen 2008). In his recent works, electronic data and network connectivity are often key elements, as for example in *Electric Shadows of Wu*, an interactive installation created in 2014 at the Vallensbæk station, near Copenhagen, playing with concepts of theatre, shadow puppetry and cinema. The installation consists of projected images and texts inspired by the Soviet novel *We* (1921) by Yevgeny Zamyatin, which are activated by the movement of passengers waiting for trains at night and in the early morning hours. The visual spectacle is determined by the travellers who become performers of words and poetic images.

Digital Dynamics

Thanks to the digital language, the image becomes information on the computer and all data can be manipulated, in contrast to the fixity of the traditional visual image in painting or sculpture. Peter Weibel once noted that: 'For the first time in history, the image is a dynamic system' (Weibel cited in Rush 1999: 170). Photography has quickly taken possession of digital language to alter and transform images. Photographs are translated into computer language by scanning, a simple process that transforms two-dimensional images into a mathematical binary. The raw material becomes malleable from the moment it becomes constituted of digits. The digital photography duo Aziz + Cucher has stated that: 'with the end of truth in photography has come a corresponding loss of trust; every image, every representation, is now a potential fraud' (cited in Rush 1999: 187–88). Digital technology cannot only be faked but can also expand the visual and creative new possibilities for a photographic work. This we find in the work of the Canadian artist Jeff Wall, who uses the computer to make montages of images that he could not otherwise do. The computer has also allowed the creation of objective reality alterations for which there is no correlation in the outside world, the surrounding reality. All of this has generated new feelings of uncertainty and instability that are connected to the absence of mimesis, that is, the system of representation of the world, which however has crumbled since the beginning of the twentieth century. Today, interactive visualization replaces representation and simulation follows mimesis. As stated by the scholar Franco Fileni: 'A continuous work of digitization leads to increasingly larger abstractions, but doing so leads further and further away from the first references' (Fileni 1999); i.e. from reality – creating a sense of a 'safe distance' from reality.

This mode of drifting away from the physical object is found not only in architecture, industrial design and design, but also in the transmission of television images, the Internet, video-games, etc. The Icelandic artist Egill Sæbjörnsson's artistic research involves the link between mental reality and phenomenal reality in an original and ironic way, sometimes reversing the positions to test the viewer and his 'safe distance' from the things that are authentic or digital. Born in 1973 in Reykjavík, and with a background in painting, drawing and music, Sæbjörnsson has always been fascinated by video and animation and in particular by the potential to replicate reality. In his installation works, the artist creates different interactive environments through everyday sculptures and objects that emit sounds or words, while video is often projected on elements of the installation. This is the case with *Ping Pong Dance* (2006), where the filmic image of two playing balls is projected to look like they are flying out of two real baskets. They move in all directions, in spite of the laws of gravity, and emit specific sounds. In this way the viewer participates in a virtual event under construction. Through the projection of videos onto objects, Sæbjörnsson expresses his interest in the connection between what we think and what is happening in the world around us. The videos can be considered a replica of reality, or vice versa. The individual constantly projects her or his thoughts onto the world as s/he registers through her or his own senses. In the installation *Kugeln* (2008), a few common objects illuminated by light beams coming from the video start emitting colours of lights and variations through the reflections. Here the projection of the video onto objects is meant as a metaphor for projection of our imagination onto reality. Other humorous video animations, such as *The Wall* (2005) and *Wall to Wall* (2008) and the musical *Bonsai* (2014), are ways to communicate and interact with various conceptions of reality. A dialogue between real and digital, between physical and virtual, is reflected both in the choice of instruments and the concepts. Sæbjörnsson says:

I have always been interested in new technologies. In a way, new technology enables us to express the way we feel in a new way and reflect on who we are in a new and often a fresh way. Sometimes expressing is better with older methods and sometimes new. I prefer doing both. For a few years, I have been looking at Virtual Reality and Augmented Reality. I am also interested in all the new chemicals that are being produced. It is always interesting to see how artists deal with new inventions. But sometimes new perceptions can also be made using old methods, put into a new context.

(Sæbjörnsson 2016)

Recently, the artist has been wondering how the computer has changed communicative relationships between people and how the computer is one of the most vital inventions of mankind as it connects us both for business and for relationships between millions of people in every moment of our day (Sæbjörnsson 2016).

Observations on the Effects of Digitalization in the Nordic Context

Today, the reproduction of light and the Nordic landscapes by contemporary artists has been reworked in the post-modern and globalized field, towards a closer attention to socio-technological nature. For example, in the practice of Laura Beloff we find important themes such as the consequences of climate change and our changing relationship with nature. The Finnish artist is always influenced by digital technology, exploring new types of relationships with the natural environment produced by networks, as in *Midnight Sun* (developed with Erich Berger and Anu Osva, 2009), in which light is transmitted from the midnight sun from Lapland in Austria in real time. Or, in *The Condition – cloned Christmas trees* (developed with Jonas Jørgensen, 2016), which raises questions concerning conditions of the planet Earth, for example: Which forms of life can survive in the future? Among the interesting questions Beloff poses in this articulate project – on the existence and commercialization of Christmas trees in Denmark, cloned to meet the aesthetic preferences of buyers, is: How can we evolve our relationship with nature when mankind designs it?

Jana Winderen, one of the most important sound artists in the contemporary Nordic art scene, makes sounds of nature yet unknown to the public known through new technologies. The advent of digitization has allowed the Norwegian artist to create an original sound archive by recording sounds from hidden sources, which are imperceptible to human senses and from places and creatures that are difficult to access, such as those coming from the depths of the glaciers and oceans. In an interview with Sonia Harmon, the artist explains about her research:

> I get surprised every time I'm out recording; there are new discoveries all the time. The first time I heard underwater insects I was in a river in Russia. It sounded like crickets, but I just thought, *what is this!* I like giving the headphones to people to listen so I can see the look that comes over their faces.
>
> (Harmon 2016, original emphasis)

The Norwegian artist scours the hidden depths of nature with the most advanced digital technologies, revealing the complexity and strangeness of the world that is invisible to most people. During expeditions, she takes several hours to record in various places, documenting those sounds that become the 'time capsule of sounds'. In the same interview, Winderen notes that ocean sounds may be rapidly different in the next couple of years due to the disappearance of coral reefs and some fish species. Her work constitutes an archive of sounds coming from the natural environment over time. Contemporary artists like Beloff and Winderen exemplify the new course of Nordic contemporary art, which seems to express a shift in interest from the romantic and melancholic inspiration of nature towards the urgent need to protect it by making the public aware of fundamental questions about how to safeguard natural resources, and by documenting some habitats before they disappear. Today, moreover, the reality of climate change and ecological issues has become a constant part of the visual imagination of all of us.

Thanks to digital culture, Nordic artistic expression was eradicated more easily than it originally was and migrated to new international influences. In the case of Iceland, a remote nation in the North Atlantic Ocean, Egill Sæbjörnsson for example explains:

I think I am very Icelandic, whatever that means, growing up in Iceland during the Cold War, when it felt like Iceland was a thousand times more isolated from the world than it is today. It was a whole different experience from visiting the tourist-loved Iceland of today. Both the ending of the Cold War and the Internet changed very much for Icelanders who are born after that time. As Iceland had almost no visual arts tradition when I was growing up, my eyes were always looking outside of Iceland. I also lived for twenty years in Berlin and Paris and have quite some central-European influence in me.

(Egill Sæbjörnsson, artist testimonial in this volume: 71)

The networkedness of Scandinavia has closed gaps between different national cultures and caused that Scandinavia today is less isolated. Digitization has affected the canons of Nordic culture to blend not only with other European cultures, or at least with a western approach, preparing countries to the flow of migration, which has occurred intensively over the last two decades in countries like Sweden, Norway and Finland. Just think of a recent speech given by the King of Norway, Harald V, on September 2016 at the Royal Palace in Oslo, who said: 'We are all Norwegians: girls who like other girls, guys who like other guys and girls and boys who love each other [...] Norwegians believe in God, in Allah, in everything or nothing. Norwegians are also those who came from Afghanistan or Pakistan, Poland, Sweden, Somalia and Syria' (King Harald V. of Norway 2016).[1] Future Nordic generations will be increasingly more genetically varied, which will have cultural and political consequences such as new behaviours and lifestyles. The multiplication of access to communication channels has already partially contributed to the opening and socio-cultural integration in the Finno-Scandinavian area, although not free from fear and rigidity, which Southern Europe has experienced for centuries, thanks to its geographic location. In a general sense, the advent of some new scientific developments, such as nanotechnology, protein engineering, biocomputing and the use of stem cells, will change the human individual into a hybrid entity, continuously transforming and redefining. Instead, human cultural autarchy will establish a new vision of the concept of humanity founded on connection with non-human otherness that goes beyond any boundary line or ethnicity.

Conclusion

Returning to the aesthetic field, in the era of 'morphing' in which every individual can alter or blend into anyone and simulations turn into reality, the question of the 'status of the visible' becomes central. The work of art becomes a 'fixed point', a still, in today's flow of thought and action. This is thanks to the art's 'uniqueness' and 'durability'. Citing the words of Hans-Georg Gadamer: 'the work of art [...] is not only the sense of the being carried to finish it. [...] here the meaning is placed on solid ground so that it cannot flow away and become confused, but remains fixed and enclosed in shape' (Gadamer [1960] 1974: 36). The work of art is the crystallization of an experience where an emotional and cognitive expertise is temporarily formed. From here, the artist's responsibility is renewed and s/he creates a work of art with her or his thoughts in the incessant flow of information. The artwork certifies the uniqueness and irreducibility of human individuality and its experience in the era of pixels. The work of art is a statement of existence; it is a time of self-assertion with respect to the changing thoughts of digital communities. Within the interrelated processes of digitization and ongoing globalization, which conform to the complexity of certain channels and partially atrophy thought and sensitivity, the artistic experience acquires great importance because it becomes a point of view transmitted to others. We only need to think of the artistic project *Fly Printer* by Laura Beloff, made together with M. A. González Valerio, which questions homogenous contemporary aesthetics causing the standardization of digital print processes and which offers an alternative experimental bio-technology. The work of art, be it digital or not, is always the sign of 'global peculiarities'. The impact of the digital dynamic of interactivity on art is profound, enabling local visual traditions to amplify to the global realm of aesthetics – through digitalization.

References

Eco, Umberto ([1962] 1989), *The Open Work (Opera Aperta)*, Cambridge: Harvard University Press.

Fileni, Franco (1999) *Analogico e digitale*, Trieste: Edizioni Goliardiche.

Gadamer, Hans-Georg ([1960] 1974), *Wahrheit und Methode (Verità e metodo)*, Milan: Fabbri.

Gilje, H. C. (2016), interviewed by Lorella Scacco, July.

Harmon, Sonia (2016), 'Hear the surprising sounds of ocean life', National Geographic, https://blog.nationalgeographic.org/2014/01/16/hear-the-surprising-sounds-of-ocean-life/. Accessed 10 January 2017.

Jacobsen, Mogens (2008), email interview by Anne Sophie Spanner Witzke and Anne Sophie Warberg Løssing, *Glemsel.net*.

La Stampa, 'Il discorso di re Harald V di Norvegia: "Siamo tutti gay e profughi"', 7 September 2016, www.lastampa.it/2016/09/07/esteri/il-re-di-norvegia-siamo-tutti-gay-e-profughi-qiMgoG3aYH9bmfLWXgEcXM/pagina.html. Accessed 10 April 2017.

Laura Beloff Official Website (2017), 'BIOGRAPHY short', www.realitydisfunction.org. Accessed 10 January 2017.

Lewin, Kurt ([1936] 1961), *Principi di Psicologia Topologica* (*Principles of Topological Psychology*), Florence: Edizioni OS.

Marchesini, Roberto (2009) *Post-human: Verso nuovi modelli di esistenza*, Turin: Bollati Boringheri.

Mogens Jacobsen Official Website (2006), 'Hørbar/Audiobar', https://www.mogensjacobsen.dk/showwork.php?pid=10. Accessed 20 October 2016.

Randomseed Official Website (2003–4), 'Seven mile boot', http://randomseed.org/sevenmileboots/text.html. Accessed 20 October 2016.

Rush, Michael (1999), *New Media in Late 20th-Century Art*, London: Thames and Hudson.

Sæbjörnsson, Egill (2016), interviewed by Lorella Scacco, September.

Note

1 Section from the King of Norway's speech on 1 September 2016 at the Royal Palace in Oslo (La Stampa, 2016).

Where the Inaction Is: The Politics of Digital Things and the Significance of the Lab... In the Practices of Laura Beloff, Kollision and Mogens Jacobsen

Morten Søndergaard

Throughout his various writings, Bruno Latour develops a method of thinking based on the notion of the 'politics of things', which he defines as the balance between human and non-human actants (Latour 2002a, 2005, 2009). The politics of things is deeply rooted in democratic issues and challenges, which Latour, amongst other references, traces back to the Nordic word for Parliament, Folke*ting* (in old Norse 'þing' denotes gathering, literally the physical place of enacting law (ruling and execution) and price-setting (commerce)). The Nordic þing, then, would be a place where the relations between humans and things are being regulated and administered – a 'parliament of things' or an 'agora'; a place where reconfigurations of the relations between human and nonhuman representation in the networked society are decided and acted out (Latour 2005). In connection to this notion of the parliament, but with other implications, Latour develops his concept of the lab as a place where experience and, one could say, the world of the parliament, is interfacing. The lab, in Latour's definition, is a place or situation in which you can experiment with alternatives to the contemporary cultural and scientific (power) structures (and metaphors) (Latour 1983). In what follows, I will be looking closer at what a *Nordic* parliament of digital things (or, the Parliament of Digital þing) might be – and show that in the practices of artists Laura Beloff, Kollision and Mogens Jacobsen the parliament turns into a laboratory where the politics of digital things are being (re)negotiated.

Other Particularities

Digital art is often defined with reference to its 'interactivity' and the technology mainly described as something affording 'interaction' and communicative situations. Rooted in a concept of human-based face-to-face communication, today the concept of 'interaction' is perhaps mainly operative as a digital design concept, which pays reference to a wider field of human-computer interaction (HCI) and user experience studies (UX). Interaction is enabling affordances, it is about making perception possible in a world, which 'unfolds itself in possibilities for action' (Wensveen and Overbeeke 2003).

However, interaction is certainly also more than a design concept. Some contemporary art historians argue that interaction is a 'digital aesthetics' that can be contextualized within a broader art-historian discourse. Christiane Paul sees Digital Art as a continuation of conceptual art and neocybernetic art by the means of digital technologies (and afforded by them): hypertext, relationality and interactivity (Paul 2015 [1999]); Katja Kwastek argues that 'the particular aesthetic experience enabled by these new media works can open up new perspectives for our understanding of art and media alike' (Kwastek 2013).

But what if we look at the particularity of digital art differently? What if the particular aspect of digital art is not interactivity at all? And what if digital art is not merely a new or different gate to experiencing aesthetically, but a reframing of what we perceive as 'real'? This chapter argues that the idea of mimesis between the phenomenology of human ontology and that of computers does not, at least not adequately, characterize a particular dynamic in Nordic digital art. The case-examples – artistic practices – I have chosen for this chapter all suggest that something different is going on behind the surfaces of interactivity.

The artists Laura Beloff and Mogens Jacobsen, and the artist-collective Kollision, are not merely experimenting with digital ontology; they are also, and more importantly for my argument, questioning how the digital emerges as a materiality – a dynamic reality of fabric, 'nature' and 'things'. They are all from the 1990s generation (born in the late 1950s or early to mid-1960s), and they represent in their variety in scopes a certain Nordic modality hinging on a social and immanent critique of 'pseudo cultural' phenomena caught up in the surfaces of a certain politics of things.

In what follows, I claim that if there is a particular Nordic art practice, this particularity must be found elsewhere than in interactive design or – aesthetics; I claim that the practices of these artists reveal an implied, often inertly, focus on the inactivity of technology and the materialities of hybrid digital life beyond certain Nordic romantic notions of big nature, utopia and 'folketing'. I argue that these artists are working mainly to reveal a distance (or inertness) of mainstream culture to what really matters (and the ironic albeit non-cynical analysis of the everyday capitalistic life as a slightly ridiculous endeavour). Instead, their works point towards, or in many cases *stages*, a different nature, places of lost ideologies (or utopias) and digital inaction. In other words: they become (what Latour has termed) agoras (gathering points) or part of a certain Nordic politics of digital things.

Action, Interaction, Inaction

Traditionally, in cultural studies, digital representation has been associated with the database and its effects on cognition in general. In his seminal study of the effect of the database on our patterns of representation, *The Language of New Media* (2001), Lev Manovich calls for a new way of understanding the database as medium – or rather, a new way of understanding how we use this new medium in particular as a cognitive reference-tool. The *language* of new media, then, is not to be understood as a new 'scientism' or 'language of computers'; it should rather be seen as a demarcation of a transformation in the configuration of our cognitive faculties using conceptual metaphors drawn from programming and computer hardware. Manovich describes a very human process, despite its apparent mask of technology: it is really about how we may understand memory as a medium with the database as a metaphor: Computers/technology and culture influence each other and we may very well discover something new about ourselves and the way we navigate ideas about our world. Thus, according to Manovich, it becomes a matter of how we represent and map empirical phenomena. In a following essay, Manovich characterizes data visualization as an 'anti-sublime ideal' because 'data visualization artists aim at precisely the opposite: to map such phenomena into a representation whose scale is comparable to the scales of human perception and cognition' (Manovich 2002: 8).

My claim is that the electronically mediated aesthetics of the artistic practices I am discussing in this chapter 'disinherit' the 'anti-sublime' ideal and all the characteristics of the 'database' and 'interaction' as cultural metaphors. Instead, a new digital dynamic emerges working in situations of inaction (ways of doing things) and materiality (ways of making things). As Jacques Rancière points out in *The Politics of Aesthetics* (2013), then aesthetics 'denotes neither art theory in general nor a theory that would consign art to its effects on sensibility' (Rancière 2013: 4). Rather, 'aesthetics refers to a specific regime for identifying and reflecting on the arts: a more of articulation between ways of doing and making, their corresponding forms of visibility and possible ways of thinking about their relationships...' (Rancière 2013: 4).

In an attempt to frame interaction in a phenomenological discourse, Poul Dourish argues that the experience of digital phenomena is based on embodied interaction (Dourish 2001). Thus HCI, according to Dourish, operates in the context of everyday embodied experience. Human action frames interaction. However, it could be argued that interaction, even embodied interaction, is a reduction of the real digital dynamics that human understanding and psychology – and art – needs to adjust to, rather than the opposite; it is a reduction of that which lies outside the bodily perception and senses, outside the a priori schemes; it is a reduction, moreover, of mathematics, and it is a reduction of data into a cultural analytical a priori. But most importantly, perhaps, interaction is a reduction of representation-aesthetics active in the perception of materiality and performance. Since it is not in itself a medium of representation but a functionalization of data processing, interaction cannot stand alone. Thus, in order to enter human experience and be part of the possible actions of perception, it has to be framed somehow. On the one hand, interaction is always dependent on the codes and algorithms of the databases it is connected to; on the other hand, the usability of these codes and algorithms has to be designed in order for the user to be able to access and use them. But this is only the case if interaction, and the mimesis to embodied experience, is the focal turning point in the study of the digital and digital art. The examples in this chapter are all indicating that the concept of 'interaction' (and all that it implies) is not the best framing for an investigation of what digital art is (in a Nordic context).

For the purpose of clarification (and in risk of oversimplifying matters), it is possible to distinguish two main theoretical sources of this critique of interaction: (1) One is coming from the field of cultural studies and the attempt to shape a phenomenology which sees computation and a 'post-human' cognition as emerging ontologies that cannot only be understood (or reduced to) enhancements of a human action field (Manovich 1996;

Hayles 2012); and (2) the other takes a different approach than the phenomenological – and basically text-based – critique of cultural analysis. Instead, this new 'continental' turn looks at materiality and reality, not as textual interpretation, but as basis for speculation about what is outside the human sphere and the reach of human consciousness, like digital materiality or a number of (quantum) physical instances and how it might affect us (Latour 2002b; Serres 1986; Pickering 1995).

As Lev Manovich points out in 'On Totalitarian Interactivity' (1996), 'interaction' is not representation but rather manipulation, since it is focused on usability: it is limiting the user's choices without making this obvious (Manovich 1996). In 1999, Manovich famously argues that the 'new media' of digital technologies contextualizes culture and language differently. His later studies go further into a study of the cultural implications of this by claiming that by the replacement of mass consumption by mass production of cultural objects by users, computation might be seen as a continuation of the 'culture industry', by imitating the mass production of cultural content and artefacts. Manovich asks, if 'the replacement of *mass consumption of commercial culture* in the twentieth century by mass production of cultural objects by users in the early twenty-first century is a progressive development?' (Manovich 2009: 321). Or, if they rather 'constitute a further stage in the development of "culture industry" as analysed by Theodor Adorno and Max Horkheimer in their 1944 book *The Culture Industry: Enlightenment as Mass Deception?*' (Adorno and Horkheimer [1944] 1969; Manovich 2009: 321). Manovich continues:

> Indeed, if twentieth century subjects were simply consuming the products of the culture industry, twenty-first century prosumers and 'pro-ams' are passionately imitating it [...] they now make their own cultural products that follow the templates established by the professionals and/or rely on professional content.
>
> (Manovich 2009: 322)

This, in many ways, returns the exploration of artistic, or creative, practice to the question of what computation brings to the table and the risk of manipulation/usability hinged on interaction, as well as reductionist naturalization of 'data' as cultural material:

> [T]he true challenge posed to art by social media may not be all the excellent cultural work produced by students and non-professionals which are now easily available online – although I do think this is also important. The real challenge may lie in the dynamics of web 2.0 culture – its constant innovation, its energy and its unpredictability.
>
> (Manovich 2009: 331)

N. Katherine Hayles takes this notion of 'unpredictability' even further in claiming that nonhuman cognition is possible and is increasingly running parallel to human cognition (Hayles 2012). Innovation and energy is a matter of what realities humans and computers construct together, without the one or the other being in complete control (there is no complete 'human' control over 'reality'). The question here is what artistic practice then is, and how can it be said to be culture.

In Manovich's perspective, highlighting his critique of a predominant scientific paradigm seeing 'data' as a separate 'language', digital representation should be associated with the database and its effects on cognition and culture in general. Computers/technology influence our conceptions of culture and the effects of this influence resonate to a large extent in the ways we use data to represent and map empirical phenomena. To Manovich, this does only implicate aesthetic expression, but, perhaps more importantly, poses an ethical challenge to artists in the 21st century.

Even though this critique does resonate with certain elements of the particular Nordic art practice I am looking at, it still seems to want to 'reduce' non-aesthetic elements and instances to an 'interactive' aesthetics. Thus, in what follows I will be following the path of the other, speculative, critique of interaction; look closer into what a *Nordic* Politics of Digital þings might be and how it frames the use of the laboratory (the lab) in the practices of Laura Beloff, Kollision and Mogens Jacobsen.

A Nordic Condition

The parliament of digital þing is evident in the bio-artistic experiments of hybrid ecology by Laura Beloff. For instance, in *The Condition – Cloned Christmas Trees*[1] (2016) the production of Christmas trees for the eternally reappearing Disney/December-event (surpassing the original Biblical 'birth' of Jesus in complete technocultural industry) becomes a visual and somewhat poetic metaphor of the anthropocene 'condition'. The work consists of a collection of nine rotating Norman baby-tree clones mounted on a wall, each fitted with a purple light. This scene emulates a real situation in the science lab where cloned trees are in fact rotated to simulate different conditions of growth – and to create the strongest trees. The aim of the science lab is the perfect technologically enhanced tree – that ultimately could grow in extraterrestrial settings.

What *The Condition* is pointing out is that nature is not a neutral or even constant 'state' of things. It is not even stable as supplier of relations between things. Nature is transitory and changeable and with human technology even more so. The romantic notion of a 'big nature' just waiting for us 'out there' is drawn into question since plant life, as an element of nature, is increasingly being constructed for certain human uses and consumption – in this case, for Christmas parties. But, as the title suggests, this is not a condition only for Christmas trees; it is a condition on a much more general level, and thus the work is speculating about the future that this might bring.

According to Beloff, *The Condition* '…draws attention to the innate, and often overlooked, sentient, agential and social aspects of plant life' (Beloff and Jørgensen 2016). However, '…its merger of organic and technological ultimately remains ambiguous and could equally be construed as a perhaps prophetic foresight of a future that is yet to come, where the natural capabilities of plants are no match for technological rationality and all that these organisms might hope for, is a technological scaffolding, that will sustain their most basic needs' (Beloff and Jørgensen 2016). Plants become metaphors of a new way of organizing things, a politics of digital matters that shapes the way we look for 'ideals' driven by rationality. Thus, plants and biological lifeforms take a seat in what I have termed the Nordic parliament of digital things, becoming part of a politics, a reality outside the human realm of ideas, effecting and affecting that very same realm of ideas (and our perception of those ideas).

This notion of *reframing* ideas and our perception of them is also the turning point of the work *BIOREAKTOR* (2013). Here, the work is a speculative turn in itself towards a new (or, at least different) perception of energy and – if one plays the language-game of physics – the search for the true effect of thermo-dynamics. Beloff argues, that 'instead of aiming at influencing the human behaviour towards more sustainable ways of using energy or proposing plausible solutions for the future, this project is focused on the underlying perception about energy and life as a symbiosis within its surroundings'. She continues: 'On the one hand, the project challenges our perception on production and consumption of energy. On the other hand, the project explores concretely a construct of hybrid ecology formed of networked technology, microorganisms and human' (Beloff and Borch 2013–14).

The bio-technologically mediated aesthetics of Beloff seemingly 'disinherits' the 'anti-sublime' ideal and all the characteristics of the 'database' and 'interaction' as cultural metaphors. There is no sublime big nature behind it all, if there ever were. Instead, a speculative digital dynamic of the real (or what might be real) emerges in her works; situations of social inaction (things do things) and materiality (things make things) proliferate.

Interfering Utopias

Throughout the practices of Kollision runs a vision: to infiltrate artistic domains. In their public designs or installations, such as *Interference* from 2014, they work from the premise of real cultural conditions and their ambiguities. This condition – differently from Beloff's method, which aims at disclosing hidden ideological framings of our conceptual understanding of the world – Kollision boils down to a few, precise technological and visual principles. These principles drive their reality-based interaction, integrating human life directly into the functionality and visuality of their design. Whereas Beloff wants to reflect on the Anthropocene and the loss of a 'big nature' (even if this is a romantic notion or not), Kollision enhances the everyday experience of public sites of former social and cultural ideals (or Utopias) by interfering with them. This is the case in *Interference*, which is a reality-based interaction design installed in a subterranean walking/biking tunnel. The passage of people through the tunnel sets off light-panels mounted on both sides of the tunnel, and a light-pattern will then follow them as they pass through it. The real interference happens, however, when two or more people pass through the tunnel. Then, a basic ambiguity of urban life becomes visible in the tunnel: it is 'based on the idea that urban life is characterized by two opposing trends: an urge to belong and be part of a community and an opposing desire to be alone and anonymous in the middle of the rush' (Kollision Official Website 2012). This basically speculative analysis of urban life by Kollision affords 'a dynamic and interactive lighting concept integrated in the tunnel walls, which focuses on creating a social space between people walking through the tunnel' (Kollision Official Website 2012). The light between people in the tunnel affords an awareness of the urban space and the passage through it.

However, as it appears from the above quote, this ambiguity is not only made visible through the interactive light-panels; it is constructed so that people are made aware that they are both individuals and citizens, anonymous yet belonging to a community. This awareness is central to the particular digital aesthetics that is an integral part of the aim of Kollision, which is to have digital stuff trickle into society via art. According to Kollision:

'Using the digital to augment physical spaces and infiltrate artistic domains is to us an almost evolutionary step to take. Digital stuff is all around us, it is only natural that it also pervades artistic practices – and that those practices in turn trickle into society, as art has always had a way of doing'.

(Kollision, artist testimonial in this volume: 95)

In this way, Kollision is nearer to Laura Beloff in the framing of their artistic method than one might think at first glance. Kollision is as much as Beloff (and Jacobsen, as we shall see) depending on lab-situations: They are indeed involved in a *Politics of Aesthetics*, which, according to Rancière, as noted above, is an articulation of ways of doing and making. The distribution of a digital sensibility and articulations between ways of doing and making that Kollision is setting a stage for is exactly where a politics of digital things emerges. With Kollision, the laboratory is the lived world of real, sensing people: Society's aesthetic atoms.

As we shall see, this understanding of the lab as not being an exclusive expert scene, nor a scene for digital nerds, receives ultimate significance in the practice of Mogens Jacobsen.

A Politics of Digital Things

[A]rt can actually make the politics of things come into its own and flourish. Instead of pulling out its teeth, art can experiment with the power of things. And that is precisely where the democratic answer to the challenge of the politics of things lie.

(Verbeek 2012: 19)

Three instruments are in front of you and at your disposal. They share similarities with the technical test-equipment from the physics department of most elementary schools. But you soon discover these instruments are different, if not in use then in their function. When you turn the knobs of the instruments, you are manipulating statistical data of the sociological and demographical kind; you are entering a game of survival.

On the first instrument, you may manipulate different parameters to create combinations of data: mixing the spread and diversity of age groups in a population. The machine tells you when you find a combination that exists in a real country. At the same time, information about different statistical facts are shown about that country. You can see the result of your interaction on the analogue and liquid crystal displays. All data is real data – about real countries and real people – don't forget that!

The second instrument gives you the opportunity to manipulate demographical parameters in a close-circuit statistical system – in the sense, 'how much money can I spend on military, without the freedom of the press being compromised?' You may now turn one of the three knobs at the time, and when the data resembles a real data-set from an existing country, all instruments light up. In this interface the country remains anonymous, however. The questions raised here are more universal and essential, like the data you encounter in studies looking to educate the world about the world without a human face – countries are reduced to combinations of statistical values only.

The third instrument gives you the chance to scroll through a wide range of different statistical values, this time controlled by a hidden 'rational' force: It contains a GPS module, which makes the instrument site specific. Therefore, it is only possible to scroll through statistical values from the country where the instrument is located. If you want to check out another country, you should move the instrument, physically, to a location within that country's borders. The situation is reversed, it seems: You are offered hard data about the world but now you need to reinvent the experimental laboratory in each country in the world to be able to make comparisons.

This is the *OECDlab* (2011) by Mogens Jacobsen. *OECDlab* is inspired by Bruno Latour and particularly his paper from 1982, 'Give me a laboratory and I will raise the world'. In this article, Latour argues that laboratories, as places of scientific experimentation, and at the very root of modern science, work/function as alternatives to more ideologically charged politics and knowledge constructions. The lab experiments with the foundation for constructing any knowledge that is different from what tradition, beliefs or maybe even prejudice tells us. By (re)visiting the basic elements of our knowledge about the world (and ourselves) from the premise of experiment and agency, Latour argues, it creates a necessary and sometimes controversial alternative to the beliefs structuring the world of politics and society. Conversely, in Mogens Jacobsen's *OECDlab*, the lab is not the control room of the world. *OECDlab* is a small laboratory for private experimentation. And – to quote Latour – 'a place where nothing special is produced' (Latour 1983: 142).

The lab is a central metaphor in Mogens Jacobsen practice: he is constantly experimenting with the core-premises of art, computers and their contexts: data-representation, surveillance, the aesthetics and realities of digital technology and politics. On another level, the metaphor of the lab is connected to the act of memory in a digital world (or rather: the world of digitization) (Chun 2016). The lab strikes a post-human and post-digital dark cord, which becomes visible in the absurdities involved: in the case of the *OECDlab*, it is a lab experimenting with the idea and construction of the lab which is limited in its connectivity to real-time data. It is not a functional lab; cause and effect are severed unless some absurd parameters are met. It is the fate of the lab, perhaps, in an age of big data and increasing control – like it may be witnessed in present-day Turkey or China, but certainly also in 'western' democracies.

Interaction: Ways of Doing Things in the LAB

For this reason, one of the sources of absurdities in Mogens Jacobsen's works are statistical numbers, or rather, the way we use them. As Mogens Jacobsen writes:

> Statistical numbers are used as tools to manage the world. Tools not only give us the ability to solve tasks, but [they] also form our understanding of those tasks. If the only tool you have is a hammer, you tend to see every problem as a nail. I meet statistical numbers almost every day; in the media, in the speeches of rulers and politicians, in finance, in business plans and in academic research. Statistics are made, chosen and juxtaposed to support particular beliefs and to substantiate arguments. Statistics are a way of looking at the world. Presented [in OECDlab] as a translucent window between me and the world, not to be looked at only to be looked through, […] I wish to draw attention to the tool, to scratch the glass and make the window visible.
>
> (Jacobsen 2011)

This notion of the translucent window is also reverberating in the (collective) work *The File Room* at the exhibition *404 FILE NOT FOUND*. As part of an exhibition in 2017 celebrating the founding of the Danish net art gallery ArtNode in 1994, it is perhaps surprising to some that digital art seems to be missing out. *404* is not about the digital as material for net art but about the politics of that digital material as part of artistic practices, which is being exhibited. Files from the ArtNode website are downloaded and the data is then plotted into a coordination system and converted into 'sculptures'; or, rather 'statistical' sculptures. They depict a probability of how they end up in the coordination system. How it would look like if we printed the data from the *OECDlab*, perhaps. As testaments of inaction, they are displayed in a glass case as if they – being converted data – were real museum 'objects'. The conversion itself, however, as well as the situation in the exhibition space, is a frozen lab-moment.

Mogens Jacobsen is questioning our real ability (or right!) to mobilize the lab. A parliament of digital things is depending on a lab that functions without political limitations. But, in effect, this assumption is more often than not out of touch with the political realities of some countries. What then becomes the artistic focus is the soft utopian gaze towards 'things that could be possible' but might not be in the present situation.

> My practice is based on things that could be possible (but not always preferable). I see it as my personal take on constructive research. At the present I feel very explorative and am working in unknown territories when working with physical materials.
>
> (Mogens Jacobsen, artist testimonial in this volume: 50)

The explorative practice of Mogens Jacobsen could be said to be in-between that of Laura Beloff and Kollision. And even though the speculative element is implied in both of the above examples, it is explicit in his artistic method as a way of setting the stage for what is possible, exploring the unknown. However, there is something in the current cognitive framing and cultural politics of things that is preventing or interfering with our ability to act. If there is a certain Nordic artistic sensibility, then it is to go where the inaction is – and establish quiet platforms in unexpected places for meditations on speculative pasts and possible futures.

The laboratory of digital things, even if expressed and developed in very different ways, can be said to be at the heart of the practices of Laura Beloff, Kollision and Mogens Jacobsen. Shared by all is the interest in experimenting with a situation we would otherwise perceive as interactive. In their practices, however, interaction is hiding a cultural and political inaction, creating a void for artistic and scientific agency to explore the unexplored or unexplorable. They are all questioning how technology and digital media is transforming our perception of the real and the world we inhabit. As artists, they go where the inaction is – to speculate about the future.

References

Adorno, Theodor and Horkheimer, Max ([1944] 1969), 'The culture industry: Enlightenment as mass deception', in *Dialectic of Enlightment*, Cambridge: Cambridge University Press.

Beloff, Laura and Borch, Martin Malthe (2013–14), 'A BIOREAKTOR 2014', http://www.realitydisfunction.org/?page_id=25. Accessed 14 August, 2016.

Beloff, Laura and Jørgensen, Jonas (2016), 'The condition – Cloned Christmas trees', http://investigations.hybridmatters.net/posts/the-condition-cloned-christmas-trees. Accessed 14 August, 2016.

Chun, Wendy Hui Kyong (2016), 'Memory', in U. Ekman, J. D. Bolter, L. Diaz, M. Søndergaard and M. Engberg (eds), *Ubiquitous Computing: Complexity and Culture*, London: Routledge, pp. 161–74.

Dourish, Paul (2001), *Where the Action Is: The Foundations of Embodied Interaction*, Cambridge: The MIT Press.

Hayles, Kathrine N. (2012), *How We Think: Digital Media and Contemporary Technogenesis*, Chicago and London: University of Chicago Press.

Jacobsen, Mogens (2011), 'OECD lab', www.mogensjacobsen.dk. Accessed 5 May 2017.

Kollision Official Website (2012), www.kollision.dk. Accessed 20 November 2016.

Kwastek, Katja (2013), *Aesthetics of Interaction in Digital Art*, Cambridge: The MIT Press.

Latour, Bruno (1983), 'Give me a laboratory and I will raise the world', in K. Knorr and M. Mulkay (eds), *Science Observed*, London: Sage, pp. 141–70.

—— (2002a), 'Morality and technology: The end of the means', *Theory, Culture & Society* 19:5–6, pp. 247–60.

—— (2002b), 'What is ICONOCLASH? Or is there a world beyond the image wars?', in B. Latour and P. Weibel (eds), *ICONOCLASH: Beyond the Image Wars in Science, Religion and Art*, Cambridge: The MIT Press.

—— (2005), *Reassembling the Social: An Introduction to Actor-Network-Theory*, Oxford: Oxford University Press.

—— (2009), 'Spheres and networks: Two ways to reinterpret globalization', *Harvard Design Magazine*, 30, pp. 138–44.

Manovich, Lev (1996), 'On totalitarian interaction', www.manovich.net/content/04-projects/017-on-totalitarian-interactivity/14_article_1996.pdf. Accessed 5 May 2017.

—— (1999), *The Language of New Media*, Cambridge: The MIT Press.

—— (2002), 'Data visualization as new abstraction and as anti-sublime', in B. Hawk, D. Reider and O. Oviedo (eds), *Small Tech: The Culture of Digital Tools* (2008), Minneapolis: University of Minnesota Press.

—— (2009), 'The practice of everyday (media) life: From mass consumption to mass cultural production?', *Critical Inquiry*, 35:2, pp. 319–31.

Paul, Christiane ([1999] 2015), *Digital Art*, New York: Thames & Hudson.

Pickering, Andrew (1995), *The Mangle of Practice: Time, Agency, and Science,* Chicago: University of Chicago Press.

Rancière, Jaques ([2004] 2013), *The Politics of Aesthetics*, London and New York: Bloomsbury Academic.

Serres, Michel (1986), *Statues*, Paris: Gallimard.

Verbeek, Paul (2012), 'On art and the democratization of things: Politics at issue', *Open – Journal of Art in Public Spaces*, pp. 5–11.

Wensveen, Stephan and Overbeeke, Kees (2003), 'From perception to experience, from affordances to irresistibles', *Proceedings of the 2003 International Conference on Designing Pleasurable Products and Interfaces*, pp. 92–94.

Note

1 Beloff realized this project as work-in-progress together with artist Jonas Jørgensen for the exhibition *Hybrid Matters* in Art Centre Nikolaj, Copenhagen, 20 May–31 July, 2016.

Visions and Divides in Icelandic Contemporary Art

Margrét Elísabet Ólafsdóttir

The ubiquity of digital technologies has been reinforced in recent decades, with the influx of smartphones, apps, social media, micro-controllers and other digital devices occupying our daily lives. Digital technologies have come to define contemporary culture with their ubiquitous presence (Gere [2002] 2009: 7). Contemporary digital culture and art have their outset in the informatics of the late 1950s and 1960s, when advances in computer and communication technologies were accompanied by various artistic experiments – for the most part in militarized countries leading research and development in the field (Couchot 1998: 133). This becomes evident when we compare countries such as, for example, the United States and Iceland. While in the 1960s the United States were leading technological developments, Iceland was an underdeveloped country with limited access to technological devices (Ólafsdóttir 2013: 173–4). The history of technologically based art is intertwined with the use of technology and media in society at large, and so it is imperative to consider the importance of access to technological devices to comprehend the intricacies of technologically based art practices and media art. In Iceland in the 1960s and 1970s, electronic and digital devices were extremely expensive and difficult to acquire, resulting in artists' limited access to technology. Other aspects – such as economic restrictions and a small homogeneous population – also played a part in the artists' approach to technologically based art and how new trends in art were assimilated by local artists. Digital technologies eventually emerged within the Icelandic contemporary art scene in the late 1990s, following the rapid expansion of the Internet and ownership of personal computers. Still, the notion of new media art, which gained its momentum at the dawn of a new millennium, was never fully embraced.

In this chapter I will study selected historical examples of artist's practices, artworks, exhibitions and experiments which reveal dynamics of opposing perspectives which have affected the way digital technologies and media have shaped contemporary art in Iceland in recent years. The chapter's theoretical background is based on discussions and debates on whether contemporary artists have adapted digital technologies by 'assimilation' to the traditional art scene – and by that refuse to recognize their differentiation as media artists. In the context of Icelandic art, an experimental phase of new technology and media art at their emerging stage, and discussions on technological specificity, has for the most part been side-stepped. Today, Icelandic artists predominantly declare their art to be non-media specific, although many have acknowledged and adjusted to the ubiquity of digital technologies.

The Age of Computers and the Internet

The first two computers arrived in Iceland in 1964 where they were installed at the Record Machines of the State and Reykjavík City – Skýrr (Skýrsluvélar ríkisins og Reykjavíkurborgar) – and the University of Iceland (Óskarsson 2001: 196). These were two official institutions without affiliations to the arts. It was not until the early 1980s, when the first Apple and Microsoft PCs were imported, that computers became accessible to artists living in Iceland and musicians and graphic designers first made use of them. Visual artists did not show any significant interest in the potentialities of computers for their own creative work until the arrival of the Internet in 1995. The Internet spread rapidly, and in spring 1996 the first multimedia event – *Craters on the Moon* – was streamed online from a concert venue in Reykjavik. The organizer was the poet Birgitta Jónsdóttir who had discovered an international community of poets online and now wanted to give Icelandic artists visibility on the Internet. She invited other poets, musicians, graphic designers and visual artists to participate in an event composed of multimedia performances, streamed from *Tunglið* or *The Moon* – a popular concert venue. The event was scheduled as part of the biannual Reykjavik Art Festival and got support from a telecommunication company and the Ministry of Education and Culture. The endeavour attracted media attention and more artists began to show interest in computers and the Internet. This was the beginning of a growing interest towards digital technology among artists

Two visual artists participated in *Craters on the Moon,* Arnfinnur R. Einarsson and Kristrún Gunnarsdóttir. Both artists had studied media and video art in the early 1990s, Arnfinnur at Duncan of Jordanstone College in Scotland and Kristrún at California Institute of Art in Los Angeles. Arnfinnur showed digitized video images at *Craters* and Kristrún was credited as the author of several videos shown as visuals with some of the musical performances. Her most noticeable contribution to the event was *The Ear* (1996), a collaborative audio-visual performance made with the composer Hilmar Þórðarson who had also studied at Cal Art. The performance included a video version of a project, which had initially aimed at creating an artificial intelligent proxy. The final version of the proxy was a representation of an ear. The online version showed an ear ready to 'listen' to Internet users through an interface. The users were invited to write their thoughts into an empty window and send them to the 'listening' ear. Although there was a deceptive discrepancy between the original, technologically ambitious idea of a human AI proxy and its actual realizations, Kristrún's online piece was effective and in tune with other successful online pieces from the period, such as Nicolas Frespechs' *Je suis ton ami(e)…tu peux me dire tes secrets* (1997) where users were invited to tell their secrets.

Craters on the Moon was simultaneously a 'conventional' performance event, presenting music, poetry and video projections, and a breakthrough event, streamed online and gathering artists interested in digital media. The event was a turning point for Kristrún Gunnarsdóttir, who in the following years continued to explore the potentials of the Internet as artistic media. She set up the webpage *Cornucopia* to present her work and create her next online piece. By that time Kristún had become active on Nettime, where on 15 December 1997 she announced the broadcast of sunshine between 11 pm and midnight until Christmas at http://this.is/cornucopia. The piece was specifically created 'for people of the northern hemisphere who miss the sun' (Nettime.org, 15 December 1997). Kristrún's background in video art comes through in these works, as in another project based on a narrative for an interactive television project. The interactive television project never got beyond the developing stage, as was the case of Kristrún's most ambitious artistic projects based on digital technology. Her last project as artist and curator was to organize the online exhibition *Takki* (or *Button*),which opened in 1998 on the site *www.takesyou.to*. The artists exhibiting at Takki were Kristrún, her collaborator, Katrín Sigurðardóttir, Hlynur Helgason, Igor Stromajer from Slovenia, Baldur Helgason and Birgitta Jónsdóttir.

Hopes and Deceptions in the Digital World

In 2000, Reykjavik was one of nine cultural cities of Europe, a status opening new possibilities to get funding for technologically based art projects. The most ambitious project in the genre was an interactive installation made in collaboration between eight artists and two computer scientists. It was conceived of and curated by Hannes Sigurðsson, the director of Akureyri Museum of Art and produced by three IT start-ups. The installation was called '@' and consisted of five independent virtual worlds created respectively by Icelandic Love Corporation, Haraldur Jónsson, Ásmundur Ásmundsson, Ómar Stefánsson and Þorvaldur Þorsteinsson. These virtual worlds could be entered from a digital field made of grids and habited by an avatar created by MY Studio (Michael Young and Katrín Ólína). The third element of the project was a soundscape created by the sound artist Finnbogi Pétursson. The dispositive of the installation consisted of three sculptural bases, each with one mouse, situated in front of a projected image. With a click on the mouse, the spectator could direct the avatar into different worlds by going through one of the 'holes' in the grid. Like Alice, the avatar would fall into a world created by one of the artists. Once inside the work, the spectator could explore it by making choices with a mouse click.

The installation first opened at the National Gallery of Iceland, along with two other exhibitions shown together under a common title: *New Visions – Digital Worlds*. The second exhibition was called *Veflist (Web Art)* and assembled pieces created by Icelandic artists for the Internet. The pieces were shown off-line in the museum and either displayed on computer screens or as video projections on walls. The curator for the exhibition, Bragi Halldórsson, had participated in the organization and design of the *Craters on the Moon* website. In collaboration with María Pétursdóttir he had organized a series of exhibitions for the temporary Gallery Fiskur during the summer 1998, accompanied by a website and followed by the publication of a CD-ROM. The core of the works shown at Veflist had first been exhibited as part of Takki, but it also showed works by María Pétursdóttir and

Egill Sæbjörnsson. The third exhibition displayed a new digital video environment *Mynd* (2000), created by Steina Vasulka.

Another major event related to the digital arts appeared in a program organized at the Reykjavik Art Museum in collaboration with eight other cultural cities of Europe in 2000. The museum hosted a net café – Café 9 – a platform for communication and exchange streamed online to and from the other cities. Among noticeable performances at Café 9 in Reykjavik was Þóroddur Bjarnason's *Parliament of Floating Discussion* – a participatory work that had previously been shown at the Living Art Museum without the use of technology. A more conspicuous contribution to net art was *Sunset* by Páll Thayer, a piece based on streaming images from web cameras around the world.

With the events in 2000 the turn of the century seemed to announce an upcoming proliferation of new media art in Iceland, but soon the initial enthusiasm, which had succeeded Craters, faded out. As a technologically ambitious work, '@' had evoked a sentiment of deception. It had promised a state-of-the-art experience, but appeared technologically imperfect to visitors. More importantly, it was seen as 'unartistic' by the local art world. Furthermore, the disenchantment encountered during the production stage of the work discouraged the participating artists from continuing in that direction. Two years later, in a survey on media art and culture in Iceland, only few artists admitted a genuine interest in digital technologies (Ólafsdóttir 2003: 68–9). One of them was Haraldur Karlsson, video studio manager at the new Iceland Academy of the Arts. The others were Ragnar Helgi Ólafsson and Julie Coadou, both recent graduates from l'École supèrieure d'art in Aix-en-Provence. Together with these artists, in 2002 I founded Lorna, an association for electronic arts, which led to my involvement with the tiny media art scene in Reykjavík. I became a participant and observer, advocating for the recognition of media art and the need to understand the implications of digital technologies within contemporary art and culture.

Based on experiences related to my involvements and theories of media art vs. contemporary art and beyond (Quaranta 2013), I want to describe the development of technologically based art practice in Iceland with the examples of two artists. These artists symbolize two different attitudes towards new media and technology, characteristic for the alleged division between 'new' media art and 'mainstream' contemporary art (Shanken 2010). In Iceland the difference was never seriously discussed. The majority of artists using digital technology have avoided the term 'media art' that emerged with the foundation of media labs and early practitioners of the Internet in the 1990s, seemingly 'afraid' of being marginalized by the more 'mainstream' contemporary art.

Contemporary vs. Media

Páll Thayer and Egill Sæbjörnsson are two Icelandic artists representative of the fields corresponding to media art and contemporary art. Páll Thayer makes a case for the media art in Iceland. He became an active member of Lorna in 2003 and initiated many projects in the following years. He organized workshops, created a festival and established important nodes in Lorna's international network. From the early 2000s he was active in a global network of media artists where he took part in discussions on sites such as Rhizome and participated in different media art festivals. Egill Sæbjörnsson, on the other hand, avoided the media art scene despite being an early practitioner of digital technology. He moved to Berlin in 1999, where he established himself as an artist while keeping his connections within the contemporary art scene in Reykjavik. Both Páll Thayer and Egill Sæbjörnsson – as many other Icelandic artists of their generation – graduated from the Iceland College of Art and Crafts. Páll Thayer studied in the mixed-media department, founded in the late 1970s. He graduated in 1999 and began to learn programming to be able to write his own codes and create net-based art. Although his early works were exhibited at Reykjavik Art Museum and the Living Art Museum, influential protagonists within the local art scene considered Páll's emphasis on programming too technical and maintained that his works were 'non-artistic'. Páll's interest in programming and further more in free and open source software, which he used as both tools and content, contributed to his marginalization within the local art scene. Egill's attitude towards technology was very different. He has said that he first came into contact with digital technology in a Photoshop course at the Icelandic College of Art and Crafts. He graduated from the school in 1997 and already in his early works began mixing real objects, photography and video. Some of his photographs were digitized and used to compose a panoramic environment, using QuickTime VR Software. These photographs were displayed on a computer screen so the spectator could explore an environment composed of still images, creating sequences with a mouse click. Egill was not interested in programming but used Quicktime Virtual in a series of works from 1998 to 2000. He created an untitled installation exhibited at Café Mokka in Reykjavík and the net pieces *Catgarden* and *Miklatún, Bollagata, Kjós,* exhibited at Veflist in 2000.

The same year, Páll Thayer created *Sunset,* a 24-hour web camera-based loop, shown at Café 9. He continued to use programming to create multi-user online pieces, such as *Looking for a Universal Harmony* (2002) and *Panse* (2003). Both offered platforms for experimental audio-visual experiences, inviting the spectators/users to participate. These works had an independent online presence and drew the attention of an international media art scene as well as a growing community of artists interested in open and free software and interactivity.

Egill continued his practice into a different direction. He began to use 2D animation software, which first appeared in video clips made to accompany the publication of his album *Tonk of the Lawn* (2000). The album was a deviation from the visual arts, revealing Egill as a musician. In 2002, these two universes of visual art and music merged in the installation *You Take All My Time* (2002–2003). It was first shown as a musical performance where Egill incarnated a country singer and interacted with animated characters in a theatrical setting composed of props and projected animations. The installation was a turning point in Egill's carrier. He continued to merge real objects and images, adding video projections, animations and dialogues. The dialogues in Egill's art take place between filmed figures or between virtual objects such as in *Ping Pong Dance* (2006) where a 3D animation brings two ping pong balls to life. The movements of the ping pong balls are projected on a wall, in front of which is a bucket. The play between a virtual image and an actual object becomes more complex in *The Box* (2009), were Egill uses 3D animation to merge virtual and actual spaces and objects. In subsequent years, he has embarked on more and more complicated projects, which he could not realize without assistance from skilled programmers.

Páll Thayer, on the other hand, joined a master program at the Concordia University in Montréal where he dived deeper into the web and into programming, relying on online data as material for his work. He used programming to re-interpret photographs available on Flickr in *On Everything* (2006) and in *Nudes Studies in Aleatoric Environments* (2008). In the former work, the reinterpretation referred to Andy Warhol's *Do It Yourself* series (1962), or 'paintings by numbers', while the latter reinterpretation resulted in 'paintings' based on seismic data collected online from different geographic centres. Both pieces had strong references to the history of painting, creating a mixture of familiarity and strangeness. These works also have a didactic quality, as they intend to make the spectator aware of different possibilities of data collected from the Internet and (re)used as material for art. Páll further explores the didactic aspect of his work in a series of program-based artworks called *Microcodes* (2009–13). In this he takes the idea of making the spectator an active participant in the development of the work further by making the code available, demystifying both the creative process and the code. As in *On Everything* and *Nudes*, the Microcodes are inspired by art history. What they do differently from paintings, or conceptual art, is that they invite the spectator to learn coding by transforming the microcode, thus becoming a creator of her or his own micro-codes, and eventually of her or his own work of art.

It is not only the attitude towards technology that distinguishes Egill Sæbjörnsson from Páll Thayer, and vice versa. Egill has concentrated on his career as an artist and has managed to establish himself as such within the global contemporary art scene. Páll Thayer, on the other hand, lived in Reykjavik where he worked full-time as an instructor and web developer. He used his spare time to organize events and workshops for Lorna and occasionally to participate in media art festivals in Europe. In 2010 he got a position as support specialist at SUNY – Purchase College and moved to the United States, where he still works. A year before he left Iceland, he founded Pikslaverk, a festival of open and free software art, held for the first time in November 2008. Pikslaverk was part of the Pixelache Network, established by Pixelache Festival in Helsinki. Pikslaverk was the second media art festival created in Iceland, 18 months after RAFLOST a festival founded within the Iceland Academy of Arts in 2007. In spring 2010, Pikslaverk and RAFLOST joined forces and organized a ten-day festival consisting of lectures, workshops and performances with the participation of local and international artists. The festival was ambitious and successful for the organizers, but the audience mainly consisted of the organizers themselves, their friends, the participants and art students from the RAFLOST student workshop. The habitual crowd of opening goers of contemporary art exhibitions was mostly absent.

Lorna Lab – In Time of Crises

Lorna had been founded in 2002 with the aim to gather artists working with digital technology and to establish a media lab in Iceland. The media lab never got on its feet as the idea did not get financial support. One argument against the media lab was that the laptop had made the need for a lab obsolete. But in 2010 things changed, at least momentarily. Iceland was going through a deep economic crisis after the banks collapsed in October 2008. The banks' downfall provoked political upheavals and protests, but in the midst of the turmoil Lorna held its first Pikslaverk festival. Thanks to a grant from a Nordic fund, the festival could invite a few foreign guests, who gave lectures and performances at the Reykjavik Art Museum. The festival also offered two workshops in SuperCollider (a platform for audio synthesis and algorithmic composition) and Perl (a programming language), held at the Iceland Academy of the Arts. The workshops attracted three young composers, all members of the composer collective S.L.Á.T.U.R. Few months later, in spring 2009, Lorna's members, Ragnar Helgi Ólafsson, Páll Thayer and myself, were invited to participate in the RAFLOST festival, coordinated by the composer Áki Ásgeirsson, also a member of S.L.Á.T.U.R.

This happened in the midst of the financial crises, which had generated an atmosphere of solidarity within the arts. There was a need to consolidate with others and that had an unexpected effect on the media arts. Before the crisis, there had been a growing interest in the creative industries and now there was a strong lobbyism in their favour. As a reaction to the crises and a predictable growing unemployment rate among designers and artists, the University of Reykjavik and Iceland Academy of the Arts joined forces and financed a space for designers and start-ups in a former saline cure factory in 2009. The project was called Hugmyndahúsið, or House of Ideas, and was meant to assist the creative industries to foster new employments. In spring 2010, House of Ideas announced the opening of a second space, called Útgerðin, in an abandoned fishing factory dedicated to art, technology and science. Before the formal opening for applications, the festivals Pikslaverk and RAFLOST were allowed to organize workshops and concerts in the empty 1000 m^2 space where part of the ten-day festival was held.

Lorna applied for a space at Útgerðin together with the artist Erik Parr, who had recently moved to Iceland from the United States, and Halldór Arnar Úlfarsson, who had recently returned to Iceland after finishing his Master of Arts in Finland. Áki Ásgeirsson, the coordinator of RAFLOST and co-founder of S.L.Á.T.U.R. also got involved and in August 2010 Halldór Arnar and the members of S.L.Á.T.U.R. moved into Útgerðin. In the course of the next five months regular group activities initiated by the artists created unexpected dynamics. The artists – and a group of hackers who were the first occupants of Útgerðin – attracted a wide range of individuals from the art community and the University of Reykjavik through workshops, lectures, informal discussions, problem solving meetings and other activities organized under the umbrella name Lorna Lab. In a few weeks' time Lorna Lab had created a large local network and continued to cultivate its connections abroad. Unfortunately the universities were reluctant to continue to use their funding on activities outside their establishments in times when their budgets were being reduced. The individuals involved in Lorna Lab and the House of Ideas tried to convince the Ministry of Education, Science and Culture and the Ministry of Industries and Innovation, to give them more support, however without success, and in February 2011, both the House of Ideas and Útgerðin were closed.

Fortunately, Lorna Labs' activities had not gone unnoticed, as Reykjavik Museum of Art invited its artists to host regular workshops at the museum. Lorna Lab had its first event in spring 2011 and held regular workshops for the next two years, until the group split up in 2012. After losing the space at Útgerðin, Lorna Lab had no fixed meeting place, which slackened the ties, and the institutional requirements of the museum were too onerous to preserve the dynamic of the group. Also, the experimental activities of some of Lorna Labs' members had attracted the attention of the departments of music and design at the Iceland Academy of the Arts, and they were invited to install a sound lab at the academy. In reverse, the visual art department was reticent towards this development and decided to distance itself from Lorna Lab members and their activities, arguing that they were too technical.

At the same time, digital technologies were having a growing impact on contemporary art on a global scale, which called for new definitions. Many claimed the beginning of post-media (Quaranta 2013) and post-Internet art (Connor 2013), meaning that the distinction between the two worlds was disappearing. Different protagonists argued whether and how these two worlds would fuse. The media art historian Edward Shanken called for a hybrid discourse, but contemporary art theorist Claire Bishop has argued that the two worlds would remain separate despite the infiltration of digital technologies into contemporary art (Bishop 2012). The evolution in Iceland points towards confirming Bishop's observation, however, it is useful to remember that the quarrel between a recognized field – and demand for legitimization of new technological practice – tends to operate with the establishing field refusing or failing to recognize the newcomer its specificity. This has happened before to older media, such as photography and video. In the 1970s, video art went from being a specific field into being merged into mainstream contemporary art practice (Movin and Christiansen 1996: 17–9).

Video Art

Video art is disposed to escape predefined definitions and categorizations due to frequent changes in technology. The effect of technological changes becomes visible when an analogue, grainy, black and white video image from the 1970s is compared with today's digital high definition colour image created with seamless mixing and editing. A black and white still from Steina Vasulka's *Violin Power* (1970–78) put beside an image from Björk's music video *Mutal Core* (2011) demonstrates how technological changes alter video's aesthetics, while it also reveals the diversity of video practices. All the same, the comparison of those video stills underlines the importance of accepting that the history of video art is intertwined with the history of technology and media. Another example of how video art and technology are mutually dependent is the paradigmatic change that took place in the early 1990s, the decade that marks the beginning of the rise of video art in Iceland and in the Nordic region at large. During this decade, projectors gradually replaced monitors as a privileged mode to exhibit video art. The display of video works shifted from single monitors and their sculptural assemblages to multiple projections on museum walls and big screens, thus bringing the video closer to cinema than monitors that referred directly to television and surveillance.

Technology supports the equipment used to make video, linking the artistic practice to artists' access to tools. The relevance of this connection becomes clear when we compare stories about how video art came into being, not only in time but also in a particular place. The universal history of video art generally starts with the story of how media technology became accessible to artists in the 1960s in a more democratic way than computers in the same decade – and how they adapted the new media into their art practices (Meigh-Andrews 2006; Spielmann 2008). Nam June Paik could be chosen as a leading character in that story, which either begins with his legendary exhibition in 1963, *Exposition of Music – Electronic Television*, in Wupptertal, Germany, or when he filmed the Pope in New York two years later. Both beginnings point to important aspects of video technology. The first focuses on Paik's manipulation of the electronic signal to distort broadcasted images of a television program, whereas the second story points to the camera he used to capture his own image material. Both versions of the story are important as they give a comprehensive understanding of the media and what it is about.

The necessity to distinguish between the global history of video art that designates Nam June Paik as its 'father' and the local version becomes evident when looking into the history and practice of video art in Iceland. Until the early 2000s, video art had not been given much attention and was more or less considered non-existing. Lack of historical and theoretical writings about early video art, and the absence of a video art archive, only seemed to confirm this non-existence. Further inquiries have shown that this absence was partly due to the artists' refusal to be labelled as video artists rather than the absence of video in art. However, this general understanding made research on video art and other media-related practice quite laborious, as it was not obvious where to find proofs of a practice that the artists affirmed did not exist. An enquiry into the main museum's collections confirmed this evaluation. The Living Art Museum, founded by an artists' association in 1978 (Guðmundsdóttir 2010) to host new and experimental art, did not have a video archive. It had held its first time-based art festival in 1981 with performances and video art that was mainly based on contributions from Gallery Die Appel in Amsterdam. Another demonstration of the lack of interest in video art in the 1980s is that the museum would wait twelve years until it organized a similar festival again in 1993. Even though video art practice began to grow in the 1990s, the Living Art Museum only had a small assortment of videocassettes kept in a box. Artists showing video in the late 1990s and early 2000s had left the cassettes in the museum. The situation was similar in the collection of the two large art museums, the National Gallery of Iceland and the Reykjavik Art Museum, where only a handful of artworks were classified as video art in 2004 (Ólafsdóttir 2004: 43–52). The question that finally emerged was: what did the museum collections tell about video art in Iceland? Was it possible that the collections did not reflect the practice?

Experimental Art

In the early 1970s, the young Republic of Iceland – founded in 1944 – was still establishing its economic independence, with a viable import-export balance. The need for balance resulted in import restrictions and high taxes on technological equipment, causing them to be excessively expensive and delaying the arrival of video technology to the country. Video cameras were extremely rare and nothing indicates that artists used them until the late 1970s. The first video made by an Icelandic artist in Iceland was a documentation of Ólafur Lárusson's performance at Gallery SÚM in Reykjavik in 1978. The artist had hung up four equally-sized glass plates onto which he painted aligned brushstrokes of colours before stabbing the plates one by one with his head at an opening. The performance entitled *Rainbow* referred to the painted colours while the recorded videotape shown in the gallery during the exhibition was in black and white. This imperfection was described by the critic Bragi Ásgeirsson, who wrote that there was nothing left to look at but broken glasses with paint lying scattered on the floor and a monitor showing 'ridiculously blurred black and white moving images' that only gave a glimpse of what had taken place (Ásgeirsson 1978: 26–7). This faintly attractive video is the first known video recording of an artist's performance in Iceland. The original tape is lost, but the performance was repeated and recorded by the national television a few years later and has been exhibited as such.

Ólafur Lárusson was one of the first artists in Iceland to seriously consider the possibilities of video technology as an artistic tool (Lárusson 1979: 9). His interest in video was in direct relation to his previous use of photography and film. He acquired a film camera and was an early practitioner of experimental filmmaking, which flourished in the mid-1970s (Valsson 2009). As an artist, he integrated film projections into performances, brought stills into installations, and mixed painting and photography. In 1976 this kind of intermedia practice inspired the founding of a new department at the Icelandic College of Art and Crafts. The department allowed students to experiment with new methods and new media, including film, photography and performance. The change was radical even though it reflected what had been going on around SÚM. Since 1939 the art college had trained students in basic skills in art and craft and graduated them with either a professional license or a teacher certificate, helping them to get a regularly paid job. Students who wanted to become artists were encouraged to continue their studies abroad although nobody expected them to be able to make a living as an artist in a country with a population of around 200,000. In the early 1970s, the students no longer accepted these premises and pushed for a change. This was implemented with a fifth year, consisting of free studio practice. It was soon replaced by an experimental 'new art' department that a few years later would be renamed as a 'multimedia' department. The new art department did not offer technical specialization but put emphasis on philosophical discussions and trans-disciplinary approaches to old and new media.

Video became part of the curriculum in the mid-1980s, but the school only possessed one camera (sometimes none) with no studio or possibility to learn post-production. Artists who had learned video abroad, typically in either Holland or the United States, all seemed to abandon the video after returning back to Iceland. A conscious approach towards change was only taken when John Hopkins became a part-time teacher in video and photography in 1990. Hopkins was determined to encourage the practice of video and new media among the students and managed to implement changes in that direction before he left in 1996. The period was also marked by a renewed interest in conceptual art, which had weakened with the revival of New Painting in the 1980s. The post-conceptual approach of the 1990s refocused on mixed-media art and declared a preference for non-media specific practice, which benefitted video and photography. Thus it was in a context of media non-specificity that video became an integral part of the art students' curriculum, and eventually of Icelandic contemporary art.

The non-media-specific approach was characteristic for the art of Þorvaldur Þorsteinsson, who in 1987 had suggested the name 'mixed-media' for the new art department. After his return to Iceland from his post-graduate studies at Jan van Eyck Academie in Maastricht, he explored mixed-media beyond the borders of established art forms. In the early 1990s he was a conspicuous figure of post-conceptual art, pursuing a carrier as a visual artist and writer of children's books, radio and theatre plays. Þorvaldur navigated between media and genre with no respect for labels and categorization, equally employing photography, ready-mades, paintings, music, film, video and even experimenting with computers in the '@' installation. Þorvaldur was influenced by artists such as Guillaume Bijl and John Baldessari and had an attitude towards media diametrically opposed to the stance that had been taken by the Icelandic video artist Steina Vasulka in the United States in the late 1960s – co-founder of The Kitchen in New York and a member of the Centre for Media Study at the State University of New York (SUNY) at Buffalo – to whom I will now turn.

Steina's Effect

Steina had not yet shown her videos in Iceland when she was first invited to participate in an exhibition in Reykjavik in 1984 with other Icelandic artists living abroad. She was the only artist showing videos, however they were not exhibited in the main exhibition hall but in the meeting room of the museum. Steina's most recent work at the time, *The West* (1983), which had been shown at Centre Pomidou in Paris a few months earlier, demanded multiple monitors to enlarge the videos' two-channel images. Finding monitors in Reykjavik in 1984 was not an easy task, and eventually Steina could only show the work on four monitors, borrowed for three days. The difficulty she encountered finding and gathering the adequate equipment for *The West* reflected a situation that the local artists making videos in those days knew only too well.

Þór Elís Pálsson had been a student of Ólafur Lárusson at the new art department of the Icelandic College of Art and Crafts. He graduated in 1979 and went to the Jan van Eyck Academie in Maastricht, which shortly thereafter hired Elsa Stansfield to establish a time-based art department with a fully equipped video studio. This was a turning point for Þór Elís Pálsson, who became fascinated with video. His graduation piece *Scarcity* was a two-channel video installation that he showed at the Living Art Museum in Reykjavik in 1982. A year later he declared in an interview that video art was 'the art of the future' (Einarsdóttir 1983: 38–9) and opened a video studio, offering to lend the equipment he had brought with him from Holland to other artists. Nobody showed up – except Steina, when she was in Reykjavik. When Ásta Ólafsdóttir (Þór Elís' fellow student from Jan van Eyck) and Sigrún Harðardóttir (who studied video art at Rijksakademie van Beeldende Kunsten in Amsterdam) returned to Iceland in 1986–7, the studio had closed.

The video fever had taken place elsewhere than within the visual arts. The first private broadcasting radio and television station founded in 1986 relied on video technology, and both the private station and the National Television needed qualified technicians. In 1987, Þór Elís Pálsson began working for the National Television as a producer. He had a vision of television as a producer and showcase platform for video art, and finally in 1991 he got the possibility to invite five artists to make videos that were shown in a four-series program broadcasted in early 1992. In the series, Þór Elís Pálsson explained video art to the television spectators and tried to prepare them for the images they were about to see. Two of his collaborators in the project were his former co-students from Jan van Eyck, Ásta Ólafsdóttir and the sound artist Finnbogi Pétursson, who also worked in television. The third artist invited was Þorvaldur Þorsteinsson. A year later Steina was invited to participate in her second exhibition in Reykjavik where she showed the video installation *Borealis* (1993) at the National Gallery of Iceland, as part of a Nordic Biennale. The exhibition marked the beginning of Steina's regular appearance in the local art scene where she eventually gained a long-deserved recognition. The installation received unanimously positive reviews, which were not unrelated to the way the installation was displayed. *Borealis* marked a shift in the presentation of video art: the installation no longer relied on monitors. Instead Steina used two projectors in front of which she placed a split beam that enabled her to divide two image sources into eight, using four semi-transparent screens situated in the middle of a dark room. Shortly after the opening of the Nordic Biennale, the Living Art Museum organized its first festival of time-based art in nine years, showing performances and videos, including tapes by Steina and Woody Vasulka. From that moment Steina began to exhibit regularly in Reykjavík and was invited to give classes at the Icelandic College of Art and Crafts. In 1997 she represented Iceland at the Venice Biennale with *Orka,* the last installation in a cycle of works – including *The*

West and *Borealis* – referring to natural phenomena with a corollary found in the elements of the videographic image (Bonin 2003).

Digital Visions

In 1999 the Iceland Academy of the Arts replaced the College of Art and Crafts. In the visual arts, the reorganization of art education meant the end of traditional disciplines, and the opening of specialized workshops. For the first time in Iceland, art students had access to fully equipped video studios with digital cameras, post-production software, computers and sensors. Haraldur Karlsson, the manager of the video studio, and Hilmar Þórðarson, from the music department, began to offer courses in new media for both students in music and visual arts. The new media subdivision offered a cross-section between visual art and music, but it was relatively short-lived. Electronic music and programming persisted and continued to develop in music, with members of S.L.Á.T.U.R. becoming teachers around 2007. At the same time, video became one of the main media of the visual art department, which was modelled after the mixed-media department of the College of Art and Crafts. What the visual arts did not offer was a substantial education in other new media and programming. I felt this strongly in my courses on histories of media art, especially after 2007, as they rarely resonated with the students' practical courses. The lack of context and dialogue on the subject of digital technologies has influenced the students' attitude and how they integrate the digital into their own work after they have become artists. We can see this in the work of Dodda Maggý, who has a strong base in video and sound – which she mastered in an unprecedented way in her exhibition *Varitions* at Berg Contemporary Gallery in 2017 – and in the works of Björk Viggósdóttir, who draws from the non-technical participation art of the 1990s, rather than interactivity relying on technological devices. Dodda Maggý's and Björk Viggósdóttir's art could thus be qualified as post-media, in the same sense as Hrund Atladóttir's works inspired by the Internet. Hrund's works refer to lives that do not distinguish between online and offline activities and experiences. They resonate with questions asked by Egill Sæbjörnsson, of whether there is a difference between actual and virtual worlds, or even between nature and technology. That question is asked in his multi-layered *Out of control* (2017), based on the characters of two trolls named Ügh and Bõögăr, shown at the Venice Biennale. For more than a century, Icelandic art has been described as being grounded in nature, but the works of Egill and Hrund invite us to ask whether the digital has not become a second nature. The fusion of virtual and actual worlds, reality and fiction, encountered in Egill Sæbjörnsson's work, also make us question the distinction, not only between art worlds, but just 'worlds'. Today, the divide between contemporary art and media art, which characterized the past decades, has collapsed. Digital technologies have become an integral part of art and culture, and the younger generation of artists are unafraid of integrating digital technologies into the sphere of contemporary art. They do so almost 'naturally', and without being concerned with the label 'too technological'.

References

Ásgeirsson, Bragi (1978), 'Samsýning í Galerie SÚM', *Morgunbladid*, 7 May.

Bishop, Claire (2012), 'The digital divide', *Art Forum*, September.

Bonin, Vincent (2003), 'Steina and Woody Vasulka fonds: Series of videotapes and installations', Foundation Daniel Langlois, www.fondation-langlois.org/html/e/page.php?NumPage=427. Accessed 9 February 2017.

Connor, Michal (2013), 'What has post-Internet got to do with net art?', Rhizome.org, www.rhizome.org/editorial/2013/nov/1/postinternet. Accessed 2 November 2013.

Couchot, Edmund (1998), *La technologie dans l'art. De la photographie à la réalité virtuelle*, Nîmes: Edition Jacqueline Chambon.

Einarsdóttir, Hildur (1983), 'Vídeó – list framtíðarinnar?' (Video – art of the future?), *Morgunblaðið*, 5 August.

Gere, Charlie ([2002] 2009), *Digital Culture*, London: Reakton.

Guðmundsdóttir, Tinna (ed.) (2010), *Nýlistasafnið/The Living Art Museum 1978–2008*, Reykjavík: Nýlistasafnið/The Living Art Museum.

Lárusson, Ólafur (1979), 'Vídeólist' (Video art), *Þjóðviljinn*, 25 April.

Meigh-Andrews, Chris (2006), *A History of Video Art: The Development of Form and Function*, New York: Bloomsbury.

Movin, Lars and Torben Christiansen (1996), 'The return of the prodigal screen', in *Art & Video in Europe: Electronic Undercurrents*, Copenhagen: National Gallery of Denmark.

Ólafsdóttir, Margrét Elísabet (2003), 'Iceland: Lost opportunities?', in Tarkka, Minna and Martevo, Mirjam (eds), *Nordic Media Culture – Actors and Practices*, Helsinki: m-cult.

—— (2004), 'Histoires courtes de la vidéo islandaise', *Art Nord*, 7.

—— (2013), 'Les arts plastiques et les technologies numérique en Islande: Histoire et 'glocalization', Doctoral thesis, Paris: Université de Sorbonne.

Óskarsson, Þorsteinn J. (2001), *Raftækni í 150 ár og þættir úr sögu rafeindavirkja (Electronic Technology for 150 Years and Elements from the History of Electronics)*, Reykjavík: Félag rafeindavirkja.

Quaranta, Dominique (2013), *Beyond New Media Art*, Bresica: Link Editions.

Shanken, Edward (2010), 'Art and technology – Contemporary art and new media: Towards a hybrid discourse', *Art Basel Conversation with Nicolas Bourriaud, Peter Weibel and Michael Joquim Grey*, artbasel.com, 19 June, https://www.youtube.com/watch?v=9p9VP1r2vc4. Accessed 1 September 2010.

Spielmann, Yvonne (2008), *Video: The Reflexive Medium*, Cambridge: The MIT Press.

Sveinbjörnsson, Bjarki (1998), 'Tónlist á Íslandi á 20. öld. Með sérstakri áherslu á upphaf og þróun elektrónískrar tónlistar á árunum 1960–90' (Music in Iceland in the 20th century: With a special emphasis on the origins and development of electronic music from 1960 to 1990), Ph.D. thesis, Aalborg University, http://musik.is/BjarkiSve/Phd/phd.html. Accessed 6 June 2018.

Valsson, Pétur (2009), 'Kvik mynd list. Tilraunakvikmyndir á Íslandi 1955–1985', Bachelor thesis, Reykjavík: University of Iceland, https://skemman.is/handle/1946/2285?locale=en. Accessed 8 May 2017.

Digital Dragons of the North: On Digital Dynamics and New Nature in Nordic Aesthetics

Stahl Stenslie

Once, advanced technologies enabled the Vikings to build exceptionally capable ships decorated with aesthetically striking dragons. These dragon ships empowered them to dominate the larger part of the world for centuries. Where are the contemporary 'dragons' of Nordic aesthetics in our current age of digital technology? Is there a genuine Nordic aesthetics within the field of media arts, or are the traditionally seen 'regional differences' in aesthetics levelled out in the racecourse of globalism? Visual art has a strong position in the Nordic countries. It is known to be vibrant, diverse and rich on expressions, but also exoticized through its focus on nature, landscape, melancholia and existentialism. It has strong traditions and is known from the immaculate decorations of the early Viking dragon ships, to Nordic Romanticism represented in the Skagen movement, to Edvard Munch's symbolist paintings of death and decay, to Hilma af Klint's spiritualist paintings. The dynamics of the digital revolution have affected the Nordic art scene particularly since the late 1980s. How has this impacted current and emerging forms of Nordic art? Where and what is the Scandinavian artistic 'magic' in this innovative, 'digitally dynamic' age? Where are the digital visionaries, these new dragons, heading?

Thirty years after the first emergence of digital artworks it can be argued, on the one hand, that the visual arts have been changed forever, but on the other, also that they have hardly changed at all. Within the three-decade long production period of electronic art in Scandinavia, one can trace the emergence of a distinct Nordic tradition in the field of Digital Aesthetics. In relation to the traditional art scene, the media arts scene is often seen to exist in a parallel dimension. The digital arts are themselves perceived in an almost digital condition: either digital tools are accepted as technological tools in the production and presentation of traditional works of art, or the use of digital tools puts art and artists into a detached 'off' position, as a practically objective field of art production. This separation of digital arts from the main field of visual arts represents a challenging division to overcome in the current aesthetic debate.

To find out about the life of contemporary 'dragons' – dragons of Nordic aesthetics in our current age of digital technology – this exposé will investigate the impacts of digital technologies and digital thinking on Nordic aesthetics from its introduction in the last millennium to the re-occurring and re-emerging focus on nature in Scandinavia. Nature has played a central role in much Scandinavian art. Particularly known is the almost pantheistic eroticism towards nature as encountered in Hamsun's literature and the known Skagen painters of the nineteenth century. In the works of Edvard Munch, nature is often at the epicentre, as an uneasy backdrop for artistic and existential investigations into outer versus inner nature.

Digital technologies have in a paradoxical way led us back to a focus on material and physical nature. The hype of virtual technologies in the early 1990s soon led us to the discovery that all things virtual are also grounded in an embodied situation inside a physical reality. After all a computer runs on a very real chip run by real electricity and put in a real room setting and real-life context. Add the contemporary focus on global warming and environmentalism, and we arrive at what can be termed *New Nature*. This New Nature is recognized through its ecocentric use of digital and emerging technologies. It is represented in recent projects such as the Finnish Bioarts Society, the *Dark Ecology* journeys as well as in educational programs such as the Master in Ecology and Contemporary Performance at the University of the Arts Helsinki.

The investigation of the notion of a Nordic aesthetics in this chapter will be primarily exemplified through the historic development of electronic and digital arts in Norway. One reason for this emphasis is the funding system for art in Scandinavia. Although there have been common cultural exchange programs within the Scandinavian region for several decades, the major funding for experimental and electronic art has been given and limited within the borders of each nation. The Arts Council Norway is an example of this. It is by far the major financial source for art projects in Norway, but with a few exceptions it only funds projects that are conceived and produced in Norway. There is therefore a tendency – then as now – towards regional thinking and developments, supportive of artistic projects and expressions specific to each and distinct Nordic nation. There is no absolute division. Art always has a tendency to slip across borders and evade limitations, but funding has advanced the logistic consequence that even if artists think globally, they actually have to work locally. One question this raises is how this impacts the spreading of artistic ideas and expressions outside the Nordic region.

A Nordic Culture of Technology

Nordic culture has a long history of being impacted by the introduction of novel technologies. Every new technology introduced into our everyday lives impacts habits and cause novel dynamics, transforming the way we think and act. In Scandinavia, the invention of the Longboat enabled Vikings to travel swiftly over huge distances – and dominate the larger part of Europe for centuries. In a global context, Edison's light bulb disconnected daily life from sunlight hours, enabling us to suddenly and efficiently work around the clock and light up the cities at dark. As Orson Welles's radio drama *The War of the Worlds* showed in 1938, radio became the first shared, real-time consensual virtual reality. Television, then, brought the world viscerally into our living room. As McLuhan comments: 'The extension of any one sense alters the way we think and act – the way we perceive the world. When these ratios change, men change' (McLuhan and Fiore 1967: 41).

Our new digital tools have underlined that statement. The digital, both as a technology and as a metaphor to think by, impacts us on a massive scale, disrupting normative behaviour and patterns of thinking. This is also so in the North. Scandinavians are known to be early adaptors and have a passionate relationship to new technologies (Dahledag 2011). It is as if we fetishize every latest gadget made, craving to possess them. One explanation for our frenzy for new tech is related to how nature governs us. Our part of the world is cold, dark, vast and scarcely populated. Without access to the best of communication tools we could expect having a much harder life, if a life at all. Scandinavians are phenomenologically formed by their natural and often harsh habitat, and now increasingly more by the new digital nature of pervasive and disruptive technologies. Scandinavia currently has one of the highest penetrations of digital technologies in the world. Basically all adults now have access to and use a computer or smartphone.[1] By now we have grown accustomed to how digital technologies have shaped our new everyday online lives, generating new expressions and forever changing the way we think and act. But a change in work and family life does not necessarily change the culturally conditioned ways of experiencing art.

Technological Art in Scandinavia

Electronic and digital culture is nothing new in the North. Electronic- and computer-based artistic expressions in Scandinavia have a rather long history, going back to the 1960s. In Norway, an early work was the composer Arne Nordheim's electronic composition *Solitaire* (Norsk Biografisk Leksikon 2013). In Sweden, the art duo Beck & Jung explored the computer as an artistic tool since 1966 (Essvik and Nordquist 2015). Also starting in the late 1960s, Erkki Kurenniemi developed some spectacular instruments for electronic music in Finland (Krysa and Parikka 2015). However, these and other experimental works hardly escaped their local turf. Beside the international success of a few individual artworks such as Marianne Heske's video and installation project *Gjerdeløa* shown at Centre Pompidou in 1980, in the 1980s there was little focus on electronic art both within and outside of Scandinavia. At the same time, the introduction of the affordable personal computer (PC) slowly but surely laid out the technological foundation necessary for building up both interest and competence within computer aesthetics, and it was labelled as 'computer art' (Essvik and Nordquist 2015).

The term *computer art* was however only used temporarily and by a limited number of artists. The reason for this was not just the limited access to advanced technologies but the high esteem of crafts in the arts. In a Scandinavian context, art making associated with industrial or high-tech production has often been slightly condescendingly looked upon. Considering the strong craft-based traditions of art making in the Nordic countries, early computer artists were met with degrading opinions such as that they were unable to craft their own art. In the beginning, art making with a computer was therefore perceived as comparable to cheating. Art was supposed to be made by humans, not by pushing buttons.

A digital artwork by the Swedish artist Jim Berggren was once confronted with the following comment: 'Oh, I thought YOU had made it', thus indicating that he was not capable of doing it himself or through his own crafting skills (Essvik and Nordquist 2015: 13). Such reactions seem misplaced considering the mentioned and almost obsessive relationship Scandinavians today have with emerging technologies in general and communication technologies in particular. Then again, art is often understood as set apart from ordinary life. Whereas communication technologies and gadgets are considered necessary parts of our lives today, art is considered something personal and virtuous coming almost directly from the soul. Even paintings, such as the famous 'Scream' by the solitary artist Edward Munch, had a hard time being recognized as 'real' art.

Added to the high esteem of handicrafts came the fundamental and painful transition between technological systems that happened in the 1990s. Understanding what digital technologies were – and what they were not – was a difficult issue. For the experimental art, the digital age came as quite a paradigmatic change. All systemic changes demand investments from users, both in cognitive adaptation and time-wise through the need to learn actual functionality of new systems. These challenges are further complicated when new technologies appear to change the whole value system of aesthetics. The digital shift that we currently experience as 'native' has not been easy, and describing and defining digital art is not a simple task even today. Is it 'art' when the artwork is exclusively made by purely digital machines? Or, is it installation 'art' when expressions combine digital sound and visuals inside an embodied environment? Still there are blurred understandings between distinctions of media. Take bioart, an art of the living that is more or less made possible due to the underlying digital support technologies, but is it digital? There are multiple directions within art that fit under its heading as 'art', but without necessarily wanting to do so. Most of the visual art today somehow incorporates the digital either as technology or as a cultural metaphor colouring the ways we see and understand.

1990s: The Golden Decade of Scandinavian Digital

The 1990s were the golden years of digital art in Scandinavia. During this time we experienced real impact and change with the digital. The emerging and digital technologies slowly but surely began to challenge and replace analogue ways of making and thinking, not just in communication industries and society at large, but also in art. In parallel to how digital technology manifested in society, digital art was progressively introduced into the Nordic landscape and began to set a real footprint. The dynamics of artistic expressions and consumption in Scandinavia was about to change. The impact of these first years of digital art laid an aesthetical foundation that is still felt today, albeit much different now two decades later.

One of the first major digital art events in Scandinavia was the 1994 International Symposium of Electronic Arts (ISEA) arranged in Helsinki. It gathered a large international community and took up both the National Museum, smaller galleries and the city landscape with novel artistic expressions. It was soon followed by exhibitions such as *Electra* (1996) at the Henie Onstad Art Center, Norway, and the 6th cyberconf with the Eon exhibition at Kunstnernes Hus in Oslo in 1997. The dynamics of a digital art in the Nordic context came to full play in the DETOX series that toured Iceland, Norway and Sweden between 1999–2005. Towards the end of the 1990s, labs in Sweden like Electrohype (Malmø) and CRAC – Creative Room for Art and Computing (1997) – and in Norway the Production Network for Electronic Art (PNEK) (2000) were formed. These initiatives occurred together with the establishment of various educational programs in art and technology, such as at the Valand Academy in Gøteborg, Sweden.

One early example of the 'digital magic' that artists made in Norway was the *Sense:Less* project (1996) by the artist group Cortex, formed by Knut Mork, Kate Pendry, Marius Watz and myself. The project was developed for the legendary, massive and later publically forgotten *Electra* exhibition. According to the project description, its installation was: '…a place for humans to experience a stranger alternate reality. Through Virtual Reality technology and a custom-made (haptic) body suit, *Sense:Less* puts the user in a multi-sensory environment. This is a dramatic space, influenced by theatre, and the users' journey through the world is an exploration of multiple personalities' (Archive of Digital Art 1996).

The installation itself was a baroque-looking, five-meter tall construction of plastic and steel (V2_ Official Website 2017). The user stood inside a semi-transparent egg, dressed in a vibrotactile bodysuit and equipped with VR goggles. Just like a real magician, users held a wand-like device that moved them inside the VR world in the direction in which they pointed. The project was later shown both at the Dutch Electronica Art Festival at V2_ in Rotterdam and at the 5th Istanbul Art Biennial. From a technological viewpoint and for the new discoveries of VR technology, such as Oculus Rift, this might sound like an extremely advanced project for 1996. It partially was, but in media archaeological terms it was also the product of the first wave of the VR frenzy that started with VPL Research and Jaron Lanier in 1989 (Steinicke 2016: 29). By 1996, VR head-mounted displays were commercially available – and affordable – with an optic resolution and real-time tracking comparable to those of today's mass market. By introducing haptics into immersive VR installations, the project somewhat approached Ivan E. Sutherland's 1965 vision of 'The Ultimate Display': a simulated, computer-rendered magic so 'real' that a virtual chair can be sit on and virtual bullets would be lethal (Sutherland 1965).

At the same *Electra* exhibition, the Norwegian artist Espen Gangvik put on a large show of his *Compustructions*, a set of 3D rendered sculptures. These were the very first digital sculptures made in Norway, from on-screen designing to the making with computer numerical controlled (CNC) milling machinery. Making sculptures without ever touching them represented a complete taboo in the art at the time in traditionalist schools of Scandinavian sculpture making. A similar challenge came from the periphery of the art world.

Marius Watz, starting out as a self-taught programmer much influenced by the early techno music scene, developed an amazing range of digitally computed graphics that became part of the Norwegian art legacy in terms of visuals. His posters and renderings put new forms and colour to the country in the 1990s. He was even commissioned to make a sculpture for the Norwegian government's public digital space, the Odin.no webpages. The Tegnemaskin 1–12 (Drawing Machine 1–12) was a software-based computer program sculpture that put a series of growing, evolving drawings onto the webpages (Norwegian Government Official Website 2017a, and 2017b). The project was initiated in 1998 and was live on Odin.no from 2003 till 2005.

Another remarkable net art initiative was the Motherboard group by Amanda Steggell and Per Platou. They staged everything from net-actionist events to elaborate theatre performances with live connections across the Internet. Today, having a live connection via the net is no special magic, but back then it brought an aura of mystery and awe into the arts. It affected the dynamics of an otherwise rather stagnant Norwegian arts community; or so at least the emerging new media artists experienced the other artistic groups. The small – but active – group of people experimenting with digital tools and expressions were definitively the avant-garde of Norwegian art during this decade. As a consequence the larger art community came to understand these unconventional, digital artists as apart and aside. This is reflected in the sharp division of artistic support programs, leaving less support for artists utilizing new technologies (such as the KNyT program of the Arts Council Norway).

The first steps of establishing a field of digital art in Norway was done in synergy between a few individual artists' artistic research and selected large-scale events, such as the mentioned *Electra* exhibition in 1996. It marked the introduction of the new media arts in Norway and was given lavish support from both the Norwegian council of cultural affairs as well as the host institution, The Henie Onstad Art Centre close to Oslo. After the three-month exhibition period, the show became one of the largest art successes ever in Norway with more than 40,000 people visting it. However, its success also became its peril. The organizers were little, if at all skilled, in handling the contemporary complexities and costs involved in running an exhibition with mostly international and overseas artists. The consequences were grave. The enormous budget deficit they amassed gave the digital arts an aura of being prohibitively expensive. That effectively put a lid on public financing and steered the arts community's focus back to where it came from: the field of hand making arts.

Although *Electra* marked the outset of electronic and digital arts in Norway, from then on the artist had to move uphill again. One of the spin-offs came the year after when the 6th Cyberconf was organized in Oslo. It was a collaboration between the University of Oslo and Norwegian Telecom (now Telenor) and with additional support from the Arts Council Norway, curated by Morten Søby, Ola Ødegaard and myself. It was an intellectually focused conference with an outlook into the – at that time – bright future of *Digitalism*; the belief in how digital technologies would fundamentally impact and forever change humanity. In parallel to the conference itself, an art exhibition named Eon was exhibited at the House of Artists (Kunstnernes Hus) in Oslo. The success of this exhibition was picked up by the

Norwegian Touring Exhibitions (Riksutstillinger) and led to the first nationwide DETOX exhibition series touring the country from 1999 to 2001. One of the leading motivations behind the first DETOX exhibition was to let Norwegian artists acquire a voice and vocabulary in relation to digital arts. Towards the end of the first digital decade, computers were still something special. As CRAC (Creative Room for Art and Computing) in Sweden wrote in 2000: 'Digitally based Contemporary art involves the purchasing of some very expensive equipment and individual artists often find the costs prohibitive' (Jon Brunberg Official Website 2017).

The DETOX series wanted to give artists a proper chance to develop art with an art form and art technique proper to its own time. More than 40 artists responded to a call for contributions. From these, eight artists and artist groups were selected. The curators' statement read: 'the new digital language provides us with new ways of experiencing the world. Both artists and the art milieu must take this into account' (Anon. 1999: 17). Like the *Electra* exhibition, the DETOX exhibition was seen by more than 40,000 visitors and created a large impact in terms of press coverage and public feedback.

Another important Nordic initiative starting up or departing in the 1990s, besides CRAC, was Electrohype in Malmø, starting up in 1999 to prepare for its first biennial in 2000. The organization was focused on computer-based art, which it formulated rather strictly: 'by computer based art we mean art made by and for computers. Art that utilize computers, art that cannot be shown or experienced without the help of a computer' (Electrohype Official Website 2017). Two decades later such a rigid statement appears odd, but in 1999 it was more representative of an avantgardistic attitude, setting Electrohype apart from most other Nordic art institutions and arrangements. Through its biennial structure, Electrohype also became one of the more important institutions for digital art in Scandinavia.

How can the extent of the digital arts in Scandinavia in the 1990s be measured? And what impact did the first steps have? Little in terms of international impact, if one looks at the then contemporary and seminal books covering the field. In Stephen Wilsons almost 'Who's Who' book titled *Information Arts*, only four artists out of 245 are mentioned that reside and work within Scandinavia – Knut Mork, Kate Pendry, Marius Watz and Stahl Stenslie (Wilson 2002). One could argue that most literature in the field of media arts has been Anglo-Centric and hence biased. Yet the lack of mentioning of Scandinavian artists is indicative of contained regional developments. Does this mean that the early media arts developed in isolation, inside of a Nordic bubble? It was certainly not based on singular events or artists suffering from communication disabilities. Digital dreaming was still expensive and although computers became more of an everyday household object they still required a substantial investment.

The Second Decade, 2000–10: Solidified Dreaming

Into its second decade, the digital arts in Norway had gained enough momentum and proved enough critical potential to somewhat appear as its own, distinct and critical art movement. The wild 1990s' dreams and seemingly endless possibilities to make strange, innovative and different art had somehow solidified into an unequal movement. One important recognition of this was the Arts Council Norway's 1999 public seminar 'Skjønnheten og Utstyret' (a Norwegian pun on The Beauty and The Beast (Equipment)). Here the needs and possibilities of digital art were mapped and described by several of the Norwegian artists and activists in the field. As the outcome, two things appeared in the early 2000s: for one, the establishment of PNEK (Norwegian National Network of production units in Electronic Art) and secondly, the establishment of the KNyT (Art & New Technology) funding program specifically for projects and artists working in the field of Art and New Technologies (Arts Council Norway Official Website 2017).

PNEK was started and funded by the Arts Council in an attempt to both help the production of new art forms and professionalize the field. Production nodes were at first established in the major cities of Oslo, Trondheim and Bergen. In their first years, these 'nodes' became central to let artists gain access to the comparatively expensive digital production tools, making computers with advanced visual software available in lab-like settings. The purpose of these open equipment labs was both learning and production. This was an upside in terms of expanding the number of digitally skilled artist, but the question is if these labs somehow took away the need for establishing educational programs inside the Norwegian art academies. For these schools it was definitely cheaper to rent equipment and teaching hours in the labs of the PNEK nodes than buying and hiring themselves. A consequence of this, which is still a problem today, was the lack of educational programs and competent teachers in the area of media and experimental art. For example, as of 2017 the National Academy of Arts in Oslo has programs and professors for all older, pre-digital craft-based art forms, such as visual art, graphics, ceramics, visual design, metal work and jewellery, but still no education or high-level teaching in digital art (Oslo National Academy of the Arts Official Website 2017). The establishing of digital programs in the other Norwegian academies have been attempted, but only half-heartedly and without securing enough resources.[2] This points to a curse-like 'success' of digital art. It was so strong, challenging and successful during its initial years that perhaps it was set apart and separated from the broader and bigger field of the visual arts too soon. Similar attempts of establishing digital arts programs have been made at other Scandinavian schools, such as the Valand Academy in Gothenburg and the KUNO driven Nordic Sound Art Master of Arts program (Valand Academy Official Website 2017; Nordic Sound Art Official Website 2017; KUNO Official Website 2017).

The establishment – and solidification – of digital art forms came to view in several successful art exhibitions and programs. In 2003 Per Platou curated a net.art archaeology exhibition titled *Written in Stone* at the Norwegian Museum of Contemporary Art (Per Platou Official Website 2003). The exhibition took an archaeological look at net art – art made for the Internet – postulating it as a 'historic' art movement. Objects and physical manifestations from the net art movement were put on display, not as art objects per se but as references and pointers to the net art that is only to be found on the Internet.

Marius Watz curated *Generator X* in 2005, an exhibition about the beauty of digital numbers. It explored the use of generative strategies and software processes in digital art, architecture and design. In the first exhibition, organized in the newly formed National Museum of Art, the focus was on the new generation of artists and designers who embraced code as a way of producing new forms of creative expression. Later, *Generator X* became a curatorial platform, but then exported out of Norway with venues in Berlin and New York. Starting in 2004, *Detox II* followed up the success of the first edition and toured Norway and Iceland before it ended up at the Moderna Museet (Museum of Modern Art) in Stockholm in 2005. The new edition involved local curators and artists at each of the eight venues it visited.[3]

These exhibitions represent the culmination of larger and coherent art exhibitions of digital art in Norway. Since 2005 there has not been any larger display, exhibition or arrangement that could be said to be representative of a 'movement' with a somehow challenging and critical stance to both the establishment and traditional divisions of art. Today, many of these initiatives from the first and second decade have either ceased to exist or changed into something different. As we step into the post-digital age where the computer, the smartphone and a constant online life, all have become ordinary tools of our everyday lives, what are the lasting effects of the digital age on Nordic aesthetics? And where is it heading?

After the relatively swift adaption to digital technologies in the 1990s, the Nordic art scene seems to have lost much of its initial momentum of actively engaging with society's digital dynamics. Looking at the Scandinavian art presentations at international biennials since the turn of the millennium, such as the Venice Biennial or Documenta, there is a consistent lack of artworks using or dependent on digital technologies. Two exceptions are the *Ichihara Touch Tales* ambisonic sound installation at the Ichihara Biennial in Japan in 2014 (NOTAM Official Website 2017) and Camille Norment's *Rapture*, a site-specific, sculptural and sonic installation in the Nordic Pavilion at the 2015 Venice Biennial. The American-born, Oslo-based artist composed and performed new music on a 'glass armonica' – an eighteenth-century instrument that creates ethereal music from glass and water (OCA Official Website 2015). Produced together with the PNEK node NOTAM, Norment attempted to create a multi-sensory space exploring the relationship between the human body and sound, using visual, sonic, sculptural and architectural stimulus into one Gesamtkunstwerk. As mentioned, a technologically-based installation like this is still an exception in the context of the established visual arts in the Nordic context, yet it is also an example of how advanced technologies play an ever more present role in enabling new expressions in the arts, even if only as underlying support.

Individual artists from Norway have continued to do remarkable works and show their art internationally. Most notably perhaps Jana Winderen, who in 2011 won the Prix Ars Electronica Golden Nica for sound art (Jana Winderen Official Website 2011). Her piece *Energy Field* consists of three sound recordings she has done with a hydrophone during travels to the Barents Sea, Greenland and throughout Norway. Her final piece is made of sound portraits of complex ecosystems woven into the landscape in such a manner '…that they feel like entirely organic extensions of it' (Kunstkritikk Official Website 2011).

Impact in Time

The question remains how and how far the digital domain has impacted contemporary Nordic artistic expressions. When Hans-Ulrich Obrist named the traditional visual art scene in Scandinavia the 'Nordic Miracle' in the late 1990s, what did he see as unique? (Bydler in Elkins 2013: 341). Perhaps this was not specifically the digital art community in itself, but rather a burst of creativity caused by changes in how digital technologies impacted Scandinavian society at large. David Basulto, the curator of the Scandinavian part in the 2016 Venice biennial of Architecture, sees a current wave of 'Nordic spirit' in the massive amount of applications that they received in an open call for participation.[4] The exhibition *Nordic Outbreak* puts emphasis on the many new expressions found across Scandinavia, reflecting 'international realities and conditions in the digital age' and revealing 'an amazing experimental energy' (Nordic Outbreak Official Website 2013). But how digital or 'dynamic' are these trends and tendencies really? To what extent are they representative of a larger impact of digital dynamics – in addition to just carefully selected examples of art of individual curators – in the sense of reflecting the digital dynamics of a Scandinavian society in transformation? These references are more likely comments to the Nordic aesthetics, an aesthetics that is highly diverse but also embedded in traditions of Nordic symbolism and melancholia. In the cross-disciplinary field of electronic music this is reflected in the practices of Fever Ray (Karin Dreijer Andersson) (Sweden) and Geir Jensen (Biosphere) (Norway).

The Nordic is often rooted in clichés, such as the mentioned romantic and existential traditions, but also marked by energetic twists, local topologies, fascinations, themes and sometimes transgressive behaviour. The curator Lorella Scacco sees examples of a unique Scandinavian aesthetics in the use of expressive gestures, such as the *New Dawn Fades* video of Norwegian artist Marit Følstad (Scacco 2009). Følstad's work shows the artist herself, starring emotionless at the camera while she is repeatedly and painfully hit by a heavy, water-filled balloon. Although digitally produced, this work cannot be said to be of a primary digital nature. This restates the question of differences and ambiguities in what can be said to be 'Nordic aesthetics'.

So, over time and looking back, digital technologies have impacted the way we make and experience visual art in the Nordic context. At the same time, one finds the visual art scene in Scandinavia to be dominated by traditional arts such as painting, graphics and sculpture. Therefore many still question if these digital dynamics will continue to affect contemporary artistic expressions in the Nordic countries. The case of digital media art in Norway is indicative of its current lack of status. Here media art is only found in a parallel dimension to the traditional art scene. For example, the Norwegian National Museum has zero pieces of digital art in its collection (Norwegian National Museum Official Website 2017). Approaching 2020, the main role of 'the digital' in art is currently as artistic production technologies naturalized into the production apparatus of traditional art. Whether we go to museums, collections, theatre, dance or opera, we experience artistic expressions produced by means of technologies. If the artwork itself is not digital, it is represented through digital media such as tablets, smartphones and screens. The digital dynamics of the golden decade have been adopted through primarily digital video and photo production and in digital reproduction through, for example, large-scale projections. The grand visions of the first Virtual Reality wave of the 1990s – where users, artwork and artists alike would merge together into one interactive, co-creational experience – have not turned out. Soon in 2020, we are still far from living that vision. Or, seen from another perspective, the vision is realized in a different form. Looking at the impact of digital communication technologies, one will find that virtually all teenagers have a smartphone and virtually all communicate on various social media platforms, such as Facebook, Snapchat and Instagram. These channels are pervasive throughout all of Scandinavia, enabling users to co-create and interact inside a virtual space, albeit different from 3D immersive media.

One exception might be the new 360 degrees VR video. This has added the possibility of making digital blockbusters out of digital art all the more likely. Yet there have been few art projects utilizing this option in Scandinavia – with the notable exception of projects such as *The Doghouse* (2014), a first-person reality film project by Makropol (DK) using 360 degrees video VR to put users inside a virtual and embodied theatre (Makropol Official Website 2017). The magic of *The Doghouse* is in how it reportedly makes users identify with the protagonist of the VR video recordings. The digital medium here becomes a phenomenological flesh.

Towards a New Nature

On the surface, digital dynamics have primarily influenced Nordic Aesthetics towards a shift into digital production and presentation techniques. However, behind that surface we now experience a cultural shift towards what can be described as a New Nature. It is nature both expanded and exploded before recombined into a new understanding. At its heart, this New Nature is recognized through its eco-centric understanding and use of digital and emerging technologies.

In his book *A Philosophy of Fear*, the Norwegian philosopher Lars Fr. H. Svendsen describes how we live with a constant and common image of fear in our societies (Svendsen 2009). While before 1989 the all-overshadowing fear was the nuclear threat, now it is the angst of global warming. This constant focus on the ecological crisis over the past decade has also influenced the arts. The term eco art is outdated and notoriously attached to the eco-movement of the 1970s and human species saving projects, such as for example the Whole Earth Catalog (Brand 1968–72). What we see now though is a return to the landscape, much like romanticism and much like what the Norwegian Painter I. C. Dahl did in the nineteenth century: inventing a glorified and ideal form of nature. However, this time it is not the landscape as a source of glorifying or even legitimizing the nation. Now it is a return to the landscape and nature as an experimental and living laboratory. Behind this apparently romantic approach lays a much darker vision of an

Earth made uninhabitable for humans because of the aforementioned global warming – by humans. Humans, many would say, are now staging their own extinction (Kolbert 2014). This is a portrait of human nature that would be Hollywood worthy, except it is no fiction. Global warming is currently very real as a social phenomenon of common fear. This is real, even if the actual predicted outcomes would never happen. The bright side of this fear is the renewed interest in nature and ecology. New technologies, such as digital biotechnologies (in connection with other digital tools), now enable artists to both explore and create quite different artworks. Digital dynamics are now impacting both a renewed focus on, as well as new examples of, nature, as exemplified in Cecila Jónsson's (SE/NO) *The Iron Ring* from 2013. In this project, the artist uses a common grass weed growing in infested, metal-rich industrial areas to extract iron from the grass' burnt remains. She is able to extract enough iron to cast an iron ring. This project would not be possible without the thinking, technologies and tools found within the circles of digital art production.

Another example is the *Dark Ecology* journeys, a collaboration between Norwegian artists and the Dutch Sonic Acts organization. Inspired by Timothy Morton's notion of Dark Ecology, the organizers set out to aesthetically explore the furthest and coldest Nordic regions between Kirkenes in Norway and Murmansk in Russia, engaging both the landscape and its local inhabitants through a chain of site-specific installations and events along the route (Dark Ecology Official Website 2016) Norwegian experimental artists such as HC Gilje and Margrete Pettersen made several land art-like, electronic installations as part of the project produced between 2014 and 2016.

The turn towards 'seeing nature anew' has become a shared Scandinavian field of interest. Nature is now again standing out as a romantic topic defining both the self and the origin of the species. The method is differing though. Famed painters, from I. C. Dahl to the Skagen painters to the social realism of Christian Krogh, tried to catch and understand nature through the frame, pigment and canvas. Now the new generation applies mixtures of scientific technologies such as DNA mapping and nanotechnology, combined with social networking, tweeting and political actionism, to extract quite new imageries and presentations of all that nature can be. These are experimental and oftentimes extreme attempts to create new forms of beauty, novel ways of understanding and alternative systems of knowledge. This interest in what we can describe as New Nature finds its protagonists in actors such as The Finnish Society of Bioart (Fi), RIXC (LV) and i/o/lab (NO). An appropriate example is the book *Field_Notes – From Landscape to Laboratory*, presenting the findings and projects from The Finnish Society of Bioart's residency and workshop program in the midst of the wild lands in Northern Finland (Beloff, Berger and Haapoja 2013). Such a venture appears almost as if taken out of the dramatic Finnish saga of Kalevalla, the national creation myth. The field report represents a phenomenologically grounded wish to stand firmly inside of physical realities, although these 'new' realities are infinitely more layered and knotted than within the first painterly approach. Doing fieldwork with your feet wet and stuck in the wet, mosquito-ridden marshlands of the North might not seem very digital, yet it is the consequence of the coming of the digital age with all its technologies, knowledge sharing and community building. The all-encompassing digitalization of our tools of perception allow us to build new imageries under the firmament of what Husserl would call our sensory Lifeworld; that is, the entire physical background and starting point for human experience and reflection (Stenslie 2010: 198).

Examples of how New Nature is expanding and coming anew is the 2016 appointment of the internationally renowned performance and bioart artist Kira O'Reilly to lead the new Master of Arts pilot in Ecology and Contemporary Performance at the University of Arts Helsinki in Finland. This is apparently a position within a field that might appear more analogue than digital, yet the contemporary context, as well as O'Reilly's background as researcher with Symbiotica, roots the practice in a solid technological fundament.

New Nature is also at the core of the European research program Renewable Futures (RF). As a response to recent quests for a more sustainable future, the RF project aims to invent new avenues for developments of tomorrow – in the cultural and creative sector in Europe. It aims at this by building cross-sector collaborations and competence, 'bringing together art and science, culture and digital technologies, sustainable businesses and social engagement of the twenty-first century' (RF Official Website 2017). A partner project is the Oslofjord Ecologies workshop, organizing hands-on collaborations (art)education, artistic research and interdisciplinary practices, actions and agency in and around Oslo, thereby turning the Oslofjord into a (potentially) vast work of meta art (Oslofjordecologies Official Website 2016).

Another example of on-going shift from the 1990s experimentation with technology-as-nature towards experiments in nature-through-technology is the CLICK festival in Denmark. The purpose of this festival is to 'embrace the future' by exploring the field between art, science and technology (CLICK Festival Official Website 2017). Such returns to nature and the renewed shift towards the physical represents a turn to post-digital, post-Internet art.

A radical artistic phenomenon now rising to the surface of everyday life is the new aesthetics produced by and for the digital machinery; what James Bridle has coined The New Aesthetic (Bridle 2013). This refers to representations in which modern reality is at display; in which computers and digital tools are progressively producing digital expressions that we humans no longer understand (Sterling 2012). This is the New Aesthetic: a kind of beauty beyond human recognition. Some might say we are going too far when producing art only for the machines. That is, if art can exist outside the anthropocentric domain. If so, then we can expect an algorithmic art emerging as a consequence of the current wave of algorithmic, deep-brain, big-data thinking.

Draconic Futures

There might not be any digital dragons left over from the virtual utopias of the visionary thinking of the 1990s, but digital dynamics have inspired and matured collaborative methods and collaborations that have spawned new and diverse practices reaching into the real and everyday world of the Nordic countries. Digital dynamics impact thinking and reflection – causing change. The new watchword is New Nature, putting the North back on the map as a place of importance, even as a test site for a 'nature future', which in the age of the Anthropocene has become the main digital dynamic, set for a comeback with a vengeance, not least as an artistic material transformable and malleable through digital technologies and the cultural thinking associated with it.

The avant-garde is always a disruption and break away from traditionalist thinking, yet in the current focus on New Nature the digital dragons return recombined and to resume the long traditions of Nordic existentialist thinking being rooted in the land and elements of 'nature brute'. The digital domain is the vessel of the foreseeable future. Here the digital dragons represent a long lost dream, a utopia and for some even a regressive romanticism. But the main question is: who and what will these digital visionaries, these dragons – this digital magic made by Scandinavian artists – be in the future? And how do we facilitate them? We should. For they are coming about like all forms of change: swift and without warning. In the age of global warming and prophesies of mass extinction we better welcome the dragons flying in than being washed ashore.

References

Anon. (1996), *Electra 96: electra manual : prosjekt for elektroniske medier*, Høvikodden: Henie Onstad Kunstsenter.

—— (1999), 'DETOX!', Olso: Riksutstillinger. https://www.nb.no/items/URN:NBN:no-nb_digibok_2010100603001. Accessed 20 January 2017.

Archive of Digital Art (1996), sens:less, https://www.digitalartarchive.at/database/general/work/sensless.html. Accessed 4 March 2017.

Arts Council Norway Official Website (2017), 'Støtteordninger', https://www.kulturradet.no/stotteordning/-/vis/kunst-og-teknologi. Accessed 4 March 2017.

Beloff, Laura, Berger, Erich and Haapoja, Terike (2013), *Field Notes – From Landscape to Laboratory*, Tallinn: Printon Printing House Ltd.

Brand, Stewart (1968–72), *Whole Earth Catalogue*, Menlo Park: The Portola Institute.

Bridle, James (2013), 'The new aesthetic and its politics', 12 June, http://booktwo.org/notebook/new-aesthetic-politics/. Accessed 22 February 2017.

CLICK Festival Official Website (2017), http://www.clickfestival.dk/. Accessed 22 February 2017.

Dahledag, Dag Yngve (2011), 'Nordmenn mest teknokåtei Europa', TU, http://www.tu.no/artikler/nordmenn-mest-teknokate-i-europa/238624. Accessed 19 January 2017.

Dark Ecology Official Website (2017), 'Journeys', http://www.darkecology.net/journey-2016. Accessed 22 February 2017.

Ekroth, Power (2007), 'Pissing on the Nordic miracle', *Artnews*, https://artmap.com/powerekroth/texts. Accessed 1 May 2016.

Electrohype Official Website (2017), http://www.electrohype.org/sve.html. Accessed 19 January 2017.

Elkins, James (2013), *Is Art History Global?* New York and London: Routledge.

Essvik, Olof and Nordvist, Joel (eds) (2015), *Den här datorn*, Gothenburg: Rojal Forlag.

Hope, Cat and Ryan, John Charles (2014), *Digital Arts: An Introduction to New Media*, New York: Bloomsbury Publishing.

Jana Winderen Official Website (2011), 'Jana Winderen wins Golden Nica at Arts Electronica 2011', http://www.janawinderen.com/news/jana_winderen_wins_golden_nica.html. Accessed 7 March 2017.

Jon Brunberg Official Website (2017), 'CRAC – Creative Room for Art and Computing', http://jonbrunberg.com/article/40/crac-creative-room-for-art-and-computing. Accessed 4 March 2017.

Kolbert, Elizabeth (2014), *The Sixth Extinction: An Unnatural History*, New York: Henry Holt and Company, LLC.

Krysa, Joasia and Parikka, Jussi (2015), *Writing and Unwriting (Media) Art History: Erkki Kurenniemi in 2048*, Leonardo Book Series, Cambridge: The MIT Press.

KUNO – An Art Academy Without Walls Official Website (2017), http://www.kuno.ee/. Accessed 4 March 2017.

Kunstkritikk Official Website (2011), 'Prestisjepris til Jana Winderen', http://www.kunstkritikk.no/nyheter/prestisjepris-til-jana-winderen/. Accessed 7 March 2017.

Lovejoy, Margot (2004), *Digital Currents: Art in the Electronic Age*, New York and London: Routledge.

Makropol Official Website (2017), www.makropol.dk. Accessed 22 February 2017.

McLuhan, Marshall and Fiore, Quentin (1967), *The Medium is the Massage: An Inventory of Effects*, London: Penguin Classics.

Nordic Outbreak Official Website (2013), http://nordicoutbreak.streamingmuseum.org/. Accessed 7 March 2017.

Nordic Sound Art Official Website (2017), www.nordicsoundart.com. Accessed 4 March 2017.

Norsk Biografisk Leksikon (2013), 'Arne Nordheim', https://nbl.snl.no/Arne_Nordheim. Accessed 4 March 2017.

Norwegian Government Official Website (2017a), 'Digital utsmykking på ODIN', www.regjeringen.no/no/aktuelt/digital_utsmykking_pa_odin/id249468. Accessed 4 March 2017.

——— (2017b), www.nasjonalmuseet.no. Accessed 7 March 2017.

NOTAM Official Website (2017), 'Ståle Stenslie i Japan', http://www.notam02.no/web/stale-stenslie-i-japan/. Accessed 4 March 2017.

OCA Official Website (2015), 'Venice Biennale 2015: "Rapture": A project by Camille Norment', www.oca.no/venice-biennale/venice-biennale-2015.1. Accessed 4 March 2017.

Oslo National Academy of the Arts Official Website (2017), www.khio.no. Accessed 4 March 2017.

Oslofjordecologies Official Website (2016), www.oslofjordecologies.net/. Accessed 22 February 2017.

Paul, Christiane (2016), *A Companion to Digital Art*, Hoboken: John Wiley & Sons.

Per Platou Official Website (2003), 'Written in stone: A net.art archaeology', www.perplatou.net/net.art. Accessed 8 February 2017.

PNEK Official Website (2017), www.pnek.org. Accessed 22 February 2017.

RF Project Official Website (2017), www.rixc.org/en/center/networks/273. Accessed 22 February 2017.

Scacco, Lorella (2009), *Northwave: A Survey of Video Art in Nordic Countries*, Milan: Silvana Editorial.

Stahl Stenslie Official Website (2017), www.stenslie.net. Accessed 22 February 2017.

Steinicke, Frank (2016), *Being Really Virtual: Immersive Natives and the Future of Virtual Reality*, Berlin: Springer.

Stenslie, Ståle (2010), 'Virtual Touch: A study of the use and experience of touch in artistic, multimodal and computer-based environments', Ph.D. thesis, Oslo School of Architecture and Design.

Sterling, Bruce (2012), 'An Essay on the new aesthetic', wired.com, www.wired.com/2012/04/an-essay-on-the-new-aesthetic. Accessed 22 February 2017.

Sutherland, I. E. (1965), 'The ultimate display', in *Information Processing: Proceedings of the IFIP Congress*, Amsterdam: North-Holland, pp. 506–08.

Svendsen, Lars Fr. H. (2009), *A Philosophy of Fear*, London: Reaktion Books Ltd.

Valand Academy Official Website (2017), www.akademinvaland.gu.se/english. Accessed 4 March 2017.

V2_ Official Website (2017), 'SENSE:LESS', www.v2.nl/archive/works/sense-less. Accessed 2 February 2017.

Wilson, Stephen (2002), *Information Arts*, Cambridge: The MIT Press.

Notes

1   The percentage of Norwegians owning a smartphone is now more than 82%: http://www.medienorge.uib.no/?cat=statistikk&medium=it&queryID=379&aspekt=oppdatering.

2   Laura Beloff was professor of media arts at KhiO in the first half of the 2000s. KhiO also took part in the Master of Arts in Nordic Sound Art for a couple of years, later KhiB in Bergen and KIT in Trondheim took part. The programme is now closed, see http://nordicsoundart.com/.

3   DETOX II visited Kirkenes: Savio-museet/Grenselandmuseet, Trondheim: Trondhjems Kunstforening, Kristiansand: Sørlandets Kunstmuseum, Stavanger: Tou Scene, Notodden: Telemarksgalleriet, Bergen: Bergen Kunsthall, Oslo: Kunstnernes Hus, Stockholm: Moderna Museet.

4   Press release for the Nordic pavilion at the 15th International Architecture Exhibition – La Biennale di Venezia, 'In Therapy: Nordic Countries Face to Face', 16 May 2016.

Conclusion: Horizons for Nordic Contemporary (Digital) Art

Tanya Toft Ag

This book examines how the digital participates in the evolution of contemporary art and aesthetics, at a time when digital dynamics are changing society and the materiality, contexts and conditions for art and artistic practice. Digital dynamics influence how social and communicational infrastructures converge and have become networked while affecting human seclusion; how the human imagination and capacity with technology has extended (e.g. with modes of digital material crafting); and how cultures oscillate between technological optimism, fetishism and scepticism. Digital dynamics diffuse computation into all dimensions of societies with mathematical, algorithmic operations, changing the materiality of matter, images and architectures, and infusing our surroundings with technologically responsive and interactive behaviours while merging real and artificial worlds. Moreover, digital dynamics affect how we increasingly engage with the world as scientific matter and in nexuses between disciplines, intentions and economies of innovation – and in collective modes of organizing and 'instituting'. These are among the digital dynamic influences examined by the authors in the book as points of departure for their chapters, shaping contemporary digital culture while conditioning how art is conceived, produced and comes into existence and effect.

Digital dynamics shape the cultures in which artists live and the sociopolitical worlds from which art derives and to which it responds. They evolve the tools available to artists for producing their art, the themes they take up and how they think about their practices and affect in the world. In perspective of the Nordic art context, and in contexts of similar technological, cultural-economic and sociopolitical conditions having evolved in the model of the welfare state in particular, this book illuminates how a current metapsychological 'image of thought' as a mode of thinking among artists is evolving with the digital dynamics that shape our world today, and how it amounts in certain orientations in artistic practice and inquiry in contemporary art.

The book casts contemporary art as an aesthetic phenomenon in a relationship of contingency and exchange with the contemporary context. With emphasis on art in which digital technologies provide an essential dimension to its conception, production, materiality and/or exhibition – hence the use of the term 'digital art' – the contingent dimension is specifically examined from the perspective of digital culture and technological innovation. While art can be said to have always been contingent with its contemporaneity, the digital dynamics that continuously advance the inscription of our human lives into digitally structured and globally networked realities simultaneously bring art and its operational tactics closer to other fields and environments alongside which the digital is evolving. We witness, as technology seeps into artistic practice and culture, how artists adapt techniques, skills, intentions and methodologies from fields beyond art such as engineering, biology and other fields of science, as well as from technoeconomic domains of media architecture, innovation design and creative industries, and from anthropology, activism and sociology and many more. We see how digital art migrates and expands into new forms and finds new inquiries with regards to what makes art and what its subject matter can be, but also in terms of an expanded notion of 'what art makes' (Rancière 2015: 18f.).

The book embraces contemporary art from the perspective of recent and current societal and technocultural influences, as phenomena of the condition of our current aesthetic regime influenced by globalization – and in the past decades particularly by digitization – and characterized by interdisciplinary encounters and liberated thinking structures.

A main motivation behind initiating this book was to nuance and broaden how contemporary art in our current aesthetic regime as a contingent phenomenon that is reconfiguring itself with the digital may be grasped, theorized, facilitated and evaluated today. The artist testimonials reveal the emergence of a number of conceptual shifts, which are identified by the book's authors and underpinning their chapters. These include an emerging shift in art's critical position from a distanced critique of cultural representations towards an embodied concern with how we are present; a shift in art's genres to concern new modes of agency rather than solely material or categorical forms of art; and a shift in artistic awareness from local collectivity to global connectivity and more universal issues guiding themes in art.

New Critical Inquiries: From Representation to Conditions of Presence

A current 'image of thought' in Nordic contemporary art is reflective of a deeply anchored critical discourse. While some artists in this context have evolved their art practices out of critical or resistant underground movements, many have attended art academies and received academic training and are schooled in educational environments informed by critical theory and critical thinking. This is mainly thanks to a regional welfare model that features free education and mobility between Nordic (art) schools and universities. The artists' testimonials reveal deep-anchored critical thinking particularly in the expression of a critical awareness of the world's representations – from images and messages on-screen to representations of 'Nordic art' as a signifying concept. Critical thinking also underpins expressions of concern about technology and the medium as representational form, as described by many of the books' contributors who have followed the adaptation to the digital in the Nordic art context – and as described by Margrét Elísabet Ólafsdóttir in her article as the root of a digital divide in the Icelandic art context.

However, the idea deeply anchored in critical theory as one of the corner stones of western artistic discourse today of art as somehow fulfilling its ethical task when positioned at a distance from society – free of the dominant societal imaginary, its technological innovations and related cultural ecologies – seems problematic if not delusional, considering how artists are culturally, socially and imaginatively embedded in the very context towards which they are thought to preserve a distance through their art. The reality is that artists live and work in cultures of representation; cultures of the visible in which images are omnipresent and integral to our life-worlds through representations in JPEGs, news features, Facebook and Instagram feeds, and in augmented visual overlays that will soon be omnipresent in our everyday experience. Artists live in representational environments and need to navigate both social and professional cultures demanding a high degree of self-representational exposure in order to be 'visible' (in order to 'be found', to be invited to exhibit, to receive grants and to attract audiences). At the same time, some artists take advantage of technologies that amplify, enhance and allow for wide distribution of their art in order to achieve greater impact. The tools and innovations that artists use to create their art are largely the same as those evolving in our digital culture; artists live within and alongside the very societal structures that they at the same time seek to problematize or engage with through their art. As such, we can consider how both conceptually and intuitively contemporary artists formulate their inquiries from a position of being part of their context and contemporaneity, rather than from a relational, distanced position to it. This ontological-conceptual shift, on which the book finds ground, matters to the ways in which we can understand the critical significance of new methodologies, materiality and conceptual matter in emerging kinds of contemporary art – especially digital art – and not least to how we can embrace new avenues of art's raison d'être in interdisciplinary and contextual nexuses that take art and artistic inquiry way beyond their conventional domains.

In some of the artists' testimonials in this book, we can locate a shift from a concern with representational form – in, for example, an image or with regards to how the world is presented to us – to a concern with what conditions *how we are present*. Some artists indicate that through a decade-long concern with the notion of representation, some artists today have moved away from being concerned with who is represented onstage or in film and how, shifting their focus more toward how we experience reality. We can find the concern with how we are present in the process-oriented work of Arijana Kajfes; in the performative, cyberfeminist work of Nuleinn (Rine Rodin and Magga Ploder), which establishes scenarios for human presence between the digital and the physical; in Hanna Husberg's work examining humans' perception and awareness of the air and atmosphere in relation to climate change; in the immersive Virtual Reality fictions of Bombina Bombast (Emma Bexell and Stefan Stanisic); and in the immersive, performative work of Lundahl & Seitl (Christer Lundahl and Martina Seitl), to name some examples.

The shift in concern from cultural representations to how we are present, or, how presence is conditioned, evokes a repositioning of the critical artist as not merely extracting faults and dysfunctions observed in society or the world and revealing these in a re-represented form to an audience, but as acknowledging her or his own subjection as embedded in this condition and formulating a critical position from within, as a critical participant.

As digital art is often time-based or involves time-based methods, this ontological shift also reflects how artists by means of digital technologies can engage with present experience in a temporal manner; for example, via time-based episodes (e.g. video art), in interruptions or interventions (e.g. interactive art, time-based guerrilla projections), in situations of participatory performance or conversation (e.g. social aesthetic art or 'relational art'), through methods of archiving temporal logs (e.g. travels or daily routines), or in experiences of temporal dislocation (e.g. perceptual journeys in cinema, VR or through mediated scenarios). In affording and furthering temporal behaviours in the art and its production, the digital offers new ways of capturing, examining, presenting and intervening in our present.[1] This evokes new modes of agency in artists' self-conception and practice.

New Genres of Artistic Agency

A second shift examined in this book concerns how the digital influences the conception of 'genres' as structuring and evolving the field of contemporary art. Western art history has taught us to organize art into categories of artistic style, material and composition. This we witness when the artists describe in their testimonials how their art develops in re-uses and cross-overs of established genres, such as drawing, painting, sculpture, installation art, photography and video – but also in the invention of new ones. More interesting than analyzing and organizing emergent genres as styles of convergence, according to established aesthetic categories or developing new categories for art as material form, we can consider how new manifestations of art revolve around what the art *does* and what the artist sets out to do – by adopting methodologies that aim to actively affect and engage with the world (Toft 2016).[2]

When surveying artistic practices today we can locate a common concern with human subjectivity as extended, repositioned or in other ways affected by technology and digital culture. This we find in, for example, explorations of themes evoking the notion of the cyborg, cyberfeminism, transhumanism, technoanimalism and avatars, artificial life and intelligence in relation to human consciousness, synthetical computational consciousness and nature. Yet artists not only deal with themes of human subjectivity in the digital age, they also conceive and produce their art as subjective beings in sync with this condition themselves. They describe, for example, how they can embody machinic behaviours through the use of technology and end up with 'generative' results, as artist Pettri Ruikka says (artist testimonial in this volume: 51); how they can 'perform as an algorithm', as artist Alberto Frigo suggests (artist testimonial in this volume: 55), or investigate what it is like to 'be a digital process' or 'a running software', as artist Carl-Johan Rosén states (artist testimonial in this volume: 48). Digital technology has afforded artists both conceptual and actual abilities to act on the world, while at the same time the reach of their art has extended magnificently. Social networks and communication infrastructures afford artists the capacity to reach mass audiences way beyond the physical site of their art and potentially achieve worldwide resonance and effect.

This results in a both real and perceived ability to 'touch' the world and potentially change a fragment of it. As nomadic, globally visible beings living and communicating within artificial social structures, artists thus develop their practices around new modes of subjective, artistic agency. In these we can locate new genres revolving around methodologies of affecting, doing, acting and changing, rather than drawing on stylistic categories.

Some genres of artistic agency have evolved from new practices of crafting in the manner of digital-aesthetic alchemy. As the digital trickles into the materials that artists use and as technological tools and programmes advance, artists can create using code and digital connections and explore ways of making and re-making aesthetic materiality – as co-producers of digital matter. In her chapter, Mette-Marie Zacher Sørensen evokes this tendency, which she describes in terms of a particular artistic attitude towards digital-aesthetic material with the concept of 'critical thoroughness'. This denotes how instead of accepting and using digital elements and tools that are readily available, artists produce digital materials from scratch. With the ability to create, manipulate, rewrite and code the digital material that makes up an expanding part of our world, artists can potentially change the frameworks and templates that structure our digital environments. They can suggest alternative experiences to those dominating our mediated experiences in digital culture, more or less independent from corporate tools and without having to support dominant technoeconomic systems. When producing the material fabric of the digital from scratch, artists become material co-producers of the world – or at least a fragment of it.

When enacting critical thoroughness toward the digital material, artists do a lot more than problematize representations: they deliberately work to create new *kinds* of representations. In his chapter, Jøran Rudi elaborates – especially with regards to 'representational audio' – on how artists working with discrete numbers in digital material – by which content becomes available for mathematical operations – create new audio materials of composed soundscapes that, when presented to us in physical locations, create discrepancies between our expectations of an environment and our immediate experiences of it. Such soundscapes potentially urge our experience of and behaviour in certain situations or environments towards other modes of associating (or, disassociating) with our experienced environment, what Budhaditya Chattopadhyay in his chapter examine in terms of intensified mobility, deterritorialization and object-disorientation of sound in digitized sound art by which traditional notions of art's site-specificity are renegotiated. Chattopadhyay examines how sound art can potentially trigger 'unsitely' and immaterial aesthetics in artistic practice, which, in a Nordic context – typically entrenched in musically structured and recognizable sound experiences that institute a sense of familiarity and discomfort, rather than comfort with the unfamiliar – could establish a sense of confidence in the 'unknown'.

Being a sound artist himself, the connection Chattopadhyay draws between how acoustic experience can trigger new forms of subjectivity and eventually impact sociopolitical consciousness bears witness to a tendency in which – by means of new approaches to the creation of digital material and the ability to create new kinds of representations – artists seize the opportunity to make artworks that directly reconfigure and rematerialize the surfaces and systems that organize everyday life experiences. In my chapter in the book, I address the potential for new political aesthetics to emerge in relation to the digital dynamic of computational diffusion; that is, how digital art directly, politically and aesthetically engages with and 'rematerializes' the real world and its surfaces and environments. I suggest that when art participates in reorganizing and rebuilding our world, it participates in *rematerializing* our environments and enacts a politically aesthetic operation by way of directly (radically) affecting the things, surfaces, structures, architectures and materialities of both solid and digital form that shape and condition our sensory experience. Through radical rematerialization, contemporary digital art may engage the concretist vision anew, as described by Jens Tang Kristensen in his chapter, taking advantage of its digitally afforded material and operating within society in direct installation as a component in our technological frameworks, and, via digital ecologies, interfaces and networks, influence societies and natures across social and geographical boundaries. And artists craft or rematerialize not only images and urban architectures but also entire platforms and artificial-phenomenological environments, what Björn Norberg, Elizabeth Jochum and Mads Dejbjerg Lind refer to as 'world-making' (crafting virtual worlds in, for example, Virtual Reality). Artists sometimes create scenarios for 'possible futures', as expressed in the testimonials by Marie Munk, Alberto Frigo and Nuleinn, which reveals a sense of agency with regards to potentially affecting actual change in the world. In reproducing, rematerializing or rebuilding our surroundings, artists come to alter our perceptual experience of feeling present and participative in the world. Ultimately, our perceptual access to the world is dependent on our ability to grasp its complexities and develop our understandings and critical positions – and actions – within it, which artists decode and make accessible to us.

As artists explore new roles for the artistic figure – as co-producer, creator or craftsperson, social or collective facilitator, investigator, narrator, advocate, poetic scientist or 'world-maker', as the artists refer to themselves across the testimonials – they simultaneously enter new domains of art to operate. In their chapter focused on VR art, Jochum and Lind characterize how artists working with this medium oftentimes operate in the spaces between artistic practice, the cultural-economic industries and the priorities of public policy, embedded in a complex network of industrial, social and cultural needs that are intertwined with political and economic imperatives. They describe how this entanglement with technological industries and imperatives of experience design entails a reconfiguration of the role of the artist, who, in a delicate balancing act – in need of securing substantial funding (sometimes private or innovation grants) in order to realize costly installations as well as proper production facilities for complex technological art productions – might become something of a professional project manager or facilitator of an innovation project, rather than a craftsperson or conceptual visionary. In assuming this role, we witness a professionalization of artistic practice and engagement with technological innovation that, from a critical theoretical perspective, might be considered to be compromising the artistic oeuvre, but that from a more pragmatic perspective might be necessary in order to secure a place for art in the technological evolution of society. From this perspective, which is also addressed by Norberg in his chapter, experimentation with immersive experiences in contemporary art reflects (and contingently develops alongside) increasingly vulnerable 'computer simulations' supported by ICT development and 'smart' technology that shape technologically developed societies today. The Nordic context has evolved at the forefront of technological innovation, with fast adaptation to digital technologies and systems and highly advanced technological solutions swiftly amalgamating the Internet and with governmental infrastructures and economies embracing visions of the smart city. The chapters of Norberg, Jochum and Lind, and my own contribution to this book, may open up for further discussion concerning the question of how new genres of artistic agency create a space for art and artistic inquiry in the discussion on how our societies currently change with technology. At stake is how art can participate – and 'institute' influence, as Jamie Allen and Bernhard Garnicnig write about – in the shaping of our perceptual and immersive experiences that increasingly condition our life-worlds and interfaces of coexistence, and eventually affect how our society is being designed and will function.

New Representations – New Nature: Horizons for Nordic Contemporary Art

Perhaps the synthesis of a reconfigured embedded critical position and new genres of artistic agency in the Nordic context will eventually reformulate a decade-long dogma of the concept of nature in Nordic art history and provide a space for more nuanced excavations of what this concept might actually mean or imply today.

One direction of change in artistic self-conception furthered by the digital reveals in the artists' descriptions of scientific, ethnographic, sociological and other world-excavating methods in their practices. With these methods the figure of the artist transforms from someone who speaks the 'truth' about the world to someone who provides access (via extraction, examination or experience) to the world in its material and phenomenal complexities. In being able to capture the world in increasingly granular ways, artists can re-represent the world to us by turning its complexities and ungraspable matter into human-decodable form; they can make visible invisible sensibilities and modify the alchemic processes that make up our environments, thus providing experiences in which we feel present in ways other than those offered by corporate, political or – in the Nordic context in particular – public sector incitements. Artist Jana Winderen, for example, describes how she uses the digital to 'obtain knowledge that could otherwise not be collected' (Jana Winderen, artist testimonial in this volume: 109). Artist Tuomo Rainio describes how '[t]he fact that we measure, analyse and prognosticate the world is paradoxically revealing the chaotic basis of nature and its processes', by which he expresses a perspective on the world as a living environment of engagement and investigation rather than a motive for depiction and representation (Tuomo Rainio, artist testimonial in this volume: 88).

Stahl Stenslie recognizes these practices among a new generation of artists who apply mixtures of scientific technologies, such as DNA mapping and nanotechnology, combined with social networking, tweeting and 'political actionism', to extract new imageries and presentations of nature. With the term 'New Nature', he evokes a return to nature as an experimental and living laboratory reflective of what he describes as a shared Scandinavian field of interest in 'seeing nature anew'. Also in the perspective of bioart – art influenced by the environmental aesthetics of biological organisms and living matter in combination with technology – Laura Beloff observes in her chapter how the recent artistic interest in exploring our relationship with living organisms and planetary phenomena in engagement with the 'actual real' redefines our relationship with nature. Lorella Scacco emphasizes the quality of interaction in art – as found in bio art but also in light installations, in installations with electronic and algorithmic elements, in interactive projections onto objects and in sound art – as a means by which artists may reconfigure experience of matter (by reconfiguring experience of being present) and affect the creation of new perceptions, through which we may rediscover our relationship to various environments, urban spaces and, particularly, nature.

Ulla Angkjær Jørgensen interestingly pinpoints in her chapter, with reference to the artistic methods of Jana Winderen, and in sync with the greater artistic attention to our conditions of presence rather than depiction of representation, how these experiences with art may evoke conceptions of our environment, namely of nature, as not a fixed phenomenon outside of us but a quality that can be sensed and perceived within us. This opens up the possibility for new human connections with nature and the 'natural' world via our sensory registry – hence, perhaps closer to a place of human sympathy or an ethical core. Such closer contact with the matter of nature in art's reconfiguration of common representations and attention to presence might simultaneously invoke a closer connection with nature's global ecosystems and their wider, global impact and urgency, as implied in the artists' testimonials; for example, in concerns over our deeper human relationships with the environment, energy consumption and with the Anthropocene itself.

In the excavation of matter and its modulation into alternative 'representations' of what the world and nature might be, artists enact an awareness and intuitive human sense of responsibility and care for matter outside of their local context and familiar world. Art then comes to challenge a tendency towards indifference that may be said to some degree to characterize the cultural mode of the historically secluded and inter-oriented Nordic region. Artist Marie Munk hints at a pacified and indifferent state of being in the Nordic society as a cultural symptom, which she relates to the 'control-obsessed' culture of Nordic conformism and homogeneity, linked to her observation of a certain disposition of citizens, especially towards the digital. We find this concern with human cultural or behavioural 'coding' under the sociocultural forces of current technoeconomic governance in the testimonials of several artists, which we can consider particular in the perspective of the Nordic context of populations traditionally trusting in and obedient to strong state governance. This concern with human subjection to the techno-politics of digital culture and its potentially habitual and cultural effects on the way we cope with everyday life as reflected across artists' practices is identified by Morten Søndergaard in terms of a cultural mechanism of 'inaction': a negative mechanism of interaction, relating to how the effects of the digital – when transmitted into physical materiality, fabrics, architectures and 'things' – affect the data materialities of digital life and eventually our behaviour, and our ways of seeing, doing and making. The representations of the 'data materialities' of our environments, whether urban, artificial or natural, thus dispose of our awareness, experience of presence and sense of what is relevant – perhaps urgent.

Engqvist explains the symptom of indifference in terms of an existential condition of boredom in the Nordic context in which people suffer from a sense of hopelessness, political depression and distress. This he ties to a loss of belief in the welfare state project, which is gradually dematerializing in the current neoliberal political climate, while the deeply anchored values of solidarity and equality emerging from a collective upbringing in the welfare state system seem to be diminishing. At the same time, the current political condition is characterized by tighter national policies on integration and immigration and the rise of right-wing nationalist parties effecting a more xenophobic rhetoric and radical values even in mainstream political and public debate, which is not unrelated to an increase in migration to the Nordic region. The Nordic region seems to have lost its sense of innocence when it comes to its role and responsibility in fending off and dealing with the current crisis of forced migration brought on by global unrest. The concern is not only with regards to a fear of terrorism but perhaps more of losing a good and secure life within the welfare state. Beliefs in values of trust, solidarity and interconnection inherent in the social democratic project of the Nordic welfare society are challenged with regards to who belongs to the 'we', and the 'pursuit of collectiveness' seems to have become a shadow of the progressive social democratic politics of another era. In this condition, representations fuelled by calculated, sensational and xenophobic rhetoric – as we have witnessed in recent years dividing the western world – dominate.

In comparison with other countries and regional contexts, however, the Nordic context remains a well-organized system with freedom of expression and few societal problems, in which the art context builds upon a more or less stable ground of public funding. From the practices of artists who work within and in response to this fairly privileged and stable context reveals a shift in focus from a sense of the 'collectivity of the state' to a sense of 'connectivity with the world'. Perhaps what we see in the artists' positioning of themselves as critically embedded in the world that they examine, as seen, for example, in the methods of extracting and re-representing data materialities, and in the new genres of artistic agency, shows ways in which the artists look beyond local dysfunction and distress towards a horizon of globally challenging questions and themes with more universal urgency. We see this, for example, in themes dealing with the construction of identity as relating to human conflict, ideological circumstances and the complexities of coexistence; in explorations of ecological imbalances, biodiversity and evolutionary thinking; and in post-anthropocentric approaches to ethical, political and climate-oriented questions that will ultimately determine our shared future. In practices dealing with such global themes, we see artists moving beyond merely representing sociopolitical dysfunctions in artistic representations to formulating and repositioning critical responses to the world anew.

Contemporary art has evolved in parallel with digital technologies and the ways in which these have impacted societies – and will continue to do so. The digital influences the matter with which artists engage, as well as the scopes, aims and tactics embedded in contemporary art; it stimulates new genres in modes of artistic agency by evoking a sense of capacity to interfere with the world, thus encouraging conceptions of art's global relevance beyond local societal and political contexts. How we acknowledge the influence of societal digital dynamics on art is relevant to how we further art's discourse; how we view, review and archive the contemporary relevance of art.

This book calls for an ontological reconceptualization of art's and artists' position of inquiry concerning both the matter and context of art. It advocates that we might advantageously try to embrace new ways for contemporary art to exercise the critical, while being contingent upon the material world (as it has always been) and significantly upon the infrastructures, materials and ecologies of digital culture, and in consideration of the artist's own embeddedness in this condition. The conception and contextualization of contemporary art in this manner prompts us to think in open-minded ways about emerging orientations in the expanding domain of art. I hope that this book will open up new ways of seeking to grasp and find value in future artistic practices whose forms and inquiries might not fit within established categories and deep-anchored discourses in the domain of art.

In particular, this book provides an impetus for foundations of inter-knowledge relevant to how we negotiate the attention paid to 'artistic quality'. This concerns how we formulate and anchor criteria for supporting and furthering artistic practices as well as how we consider the 'value' of art today (and in the future), beyond pragmatic, potentially measurable aims. Perhaps – beyond evaluations based on pre-established conceptions of genres and markers of quality – art could be acknowledged – and evaluated – in terms of an expanded, horizontal domain of the 'field of art'. Along this line of thinking, we could be asking:

- Where is the value in testing cultural limits and exploring new aesthetic alchemies and materials in the nexus between art, technology, innovation and other domains?
- Where is the value in engaging methods from other exploratory practices, in overlapping knowledge or value systems, or in finding places for art at the interfaces of our environments and architectures?
- What would happen if we valued experimentation and affect equally with reference and form?

We cannot predict the directions art will take, but we can point to dynamics that influence it and examine what in our contemporaneity seems to enable and motivate art's inquiry. Hopefully, this book will serve as a valuable resource for lecturers, artists, curators, researchers and others as a source of insight into how artists currently think of the digital as influencing their art, and how art and art's inquiry are changing with the digital dynamics that are shaping our world and societies. With their plurality of voices, methodologies, philosophies and inquiries, the many participants featured in this book contribute to archiving a current 'image of thought' that is evolving with the digital, which we might look back upon in the future when questioning how the current unimaginative manifestations and methodologies of art came about, and what they did to the world.

References

Rancière, Jacques (2015), *The Politics of Aesthetics*, ed. and trans. Gabriel Rockhill, London and New York: Bloomsbury Academic.

Toft, Tanya (2016), 'What Urban Media Art Can *Do*', in Susa Pop, Tanya Toft, Nerea Calvillo and Mark Wright (eds), *What Urban Media Art Can Do – Why When Where & How*, Stuttgart: av edition, pp. 50–63.

—— (2017), 'Images of Urgency: A Curatorial Inquiry With Contemporary Urban Media Art', Ph.D. dissertation, Copenhagen: University of Copenhagen.

Notes

1 I elaborate on art's temporal dimension as a quality of intervening in situations of presence and temporal experience in 'Images of Urgency: A Curatorial Inquiry With Contemporary Urban Media Art' (Toft 2017).

2 For a description of the contemporary art perspective concerning what the art *does* as opposed to what the art *is*, see my introduction 'What Urban Media Art Can *Do*' (Toft 2016).

Notes on Authors

Tanya Toft Ag (Ph.D., Copenhagen) is a curator, researcher, writer and lecturer examining urban media aesthetic phenomena and (media) art's engagement with societal and urban change, in a global perspective. She was curator and led the artistic research program at the Screen City Biennial 2016–2018 (Stavanger), co-curated *Nordic Outbreak* (2013–14) presented by the Streaming Museum in New York City and across the Nordic region and the *SP Urban Digital Festival* 2013 and 2014 presented by Verve Cultural in São Paulo. Other exhibitions include *Voyage to the Virtual* (2015) at Scandinavia House, *Here All Alone* (2015) in a factory in Copenhagen and *Play!* (2013 and 2014) at the SP Urban Digital Gallery in São Paulo. She is editor of *Digital Dynamics in Nordic Contemporary Art* (Intellect, 2019) and co-editor of *What Urban Media Art Can Do – Why, When, Where, and How?* (av edition, 2016). In 2017 she co-initiated the globally networked Urban Media Art Academy. In 2018-2020 she is a research fellow at School of Creative Media, City University of Hong Kong.

Jamie Allen was born in Canada and is an artist and scholar. He has been an electronics engineer, a polymer chemist and an exhibition designer with the American Museum of Natural History. Allen works, learns and teaches all over the world. Allen is Senior Researcher at the Critical Media Lab in Basel, Switzerland and Canada Research Chair in Infrastructure Media & Communications at NSCAD. His Ph.D. at the European Graduate School under the supervision of Siegfried Zielinski and Avital Ronell was awarded in 2015 (summa cum laude). He is occupied with the reconstitution of institutions such that they reflect the importance of generosity, friendship and love in knowledge practices like art and research.

Laura Beloff (Ph.D.) is Associate Professor and Head of the Ph.D. School at IT University of Copenhagen. She is an internationally acclaimed artist who has been actively producing works and exhibiting worldwide in museums, galleries and art events since the 1990s. She has been a recipient of various grants, art residencies and awards. In 2014 she, along with partners, received the largest art grant within Nordic countries from the Nordic Cultural Fund. Her research interests include practice-based investigations into a combination of information, technology and organic matter, which is located in the cross section of art, technology and science. Her research engages with the field of art and science, biotechnologies, biosemiotics, biomedia and information technology in connection with art, humans and society.

Budhaditya Chattopadhyay (Ph.D. in artistic research and sound studies from Leiden University, The Netherlands) is an Indian-born artist, researcher, writer and theorist. His work inquires about the materiality, site-specificity and objecthood of sound and addresses the aspects of subjectivity, contemplation, mindfulness and transcendence inherent in listening. He has received several fellowships, residencies and international awards, and his works have been widely exhibited, performed and presented. He graduated from the national film school of India specializing in sound and received a Master of Arts degree in new media from Aarhus University, Denmark, writing on sound art. Between 2018–2019, Chattopadhyay is a Mellon Postdoctoral Fellow at the Center for Arts and Humanities, American University of Beirut.

Jonatan Habib Engqvist is an independent curator and theorist, with a background in philosophy and aesthetic theory. Previously, he has been project manager for visual art at Iaspis (2009–14) and curator at Moderna Museet (2008–09), and has worked with art, architecture and technology at The Royal Institute of Art in Stockholm (2005–07). He has curated a number of large international exhibitions, including *Survival Kit 9* in Riga, Latvia; *Sinopale 6*, Sinop, Turkey (2017); *(I)ndependent People*, the visual art focus of Reykjavík Arts Festival 2012; and *Tunnel Vision*, the 8th Momentum biennale in Moss, Norway 2015. He is the curator of *Children of the Children of the Revolution* at Färgfabriken in Stockholm (2018) and *New Småland* on commission by four art museums and a university (2016–19). His books include: *Big Dig – Om passivitet och samtidskonst* (CLP Works, 2018); *Studio Talks: Thinking Through Painting* (Arvinius+Orfeus Publishing, 2014); *In Dependence – Collaboration and Artists' Initiatives* (Torpedo Press, 2013); *Work, Work, Work – A Reader on Art and Labour* (Steinberg Press, 2012); *Dharavi: Documenting Informalities* (KKH, 2008).

Bernhard Garnicnig founded the Palais des Beaux Arts Wien (www.palaisdesbeauxarts.at) in 2013 and was its Very Artistic Director until 2018 and is now its Head Janitor. In 2014 he co-founded Supergood (www.supergood.today), a nomadic movement in the ambiguous space between product and performance. In 2012 he co-founded the Bregenz Biennale (www.bregenzbiennale.com), a festival for ephemeral and impermanent forms of art in his lakeside hometown. In 2011 he co-founded *continent.* (www.continentcontinent.cc), a para-academic journal for thought in its many forms. He likes to work with friends and to make friends through work and has shared this process and its results in galleries, artist-run project spaces and research institutions all over the world, most recently at the Haus der Kulturen der Welt, Nikolaj Kunsthal Kopenhagen, MAAT Museum Lisbon and Kunsthalle Wien.

Elizabeth Jochum (BA Wellesley College; MA, Ph.D., University of Colorado, USA) is an Associate Professor at Aalborg University (DK) and the co-founder of Robot Culture and

Aesthetics (ROCA) research group at the University of Copenhagen (DK). Her research focuses on the intersection of art, robotics and performance. She is a member of Aalborg U Robotics and Erasmus Mundus Media Arts Cultures graduate faculty. Her research has appeared in *Theatre Journal*, *Puppetry International* and in the edited volumes *Routledge Companion to Puppetry and Material Performance*, *Robots and Art: Exploring an Unlikely Symbiosis* (Springer) and *Controls and Art* (Springer). She is the author of *Inclining East: Kabuki and Interculturalism in Contemporary Theatre* (VDM Verlag).

Ulla Angkjær Jørgensen (Ph.D.) is an Associate Professor of Art History at the Norwegian University of Science and Technology. Her research focuses on Nordic twentieth-century and contemporary art, feminist art history, post-colonialism, visual culture, globalization and technology and the arts. She has participated in interdisciplinary research projects on gender and aesthetics, Nordic art and globalization, and at present she manages the network and project 'Gender and Diversity in Nordic Art Museums'. Her publications include the book *Kropslig kunst* (Museum Tusculanum, 2007), chapters in *Globalizing Art* (Aarhus University Press, 2011), 'From Sign to Signal' (*Journal of Aesthetics and Culture* 2012), and *Kjønnsforhandlinger* (PAX Forlag, 2013) and *Sámi Art and Aesthetics* (Aarhus University Press, 2017). In 2015, she was the co-curator of the exhibition *Women Forward!* at the Museum of Contemporary Art in Roskilde, Denmark.

Jens Tang Kristensen (Ph.D., Postdoc, Department of Arts and Cultural Studies, University of Copenhagen) is working with topics related to the Danish Concrete art from 1940 to the present, and the relation between this movement and the spontaneous art, primarily focusing on *Linien II* and *CoBrA*. He has published articles about national identity, art, archaeology, modernism, avant-gardism, contemporary art and politics in general. In 2017 he worked together with the Danish artist Claus Carstensen in collaboration with Den Frie Udstillingsbygning in Copenhagen and The Museum of Religious Art in Lemvig on their international book-and-exhibition project: *Becoming Animal*. In 2011 he also worked with the artist Sarah Pierce on the exhibition project *The Research Programme* at Charlottenborg Kunsthal in Copenhagen.

Mads Deibjerg Lind (BA in art and technology from Aalborg University) is currently a graduate student in lighting design at Aalborg University Copenhagen. He was employed at BIBIANA Danmark and Utzon Center, where he developed activities and events to foster creativity between children, art and technology. His research focuses on experience design with emerging technologies, with an emphasis on virtual reality and light. He has designed public light installations in the region of Copenhagen.

Björn Norberg is a curator based in Stockholm and Uppsala in Sweden and has been active in the field of art, science and technology for more than two decades. He has curated exhibitions at Kiasma in Helsinki, Museet for Samtidskunst in Roskilde, Bonniers Konsthall in Stockholm, The National Museum of Science and Technology in Stockholm, Bildmuseet/ Umeå University in Umeå, Reykjavik Art Museum and Moderna Museet in Stockholm. He is curator and artistic leader at Dome of Visions at KTH – Royal Institute of Technology in Stockholm and has lectured at universities such as Stockholm University, KTH – Royal institute of Technology, Konstfack University College of Arts, Crafts and Design, Royal Institute of Art, Uniarts in Stockholm, KuvA in Helsinki, Valand Academy/University of Gothenburg, Blekinge Institute of Technology, University of Gävle and more. He is part author and co-editor of the anthology *Get Real!* published by George Braziller, and has published texts both in Sweden and abroad.

Margrét Elísabet Ólafsdóttir (Ph.D., University of Pantheon-Sorbonne, Paris) is Assistant Professor at the University of Akureyri in Iceland. She has been active in the field of media art since 2002 when she co-founded Lorna, an association of electronic arts. In 2010 she co-founded Lorna Lab, an interdisciplinary platform for art, science and technology, and has been the organizer of the Pikslaverk Festival since 2008. She was the curator of the exhibition *Video Art in Iceland from 1975 to 1990* at the Reykjavik Art Museum in 2013, and the *Melting on Ice* workshop and exhibition at Kling & Bang in 2015. She was a part-time teacher at the University of Iceland and the Iceland Academy of Arts from 2005 to 2015. She has been writing on art and culture since 1987.

Jøran Rudi had his first academic training in social sciences, followed by a few years as a rock musician in one of the influential bands that emerged in the end of the 1970s. After studying computer music at New York University, he founded and directed NOTAM from 1993 to 2010 when he stepped back to a researcher position. His research interests span across educational issues arising from the use of music technology via studies of artistic genres such as music, music animation, soundscape and sound art, to more conventional musicological work with a historical orientation. As a composer, he has developed a portfolio of works for electronic instruments and/or fixed media, as well as for dance, film, performance art, installation and multimedia. His most significant artistic contributions are the computer music animations made in the mid- to late 1990s.

Lorella Scacco is a curator and journalist with a background in the history of contemporary art and aesthetics. She teaches phenomenology of contemporary art at the Italian Academies of Fine Arts and has realized lectures and seminars at several universities, academies and foundations in Italy and abroad. She has curated exhibitions and edited catalogues for contemporary art exhibitions in public and private spaces in Italy and abroad, including *Artext*, La Triennale, Milan (2006), *Mobile Journey*, 52nd Venice Biennale (2007), *The Hot Season – Italian Art Now*, Stenersen Museum, Oslo (2008), *Social Videoscapes from the North*, Pro Artibus Foundation, Finland and Careof DOCVA, Milan (2013). She has contributed to specialized art magazines and is the author of *Estetica mediale. Da Jean Baudrillard a Derrick de Kerckhove* (Guerini, 2004),

Northwave: A Survey of Video Art in Nordic Countries (Silvana Editoriale, 2009) and *Alberto Giacometti and Maurice Merleau-Ponty: A Dialogue on the Perception – Phenomenology of Art Experience* (Gangemi, 2017). She is currently a PhD candidate at the University of Turku, Finland.

Morten Søndergaard is Associate Professor and Curator of Interactive Media Art at Aalborg University. He holds an MA in Modern Culture and a PhD in Performance Design. He is co-founder and member of the Consortium Board of the Erasmus Mundus Master in Media Arts Cultures. He was Curator/Deputy Director at the Museum of Contemporary Art in Roskilde (1999–2008). He was head of the Culture Denmark advisory board and member of the New Media Forum, both hosted by the Danish Ministry of Culture (2003–07). He was co-founder and board-member of the LARM audio research project 2010. Same year, he commissioned Stelarc's Internet Ear Project for the exhibition *Biotopia – Art in the Wet Zone*. He was Senior Curator of the re-new festival of digital arts in Copenhagen (2010–12). He curated the 'Unheard Avant-garde (in Scandinavia)' section at the Sound Art – Sound as Medium for Fine Art at ZKM, 2012. Co-founder and chair of ISACS – the sound art curating conference series (with Peter Weibel). Co-founder and chair of POM – Politics of the Machines conference series (with Laura Beloff).

Mette-Marie Zacher Sørensen (Ph.D.) is Assistant Professor in the Department of Culture and Communication at Aarhus University in Denmark. She is an interdisciplinary scholar interrogating current relationships among computer science, art and communication. Her recent publications include 'Quantified faces: On surveillance technologies, identification and statistics in three contemporary art projects', *Digital Culture and Society* 2:2 (2016) and 'Words with cybernetic senses: Questions of multimodality, programming and liveness in digital poetry', in *Beyond the Literary*, eds. Sarah Paulsson, Anders Skare Malvik and Roger D. Sell (John Benjamins Publishing Company, 2016).

Stahl Stenslie (Ph.D., The School of Architecture and Design, Oslo) is an artist, curator and researcher specializing in experimental art, interactive experiences and disruptive technologies. His artworks challenge our ordinary ways of perceiving the world. Keywords are somaesthetics, unstable media, transgression and the numinous, and the technological focus in his works is on the art of the recently possible – such as (1) panhaptic communication on Smartphones, (2) somatic sound and holophonic soundspaces and (3) open-source, disruptive design for disruptive technologies such as low-cost 3D print of functional and lethal art-weaponry. Currently, he is teaching and researching as an Obel Professor in Art and Technology (opplevelsesteknologi) at Aalborg University, Denmark. He is also the director of PNEK – Production Network for Electronic Art, Norway, www.pnek.org. He has been exhibiting and lecturing at major international events (ISEA, DEAF, Ars Electronica, SIGGRAPH). He represented Norway at the Ichihara Biennial (Japan 2014), 5th biennial in Istanbul, Turkey, co-organized 6cyberconf and won the Grand Prize of the Norwegian Council for Cultural Affairs.

Index

264; technological 267; urban 356,
357, 360; user interface 253, 280, 318
Institute of Contemporary Arts (ICA) 133
Institute of Light 136
instituting 10, 12, 145, 147, 148, 149, 150, 184,
351; institutionalization *157. See also*
New Institutionalism
institutional: analysis 148, 149–150, 151–153,
154–157, 262; anti-institutional
technocentric developments 151,
156; institutional becoming 154;
institutional experimental sites 12
Institutional Critique 119, 150, 151–152, 153,
154, 262
interactive: art 14, 106, 138, 238, 246, 249, 267,
290, 291, 292, 298, 312, 354, 358; artists
290; aesthetics 14, 307; behaviors 50,
51, 52, 57, 122, 137, 164, 165, 171, 261,
263, 271, 351, 354, 355; context of art
196n.11, 290, 343; devices 289–290;
installations 57, 87, 100, 106, (pl. 12),
211, 212, 138, 183, 190, 196n.11, 246,
249, 265, 291, 294, 295, 309, 358;
design 304; media 189; methodology
190, performance 96, 265; institutes 87,
106, 153, 214; technology 56; television
319; visualization 295; interactivity of
video games 58
Interactive Institute (Sweden). *See* RISE
Interactive Institute
interdisciplinary fusion in art ix, 13, 49, 59,
64, 135, 147, 234, 252–253, 262, 345,
352–353, 360
Interference (2014 installation) 308–309
International Symposium of Electronic Arts
(ISEA) 214, 234, 236–237, 367
Internet: art about 93, 282, 319, 329; art
with 338, 340, 318; theme in art 85,
97; and artistic research 37, 40, 41,
49, 59, 60, 138, 235, 322; and artistic
independence 97; and marginalization
of artists in Iceland 320; Commons-
oriented process 85; connectivity and

its consequences 35, 102, 235, 237;
commercialization 82; and culture 58,
71; dependence on web technologies
175; dissemination platform 10, 36,
51; emergence of 71, 75, 83, 232–234,
236, 297, 317–318, 318; generation
raised on 236–237; hoaxes 237;
and hybridity 291; influences on
art and art world 89, 97, 106, 108,
134, 139; infrastructure in Sweden
240; changing art institutions 153,
155–156; and manipulation 239;
as mirror of narcissism 121; net art
340; and networked phenomena 10;
personalization and filtering 11, 121;
piracy 135; social environment 64; and
spectacularization; Bernard Stiegler on
281, 284; technological changes of 233
Internet of Things 239, 240, 264
Inter_Skin (1993–94 installation) 222
interventionist art practices: in artists'
practices 59, 105, 132, 139, 190–192;
computer-based 134; new modes of
168, 354; of the post-war avant-garde
129, 130, 136; site-specific 95; of
sound 186; tools 153; types of 266; of
Virtual Reality 255
The Invention of Art (2005 book) 282–283
i/o/lab 215, 224n.5, 224n.6, 344
Iraq war 90
IRCAM (Institut de Recherche et
Coordination Acoustique/Musique)
173
The Iron Ring (2013 project) 344
Irwin, Robert 73
iSynx (art project) 169–170
Iversen, Marie Kølbæk 55, 56, 91–92, 103,
(pl. 11), 273

J

Jacobsen, Mogens 34, 49–50, 75, 98, (pl. 12),
171, 294, 303, 304, 307, 309, 311–312

Z
Zamyatin, Yevgeny 294
Zelig (1983 film) 165, 177n.2
Zendai MOMA Intrude Project 105
Zetterqvist, Johan 124n.2
Zimmerman, Eric 59

Žižek, Slavoj 90, 106, 135, 178n.4
ZKM 100
Zoomorph (app) 104; *Zoomorph App and Test Images* (ph. 14)
Zuckerberg, Mark 236, 247